THE WILD-FOWLER

A TREATISE ON
FOWLING, ANCIENT AND MODERN
DESCRIPTIVE ALSO OF
DECOYS AND FLIGHT PONDS
WILD-FOWL SHOOTING WITH GUNNING
PUNTS,
SHOOTING YACHTS, &C.; ALSO FOWLING IN
THE FENS AND IN
FOREIGN COUNTRIES, ROCK-FOWLING, &C. &C.

BY

H. C. FOLKARD, ESQ.

British Library Cataloguing-in-Publication Data
A catalogue record for this book is available from the
British Library

CONTENTS

Shooting Wildfowl

Wildfowl hunting or shooting is the practice of hunting ducks, geese, quail or other wildfowl for food and sport. In many western countries, commercial wildfowl hunting is prohibited, and sub-genres such as duck hunting have become sporting activities. Many types of ducks and geese share the same habitat, have overlapping or identical hunting seasons, and are hunted using the same methods. Thus, it is possible to take different species of wildfowl in the same outing – waterfowl are by far the most commonly hunted birds though. Waterfowl can be hunted in crop fields where they feed, or, more frequently, on or near bodies of water such as rivers, lakes, ponds, swamps, sloughs, or oceanic coastlines.

Wild wildfowl have been hunted for food, down and feathers worldwide, since prehistoric times. Ducks, geese, and swans appear in European cave paintings from the last Ice Age, and a mural in the Ancient Egyptian tomb of Khum-Hotpe (c. 1900 BC) shows a man in a hunting blind (a covering device for trackers) capturing swimming ducks in a trap. Wildfowl hunting proper - with shotguns - only began in the seventeenth century with the invention of the matchlock shotgun. Later flintlock shotguns and percussion cap guns have also been used, but in general shotguns have been loaded with black powder and led shots, through the muzzle, right up until the late nineteenth century. The history of shooting wildfowl is very much tied up with the development of the shotgun. It was the semi-automatic 12 ga. gun, developed by John Browning in the very early twentieth century which allowed hunters to shoot on a large, commercial scale. Once wildfowlers (primarily in America and Europe) had access to such guns, they could become much more proficient market hunters. They used a four-shell magazine (five including the one in the chamber) to rake rafts of ducks on the water or to shoot them at night in order to kill larger numbers of birds. Even during the great depression years, a brace of Canvasbacks could easily be sold, but legislation was gradually brought in to prevent such practices.

Early European settlers in America hunted the native birds with great zeal, as the supply of wildfowl, especially waterfowl on the coastal Atlantic regions seemed endless. During the fall migrations, the skies were filled with birds. Locations such as Chesapeake Bay, Delaware Bay and Barnaget Bay were hunted extensively. As more immigrants came to America in the late eighteenth and nineteenth centuries, the need for more food became greater. Market hunting started to take form, to supply the local population living along the Atlantic coast with fresh ducks and geese.

Men would go into wooden boats and go out into the bays hunting, sometimes with large shotguns – and they could bring back one or two barrels of ducks each day. Live ducks were used as decoys, as well as bait such as corn or grain to attract other wildfowl.

There are several items used by almost all wildfowl hunters: a shotgun, ammunition, a hunting blind, decoys, a boat (if needed), and various bird calls. The decoys are used to lure the birds within range, and the blind conceals the hunter. When a hunter or hunters sees the wildfowl, he or she begins calling with an appropriate bird-call. Once the birds are within range, the hunters rise from the blind and quickly shoot them before they are frightened off and out of shooting range. Duck or goose calls are often used to attract birds, but sometimes calls of other birds are simulated to convince the birds that there is no danger. Today, due to the ban on lead shots for hunting wildfowl over wetlands, many wildfowlers are switching to modern guns with stronger engineering to allow the use of non-toxic ammunition such as steel or tungsten based cartridges. The most popular bore is the 12-gauge. Only certain 'quarry' species of wildfowl may legally be shot in the UK, and are protected under the Wildlife and Countryside Act 1981. These are Mallard, Wigeon, Teal, Pochard, Shoveler, Pintail, Gadwall, Goldeneye, Tufted Duck, Canada Goose, White-fronted Goose, Greylag Goose and Pink-footed Goose. Other common quarry targets for the wildfowler include the Common Snipe.

An intimate knowledge of the quarry and its habitat is required by the successful wildfowler. Shooting will normally occur during the early morning and late afternoon 'flights', when the birds move to and from feeding and roosting sites. A long way from the market hunters of the eighteenth century, current wildfowlers do not search for a large bag of quarry; their many hours efforts can be well-rewarded by even a single bird. Wildfowling has come under threat in recent years through legislation though. Destruction of habitat also has played a large part in the decline of shooting areas, and recently in the UK 'right to roam' policies mean that wildfowlers' conservation areas are at risk. However, in most regions, good relationships exist between wildfowlers, conservationists, ramblers and other coastal area users. In America, the situation is rather different, due to the concerted efforts of J.N. Darling in the 1930s. He urged the government to pass the 'Migratory Bird Hunting Stamp Act' better known as the 'Federal Duck Stamp Act', which required hunters to purchase a special stamp, in addition to a regular hunting license, to hunt migratory waterfowl. This scheme has funded the purchase of 4.5 million acres of National Wildlife Refuge land since its inception in 1934. The Duck Stamp act has been described as 'one of the most successful conservation programs ever devised.' Thanks to such efforts, which maintain the natural habitats of wildfowl, and especially of waterfowl, the sport is still enjoyed by many, all over the world.

LONDON.
LONGMAN'S & C? PATERNOSTER ROW

The day for Ducks.

PREFACE

TO

THE THIRD EDITION

A NEW EDITION of this work being required, the Author has availed himself of the opportunity of revising it throughout, and of making considerable additions to it in various parts, the results of further experience and research; particularly with regard to some curious and interesting arts of Fowling as practised in foreign countries.

With a view to the production of a less costly volume, the present edition has been printed on a thinner paper, and with a fuller page, though of somewhat smaller dimensions; so that, although the new volume is less bulky in appearance, it is in fact a considerable enlargement of the preceding edition, and contains more matter, in a more compact form, with the whole of the Steel Plate and Wood Engravings that were contained in the previous editions. In its present form it is hoped that the new edition may be found as acceptable as the two previous ones.

LONDON: *February* 1875.

INTRODUCTION

'Form'd on the Samian school, or those of Ind,

There are who think these pastimes scarce humane;

Yet, in my mind (and not relentless I),

His life is pure that wears no fouler stain.'

ARMSTRONG.

AMONG the various country sports and recreations of the English gentleman, there is one which, singularly, has hitherto remained in a state of neglected and unexplained obscurity, so far as regarded in a literary point of view; whilst every other sport—from fox-hunting down to boxing—has formed the subject of a separate treatise, wherein is practically and theoretically explained and illustrated the particular recreation of which it treats.

A volume upon Wild-fowling, with its instructive and pleasing varieties, justly demands a place in our libraries by the side of works devoted exclusively to other sporting pursuits, neither more nor less exciting and amusing.

In addition to the ordinary means of wild-fowl *shooting* are the more interesting *arts* of 'the decoy,' and means of capturing wild-fowl alive; the flight-pond, and its notable concomitants; with various other remarkable methods of fowling, both ancient and modern.

There are so many different species of wild-fowl, each with its peculiar habits, and therefore requiring different methods of capture, that to give a faithful history of the sport, and its varieties, otherwise than in a volume devoted expressly to the purpose, must necessarily be abortive and unsatisfactory.

The Author is quite conscious that the undertaking is a bold one; and if he had not a certain degree of confidence in his own personal experiences in this, for years past, one of his favourite recreations, also long since felt the requirements of a work of the kind, he would not have attempted to supply the want.

The enquirer will do the Author the favour to bear in mind that he does not profess to give ornithological delineations or descriptions of the various species of wild-fowl, other than those which may have suggested themselves from personal observation and familiarity with the habits of the birds; and such as are necessary for explaining the pursuit of Wild-fowling: ornithology as a science being a subject foreign to his purpose, and already abundantly treated of by many distinguished authorities.

To know something of the ingenious methods of taking wild-fowl must be useful to all men; and more especially those about to reside in foreign countries, who should remember that there are wild-fowl in all parts of the world; and perhaps such men may at some time or other find it highly expedient to exercise some of the ingenuities and means of capture which have been employed in this and other countries with a success almost beyond credibility.

The art of Wild-fowling, as regards capturing the birds alive, demands, in the first place, a familiar knowledge of the habits and instincts of the birds.

It may be imagined a very tantalising situation, to be placed in a country where hundreds of wild-fowl are daily in the habit of thronging the inland waters, and yet to find oneself so uninstructed in the art of fowling as to be unable to capture a bird; whilst if it could be successfully employed in taking them they would afford the most abundant and inviting table-luxuries in the land. An individual so situated would naturally ask himself, as he gazed from day to day upon the feathered occupants of the waters, 'How are these birds to be taken?' It is our purpose, in these pages, to explain to him, not only how and when to pursue them with dog and gun, but how to take them alive, in large numbers; and, whether on the open waters, savannas, or otherwise, to shoot them, both by night and day.

The flight-pond, with the curious and interesting proceedings connected with it, has hitherto, as a subject of literary diversion, remained in obscurity; no author (as far as I have been able to discover) having ever attempted an explanation, beyond the few unsatisfactory observations, occupying but a few lines, in vol. iii. of Daniel's 'Rural Sports,'[1] and which (if the Author may be forgiven for the assertion) tend rather to mislead than instruct the enquirer; yet, strange to say, they appear to have been copied and re-copied by subsequent writers, as their only text upon the subject.[2] The Author has therefore endeavoured to lay before his readers a full description of the quaint contrivances which have been invented by our forefathers for capturing a cunning and whimsical species of wild-fowl, that defied the efforts of the most experienced decoyers, but which fell victims by thousands to another means, almost as ingenious as the decoy.

The subject of 'Ancient Methods of Capturing Wild-fowl' has been compiled from the oldest and most reliable sources; and, in some respects, from authorities of great antiquity, and books of extreme rarity.

The latter portion of the work, which is devoted to the subject of 'Wild-fowling in Foreign Countries,' is not entirely the result of the Author's individual experience, but has been carefully compiled, after diligent research in books of travel, history, and philosophy: a task which, though laborious, has been an agreeable one, because considerably facilitated through the ready access which the Author has had to the British Museum and other public and private libraries.

Those who are familiar with the migratory habits of wildfowl, and who have travelled in Northern Europe, and seen the myriads of aquatic birds which inhabit those quarters, and in winter are driven Southward by the severity of frost, will bear the Author out in the opinion that there must always be wild-fowl annually visiting our shores, in greater or less numbers, according to the temperature of the season.

An old-fashioned winter will assuredly bring with it old-fashioned sport; in proof of which we have only to refer as far back as the season of 1846–7, which is long subsequent to the drainage of the great Bedford Level;[1] and we find the wildfowl shooter enjoying sport to his heart's content. In that winter, the London market was so abundantly supplied, that wild-ducks were sold at two shillings per pair, and snipes at fourpence each; and in Devonshire snipes were so numerous as to be sold at one halfpenny each.[2] During the same winter, to the Author's own knowledge, wild-ducks were sold in country towns at one shilling and sixpence and widgeon at one shilling, per pair.

In severe winters the markets are always crowded with wild-fowl; and it stands to reason, that when the surfaces of the Northern countries—as Lapland, Sweden, Norway, and parts of Russia—are deeply buried in snow, wild-geese, and such fowl as feed inland, are compelled to migrate to more genial climates; and England—a salubrious island—situated as she is in the direct track of the myriads of migratory birds from the hyperborean latitudes, offers the first, the fairest, and most inviting retreat to those aërial wanderers.

Few but those who have seen them would believe in the immense flights of wild-fowl which in severe winters visit our coasts—flights which, when they have alighted, cover acres of water. But the sportsman and decoyer complain of a great decline in the sport of late years; though this is, in a measure, to be accounted for by a succession of mild winters; so that nothing like the success of good old times has attended their pursuits. Nevertheless, in further proof of the assertion that 'the sport is good as ever, in hard winters,' we may refer to a still more subsequent season—that of 1854–5, which was the hardest winter on record since 1846–7; and we find the sport in no way inferior to that of former years, when the season has been of about equal severity, with similar duration of frost.

However, we cannot help looking back with regret at the mischief done to our sport by the drainage of fens, swamps, and moors. Such places, in their wild and uncultivated state, were the very nurseries where hundreds of wild-fowl were annually hatched and reared: more particularly the fens and broads about the Eastern coast, which, from the favoured situation they occupy, were always the first resting-place of wild-fowl, after crossing the sea from Northern countries; and thus became the very haunts and places of refuge of immense flights of aquatic fowl; and to this day, the few remaining fens which have been undisturbed by the powerful arm of modem cultivation are their best and last strongholds. There are also still remaining several private preserves for water-fowl, where the wild-duck lays her eggs and rears her nestlings in unmolested security.

It is the flat-lying counties of England, intersected by broadwaters, tidal-rivers, and savannas, that afford the Wild-fowl-shooter the greatest amount of diversion.

The subject of the 'Shooting Yacht,' with experiences of shooting under sail, have never been collectively published. The sport was little understood, and seldom resorted to, in the days when Colonel Hawker wrote. Punting was then also, comparatively speaking, in its infancy, when contrasted with the perfection to which the art has since attained; for when the birds became scarce and more wary, the ingenuity of the punter was taxed to the utmost; and a greater perfection in the art has thus been acquired.

The whole of the subjects treated of (except as regards ancient and foreign methods of capturing wild-fowl) are explained chiefly from the Author's own experiences; and wherever he has borrowed assistance from others he has been careful to acknowledge it.

It may be proper here to allude to a vulgar error which appears to exist in the minds of some persons, that there is a fishy flavour about all wild-fowl, which renders them unpalatable as an article of food. Such, however, is altogether erroneous; the only birds which possess that disagreeable odour in their flesh being those which subsist on fish; and for the purpose of catching and holding such. Nature has gifted them with superior powers, and a beak totally different to that of other water-fowl. The fishy-flavoured fowl have serrated beaks, the interior mandibles of which, with their shark-like teeth, are exquisitely formed for holding, with firm grasp, the most slippery of the finny tribe. These are, for the most part, of the species diver and merganser; and their flesh is not palatable. Those which are so much esteemed as table delicacies do not feed on fish, nor have they the power to catch them: their food consists of duck's-weed (*lens palustris*), grasses, and other inland herbage, which can have no tendency to give them the flavour complained of; whilst the high prices which wild-fowl, such as teal, widgeon, duck and mallard, sea-pheasants, brent-geese, pochards, and others, constantly fetch in the London and country markets, show the esteem in which they are held as delicious and wholesome luxuries.

It has been the Author's endeavour, throughout these

pages, to render them amusing as well as instructive, a task by no means easy where so many practical details have to be stated with care and particularity; nevertheless, with that view, he has occasionally, but very sparingly, interspersed anecdotes of his own adventures, and only where he has thought it the readiest and most agreeable means of imparting amusement as well as instruction to the enquirer.

With a modest conviction that he will not be accused of writing a book upon a subject with which he is not familiar, the Author nevertheless regrets that the effort has not been made by one more competent; for he feels certain there is much more which might, and ought to, form part of a volume devoted exclusively to the subject.

[1] And these appear to have been borrowed from Montague's 'Ornithology.'

[2] Professor Yarrell, in his book of 'British Birds,' mentions the flight-pond; but he approaches the subject with the same uncertainty, and throws no new light upon it.

[1] *Vide* Well's 'History of the Fens:' A.D. 1830.

[2] Howitt's 'Year Book of the Country.'

THE WILD-FOWLER

CHAPTER I

FOWLING

'Aucupium felix festinaquè copia præda.'

BARGÆUS, DE AUCUPIO: ANXO 1566.

IN Greek this sport is termed ὀρνιθοθήρα; in Latin, *aucupium*, from *avis*, a bird; and *capio*, I take. It signifies the art of decoying, capturing, or killing birds *feræ naturæ*, by means of decoy-ducks, dogs, guns, rapacious birds, nets, snares, bird-lime, bird-calls, or other artifice; and whether used upon land or water.[1]

The Saxon dialogue upon the Art of Fowling is thus expressed:—

Q.—How do you catch birds?

A.—I catch them many ways: sometimes with nets, sometimes with nooses, sometimes with bird-lime, sometimes by whistling, sometimes with hawks, sometimes with gins.[2]

It is one of the most ancient, as well as most natural, arts known to mankind; and in every nation has called forth the earliest cunning of the people. There are frequent allusions to

21

it in the Scriptures; more particularly in the Old Testament, as to the 'snares of the fowler;' and there can be no doubt but such were used many centuries before Christ.

As different species of birds have different habits, so the method of taking them differs, in accordance with such habits. Such portions of the art as relate to the capture of wild-fowl and fen-birds are by far the most attractive, varied, and extensive, and to those particular branches our discourse will be more especially devoted.

It is a pleasant and useful diversion, abounding with varieties as attractive and instructive as they are exciting and exhilarating.[1]

There is no branch of the art of fowling possessing so great an amount of attraction, or requiring so much skill, as is necessary for proficiency in the art of capturing water-fowl; and, besides, there is no one which offers so many examples of instinct.

It appears, however, to have been a sport distasteful (because, probably, very imperfectly understood) to that earliest of writers upon sporting literature—Dame Juliana Barnes, *alias* Berners. That antiquated and distinguished sportswoman draws a very forlorn and miserable, though amusing, picture of an ancient fowler; showing him up, in her peculiar style of language, as the very object of pity, disappointment, and misery;[2] but her remarks can only be read as applying to taking birds with nets, gins, and such like contrivances—other portions of her work being dissertations specially in praise of hawking, as a distinct branch of the pursuit, and in which she appears to have been a proficient, and evidently familiar with the art of capturing wild-fowl with rapacious birds.

Both ancient and modern fowlers agree as to the necessity of knowing something of the haunts as well as the habits of wild-fowl, before success can be confidently looked for in any branch of the pursuit. There are certain places in the Fens preferred by wild-fowl to others; and the same is to be observed of such fowl as do not venture far inland; but, as the subject will be briefly discussed in subsequent pages, under the different heads applicable to each particular species, we only speak here in general terms as to their haunts and habits. The knowledge of this branch of the art possessed by the ancient fowler was by no means so superficial as may have been supposed: it was of the essence of his success to be well informed on this head.[1]

The favourite daily resorts of the smaller species of wild-fowl, as duck, teal, and such like, are sequestered lakes, ponds, and arms of the sea. At twilight, in the evening, they change their quarters to fens, moors, and bog-lands, where they find their best and most abundant food. The wilder and more uncultivated the country, the more it is frequented by wild-fowl; provided it be a moorish or sedgy and fertile soil.

During great and heavy rains they resort to flooded meadows, delighting to dabble in shallow water, where easy access can be obtained to the bottom without immersing their whole bodies. They are particularly partial to such swamps and morasses as are intersected with small islands and mounds. Widgeon prefer saline feeding-grounds, and do not generally seek their food so far inland as ducks and teal. Brent geese confine themselves exclusively to the sea by night, and frequent saltwater rivers and bays during the day. Grey-lag geese are devotedly attached to fields of green wheat, and extensive moors and savannas.

From this mere cursory glance at the habits of wild-fowl, the variety of the diversion will be at once apparent to the reader; and it will be perceived that a familiarity with the haunts as well as the habits of the different species is of paramount importance to the wild-fowler.

Wild-fowl are by far the most subtle of all birds: it is their very nature to be so, accustomed as they are at one season of the year to wild and uninhabited regions, and at another to the incessant persecution of the fowler; but they are nevertheless the most attractive objects of the sportsman's diversion, both physically and gastronomically. They are birds of marked discipline, flying in rank and marching in a body; and when an enemy (as a hawk or weasel) ventures to disturb their privacy, and an attack upon the intruder is contemplated, it is always made in troop. Both by night and day they have sentinels on constant duty, to give warning of the enemy's movements; and so vigilant are they, and so awake to suspicion, that more than ordinary perseverance and ingenuity are requisite on the part of the wild-fowler to ensure success. They are fond of assembling in large numbers, particularly in cold weather: when dispersed, they appear unsettled, and less capable of taking care of themselves.

Wild-fowl, as a dietary article, were always esteemed luxuries; and by the ancient as well as the modern Apician their flesh has been considered more wholesome, and easier of digestion, than that of tame fowls. Yet in former times it would seem that the distinction between such fowl as are now classed among dainties, and such as are mere carrion, was not then observed. Swans, cranes, and curlews were priced highest.[1] Sea-gulls, as well as several other such unpalatable morsels, were deemed fit articles of food for the nobleman's table:[1] and by way of further illustration of the extraordinary taste which prevailed in those days, it may be added that some of the most delicious birds that fly, as teal for instance, were excluded from the table when any other sort of wild-fowl could be had.[2]

The arts and contrivances for taking water-fowl alive are chiefly of very ancient origin, and some of them are most quaint and amusing. The authors who have written upon the subject are few in number, but they have left some highly instructive accounts of their ingenious arts; many branches of which have been but little used since the numbers of wild-fowl bred in this country have so considerably decreased, through the extensive drainage of their original breeding haunts, for the purpose of acquiring and fitting the land for the more profitable pursuits of agriculture.

The age when decoys were prevalent may be appropriately termed the 'middle age' of wild-fowling; all previous systems of taking wild-fowl by nets, snares, lime-strings, lime-twigs, lime-rods, and otherwise, sink into insignificance when compared with the peculiar ingenuities of the decoy, and the subsidiary schemes of the flight-pond. But after the mischief incurred to decoys by the ubiquitous system of land-draining, the successes of the decoyer were considerably diminished; and at the present day, the most common modes of wild-fowling, and those in greatest repute, are by means of the gunning-punt, shooting-yacht, and stanchion gun.

There cannot be a stronger proof of the unfamiliarity of the present age of sportsmen with the ancient and original art of wild-fowling, than by reference to the erroneous terms which are applied to the pursuit by many modern sportsmen; and it is only from the lips of a few 'ancient fowlers,' however illiterate, that we hear the correct version of sporting terms applicable to wild-fowling. Thus, modern sportsmen speak of every large number of wild-fowl as a 'flock' (a term chiefly appertaining to sheep), and this whether ducks, geese, widgeon, or whatever else; whereas the term 'flock' is improper as applied to any distinct species of wild-fowl, and should only be employed when speaking *indefinitely* of wild-fowl, or a mixture of wild-fowl, not knowing of what species they are. Errors of this sort are seldom made in respect of other field sports without at once bringing down a shower of ridicule by the better-informed upon the head of the more ignorant one.

To speak in the present day of a 'flock' of partridges, instead of a 'covey,' would so offend the ears of the most superficial sportsman, that he would look with contempt upon an individual who so applied it; and yet the term 'flock,' as applied to wild-fowl, is equally erroneous as if applied to partridges, and quite as inexcusable when coming from the lips of a sportsman. But in consequence of the indifference with which the subject of fowling has been treated of late years, we find the most learned ornithologists of the day, throughout their voluminous histories, guilty of these inexcusable blunders. Writers upon sporting literature, one and all, commit similar errors; and though they apply correct terms to game and birds of the land, water-fowl are invariably classed by them in 'flocks.'

The ancient and modern terms, as applied to water-fowl when *congregatus*, are as under:—

Ancient.[1]

27

A *teme* of swannys.

A *gaggyllyng* of gese.

A *teme* of dukys, or

A *padelynge* of dukys.

A *sorde* of malardys.

A *spryng* of telys.

A *doppyngg* of scheldrakys.

A *coverte* of cootes.

A *herde* of corlewis.

A *sege* of heyronys.

A *congregaçon* of plovers.

A *dysseyte* of lapwynges.

A *herde* of cranys.

Modern.

A *herd* of swans.

A *gaggle* of geese (when on the water).

A *skein* of geese (when on wing).

A *paddling* of ducks (when on the water).

A *team* of wild-ducks (when flying in the air).

A *sedge* of herons.

A *wing* or *congregation* of plovers.

A *desert* of lapwings.

A *walk* of snipes (in allusion to the ground they use).

A *sord* or *suit* of mallards.

A *company* of widgeon.

A *flight* or *rush* of dunbirds.

A *spring* of teal (in Norfolk sometimes a *coil* of teal).

A *dopping* of sheldrakes.

A *covert* of coots.

A *herd* of curlews.

A *wisp* of snipes signifies a few.

A *fling* or *cloud* of oxbirds (when on the wing).

A *hill* of ruffs.

A small number of wild-fowl, as ducks and geese (about thirty or forty), is termed a *trip*. The same of widgeon, dunbirds, or teal, is termed a *bunch*; and a smaller number (from ten to twenty) is called a *little knob*.

Of swans it would be said a *small herd*; and sometimes of geese a *little gaggle* or a *small skein*; and so of ducks a *short* or *long team*.

Let us hope the character of the English sportsman is not so far degenerated, or the respect he owes to ancient authorities so far lost sight of, as to induce him to use the inapplicable term 'flock' to every, or any, description of wild-fowl. It should be borne in mind that, as we derive our laws and our purest sciences from the ancients, from the same source sprang our national sports; and the arts, systems, and terms in connection with such have been handed down to us from generation to generation, because none other express so faithfully the meaning intended to be conveyed.

----

[1] Markham thus defines the art: 'Fowling is an art of discerning and understanding how to take all manner of

fowle; and it is to bee applied or used two severall waies—that is to say, either by enchantment or enticement, by winning or wooing the fowle unto you with pipe, whistle, or call, which either beguileth them with their own voyco, or amazeth them with the strangenesse of the sound; or else by engine, which unawares surpriseth and entangleth them.'—*Hunger's Prevention, or the Art of Fowling*. By Gervase Markham. A.D. 1655.

Blome gives the following definition; 'Fowling is an art for the taking all manner of fowl, either by enticement or enchantment; as calls, intoxicating baits, or the like; or else by guns, nets, engines, traps, setting dogs, &C.'—*The Gentleman's Recreations*. By Richard Blome. A.D. 1686.

Udall, in his 'Flowers of Latine Speaking,' says *Auceps*: 'properly a fowler, and *aucupium* is foulynge, and, by a metaphore, it is for all maner of wayes, to geat any thynge by wiles, traynes, or crafte.'—*Vide* also 'Bargæus, de Aucupio:' a Latin poem on Fowling, published at Florence in the year 1566.

² 'Quo modo decipii aves? Multis modis decipio aves,

aliquando retibus, aliquando laqueis, aliquando glutino, aliquando sibilo, aliquando accipitre, aliquando decipula.'— *Cott. MS. Tib A. 3. Plut.* p. 60.

[1] Burton, in his 'Anatomy of Melancholy,' speaking of 'Exorcise rectified,' says: 'Fowling is more troublesome, but all on't as delightsome to some sorts of men, be it with guns, lime, nets, glades, grnnes, strings, baits, pitfalls, pipes, calls, stalking-horses, setting dogs, coy-ducks, &c., or otherwise.'

[2] 'The dysporte and game of fowlynge me semyth moost symple, for in the wynter season the fowler spedyth not but in the most hardest and coldest weder; whyche is greuous. For when he wolde goo to his gynnes he maye not for colde. Many a gynne and many a snare he makyth, yet soryly dooth he fare. At morn tyde in the dewe he is weete shote vnto his taylle.'— *The Boke of St. Albans.* By Juliana Barnes, A.D. 1496.

[1] Markham observes: 'The first and prineipalest thing our skilfull Fowler hath to learne is the knowledg of the haunts or places of residence where these Fowle for the most part abide.'

[1] *Cott. MS. Nero. A.* vi.—Proclamation that poulterers shall not charge more than the prices following (8 Edw. II.):—

		s.	d.
For the best Teal		0	2
„	River Mallard	0	5
„	Plover	0	3
„	Curlew	0	10

In 1302 the tariff was :—

		s.	d.
For the best Mallard		0	1½
„	Heron	0	6
„	Plover	0	1
„	Swan	3	0
„	Crane	1	0

In 1274 :—

		s.	d.
For a Mallard		0	3½
„	Wild Goose	0	4
„	Wild Duck	0	1¾
„	Heron	0	6
„	Curlew	0	3
„	Plover	0	1
„	Swan	3	0
„	Crane	3	0

Introduction (by J. M. Kemble) to 'The Knights Hospitallers in England. Printed for the Camden Society in 1857. Pp. li. lii.

[1] 'Mounethly. Item it is thought good that *Sec-gulles* be hade for my Lordes owne mees and non other so they be good and in season and at jd. a pece or jd. ob. at the moste.'—*Northumberland Household Book, temp. Hen. VIII.*

32

[2] 'Item it is thought good that noo *Teyllcs* [Teal] be bought, bot if so be that other Wyldefowll cannot be gottyn and to be at jd. a pece.'—*Ibid.*

[1] *Vide* 'The Boke of St. Albans.'

CHAPTER II

ANCIENT METHODS OF CAPTURING WILD-FOWL

'Aucupans omnes rumusculos populari ratione.'

PLAUT., TRUCUL., &c.

IN primitive ages, sporting pursuits were followed rather as a necessary occupation than an occasional recreation. The Greeks were especially fond of field sports, as it is clear from the accounts transmitted to us by Xenophon. Ulysses instituted such diversions after the conquest of Troy: they received commendation from Plato, as the sources of renewed enjoyment to those who suffered either from domestic calamities or the injuries of war.

At a later age, many of those who were not engaged in agricultural pursuits depended upon their skill as hunters and fowlers for their daily subsistence. At an early age there were fowlers well skilled in their art, who caught wild birds in nets and traps, and by various other devices; bestowing greatest pains on taking water-fowl, which were more highly prized for the table than such birds as frequented districts far removed from the coast. The nets most generally employed by the Greeks for capturing wild-fowl were similar in many respects to those of the ancient Egyptians, which will be spoken of under the head 'Egyptian Fowling.' The day, or clap-net, was spread flat on the ground after the same manner, in rhomboidal form, the interior network of which represented a square, termed the βρόχος[1] or strangling part.

The *argumentum* was one of the principal nets or machines of the ancient fowler, and was chiefly useful in taking wild-fowl on the surface of the water.[2] It was a machine very similar to a French quail-pipe; that used for water-fowl was not unlike a modern decoy-pipe. The art of decoy, however, was not then known; the birds were not decoyed into the argumentum, but driven.

The *panthera*[3] was a kind of purse or drag net, used by ancient fowlers for taking water-fowl, and was the largest description of net known for the purpose. Wild-fowl were captured in the panthera on land, whilst feeding at night in the fens; it was also hung upon poles, and extended along the banks of rivers, according to the turns of the current, the fowler, meanwhile, keeping watch over the movements of the birds.[4]

The *curbaculum* was simply a trap employed by the fowlers of old for taking birds in the snow.[5]

Ancient fowlers are said to have been gifted with an art

of enchantment, whereby birds were enticed into snares, or otherwise became captives to the fowler's artifices, through the means of bird-calls, and other devices for attracting their attention, or amusing them in such a manner as to excite their curiosity; and for this purpose the fowlers used to clothe themselves in feathered jerkins,[1] and dance with particular motions and gestures in the presence of such birds as they sought to capture.

The methods of taking wild-fowl with horse-hair nooses and springes are very ancient. They were used by the Anglo-Saxons both by night and clay, and were employed in the fens as well as by the margins of lakes, rivers, and pools, the snares being sometimes placed under water.[2] They were also frequently planted in plashes, made by breaking the ice, because of the greater resort of wild-fowl to such puddles in severe weather, and consequently with the greater prospect of success.[3] Springes were also made with a running knot, and set with sticks freshly cut from a growing elm, or other tree of flexible substance; and such were freely employed for taking snipes and woodcocks.[4]

Ensnar'd and hamper'd by the soul,

As nooses by the legs catch fowl.[5]

These ancient devices for taking wild-fowl by the neck or legs, and frequently by both, were highly successful; they were simply by means of nooses or running knots, made of horsehair (generally black or dyed), fastened to stakes, and placed in small openings among sedges and rushes, or in any such places as the fowler, from his previously acquired knowledge of their haunts, deemed most favourable to his pursuits. Two or three of the nooses were secured to each stake; and as many as three or four dozen stakes so fitted were occasionally in use at the same time, pricked out in a small space frequented by wild-fowl. It was a favourite practice of the ancient wild-fowler to set snares of this description in marshes and plashes where the water was not above a foot and a half in depth; and by scattering handfuls of grain two or three days in succession, about the spot best adapted to his purpose, the snares were spread with greater prospect of success.

Archery was anciently a mixed military and sportive exercise, and was successfully used in fowling. In the sixteenth century, when shooting with the long bow had become so perfect an art, it was esteemed above all other contrivances for taking wildfowl; and for some time after the invention of guns, the long bow was preferred as the best and most practicable means that could be employed for the purpose.[1] A statute was accordingly passed prohibiting the taking of wild-fowl in any other manner.

To such perfection had the art arrived in those days, that we find the same author asserting elsewhere that shooting with the 'longe bowe' was declared the 'principal of all other exercises,' for he adds—'And, in myne opinion, none may be compared with shootyng in the longe bowe, and that for sundry vtilities that come thereof, wherein it incomparably excellethe al other exercyse.'

It is also stated that some of the archers of those days were enabled to fly their shafts with such unerring precision, that their aim was always directed to the *head* of any large bird, rather than the fairer mark presented by the body; and that wild-fowl so bagged were of greater value, and more saleable, because of there being no wound in the flesh. A circumstance is also recorded of small birds being placed on the back of a cow, and killed with bow and arrow without injury to the animal.[2] Accomplishments of this nature would seem almost to vie with those of William Tell.

The diversion of falconry as appertaining to the capture of wild-fowl is not near so ancient as that of taking them with nets, snares, and traps. Flavius Blondus, who wrote in the fifteenth century, negatives the assertion that falconry was a pastime of the ancient Greeks, and positively affirms that no nation or people were accustomed, previously to the thirteenth century, to catch either land or water-fowl with any rapacious bird trained for the purpose. And Rigault is of the same opinion.[1] Pancirollus and Salmuth also both concur.

The Roman laws distinctly recognise this method of fowling—

'Ne is qui duntaxat iter per fundum meum fecerit, aut avem egerit venatusve fuerit, sine ullo opere, hoc interdicto teneatur.'[2]

Fowling by means of rapacious birds must have been used in Italy at a very early age, for it is spoken of both by Martial and Apuleius as an art generally known and practised in that country.

Ælian mentions that in Thrace hawks used to accompany the fowlers when they went in quest of birds in the fens. The fowlers, having spread their nets, remained quiet; whilst the hawks flew about, terrifying the birds, and driving them into them.[3]

The same author also states that the Thracians, when they caught birds, used to divide them with the hawks, by which means they rendered them faithful partners in fowling; and that, if they had not given them a share of the booty, they would have been deprived of their assistance.[4]

This division of the prey between the fowler and his hawks is also mentioned by Pliny—'Rursus captas aucupes dividunt cum iis.'[5]

The rapacious birds used for the purposes of fowling were termed ἱέρακες by Grecian authors. Pliny terms them *accipitres*.

There are curious assertions in a book ascribed to Aristotle, that in Thrace falcons were so perfectly trained as to answer to their names, and go direct to the fowler when called; and that they used to bring to him, of their own accord, whatever prey they had taken.

The ancient falconer delighted to make wild-fowl his quarry: the pursuit of such birds was his favourite diversion, as will be seen on reference to the earliest treatises upon that once princely and popular recreation.[1]

Falconry is still practised, in some countries, with all the spirit and enthusiasm of the good old times. In Hungary particularly hawking-parties are highly attractive,[2] and of frequent occurrence. In that country, as in England, the heron is the favourite quarry.

The nobility of Mingrelia practise falconry, particularly for the purpose of capturing wild-fowl. They pursue the sport on horseback, and carry a small drum at the pommel of the saddle; and by beating the drum they put up the birds, and then fly their hawks at them.[3]

Hawking is said to have been constantly in use in England down to the year 1725, when *shooting flying* was introduced, to the great astonishment of the Dalesmen.[4]

Some of the early English poets make marked allusion to water-fowl as the falconer's best quarry:

'No fellow to the flight at brooke, that game is full of glee.'[5]

'The duck and mallard first, the falconer's only sport.'[6]

Hawks were specially trained for capturing water-fowl, and a species termed the 'Rammage Lanner' devoted exclusively to such quarry.[7] The goshawk, ger-falcon, jerkin, haggard falcon, and tassel-gentle were also taught to fly at wild-ducks that were found in ponds or other inland waters. This was esteemed most exciting sport, and the wild-duck a good prey;[8] but the heron was always considered the falconer's noblest quarry.

Hawking was also a sport in which the gentler sex freely indulged; no expedition of the kind was deemed complete unless graced with the presence of a lady-falconer. The engraving opposite represents that method of falconry as practised in the Fens about the fifteenth century. It was usual, on excursions of the kind, to be accompanied by a water-dog, because the hawk and its prey sometimes both fell in the water; and in their struggles, the wild-fowl, from its greater power when on the surface of that element, frequently imperilled the safety of the hawk by plunging and diving. The fowler, meanwhile, watching his bird, in case of danger would send the dog to the rescue, which was so trained that it never attempted to injure the hawk, but seized the mallard, or whatever fowl it might be, and brought it to its master.

The Fen-Fowlers of Old

During the age when falconry and archery were considered the first and most distinguished pastimes in the land, sportsmen were extremely tenacious about the preservation of wildfowl, and more especially after the passing of the bill against 'shootynge with hayle shott,'[1] in reference to which an original letter from Sir E. Bedingfield to the Earl of Bath, written about that time (1548), shows the strong feeling then entertained as to the preservation of wild-fowl as quarry for the falconer.[2]

Some of the contrivances of the ancient fowler, previous to the invention of decoys, strike us at the present day as exceedingly grotesque and simple; but, as they are transmitted to us by authors of reliable authority in those days,[3] and by them asserted as the best and most effectual means of taking wild-fowl, we are bound to believe that some, at least, of these manœuvres were highly successful. Nets of various forms and sizes were also freely employed; and those used for taking the largest sort of wild-fowl were made of strong pack-thread, with large meshes, at least two inches in extent from 'poynt to poynt.'

One of the most successful methods of taking wild-fowl was with a net of the kind, twelve yards in length by eight in breadth, which was as large as one man could dexterously manage or overthrow. This net being verged on each side with a stout cord, it was stretched on poles, and spread flat upon the ground, at least two hours before twilight, in the most favoured haunts of wild-fowl known to the snarer. The manner of working the net was, by staking the two lower ends firmly to the ground, but leaving sufficient play to admit of its being thrown over without drawing the stakes or unhinging the loops or fastenings;[1] and a line being connected with the upper verge, and rove through a hole in another stake, about six yards in front of one of the lower corners of the net, it was then of sufficient length to extend to the fowler's hiding-place, which was generally about twenty or thirty yards from the net—a mere temporary screen or embankment of turf and dried grasses; and, with such arrangements complete, and having carefully strewn a few handfuls of short grass over the surface of the net, and placed it so that no obstruction might prevent its being suddenly thrown over, the fowler was supposed to await patiently the arrival of the birds. Sometimes a live heron, or other species of wild-fowl, was secured to a stake, as a 'stale'[2] for enticing others; and when a satisfactory number of birds had come within a scope of the net, by suddenly drawing the line the snare was cast over them, and they were thus taken captive. 'The proceedings,' Markham observes, 'might be continued during twilight of an evening, and early in the morning, until the sun had risen half-an-hour, but not later.' This system of fowling was performed with equal success upon the plover species as upon the larger sort of fowl, which are in the habit of feeding on and frequenting marshes and fens by night.

It is somewhat remarkable that so rustic a style should have been practised after the fowling-piece came into use; but it seems to have been long preferred to the matchlock, notwithstanding that the fowler, in his hidden position, whilst attending the net, was within deadly range, with powder and shot, of any birds which came to his snare.

The method of taking wild-ducks in the Fens, with the clap-net, is described and illustrated by Peter de Crescentius,[1] as are also several other methods of land-fowling.

One of the most singular artifices recorded of the ancient fowler is that of employing four hungry ducks as the chief instruments of his art. Having spread an ordinary clap-net upon the ground, and scattered a few handfuls of corn within scope of its meshes, two men are stationed in a place of concealment, at some little distance from the spot, who hold the check-rope in their hands, in connection with the net, at command. The four hungry decoy-ducks are then let out, and permitted to taste the food, when they are immediately driven away by men with staves. The famishing ducks then fly for food and refuge to the neighbouring fens, but return in a short time, accompanied by many followers; which, alighting with the hungry decoy-ducks between the folds of the net, and feeding greedily upon the scattered grain, the fowler is immediately enabled to capture them. This method of fowling is thus described in Latin, in a work of great curiosity,[2] which bears a well-executed engraving of the proceeding:

> 'Arte nova instructos Anates fallax habet Auceps.
> Quatuor: bis urgente fame proponitur esca:
> Verum ne comedant baculis terrentur: ut inde
> Avolitent redeantque Anatum comitante caterva.'

A very remarkable device for capturing cranes is also described and illustrated in the same work. The fowler, having made up a number of paper hoods in conical shapes, places them in a locality commonly frequented by such birds, in holes or furrows in the ground with the points of the cones downward: he then baits each of them with a small fish, which he places inside, at the very point or bottom of the hood; and, having bedaubed the interior of the paper with bird-lime, the traps are ready. The hungry cranes, coming to their haunts, eagerly thrust their heads into the hoods to seize the fish, when, the bird-lime sticking to their feathers, and the hoods covering their eyes, in that hoodwinked dilemma they are unable to fly, and so become captives to the fowler. The artifice is thus described in the Latin text from which, assisted by the illustration, our description in English has been written:

> 'Auceps è chartis confectos arte cucullos
> Interius visco linit: in scrobibus locat: indit
> Pisa: venit Grus esuriens: rostrum ingerit: hæret
> Charta oculos velans, volucri prohibetque volatum.'

A similar device is mentioned by Blome as 'a very pleasant way of taking pigeons, rooks, and crows;' but, instead of a fish, being used as a bait, a few grains of corn are put at the bottom of the hood. The plan is recommended to be used in ploughing-time, the hoods being placed in the furrows, and baited with lob-worms.

Another ancient method of fowling appears to have been practised with remarkable success upon the smaller sort of wildfowl, which for the most part frequent, and feed upon the water at night. The nets employed for this purpose were simply what are termed at the present day 'flue-nets,' and such as are used for taking fresh-water fish in narrow waters. For the purposes required by the ancient fowler, these nets were two and a half or three feet in depth, and of lengths in proportion to the width of the river or extent of the water over which they were employed.

A number of these were thrown across a stream, at various distances apart, and staked down at each end to the bank, in such a manner that the lower part, which was weighted for the purpose, might sink about half a foot under water, but not deeper; the remainder or upper part of the net standing in a bowline, about eighteen inches above the surface, and the rods supporting it being flexible, so that, when any fowl struck against the net, the rods yielded to the pressure, and gave scope for entanglement. Some of these nets were also placed along the banks of rivers and ponds, and among rushes and swamps, in the fens and in other such resorts of wild-fowl; and it would seem that the fowler, by judiciously arranging his nets in the manner described, was frequently rewarded with abundant success.[1] The time of day for this mode of fowling was evening, the nets being spread just before sunset. The principal feature in the art was that of being familiar with the habits and haunts of the birds; so that, when they were searching for food by the banks of the water or elsewhere, they became entangled within the meshes of the net; and, it appears, an experienced fowler would so place his nets that every fowl which approached the bank inevitably fell captive to his snares.

The nets for taking wild-ducks and Pochards were sometimes placed entirely under water, several live decoy-ducks being tethered to stakes near by. In nearly all the artifices used by the ancient fowler decoy-birds were freely employed.[1]

———————

[1] Pollux, v. 4.

[2] 'Argumentum: Machina, qua aves in aquis capiuntur.'—*Du Cange.*

'De argumentis vero, per quae aves possunt capi super aquam.'—*Charta Childe-berti Regis pro Monasterio S. Germani Parisiensis.*

[3] 'Panthera posita ab aucupe.'—*Ulpianus.*

Panthera is also a term applied by the lower Normans to nets used for taking all kinds of birds, whether land or water-fowl: 'Normanni inferiores Pantiere vocant rete quo capiuntur aves maritimæ.'—*Martinii.*

Panthera is also a word used by Peter de Crescentius (who

flourished about the middle of the thirteenth century), in his 'Opus Ruralium Commodorum sivo de Agricultura.'

[4] 'Andr. Floriac. in Mirac. S. Bened. MSS., lib. iii.: Dum casses retium, quas vulgo Pantheras vocant; hinc inde porrectis amicibus fluminis alternis protenderet ripis, et volucrum pervigil excubitor præstolatur capturam, etc.'—*Du Cange.*

[5] 'Curbaculum: Instrumentum ad capiendas aves tempore nivium.'—*Petrus do Crescentius*, lib. x., *De Agricultura.*

[1] Fosbroke's 'Encyclopædia of Antiquities.'

[2] Blome's 'Gent.'s Rec'

[3] *Vide* 'The Compleat Sportsman.' By Giles Jacob, A.D. 1740.

[4] *Vide* 'Jewell for Gentrie.' By Jno. Helme, A.D. 1614.

[5] Hudibras.

[1] 'I shall hereof more speake in an other place, and retourne nowe to the seconde vtylitee founde in shotynge in the longe bowe, which is kyllye of deere, wylde fowle, and other game; wherein is bothe profyte and pleasure above any other artyllery.'—The boke named *The Governour*. By Sir Thomas Elyote, Knyght. 1557.

² Carew's 'Cornwall,' p. 73A.

¹ *Vide* also Jos. Scaliger, 'Comment, in Cirin.,' fol. 344. Also, Preface to Scriptores Rei accipitrariæ.

² Digest, lib. xliii. tit. 24, s. 22.

³ 'Eos in Thracia auditione accepi ad hanc rationem cum hominibus per paludes societatem aucupandi coire: homines expansis retibus quiescero, accipitres autem supervolantes exterrere aves, ac intra retium ambitum compellere.'—*Ælian. Hist. Anim.* lib. ii. cap. 42.

⁴ 'Thraces si quas ceperint aves, cum accipitribus partiri, eosque turn ad aucupii societatem fidos habere; sin cum his earum partem, quas ceperint, avium non communicaverint, aucupii sociis privari.'—*Ibid.*

⁵ Pliny, lib. x. cap. viii. s. 23.

⁶ De Mirabilibus Auscultat. cap. 128.

¹ Seo also 'De Arte Venandii cum Avibus'—a work of extreme scarcity, printed at Augsburgh, anno 1596, from a MS. belonging to Joachim Camerarius, a physician at Nuremberg.

² 'Rambles in Search of Sport.' By the Hon. F. St. John. A.D. 1853.

[3] 'Travels in Persia and the East Indies.' By Sir John Chardin. 1643.

[4] Whitaker's 'Richmondshire,' vol. i. p. 309.

[5] Turberville.

[6] Drayton.

[7] Latham's 'Faulconry,' book ii. A.D. 1658.

[8] Latham, book ii.

[1] 2 & 3 Ed. VI. cap. 14.

[2] 'My good Lorde,—I beseech yon to take knowledge to move as you shall think good for a redresse to be had for such persons as dayly do shoote in hancle-gonnes, and beat at the fowles in ryvers and pyttes, so as ther is no fowle that do remayne in the countrye; a man disposed to have a flight wt. hawkes may seeke tenn myles ere he fynde one coople of fowls to fly at, wheare in all yeres past there shulde have been founde in the same places vc. coople of fowls. I have spoken to the clarke of the peace with in Norfolk, who asserteyned me by his book, not to be above the number of iij persons entered into his booke for to shoote in gonnes, but surelie I think ther be wt. in this shyre that claylie doth exercyse and practyse shooting at fowle wt. there gonnes not so few as three

score of which number I cannot hear of any that may spend of lands being their owne above iiij scr. lb. by yere. If this be not reamyded, you wt. all the rest of the nobilitie may put forth your hawkes to breede and to keepe no more. And thus I beseeche God to have yor. Lordshippe and my good Lady your wyffe in moche honor. Yors. to comaunde,—EDMUNDE BEDINGFIELD.'—Vide *The History and Antiquities of Hengrave.* By John Gage, Esq., F.S.A.

³ Gryndall on 'Fowling:' 1596. 'A Jewell for Gentrie:' 1614. Markham on 'Fowling:' 1655. Cox's 'Gentleman's Recreations:' 1686. Blome's 'Gentleman's Recreations:' 1686: &c., &c.

¹ 'So that the nets may rise upon those stakes, to open and shut as upon so many payre of hinges.'—*A Jewell for Genlrie.*

² Call-bird.

¹ Book x., cap. 20.

² Venationes Ferarum, Avium, &c.; depictæ a Joanne Stradano, editæ a Philippo Gallæo; Carmine illustratæ a C. Kiliano: no date.

¹ 'And thus without fayle, where plenty of Fowle are, you shall take plenty: and where they are the scarcest, yet you shall have an equall share without much trouble.'—*Hunger's*

Prevention.

[1] 'They that would employ themselves in taking ducks and mallards with nets &c. shold always have some wild ones reclaimed, and made tame for that purpose; for the wild will never accompany themselves with those of the real tame breed.'—-Blome's *Gentleman's Recreations*.

CHAPTER III

ANCIENT METHODS OF CAPTURING WILD-FOWL—continued.

'With seeds and birdlime from the desert air,
Eumelus gather'd free, though scanty, fare.
No lordly patron's hand, he deign'd to kiss;
No luxury knew—save liberty—nor bliss.
Thrice thirty years he lived, and to his heirs
His seeds bequeath'd—his birdlime, and his snares.'

Translation by MILTON.

THERE was also a method much in vogue, previously to the invention or discovery of decoys, of taking wild-fowl with lime-strings,[2] made of pack-thread or string, knotted in various ways and besmeared with bird-lime; these were set in rows about the fens, moors, and other feeding haunts of the birds, an hour or two before morning, or evening twilight. The plan was to procure a number of small stakes, each about two feet in length, sharpened to a point at the nether end, and forked at the upper. These were pricked out in rows about a yard or two apart, some being placed in a slanting direction, and each stake siding one with another within convenient distances, of four or five yards, so as to bear up the strings, which were laid upon the crotches, and placed loosely about eighteen inches above the ground. The lime-strings were thus drawn from stake to stake in various directions, and lightly placed between the forks at the top of the stakes, some rows being higher than others; and in this manner the whole space occupied by the stakes was covered with lime-strings, as if carelessly laid in wave-like coils, or placed in different directions, the ends being secured to the stakes with slip-knots, so that upon slight strain the whole of any string which might be touched by the bird became instantly loose; and sticking to the feathers, the more it struggled to free itself, so much the more the string twisted about it: and thus the bird was quickly entangled, and became an easy prey. In this manner numbers of wild-fowl of the largest species were taken at night, at the moment of swooping over the ground at a very low flight, just before alighting. And it would appear that this method of fowling was particularly successful in taking plovers, which generally alight on the ground thickly congregated together.

A similar method was employed for taking wild-fowl with lime-strings placed over the surface of rivers and ponds frequented by those birds, and apparently with remarkable success. For this purpose it was necessary to procure a waterproof birdlime wherewith to dress the strings, which were knotted in a similar manner to those employed for taking birds on land. The strings so prepared were placed at an elevation of about two feet from the water,[1] and arranged in serpentine coils from stake to stake; the stakes being forked at top, and of similar form to those last described, but of sufficient length to reach the bottom of the water and obtain a firm fixing in the mud. Some of the stakes were placed on the bank of the water, or in any manner so that the lime-strings could be drawn across and about the surface in different directions, resting here and there on some or other of the stakes, or any boughs or branches of overhanging trees, in such a way that the birds, when in the act of alighting on the water at night, might strike against the lime-strings and become therein entangled.

The principal secret of success in this and the preceding device was that of placing the lime-strings, in shady places, over the most assured haunts of the birds; and it was only obtained on dark nights or in good shade, for whenever there was sufficient light for the birds to see the least sign of the snare spread for them the fowler had no chance of making any captives.[2] And, as wild-fowl in their descent, just before alighting on the water, diverge from their accustomed angular figure, and spread themselves more in a broad front line, a whole flight sometimes came swooping into the fowler's snare all at once.[1]

Another ancient mode of fowling was by means of lime-twigs—

'Various, too, the snares he'd spread;
Along their paths he'd lime-twigs lay,
Or spread the hair-noose in their way'—

the size and strength of which were in accordance with the size and strength of the birds expected to be captured; but light, flexible, and slender, that they might twist and cleave to the feathers. Twigs taken from the willow tree were best adapted, and most generally employed, for the purpose. A number of these twigs, or rods, being placed about the most frequented feeding haunts of wild-fowl just before twilight of a winter's evening, and a stale or two made fast to stakes in a vacant place among the lime-rods, the fowler hid himself at a convenient distance, where he held in his hand a string in connection with the *stales*,[2] that he might rouse and cause them to flutter and 'quack!' so as to attract the attention of flights of fowl that might be passing over in the air; which, on alighting among the lime-twigs, became besmeared about their feet and feathers with birdlime, and being unable to release themselves, they were held down, and prevented from flying by the adhesive properties of the lime, and so easily captured; for the more they struggled to release themselves the sooner they became helpless, and unable to fly.

In placing these lime-rods it was necessary to take particular observation of the furrows and water-rills, where the fowl usually stalk and paddle for worms, flot-grass, roots, and such like; and to note where several furrows meet in one, or branch off into smaller divisions, and in such places to set the rods.

The lime-twigs employed for taking wild-fowl on land were also frequently applied to the purposes of taking them by water, the twigs being planted partly above and partly under water, with a few call-birds among them, secured to stakes in the manner already described. The whole was a very attractive and often highly successful method of fowling, and was employed by day as well as night, particularly in shallow pools and inland waters—the daily haunts of duck, widgeon, and teal. The services of a good water dog[1] were considered essential for the purpose of capturing the birds, which dived with much avidity, notwithstanding that the twigs might be sticking to their feathers.

It would appear that a considerable amount of skill and experience was necessary in placing these lime-twigs for fowling by daylight, or the birds would not alight among them.

This art was often successfully performed upon large gaggles of grey geese; the lime-twigs being of extra size, and the lime of double strength. A number of these twigs (or rods, as they were sometimes called) were placed in open fields amongst green wheat, on which the species grey-lag are particularly fond of feeding. And, it seems, the fowler had to pay special regard to the colour of the rods, that they might resemble as nearly as possible the soil on which they were placed, and so excite as small an amount of suspicion as could be. But without a thorough knowledge of the most favoured haunts of the birds these methods of fowling with lime-twigs could not have been attended with any proper result. A regard to the season of the year and the number of birds about the coast was also an important consideration. In some cases success might be obtained by the fowler's cunning in disturbing the birds from other haunts near at hand, when they would probably fly directly to those where his own snares were spread.[2] But it must have been, at all times, a very uncertain and precarious method of fowling.

The appropriation of birdlime to the purposes of taking wild-fowl has been known during many centuries. It is mentioned by Plutarch as one of the fowler's devices in early clays; and it was also freely practised in France and Holland, and on various parts of the continent, as were also many of the devic es alluded to for taking them with nets.[3]

The mischievous practice of capturing wild-fowl by aid of poisonous drugs was formerly considered a fair method of fowling. It is fully treated in Blome's 'Gentleman's Recreations,' where instructions are given for mixing and making 'the composition and baits for intoxicating of fowl, and yet without tainting or hurting their flesh,' the ingredients for which comprise simply, corn or seeds steeped in mix vomica, wine lees, or juice of hemlock. The author of 'A Jewell for Grentrie' publishes this disreputable art as a great secret, as will be seen from the extracts below.[1]

This derogatory system of fowling is also alluded to in the 'Song of the Poacher,' published in vol. ii. 'Annals of Sporting.'

'Or barley, oats, or wheat he'd use,
Steeped in the Indian berry's juice,
Which by the heedless birds devour'd
Makes them fall senseless and o'erpower'd,
At once a rich and easy prey.'

Besides the two recipes below, the author of 'A Jewell for Gentrie' puts forth another 'excellent way to make a baite to catch wild geese, and wild duckes, and all other sorts of fowle.' It consists in simply steeping the seeds and roots of 'Belenge' in water, and, when well soaked, laying it in places the resort of wild-fowl; when, if the birds eat it, they are said to 'sleepe as if they were drunke,' and in that state the fowler is enabled to take them without difficulty. It is added, that if brimstone be mixed with the bait, the birds 'fall downe and die;' but in order to keep them 'that they die not, you must give them to drinke oyle olive, and shortly after they will revive againe.'[2]

In centuries past, a most destructive and reprehensible system of fowling was pursued, whereby thousands of wild-duck and teal were taken during the moulting season—

'For sure unless in me, no one yet ever saw
The multitudes of fowl in *mooting* time they draw.'[1]

When, having lost many of their feathers, they were unable
to fly, and their young being only half-grown, in this helpless
condition old birds and young were driven into tunnel-
nets and secured. It is one of the most ancient systems on
record of taking water-fowl in very large numbers. It was a
practice extensively resorted to in the fens of Ely, Norfolk, and
Lincolnshire, about Crowland and elsewhere.[2] Ducks, teal,
widgeon, and other birds of the kind were taken in numbers
which appear almost incredible. The manner in which it
was conducted is as follows: Two very long nets, or rather a
number of nets spliced together, were placed in line in the
water, so as to form two sides of a triangle, at the narrow
extremity of which were one, two, or three conoidical nets,
resembling decoy-pipe and tunnel-nets; the opposite angle of
the space encompassed was left entirely open, and thus a broad
expanse of water was enclosed on each side and at the farther
extremity. The sedges and surrounding haunts of water-fowl
were then beaten by a great concourse of men in boats, who
drove the helpless fowl within the space enclosed, by splashing
and dashing with long poles and staves; and so, by degrees,
they were driven into the tunnels and captured. Many birds,
which might chance to strike against the side-nets during
operations, became ensnared before reaching the tunnel,
and were taken up generally by the person to whom the net

belonged; and there were usually a combination of owners, the nets being linked one to another, so as to enclose as large a space as possible. Latham has recorded an instance in which *two thousand six hundred and forty-six* wild-fowl were taken during the short space of two days on a mere near Spalding, in Lincolnshire; and Willughby states that at a fowling-party engaged in this pursuit as many as *four hundred boats* used sometimes to meet, and that *four thousand mallards* have been taken at one driving in Deeping Fen.[3]

These proceedings were considered so disreputable and injurious to the preservation and increase of wild-fowl as to demand the attention of the legislature, and led to the passing of that curious, and at the present day amusing, statute, 25 Hen. VIII., cap. 11, intituled 'An Acte ayenst the Destruccyon of Wyld-fowle;' wherein, after setting forth that before that time there had been plenty of wild-fowl, but that in consequence of clivers persons inhabiting the districts where wild-fowl breed, having in the summer season, 'at suche tyme as the seid olde fowle be mowted and not replenysshed with fethers to flye, nor the yonge fowle fully fetherede perfyctfy to flye, have, by certen nettes and other ingyns and polycies, yerely taken great nomber of the same fowle, in such wyse that the brode of wylde-foulle is almoste thereby wasted and consumed, and clayly is lyke more and more to wast and consume yf remedy be not therefore pvyded.'

The statute then provides against taking wild-fowl by such means between the 'last day of Maye and the last day of August' in any year, thereby putting a summary stop to such destructive proceedings.

A statute was also passed in Scotland in the reign of James II., A.D. 1457, prohibiting the destruction of wild-fowl during the moulting season.[1] Blome also speaks of this system of fowling, and states that numbers of wild-fowl were easily taken in the fens, in moulting time, with the assistance of a water-spaniel, by simply driving them into narrow creeks where tunnel-nets were previously fixed.

Notwithstanding the statute of 25 Henry VIII., it appears that in subsequent reigns it was often infringed; and though Markham, who wrote in 1621 and 1655 upon the art of fowling, makes but cursory mention of taking wild-fowl by driving, Willughby, who wrote in 1678, gives a full description of it. The omission by Markham was probably intentional, because of the illegality of the proceeding after the statute of Henry VIII. above cited.

In reference to the wholesale capture of wild-fowl which prevailed previous to the passing of the statute alluded to, it is worthy of remark that many fens and other strongholds of wild-fowl were then in their wild and natural state; no draining pipe had then found its way beneath the surface, but the whole country of the fens afforded every requisite protection, and encouragement to the breeding and rearing of water-fowl. No wonder, then, that their numbers should have been so great, that as many as three and four thousand should have been taken at a driving; and this, it must be remembered, in the summer season.[1]

The numbers now bred annually in the English fens are too insignificant to make it worth while resorting to such unsportsmanlike proceedings as those just described; and setting aside the undignified nature of the pursuit, it is one not very likely to be revived in this country, the few wild-fowl which now stay and breed with us during summer having become of too rare a curiosity to be destroyed when in a helpless condition by any person aspiring to the character or position of an English sportsman.

There can be no doubt but this ancient system of driving wild-fowl up tunnel-nets when unable to fly, as already described, was directly or indirectly a means which suggested the contrivance of the Decoy—a laudable and ingenious pursuit, explained in subsequent chapters.

---

[2] Hunger's 'Prevention.' Blome's 'Gent.'s Rec.,' &c.

[1] Blome.

[2] 'And be sure to take this caution, not to use these strings in moonshine nights; for the shadow of the lines will create a jealousy in the fowl, and so frustrate your sport.'—*Blome.*

[1] Hunger's 'Prevention.'

[2] Decoy-birds.

[1] 'Neither shall you in any wise come without your water dogge, for he is a main instrument, and a servant of such use, that without him in this place you shall loose half your gettings, therefore in anywise he ever sure to have him at your heeles.'—*Markham.*

[2] Hunger's 'Prevention.'

[3] *Vide* Le parfait Chasseur; par M. de Selincourt: 1683. Le Traité des Oiseaux de voilière; ou, Le parfait Oisleur. Traduit en partie de l'Ouvrage Italien d'Olina: 1774. Also Traité de toute Sorte de Chasse et de Pêche; contentat, la manière de faire, racommoder et teindre toutes sortes de fillets; de prendre aux pièges toutes sortes d'oiseaux et bêtes à quatre pieds: un Traité de la Volerie et des Oiseaux qui y servent, &c.: à Amsterdam, 1714; 2 tomes. And see also, 'Amusemens do la Campagne, ou Nouvelles Ruses Innocents qui enseignent la manière de prendre aux piéges toutes sortes d'Oiseaux,' &c.: par le Sieur

L. Liger: à Paris, 1753.

[1] 'A rare secret to catch fowle, as geese, duckes, or birds:—Nuxe vomica, otherwise called in English spring nut; put a pretie deale of that sod in a peake of barley, or as little as you thinke good, or fetches, or wheat, and being strowed where wilde geese, or wild duckes come, and as soone as they eate of this, they will sound, and you may take them with your hand.'—*A Jewell for Gentrie*, Printed for Jno. Helme. A.D. 1614.

'Another pretie way to make birds drunke that you may take them with your hand:—Take wheat or fetches, or any other seede, and lay the same in steepe in lees of wine, or in the juice of hemlocke, and strow the same in the place where birds use to haunt, and if they eat thereof, straightwaies they will be so giddie that you may take them with your hand.'—*Ibid.*

[2] The restorative properties of 'sallet oyle' with 'white wine vinegar' are recommended by Blome to be given to fowl as soon as captured, for the purpose of correcting the ill effects of the poison.

[1] Drayton.

[2] Willughby.

[3] This is one of the principal fens mentioned by Wells, in his 'History of the Drainage of the Great Bedford Level;' it is also referred to by Dugdale, as formerly ten miles in breadth, and containing 27,000 acres.

[1] 'Item anents the keping of birds and wylde fowlys that ganis to eit for the sustentacione of man as pertriks pluvors wylde duks and sik lik fowlys it is ordanyt that na man distroy thar nests nor thar eggs nor zit sla wilde fowlys in mooting tyme quhile thai may not fie.'

[1] Daniel, in his 'Rural Sports,' also mentions a record of this driving of the old birds, at Spalding, when unable to fly, and states—'That at the duking, on Thursday last, were taken up one hundred and seventy-four dozen of mallards or drakes, moulting; and on Monday forty-six dozen anda-half: in all two thousand six hundred and forty-six mallards.'

In 'Fuller's Worthies of England,' by Nuttall, it is also stated, in allusion to the great abundance of wild-fowl taken by the fowlers in this country—'In the month of August three thousand mallards, with birds of that kind, have been caught at one draught, so large and strong their nets,' vol. ii. p. 263.

CHAPTER IV

EGYPTIAN FOWLING

'I scorn th' Egyptian fen which Alexandria shows,
  Proud Mareotis, should thy mightiness oppose,
Or Scythia, on whose face the sun doth hardly shine,
Should her Meotis think to match with this of mine.'

DRAYTON.

THE history of the Egyptians, with their manners, customs, arts, sciences, and recreations, is contained in illustrative figures and monuments rather than in written record; and probably no more faithful source could be resorted to for the purpose of acquiring a knowledge or familiarity with the habits of that people, and more especially with their remarkable methods of fowling, than by closely looking into those graphical and valuable delineations of art and science, each one of which is a study in itself. So exquisite are many of those figurative, representations of the art of fowling, that it is one of the recreations of that ancient people which can be as correctly relied on, traced, and described as any branch of their pursuits. All classes of the ancient Egyptians delighted in the sports of the field;[1] and in none have they left more satisfactory record than in this, which was one of their favourite diversions.

The valley of the Nile, with its extensive and luxuriant resources, has always been a much frequented resort of waterfowl; affording endless diversion to the Egyptian sportsman, and handsome remuneration to those who pursued the avocation of fowling as a means of livelihood.

The bow and arrow appear to have been the primitive instruments employed by the ancient Egyptian fowler for the purpose of taking wild-fowl; the arrows chiefly in use for such purpose being armed with a sharp-edged iron plate of crescent-like shape.[2] But it appears this art was not attended with that success which resulted from the 'throw-stick,'[3] the more favourite method of fowling.

The 'throw-stick' was a flat-shaped missile, made of hardened heavy wood, of from fifteen to twenty-four inches in length by one and a half in breadth, and about half an inch in thickness, the outer edge being thin and rather sharp. The upper end of the stick was slightly curved, the whole being similar in form to the boomerang of the New Hollander.

An expert fowler was able to throw this weapon a considerable distance, and with remarkable accuracy; and it appears from some of the plates of Egyptian bird-catching that the fowler's-aim with the throw-stick was chiefly directed at the neck of the bird, and that it was an art more particularly adapted to taking wild-ducks, geese, herons, and birds with long necks, rather than others.

The Egyptian fowler was accompanied on excursions of this kind by two or more attendants, some of whom were children, and all had certain duties to perform, being placed in relative positions in the fowler's boat. The water-fowl were either approached under ambuscade of rushes or papyrus, or the fowler and his assistants placed themselves in concealed positions, and, by aid of decoy-birds, enticed the fowl to advance. The duty of the youngest or smallest occupant of the boat appears to have been that of attending the decoy-bird, which in every representative scene of the kind stands on the prow of the boat; the fowler also holds one or more live decoy-fowl in his left hand; and it would seem that the object of such proceeding was to entice the wild-birds to fly near the captives, that the fowler might have the more favourable opportunity of discharging his missiles, and with greater certainty of success. These decoy-birds were held up by the fowler above the level of the reeds or other ambuscades; and from the fluttering position of their wings it seems reasonable to suppose that, at certain junctures, the fowler, by squeezing their legs, or some other manœuvre, caused them to call out, and so attract the notice of others, the immediate objects of his diversion.

On the wild-fowl rising suddenly from the water, or

approaching in their flight within range, the fowler threw his missile with such force and precision as to break the neck of the bird aimed at. And it would appear that an expert fowler was able to discharge three or more of these missiles, one after another, in rapid succession, and with unerring effect. To assist him in his dexterous performances it was the duty of one of his attendants to hand him other 'throw-sticks' in instantaneous succession, as he discharged them at the birds.[1]

Another attendant, who is represented as a young girl, stands close behind the fowler during his performances, and has her right hand firmly grasping his waist; evidently for the purpose of supporting and steadying him in his critical position as he stands in the boat, and so preventing any overbalance caused by extraordinary exertion in throwing the stick, and whereby, but for the temporary fulcrum of the attendant's hand, the fowler might fall overboard. Another attendant holds his leg, as if for the additional purpose of steadying his position and preventing his falling over the gunwale of the boat in which these operations are conducted. The boat itself is also held, as if by a temporary anchor, by the hand of one of the crew grasping a bunch of growing papyrus or lotus.

The fowler is also represented as attended by a cat, in the act of retrieving the struck birds; but this feline assistant was probably employed to retrieve those only which fell on land, or among sedges growing on a soil too rotten to bear the weight of human foot. It is impossible to imagine that the Egyptians, with all their renowned skill in training animals, could have so taught a cat as to employ it for retrieving from the water— an element always obnoxious to such animals; and, as there are no illustrations of the cat swimming in pursuit of the fowler's game—though there are several showing it retrieving waterfowl from the papyrus and banks of the water—we are disposed to believe that the services of this domestic attendant were employed exclusively to retrieve on land, and from such unapproachable places as those already alluded to.

The punts employed by the ancient Egyptian fowler were constructed of the trunk of the papyrus,[1] and were propelled by a setting-pole or paddle with a blade at one end. In a frail little bark of this nature he glided noiselessly in pursuit of his diversion among the sedges of the Nile, where wild-fowl have always been abundant, though more especially so at the periods of inundation.[2]

Many of the fowlers' traps and nets that are used in England at the present day for catching wild birds on land are very similar to those employed by the ancient Egyptians;[3] more especially the clap-net, which is nearly identical, though probably the Egyptian net was the larger, as the united strength of several persons appears to have been necessary for pulling the rope by which the net was suddenly collapsed.

This was evidently a very successful means by which they

captured wild-geese and ducks, as there are many different representations of it in the plates;[4] and it seems to have been more particularly employed for taking these and other waterfowl, for which purpose it was placed flat on the ground, in the fens or other haunts of such birds; and, a long rope being connected with the collapsing apparatus, five or six persons were stationed at the farther extremity of the rope, whose duty it was to take the end of it in their hands, on a given signal from the fowler,[1] and by drawing it suddenly and sharply it collapsed, and encompassed any birds which might have been lured within its circumference.

The spot usually selected for these operations seems to have been one where a sufficient ambuscade could be had within sight of the net, behind which the λινόπτης[2] placed himself; and from this place of concealment he watched the arrival of the fowl, and signalled to his assistants when to get ready, and when to draw the rope and close the net.

The practice of salting quails, ducks, and small birds, in Egypt, mentioned by Herodotus,[3] is confirmed by the sculptures, drawings, and representations; in which figures are shown in the act of plucking, salting, and preserving them in this manner, and depositing them, when cured, in jars. Champollion gives clear and beautiful engravings of the whole process.[4]

The illustrations also testify that swans and wild-geese were hunted and captured by dogs during the moulting season, when unable to fly.[5] There are two or three other methods of ancient Egyptian fowling exhibited by the original authorities, the precise intention of which is only partially explained, in consequence of mutilation to some of the figures.

---

[1] 'Manners and Customs of the Ancient Egyptians.' By Sir John Gardner Wilkinson, F.R.S., &c, vol. iii. cap. 8.

[2] 'Champollion-le-Jeune, Monuments de l'Egypte,' vol. iv. elephant folio. This is a most costly and elaborate work; it occupied ten years in completion. The engravings are executed in the highest style of perfection, and the entire work is printed on large folio sheets, comprising five volumes. It contains graphical illustrations of the whole of Bossellini's plates of Egyptian Antiquities.

[3] Wilkinson's 'Ancient Egyptians,' vol. iii. cap. 8.

[1] Sir G. Wilkinson states, in a note to his amusing work, that the Irish frequently use the 'throw-stick' for the purposes of fowling, after the manner of the ancient Egyptians.

¹ Conf. Lucan, iv. 136. Pliny, xiii. 11. Plut. de Isid, s. 18.

² Wilkinson, vol. iii. cap. 8.

³ The Egyptian bird-traps were employed for taking land-birds. This work professes to treat of water-fowl only.

⁴ *Vide* 'Champollion,' vol. ii. plate cxxxxv.; vol. iv. plates cccxciv. and CCCLXXVII. (*bis*).

¹ 'Un homme caché dans les tiges de papyrus indique le moment où l'on doit tirer la corde passée autour d'un poteau.'—*Champollion*, vol. iv.

² The fowler performing this part of the operations was so styled by the Greeks.—Vide *Julii Pollue. Onomasticon.*

³ Lib. ii. 77.

⁴ Vol. ii. planche CLXXXV., No. 2: 'Préparation des oies pour être conservées dans des jarres.'

⁵ Vol. ii. planche CLXXI.

CHAPTER V

THE HISTORY OF DECOYS.

'Tow'rds Lincolnshire our progress laid;
We through deep Holland's ditches made,
Fowling and fishing in the fen.'

DRAYTON.

IT seems quite unaccountable that none but mere cursory accounts of the decoy should hitherto have issued from the pens of any of the numerous contributors to the literature of field sports and recreations: such, however, is the fact, that no complete description of it has ever been published.

It cannot have been that the subject was not sufficiently attractive to demand the attention of the general reader as well as of the more careful enquirer, since, as regards natural history, rustic art, and ingenuity of contrivance, there are none to equal it; and, when it is considered that to this day the chief supplies of wild-fowl to the London and provincial markets are furnished from decoys, it is the more singular that so little has been made known as to the means which are used for taking them.

Decoys of long standing have sometimes been considered of sufficient importance to be mentioned by topographers;[1] but beyond a slight notice of the existence of such places, no further information has been given regarding them: they have also, on several occasions, been the subject of law-suits.[2]

Truly, the pursuits of the decoyman are such that, to insure success, they must be carried on almost in solitude. The gate of the decoy-grounds is generally closed against all enquirers, because of the quietude necessary to be maintained in conducting the operations, and consequently the secrecy of the art; and this may, in a measure, account for the unsatisfactory manner in which the subject has hitherto been approached in a literary point of view.

The proceedings within the quiet enclosure of the decoy, where Nature reveals some of her most admirable works, and animal instinct appears in its most bewitching garb, cannot fail to exalt the feelings of man, and teach an exceedingly amusing and instructive lesson; for there, within the precincts of the decoy, alone and unobserved, the solitary fowler is afforded an opportunity of acquiring such a knowledge of the habits and instincts of some of the most interesting of the feathered web-footed tribe as cannot be acquired elsewhere.

It is clear that our continental neighbours were, long ago, thoroughly awake to the art of taking wild-fowl by decoy, which they considered the most attractive sport in the world.[3]

And it is evident that decoys were constructed in Holland with great skill, and employed very successfully; for we find it suggested by a French writer of authority that large estates belonging to lords of manors, and possessing the conveniences for decoys, should be provided with such. But it is specially recommended that fowlers from the Netherlands should be hired to construct them, who should bring with them trained ducks, which, mixing with wild ones during the night, would return in the morning to the decoy, and entice several of their new acquaintances to follow them.[1] The same author carefully abstains from enlightening his readers upon the subject; but simply states, he shall say nothing upon the construction of the said decoys, nor of the manner in which the wild-ducks are taken, because, he adds, it is necessary to see the decoys made, and learn from thence all the tricks that are used for taking as many as may be desired.[2]

An early English writer upon fowling[3] is equally guarded in his remarks upon the decoy; and although he states that a long discourse might be written upon the subject, he simply follows in the steps of the French writer, by recommending his readers requiring information upon decoys to inspect those already made.[4]

The invention of the decoy appears to be the result of rural ingenuity, and may be traced to an age of antiquity, though it seems to have been unknown in Bracton's time. Blomefield, in his 'History of Norfolk,'[5] says decoys were invented by Sir William, son of Sir William Wodehouse,[6] who lived in the reign of King James I. It is, however, but a bare assertion, and stands unconfirmed by any other authority; nevertheless, the high character of that author's writings is sufficient warrant of their authenticity. In a very important case,[1] which was heard before Lord Holt in 1706, it was stated that decoys had not then been of long standing.

After examining some of the earliest authorities upon the subject of fowling, we find them awake to various crafts for taking wild-fowl in large numbers with nets and by other contrivances, some of which have been already referred to under the head 'Ancient Methods of Capturing Wild-fowl;' and the stat. 25 Henry VIIL, cap. II,[2] is conclusive as to the fact of wild-fowl being taken by thousands during the moulting season; and it would therefore appear that thousands of wildfowl must have been bred every year in England; while from the accounts as to these proceedings, which have been handed down to us by the authorities before referred to, it is clear that this was a very different proceeding to that of the clecoy. It seems that wild-fowl, when unable to fly (and when, in fact, out of season), were *driven* into a remote corner of a large space of water, and then up a pipe of net-work, and finally into a collapsible trammel, very similar to that which is employed by decoyers at the present day. The main feature, therefore, in the subsequent invention of decoys, is the part performed by the dog, which, combined with the services of the 'coy-ducks,' as they were anciently called,[3] constitutes the chief secret of the art. Thus it differs from the other proceeding, inasmuch that, instead of *driving* the fowl, they are enticed into the decoy pipes. Ray, who wrote in the year 1678, attributes the invention of decoys to the Low Dutch; but it would seem that the art was at that period very imperfectly understood, though he speaks of large numbers of duck, mallard, widgeon, and teal being taken in the '*winter-time*' by decoy. The author of the 'Encyclopaedia Metropolitana,' in allusion to the *panthera* and *argumentum* which were used by the wild-fowler of the thirteenth century, speaks of the latter as probably appertaining to a decoy; but there is no authority for such an assertion.

The *argumentum* appeals to have been a pipe or tunnel of net-work, with which the ancient fowler captured both land and water-fowl by simply driving them into it; but there is not the smallest trace of evidence to prove that the birds were decoyed or enticed; on the contrary, all the authorities tend to show that land and water-fowl were *driven* into the *argumentum*.[1]

The method of forming the original decoy-pipe was by thrusting flexible rods into the bank on either side of a ditch or channel leading out of the decoy pond, and bending them over so as to span the ditch and form an arch, the upper ends being bound together in pairs all the way up the pipe, those at the entrance forming much the largest and widest span, and so gradually becoming smaller and narrower towards the tail end of the pipe. The poles so bent and fastened were then covered with netting, and thus a cylindrical passage was formed, after the same manner as a modern decoy, but in a rougher and less elaborated style. The reed-screens were placed obliquely, and employed in a manner precisely similar to those in a modern decoy; and at the exit of the pipes, extra reed-screens were set up, for the purpose of screening the fowler and his operations from the sight of the birds.

In further proof of the imperfect manner in which the art was then understood, it is not mentioned by the authorities referred to that the dog is an indispensable assistant to the decoyer, but merely that 'Some train up a whelp for this sort of fowling,[2] and teach him to compass the reed-screens, and show himself "*behind* the birds:" 'an assertion which must be erroneous, because the part which the dog enacts is in *front* of the birds: they must be enticed a certain distance up the pipe before they can be driven. Willughby is evidently wrong in his notion that 'the dog terrifies the birds and drives them forward;' if the dog 'terrified' them they would take wing and leave the decoy, so also if he attempted to 'drive them forward;' yet his subsequent remarks would seem to suggest that he knew something of the art, for lie adds, 'Those behind him he allures and tolls forward, they following him, to gaze at him, as a new and strange object.'

The sources from which the author of that work compiled his dissertation upon the decoy were evidently loose, scanty, and inaccurate. The whole space devoted to the subject occupies barely one page in the volume. Nevertheless, from that time (1678) to the present, there has been no attempt by subsequent writers to explain the errors of their predecessors.

Bewick's[1] description of a decoy and method of using it is wild, theoretical, and erroneous: he speaks of the operations being always conducted *by night!* thus proving at once that he knew nothing of the art, the operations of capturing wildfowl at the decoy being always performed by daylight; and, indeed, there are seldom any wild-fowl in decoys at night. They generally leave at twilight in the evening, and repair to fens and meadows, where they remain until morning; and if it so happens (as it does sometimes) that a few birds remain all night in the pond, the decoyer could not see to perform his operations, which of necessity require daylight for being put into practice.

Wilson, in his 'American Ornithology,' copies all his information on decoys from Bewick, consequently adopts all his errors; and he likewise alludes to the operations of the decoyer as being conducted in the evening.

It is possible, though, it is hoped, not probable, that some persons, having constructed decoys on their estates, and being unacquainted with the decoyer's art of capturing wild-fowl, may have adopted the erroneous instructions of Bewick or Wilson, by attempting to take the birds by night, and have found the attempt so utterly useless that they abandoned the pursuit without venturing to differ from those authorities, or thinking for a moment that *daylight* must be the proper time to work a decoy.

The editor of the 'Encyclopaedia Metropolitan a' is also wrong in stating that '*towards evening* the decoyman prepares for working the pipe and *driving* the wild-fowl.'

Brande, in his 'Dictionary of Science,' falls into the same error. Under the head 'Decoy,' he states that the fowl are *driven* up the net by the dogs.

Several other writers have followed the text of these authors, and no one has yet ventured to contradict their fallacious theory.

The erroneous assertion that the fowl were driven into the decoy-pipe has thus become lamentably mischievous, as writers one after another have copied that absurd notion. And what is more astonishing than all is, that Mr. Wells, in his 'History of the Fens,' is equally guilty with his predecessors of this popular error. He observes on the art of decoying wild-ducks:[1] 'Sometimes, however, from their extreme shyness and caution, the tame duck does not succeed in trepanning others; in such cases, the decoyman employs a small dog, which, by *swimming about* amongst the rushes and reeds, and *alarming* the wild-fowl, *drives them up the mouth of the net!*[2]

It is possible that Mr. Wells may never have been within the grounds of a decoy; but certainly he was not familiar with the art of decoying wild-fowl, or he would not have asserted that the dog either 'swims about the rushes,' 'alarms the wildfowl,' or 'drives them up the mouth of the net.' For, in truth, the dog does neither; he is not sent into the water at all during the operation; instead of alarming the birds, every possible precaution is taken to avoid such a proceeding; and as to driving the fowl into the pipe, it is never attempted—they must be *enticed* by the dog, not driven. The only time of year when they can be driven is when they are moulting, and unable to fly—a season during which decoys are not exercised.

The term 'rising,' as applied to a decoy, implies that the wild-fowl leave it and go elsewhere; and this term has been too frequently misunderstood by those who imagined that the birds were captured by night, instead of by day; and they have supposed that, because wild-fowl feed at night, they were captured in the decoy at night, and that the 'rising of the decoy' meant the time to commence operations, whereas it implies the very reverse.

But of all the glaring absurdities ever published upon the subject, none are so ridiculous as the article under the head 'Decoy' in the 'Pantalogia.'[3] The writer starts off with the false notion that at the rising of the decoy, in the evening, the sport commences, and gives his readers to understand that a net covers the *entire pond*, reed screens and all! He also says, the wildfowl *pass over the screens*, and become *completely surrounded by the suspended net!* The writer then proceeds to say that, if the wild-fowl are inactive, the dog receives a signal 'to *paddle* at a little distance; and they are sure to advance, in the hope of catching and devouring what they *suppose to be small fishes* rising to the surface of the water!' In conclusion, this deluded writer states that, after the decoyman shows himself, the wildfowl follow the trained birds into the respective pipes.

From first to last, the whole of the article in the 'Pantalogia' as to the decoy is unpardonably erroneous, and tends not only to mislead the inquirer, but to confuse him as to every principle connected with the ingenious art of decoy, and is also directly at variance with the common instincts of the birds.

Blome's[1] description of a decoy-pond, with 'some directions concerning the same,' is free from error as far as it goes; but as it occupies only two-thirds of a column, or half a page, it is but a very meagre account.

Pennant[2] also gives a far more truthful description of the decoy than many of his predecessors, though it is a very brief one, the whole occupying but three pages. Oliver Groldsmith also gives a very fair description of a decoy and the proceedings in connection with the capturing of wild-fowl thereat.[3]

Lubbock's[4] description is entirely reliable, and much fuller than that of any previous writer upon the subject: he gives truthful and interesting details of the decoy.

Lubbock writes without reference to any standard work on fowling, but simply puts forth a pleasant little volume on the 'Fauna of Norfolk,' with such information regarding decoys as he himself possessed, combining with his own experience some excellent suggestions from a Lincolnshire decoyer.

---

[1] Blomefield in his 'History of Norfolk;' Watson in his 'History of Wisbech;' Morant in his 'History of Essex;' Palmer in his notes to Manby's 'History of Great Yarmouth;' Lipscomb's 'Buckinghamshire,' and others.

[2] Holt's 'Rep.' p. 14. 11 East 574. 2 Camp. 258.

[3] 'Il se fait en ces mares les plus beaux coups du monde.'— *Le Parfa it Chasseur.* Par M. De Selincourt. A.D. 1683.

[1] 'Quand un terre est fort seigneuriale, de grand étenduë, qu'il y a des étangs, de grandes prairies, de grand marais, on y doit faire des canardières, et pour cet effet, on doit faire venit des gens du païs bas pour les construire; lesquels apportent

avec eux des canards dressés qui se meslent parmi tous les autres sauvages toute la nuit, et le matin ils reviennent à la canardiére et en emmènent avec eux plusieurs sauvages.'—*Selincourt.*

[2] 'Je ne dis rien de la construction desdites canardières, ou de la façon et manière dont on prend les canards sauvages qui sont amenés par les privés, parce qu'il faut voit faire les canardières et apprendre d'eux toutes les ruses dont ils se servent pour en prendre tant qu'ils veulent.'—*Ibid.*

[3] Blome.

[4] 'The manner of doing it, and the making of the decoy pond, with the several apartments belonging to it, requires a long discourse; nor, indeed, can any particular rules or directions be given therein, as being variously made, according to the situation of the place, which must be considered; so that such as would make any had best inspect some already made, which are frequent in divers parts of this kingdom, especially in Lincolnshire, Cambridgeshire, and such-like fenny countries.'—*Blome's Gentleman's Recreations.*

[5] Vol. v. folio edition.

[6] The alleged introduction of decoys by Wodehouse is repeated by Mr, Palmer, in his notes to 'Manby's History of Great Yarmouth,' vol. i. p. 287.

[1] Keeble *v.* Hickeringall; and see *infra* 'The Law of Decoys.'

[2] 'An Acte ayenst Destruccyon of Wyld-fowle.'

[3] Willughby's 'Ornithology.'

[1] *Supra*, p. 8.

[2] Willughby.

[1] Bewick's 'Ornithology.'

[1] Wells, p. 447.

[2] In Watson's 'History of Wisbech,' p. 471, is a similar erroneous description of the proceedings at the decoy. Indeed, Wells's narrative appears to have been copied from Watson.

[3] 'Pantalogia:' 16 vols. 4to. Published 1813.

[1] Blome's 'Gentleman's Recreations.'

[2] Pennant's 'Natural History.'

[3] 'A History of the Earth and Animated Nature,' By Oliver Goldsmith, M.B. vol. iii. pp. 418, 419. Edition 1824.

[4] Lubbock's 'Fauna of Norfolk.'

CHAPTER VI

THE HISTORY OF DECOYS—continued

'Thick as the feather'd flocks in close array,
O'er the wide fields of ocean wing their way;
When from the rage of winter they repair
To warmer suns and more indulgent air.'—PITT.

IT is easy to imagine that in centuries gone by, before the use of fire-arms became general, the inhabitants of the fen countries endeavoured to devise a more liberal scheme for capturing some of the winter visitants of those regions, which assembled in such vast flights; but to take them seemed almost impossible, though it would appear as if they were sent in such abundance by Providence to be food for those who might succeed in capturing them. No wonder, then, that the ingenuity of man should, even in those days, have discovered a stratagem whereby to lure the eagerly-sought aquatic tribe within the meshes of a decoy, and thus to make them an easy prey.[1]

At the present day decoys are not confined to England alone, but are employed with considerable success in various parts of the Netherlands, and some other countries where the aquatic species resort. From the effects of land-draining, which has been carried on to such an extent of late years, the haunts of wild-fowl have been so much disturbed, and in many places so entirely destroyed, that the numbers now taken in England have greatly fallen off; a circumstance much to be regretted by English sportsmen. The extensive fens of Lincolnshire—formerly the great wild-fowl preserves of this country—are now drained and cultivated, and there is no longer any secure resting-place there for the wild-duck and her nestlings. Those fens formerly abounded with decoys. The most skilful decoyers in the land were the Lincolnshire fenmen, and numbers of poor families were entirely supported by the returns of those decoys. But it is not to that county alone that the drainage system has been confined; the counties of Huntingdon, Norfolk, Cambridge, and in the south, Somerset, and, indeed, almost every county, more or less, have each in their turn been encroached upon, the haunts they offered the web-footed species disturbed, and the spade and draining-pipe have completely uprooted the substance, and drawn off the means of subsistence of the feathered aquatics of those parts, which have been thus driven to seek shelter in foreign lands. Thousands of wildfowl of various species were annually bred in the fens alluded to; they were there at all seasons of the year, though very much more numerous during winter than at any other time.

There is no doubt but the existence of extensive tracts of fen-land was the direct means of keeping wild-fowl together, and of encouraging them to breed in this country; and after the formation of drains in the fens, and cultivation of the soil, they were at first captured in decoys with less difficulty, and in greater numbers, because they were not scattered over such a wide extent of water, but resorted to smaller pools, where the decoyer was enabled to practise his artifices upon them with greater chances of success. A very logical plea as to land-draining being beneficial to the purpose of decoys is appended in the note below.[1]

But there is not now a tenth part of the fen and bog-land in this country that there was formerly, consequently the numbers of wild-fowl have much decreased. The winter visitants do not stay and breed with us in such numbers as they used to do; but those which halt during winter on English soil return on the annual emigration of wild-fowl to the north, in the early spring of the year, and breed in vast numbers on various parts of distant shores where food and shelter may be had.

Another fatal obstacle to the increase of wild-fowl is, the destruction of their nests by taking the eggs—a mischievous system still pursued in some parts of the fens during the laying season.

In former days there were, in various parts of the counties alluded to, many bogs and morasses which seemed almost impenetrable, and offered admirable asylums to the feathered emigrants of the frozen regions. The great desideratum seemed to be, to secure as large an extent of inland water for the purposes of decoy as could be had; and thus we find many decoy-grounds consisting of a preserve of several hundred acres of land and water. The Watton Decoy, in Yorkshire, alone, had a range of a thousand acres of land and water. Decoys have also formed the subject of special and heavy compensation to the proprietors, when destroyed by the drainage of neighbouring lands; and we find in several private Acts of Parliament for permitting the drainage of moors and fens, special provision is made for compensating the proprietors and occupiers of such decoys as may be injured by the operations. Decoys were formerly very lucrative concerns: the quantities of fowl sometimes taken in them by the Lincolnshire fowlers of fifty years ago would exceed the belief of anyone unacquainted with the operations. Pennant says he was assured by several Lincolnshire decoymen that they would have been glad to contract, for years, to deliver their ducks at Boston at 10*d.* the couple. And to the author's own knowledge wild-fowl were sometimes so abundant, and such numbers captured, that the Essex and Norfolk decoyers were glad to sell wild-ducks at *Is.* per pair. The neighbourhood of Croyland in Lincolnshire was formerly famous for its decoys, and was in fact the very centre of the wild-fowler's ancient domain. Within the last fifty years the town itself derived its greatest commercial gain from the numbers of wild-fowl taken in its vicinity. It is mentioned in a topographical description of Croyland Abbey that the people employed at the decoys have captured as many as *three thousand* wild-ducks at once in the decoy-pipe. And even at the present day (1874) the principal resorts for wildfowl (which still are always very numerous during sharp winters) are at Croyland and Corobit washes and the neighbourhood.

In former days decoys were generally let to fowlers at annual rents, and such as could not afford to embark in expensive undertakings rented small pools, and carefully selected spots in the fens, where they constructed in the most rustic fashion their own decoys, having merely a nominal rent to pay for the occupation of the land, sometimes not more than 5*l*. per annum, and seldom exceeding 30*l*.

The Norfolk Broads[1] would appear from their geographical position to be peculiarly adapted as a refuge, feeding ground, and nursery for wild fowl; situated as they are on the most eastern extremity of the English coast, within a sort of triangle, which may be pretty accurately defined on a map of the locality by drawing an imaginary line from Lowesto ff to Norwich, and from thence to Happisburgh,[2] with a projecting coast line of more than eighty miles in length, and containing many hundreds of broad acres in extent, no readier or more inviting refuge could be found: and, as regards a feeding-ground, these broads abound with what most wild-fowl chiefly delight in, viz., shallow water, beneath which lies plenty of grass, duck-weed, and other rich fattening food, within easy reach of the surface; and occasionally a suitable cover for nesting, in the shape of little islands of grass, reeds, sedges, and low-growing cover, with here and there an alder-carr,[1] and a few scattered willow-staddles and birch poles.

In many parts these Broads are still very inaccessible to any but hardy fowlers, naturalists, and others well equipped for treading the soft morass, and occasionally wading knee deep in mud and water.

The Norfolk Broads vary in extent from the small pool called a 'pulk' to the wide-spreading lake known as Hickling Broad, which has an area of four hundred acres or more of shallow water, not more than four feet and a half in depth, except in a very few places.

The other principal broads in this locality are, Horsey Mere, containing about 130 acres and lying within a mile of the sea, Heigham Sounds, Lake Lothing, Oulton and Fritton waters, Barton, Eollesby, and Filby Broads, South Walsh am, Banworth, and Hoveton Broads, and Breydon water; the latter covering about 400 acres and lying at the back of the Town of Yarmouth, and formed by the confluence of the Rivers Waveney, Bure, and Yare.[2] At Fritton and Ranworth there are decoys still in working order. Until of late years, at all seasons of the year, these broads were the favourite haunts and breeding-places of hundreds of wild-fowl of various species, and in the winter months they literally swarmed with wild-fowl: so that the manner of estimating their numbers was expressed by the supposed extent of acres of water the flight or flights appeared to cover; and no one who has not visited the broads, or some other such localities, and seen the large flights of wild-fowl which assemble in favourite feeding-grounds, can form any conception of the countless thousands which even now in severe winters may be seen in those parts. At the present day, however, but comparatively few are bred in those waters, except in places watched and preserved; and there are not now so many decoys kept up for the profit alone as formerly, because of the uncertainty of taking a sufficient number of birds to pay the expenses attending them. There is also Scoulton Mere, a solitary but extensive broad, covering, with the island in the middle, over 70 acres, lying almost in the centre of the county of Norfolk, 25 miles from the sea, and without any river communication with it. Tradition says of this mere that it is but a fragment of the ancient estuary which once divided the county.

In the midst of Scoulton Mere, and bristling with reeds and a few scattered willows, is a boggy but favoured and profitable island, which from time immemorial has been the chosen resting-place of thousands of the black-headed seagulls: and notwithstanding that more than thirty thousand of their eggs are taken from the island in an average season, many thousands of birds are hatched and reared there under the protection of a fowler.

Decoys, so far from driving wild-fowl from a chosen locality (as is supposed by some persons not intimately acquainted with the habits of water-fowl), are the direct means of encouraging them to stay and frequent that particular part of the coast; and, as a general rule, the more decoys there are in the neighbourhood, the greater are the numbers of wild-fowl on and about the coast, marshes, and lakes.

In the good old times, when hundreds of decoys were in active operation in the fens, and when guns were fewer and far less freely used than now, there was no difficulty in securing in the surrounding neighbourhood the quiet and repose so necessary to successful operations at the decoy. Consequently the more numerous the decoys, so much the more extensive and complete were the surrounding preserves. Notwithstanding the great captures which are sometimes made, a decoy is nevertheless a preserve for wild-fowl; and as it is necessarily situated in a very secluded part, when once a number of water-fowl have discovered it they invariably visit it at regular intervals, frequently enticing swarms of followers to the same delusive repose, until the fowler, finding the numbers considerable, proceeds to put in operation his ingenious contrivances, and often with such success as to take in the course of an hour several hundred birds. The proceedings are conducted with so much caution and such profound silence that, were there as many more birds upon the open water of the decoy as those allured into the fowler's fatal snare, they would be quite unconscious of the wholesale and deliberate slaughter of their companions which may be going forward in a remote corner of the decoy, whilst the unsuspecting are revelling in the rich dabblings of the grassy mounds and shallow bottoms of the pond, screened from view of the others by thickly-planted underwood, reeds, and other contrivances.

A succession of mild winters, combined with the facts before stated as to the drainage of fen-lands, have been the cause of many decoys being done away with and of others remaining unemployed, whilst some have been entirely cleared of the pipes and apparatus; and the occasional pairs of ducks and small flights of wild-fowl which alight in the old decoys are now despatched with the shoulder-gun, and brought to hand by the retriever or water-spaniel. Still there are yet remaining, and probably always will be, several well-conducted and carefully-watched decoys in various parts of this country, though the author ventures to predict, from the experiences of late years, there will be only a few kept for profit, but rather exclusively, and as a valuable appurtenant to a country seat; a preserve for wild-fowl affording amusement to the proprietor and his friends, and always remaining an object of interest and curiosity to all, whether strangers or persons familiar with its attractions. And, certainly, a decoy is a far more agreeable feature in a park than a rookery; in addition to which, the sport attending a decoy extends over many months, whilst the murderous onslaught upon the rooks lasts but a few weeks at most. There is much opportunity for the exercise of skill and pleasing excitement attached to the one, but little else than wanton cruelty, danger, and clamour to the other.

The golden days of the decoy appear to have passed away, and we find that many of those places which were formerly kept up at considerable expense are now merely employed as an agreeable recreation to the country squire, or some enterprising clergyman who may be fortunate enough to have a residence near the sea-coast, with a decoy-pond attached to the glebe. But there are undoubtedly places as fitting as ever for decoys on many of the principal estates of extensive land-owners in this country, particularly in the counties of Lincoln, Norfolk, Suffolk, Essex, Dorset, Devon, and Somerset, where lakes and ornamental waters adorn their finely timbered parks, and afford the passing wild-fowl the quiet retreat they seek in their long flights over the country, in quest of inland waters. Decoys might be planned and cultivated with considerable success, even at the present day, on most of such estates, and at a cost which may well be termed 'trifling' in comparison with the money expended by the same land-owners in the breeding and rearing of pheasants.

In some instances where land has been reclaimed, and

wild and dreary waste brought into a state of cultivation, the haunts of the wild-fowl have been protected. Holkham, the seat of the Earl of Leicester, is a striking instance of this.[1] The ornamental and extensive lake in the park, studded with the most inviting islets, is as much or more than ever the frequented haunt and breeding-place of vast numbers of wild-fowl, which, of course, are as strictly preserved for the diversion of the noble proprietor and his guests, as the game in the surrounding coverts.

Mild winters seldom afford the decoyer an opportunity of taking wild-fowl in large numbers; but in hard winters the chances are in no way inferior to those of the good old times. The British islands, from their position on the globe, offer so fair a retreat to the myriads of wild-fowl, which are annually driven from northern latitudes by the severity of weather, that there will always be sport for the wild-fowler more or less in proportion to the strength and duration of the frost. During the season of 1854–5, which was the sharpest winter we have had for many years, several large flights were taken in the English decoys. But no such large profits have been made of late years as formerly, because of the negligence with which those places have been kept up. A clear profit of from 200*l.* to 500*l.* in a season used to be but an average return for a complete decoy; and many instances of extraordinary luck are recorded (some traditionally known to the author)—of 600*l.*, and even 800*l.*, being cleared from a single decoy in one season.

The author was also acquainted with the aged proprietor of an estate in Essex, on which there is an excellent decoy-pond, now entirely neglected and unused, but which, has in several seasons, some forty or fifty years ago, yielded the worthy old squire a clear 800?. for one year's profit! as can be proved not only by the verbal testimony of some members of the family and others living in the neighbourhood, but also by the book of receipts and disbursements of that period. And this is far from being a solitary instance.

Mr. Daniel mentions, in his book of 'Rural Sports,' that in the year 1795 a decoy at Tillingham, in Essex, then in the occupation of Mr. Mascall, after payment of every expense, yielded a profit of upwards of 800*l.*, and the only birds taken were duck and mallard.

The same author states that 'in 1799 ten thousand head of widgeon, teal, and wild-ducks were caught in a decoy of the Rev. Bate Dudley, in Essex.' And again, in the 'Supplement' to his 'Rural Sports ': 'In the year 1765 there were caught at Dowesby, in Lincolnshire, 1,075 dozen and 8 wild ducks [or 12,908], which, on the average, fetched 7*s.* per dozen [or 376*l.*].

Pennant mentions that, by an old account of the number of wild-fowl caught in ten decoys in the neighbourhood of Wain-fleet, it appears that 31,200 were taken in one season.[1]

The Rev. F. O. Morris, in his 'History of British Birds,' says—'I am informed that, at the decoy of Watton in Norfolk, nearly four hundred ducks have been known to be taken in one day.'

At the present day (1874) the chief supply of wild-fowl to the London markets is from English decoys. The number received from the 'gunners' is small in comparison with those that are sent from decoys; and the decoy-fowl being free from shot wounds are always preferred, both by dealers and buyers. The proprietor of a well-managed decoy may always fairly reckon on a few 'good days,' even in the mildest winters, on some of which he sometimes succeeds in taking from 200 to 300 fowl in one day; and often several of these lucky days intervene during every season.

In Watson's 'History of Wisbech 'mention is made of a decoy at Leverington. Mr. Wells, who wrote in 1830, speaks of three decoys as then existing in the vicinity of the Great Bedford Level, namely, one in Borough Fen, near Thorney, then the property of Sir Culling Smith, Bart.; another in Holme Fen, near Stilton, then the property of the trustees of the late Captain Wells; and a third at Lakenheath, in the county of Suffolk, the property of William Eagle, Esq.

The same author also speaks of another decoy which was originally formed on the borders of the fen at Chatteris; but adds that 'no vestige of it now remains, except the wood by which it was surrounded, and which is called "Coy Wood" to this day.'

The 'Six Hundred Decoy' was situated on an island in the very heart of the fens. The pond contained about three acres of water, was well sheltered, and distant from disturbance. It became so great an asylum for wild-fowl during the breeding season that (upon the authority of Fen-bill Hall[1] and divers decoymen) the whole island was covered with nests, so that 'it was apparently impossible for one egg to drop without hitting another.' And according to the same authority the fowl were sometimes so numerous, and in such myriads, that when disturbed the noise they made was not unlike distant thunder.

Within the lordship of Boarstall, in Buckinghamshire, is an ancient decoy-pond of about three acres, for wild-ducks, teal, widgeon, &c, which abound in the contiguous marshes called Otmoor.[2]

The decoy at Oakley Hall, in Essex, may also be mentioned as one which was formerly very lucrative, and yielded the late proprietor many hundreds of pounds annual profit, but is now not attended as a decoy, so few are the birds which visit that immediate locality in comparison with the traditions of old times.

There was also a decoy at Beaumont-cum-Moze, in Essex, which has attained some historical notoriety through being the subject of a lawsuit in the year 1809, when, at the trial of the case before the then Lord Chief Baron Macdonald, the plaintiff (proprietor of the decoy) obtained a verdict, with 40s. damages, against the defendant—a punter—for wilful disturbance to the decoy, in shooting wild-fowl within two hundred yards of the plaintiff's pond.[1]

There are two very attractive decoys at Pur dies Hall, Nacton, in the county of Suffolk, which at the date of the first edition of this work were kept up at considerable expense, and in as perfect order as any in the county. They were then in the occupation of Mr. Hillen, the lessee of the farm.

There is also another in equally perfect condition in the same neighbourhood, on the estate of George Tomline, Esq., on the banks of the river Orwell, in Suffolk.

The county of Somerset was also well furnished with decoys, particularly in and about its low-lying moors, where, in numerous places, traces are still to be found of many an ancient decoy—the pond, the decoyman's cottage, the curved ditches, and the plantation around—but in many cases now overgrown with brushwood, tall reeds, and wild herbage, as in the case of that well-planned and formerly flourishing decoy near Aller and Langport in that county; for since the draining of the moors the profits of most of the Somersetshire decoys have been too precarious to give encouragement to the proprietors to afford the necessary outlay required for keeping them up. There was also a decoy of considerable importance and profit on Godney Moor, at Lower Godney, near Glastonbury, and some others in the neighbourhood. But now, the good old decoys of Glastonbury, which in years gone by so well supplied the refectories of that once famous monastery, have, like others in the county, long since fallen into decay, and are now looked upon almost as curiosities of the past. But there are yet living those who remember the time when Sedgemoor had many decoys, which yielded to their proprietors considerable annual profits.

In Ireland there are several decoys, though they are supported with less vigour than formerly, for the same reasons as those suggested by experiences in England, viz., the system of land-draining and the unprecedented succession of mild winters with which we have been visited, and consequent scarcity of birds. The decoys at Lismullen and Mountainstown, in the county of Meath, and Ballynakill, in Kildare, are fair specimens of Irish decoys.

It appears that many wild-ducks are taken in decoys in Germany, and that there is a very important one on a lake situated in the centre of a wood in the vicinity of Carlsruhe, and belonging to the Grand Duke.[1]

There are probably, even at the present day, more decoys both in this and other countries than many persons would suppose, and, where expense is no object to the proprietor, the agreeable and peculiar pleasures attached to the pursuits of the decoy are generally of too interesting and attractive a character to induce country gentlemen to abandon them or permit them to fall into ruin; for although several mild, and consequently unfavourable, winters may follow in succession after a hard and severe one, the latter never fails to compensate the modern decoyer according to the fashion of olden times.

Mr. Stevenson[2] mentions a curious circumstance arising out of the altered condition of the marshes in the neighbourhood of Holkham, the seat of the Earl of Leicester, and the closing of decoys, once so profitable in Norfolk. He says that of late years, since both the Holkham and Langham decoys have ceased to be worked, flocks of widgeon have resorted to the lake in Holkham Park during the day-time, a few only appearing at first, but their numbers increasing during each successive winter.

---

[1] Daniel, in his 'Rural Sports,' gives an account of an attempt which was made by the Maldon decoy-owners to stop the punters from shooting in the public river within a certain distance of their ponds, and quotes the opinion of counsel taken upon the subject.

¹ 'And that decoys are now planted upon many drained levels, whereby greater numbers of fowls are caught than by any other engines formerly used; which could not at all be made there, did the waters, as formerly, overspread the whole county.'—*Dugdale on Embanking*, A.D. 1772.

¹ 'Broad' is a provincial term signifying an extensive expanse of shallow water, or the widely expanded wings of a river.

² Pronounced and frequently spelt Hasborough.

¹ Alder-carr, a local term for a copse of *Alder trees*.

² Lubbock's 'Fauna of Norfolk' contains a geographical description and a map of the Norfolk Broads.

¹ 'It was about the years 1725 and 1726 that the Earl of Leicester, determining to fix his family seat at Holkham, after making several purchases of intermixed lands and estates, began to enclose the parish of Holkham. In 1728 he built a new farmhouse, &c, on the distant fields on the west side of the parish, at a place called Longlands. In 1735 he built another farmhouse upon the old heath, on the east side of the parish, at a place called Brenthill, and enclosed and cultivated the heath-land; thenceforward, he gradually proceeded with enclosing and improving the whole parish, dividing to himself, round about where he intended to build his seat, and enclosing with pales, a park containing about 840 acres of

land, and therein made many plantations of wood, laid out lawns, gardens, water, &c, with many useful and ornamental buildings, and nearly completed his manor-house, begun in 1734, before he died.'—See Stacy's *History of Norfolk*.

[1] And see Goldsmith's 'History of the Earth and Animated Nature,' vol. iii. p. 420, Edition 1824.

[1] Fen-bill Hall, the author of some curious (but vulgar and illiterate) tracts bearing the specious title, 'A Sketch of Local History relating to the Fens;' with a life of the author, born 1748, published at Lynn 1812. The following are some of the most presentable extracts, conveying a fair idea of the aquatic bird-land of the locality. Speaking of himself, he says he was

'Bred where whole winters nothing seen,
But naked flood for miles and miles,
Except a boat the eye beguiles;
Or coots in clouds by buzzards teazed,
Your ear with seeming thunder seized;
From raised decoy, there ducks on flight,
By tens of thousands darken light.'

And again—

Born in a coy, and bred in a mill,
Taught water to grind, and ducks how to kill.

. . . .

Laying spring-nets to catch Ruff and Reeve;
Stretched out in a boat with a shade to deceive;
Taking geese, ducks, and coots, with nets upon stakes,
Riding in a calm day to catch moulted drakes,
Gathering eggs to the top of one's wish;
Cutting tracks in the flags for decoying of fish.'

And again—

'Where ducks by scores traversed the fens,
Coots, didappers, rails, water hens,
Combined with eggs to charge our pot,
Two furlongs circle round the spot,[1]
Fowl, fish, all kinds the table graced,
All caught within the self-same space;
As time revolved, in season fed,
The surplus found us salt and bread;
Your humble servant, now your penman,
Lived thus a simple, full-bred fenman.'

[2] Lipscombe's 'Buckinghamshire,' vol. i. p. 88.

Then an island of but few perches; the author the last person living who was born upon it.

[1] This case is well known among members of the legal profession as that of 'Carrington *versus* Taylor,' and is reported in 11 East, p. 571, and 2 Camp. 258. *Vide post*, 'Laws relating to Decoys.'

[1] 'Rambles in Germany.' By the Hon. Ferdinand St. John. 1853,

[2] See 'The Birds of Norfolk.' Introduction.

CHAPTER VII

THE DECOY-POND.

'Ergo avidas si forte anates captare libebit,
Atque alias liquidis quascunque paludibus ulvæ
Delectant molles, captique in gurgite pisces
Palmipedum genus alitium: torpentia propter
Stagnaque velocesque amnes, deducere fossam
Perge celer tenni refluentem leniter unda.'

BARGÆUS DE AUCUPIO.

A DECOY is a place set apart for the enticement, resort, and capture of wild-fowl,[1] and is simply a pond or small lake, having one or more semi-circular arms, or tapering ditches, spanned with nets; the situation of the whole being in a retired locality, and surrounded with thickly-planted trees and underwood.[2] It is contrived for the purpose of alluring wild-fowl to resort there, and by various stratagems, to entice them up these narrow arms of water: their retreat is then cut off, by the fowler suddenly making his appearance from behind a place of concealment, when the birds, in their fright and endeavour to avoid him, rush forward up the curved arm of water, probably thinking to make their escape at the other end, but ultimately finding themselves enclosed in a tunnel-net.

A decoy is one of the most ornamental acquisitions to a private landed estate that can well be imagined, and at all times presents an object of amusement and attraction. When properly managed and kept strictly quiet, it makes an admirable nursery for wild-fowl, and may also materially assist in the preservation of game.

It is also a pleasing and satisfactory resort in summer for the naturalist, where much is to be learned of the habits and instincts of water-fowl, though it seems that, for some reason or other, naturalists and inquirers could seldom obtain admittance.[3] In winter, though sport cannot always be had elsewhere, there is scarcely a day but amusement of some kind may be found at the decoy.

It requires much good judgment to plan a decoy-pond so as to insure success in taking wild-fowl in numbers sufficient to answer the purpose, or repay the expense of outlay and keeping up.

The place chosen for the decoy must necessarily be a secluded spot, far removed from public highways, footpaths, railroads, canals, and other interruptions. The 'twang!' of the rifle or the 'bang!' of the shot-barrels must never be heard within its precincts. No crack of the whip or huntsman's horn, no sound of human voice, of cart-wheel, or horse's hoof, must reach the lonely spot, particularly whilst birds are known to be resting or feeding there; silence and undisturbed tranquillity must predominate and be observed at all times in the locality of the decoy. The success or failure of the enterprise, both as regards enticing the birds to alight in the open water, and the ultimate proceeding of alluring them up the pipe, depends mainly on the quietude of the whole scene around, and the absence of all interruption to the decoyman and his dog; to accomplish which effectually, the proprietor must secure possession of surrounding lands to such an extent as to be able to command the necessary calm, and subdue all disturbance and interruption. Wells, in his 'History of the Fens,'[1] observes that the decoy 'should be surrounded by forty or fifty acres of plantation.' But this must depend on the size of the pond and nature of the locality.

The pond itself should be surrounded with trees and copse, and near the water's edge reeds and sedges should be cultivated and permitted to flourish, all of which tend to preserve the quietude of the water, and afford security and shelter to the birds. The decoyman's cottage should be near, though not within four or five hundred yards of the pool; it should be well sheltered and hidden by trees and shrubs, and the pathway leading to the pond should be under the cover of a quickset hedge or through a sheltered lane.

The fens around should be as carefully kept quiet and unmolested as the decoy itself, and where this can be done, hundreds of wild-fowl are bred, even at the present day, both in the surrounding fens and about the sedges and underwood of the decoy; and it should be remembered that these are the very birds on which the decoyman's hopes chiefly rest: to the tamest of them he looks for his decoy-ducks, and to the wildest to bring flights of others into the pond, on returning in the morning from their midnight excursions.

In former days, much difference of opinion existed as to the extent of water best adapted for the purposes of a decoy; and, it being at all times pleasing to the eyes of a wild-fowler to see large numbers of the duck tribe within the precincts of his domain, it was considered advisable to obtain as wide a surface of water as possible; and, whilst from forty to fifty acres have frequently been set apart for the purpose, instances have been known of seventy and eighty acres of water being entirely so appropriated. But experience has long shown that more wildfowl are taken in small decoys than in such extensive ones as those alluded to. It is always difficult to induce birds to 'pipe' in a very large decoy, though acres of the water may be covered with them; and whilst at the neighbouring pools, only three or four acres in extent, the decoymen of more humble pretensions are probably taking their scores and hundreds daily, perhaps the other catches none.

These extensive spaces of fresh water, or small lakes, as they may truly be called, afford splendid preserves, but are not well adapted to the purposes of decoy; a safe retreat for wildfowl at all times, and shelter from the gunner and the storm; but the birds are not to be got at so readily, nor the pond worked so handily as a small pool. Thousands of wild-fowl used to frequent these large decoys at all times of the year, though in far increased numbers during the winter season, spending the greater part of the day on the water and its banks, where undisturbed; and at twilight—or 'flight-time,' as it is termed—they leave their daily haunts, to seek for food in marshes and fens, perhaps many miles distant.

The extent of a decoy-pond should not be more than four acres: those averaging from two to three acres are best. Many instances are known of a single acre of water, in the fens, yielding more profit to the decoyman, during the year, than any other above that size; but these have always been in the locality of small lakes, fens, and pools. It is easy to account for the better success attending small decoys: the birds may generally be 'worked,' if the fowler understands his business and his dog and decoy-ducks are well trained, the confined extent of the space of water materially assisting his operations; and if there be several working-pipes placed at different parts of the pond, so as to suit the chances of the wind, success will be more frequent. Whereas, on a vast extent of water, there may be swarms of wild-fowl, but none within hail of the pipes, or near enough to regard the enticements of the decoy-ducks or the singular befoplings of the dog.

In a perfect decoy there are generally several pipes, so as to suit at least every cardinal point; and the best and principal pipes tail-off in an east, north-east, or south-east direction, those being the quarters from which most sport may be expected, and are also the winds which bring most wild-fowl to our shores. It must depend on the wind as to which pipe the birds will take to, bearing in mind that they must always be decoyed *towards* the wind, it being invariably found a useless task to attempt enticing them to leeward.

In addition to the space actually covered with water there should generally be enclosed an average extent of ground, of from fifty to a hundred yards in width, all around the pond, which ought to be planted with much discretion, so as to give a quiet aspect to the whole, but leaving a careless-looking opening in the plantation at the course of every pipe, so as to admit a current of air from whichever quarter the wind blows. No very large trees, as oaks and elms, should be planted about the decoy, but those of inferior growth, as the birch, the willow, alder, and others; besides which a thick underwood should cover every vacant space; and nearer the banks of the pool should be borders of reeds and rushes.

In some decoys the whole pond is enclosed by a reed fence about four feet in height, the object of which is to prevent the decoy-ducks leaving the place. It is best, however, to dispense with so much fencing, because wild-fowl are shy of entering a space too much enclosed by artificial means. Besides, the fencing prevents their becoming familiarised with the growing cover, sedges, and rushes, in which many of the birds visiting the decoy late in the season would probably stay and breed.

The banks of the decoy, near the entrances to the pipes, are to be kept smooth and clean, as basking-places for the fowl; gradually sloping to the water's edge, that the birds may readily step upon them and rest there. When so at rest they are said to be 'banked.' It is not unusual for wild-fowl to sit several hours of the day 'in bank,' when they are undisturbed. (These are not merely *termly* sittings *in banco!*)

When a new decoy has been made, though in a neighbourhood where there are many others, and generally a good number of wild-fowl, the proprietor must not be disheartened if he meets with little or no success in the first year or two, though his neighbours may take vast numbers during the season. "Wildfowl are by nature addicted to following their leaders, which are generally old birds, and very often bred in the locality they most frequent; these prefer going to old quarters, where they have previously experienced quiet and repose, to venturing upon a new-made decoy, which always has a degree of suspicion about it. This, and the uncertainty as to the flight of birds, are alone sufficient to give courage to the proprietor of the new decoy, who may fairly hope for success in the following season. If, during the first two years, he takes sufficient to pay the expenses of attending and working the decoy, he ought to be well satisfied.

In addition to the screens which are placed along the bank outside the pipe, there are generally others about the mouth or entrance, skirting the resting-places where the birds are encouraged to sit; and other parts of the pond are so fenced or planted that they could not, if they would, sit upon the bank in any other places than those where the fowler wishes them.

There should also be a few tufts of grass, small mounds, and tiny islands in the pond, near the entrances to the pipes. These are termed 'accommodation tufts.'

It is desirable that the pond should not be deep, but, on the contrary, shallow; and the more abundantly the pond-weed grows at the bottom, the better.

The pond should also be constructed with proper dams and sluices, so that the depth of water may be regulated and kept at a suitable level.

Decoys which are kept up regardless of expense, and more as a recreation than otherwise, should be provided with a small grotto or watch-house, from which the decoyer may be enabled to make his observations. It should be placed among the trees, and well-hidden, but in such a position as to command a view of the whole space of water.

---

[1] In legal language it is termed a 'vivarium.' *Vide* 2 Coke's 'Institutes,' p. 100; and Holt's Bep. p. 14.

[2] Lubbock gives the following definition: 'A decoy is a sequestered pool, with curving ditches, and of depth of sixteen or eighteen inches of water, dug from the main water, and covered with a net; and that the fowl are taken by alluring them from the main water into these fatal retreats.'

[3] Lubbock, speaking of the privacy of decoys, remarks: 'And here, in fact, the knowledge of many, even of naturalists, terminates, for it is not always an easy task to obtain admission to a decoy.'

[1] P. 447.

CHAPTER VIII

THE DECOY-PIPE

HAVING now given a description or outline of the pond and plantation surrounding it, the most important part of the decoy has now to be described, viz. the decoy-pipe. The *pipe* is formed by digging a shallow ditch or arm of water, about six or eight inches in depth,[1] leading directly from the main pond into the plantation or decoy-grounds, to an extent of from sixty to seventy or eighty yards. It is planned in semi-circular form, with a rather sharp curve. The object or advantage of the curve is twofold. In the first place, it is the twist of the pipe which deceives the birds, when enticed within it, and induces them to imagine they are going out at the other end, when the decoyman shows himself and cuts off their retreat; in the next place, the curve assists the fowler in performing his operations without disturbing the decoy-pond, and in such a manner that his actions and those of the deluded birds may not be seen by others remaining on the open water. Some decoys of modern construction are provided with water-pipes and taps for turning the water on and off at pleasure in the decoy-pipes. In others a constant stream is kept up from end to end in the pipe; the advantages of which are, that in frosty weather the pipes may the more easily be kept free from ice.

The width of the pipe at the mouth is immaterial—it varies according to circumstances; but, generally speaking, is from twenty to thirty feet, and gradually diminishing to two feet at the upper end, where it terminates with a tunnel-net, generally upon dry land.

The whole of the pipe is spanned and covered with a light netting, spread upon semi-circular bars of iron-rod, placed about three or four feet apart, or at such convenient distances as may be found necessary, the ends of the rods being stuck in or secured to small wooden posts driven into the bank on both sides of the pipe, and standing a few inches above the ground: those on the inner side of the curve are close to the water, whilst those on the outer side are about two feet from the brink, in order to leave sufficient space for the dog to perform his antics. The whole are neatly arranged, and form a light and lofty arch, about twelve feet above the surface of the water at the main entrance, but tapering with the gradually narrower form of the pipe to the extreme tail, which is completed with a collapsible tunnel-net spread upon small hoops of iron or brass rod—the diameter of the largest, or that nearest the mouth, being about two feet. This net is of various lengths, from six to ten feet, according to the sort of success anticipated: it is hung upon the end of the pipe, which, for the purpose of receiving it, is fitted with hooks and clasp; and the tail-end being drawn out and looped to a small stake, it forms a graceful continuation and termination of the pipe.

The whole of the iron framework of the pipe should be as lightly constructed as possible, especially at the broadest part. The network must be made of stout twine or small cord. The size of the meshes, at the extreme entrance of the pipe, should be large enough to admit the body of a wild-fowl with its wings folded; but a few yards farther up the size of the mesh should be a little smaller: beyond the screen, smaller still. The lower part of the iron framework, on the side next the reed screens, should be left open as far up the pipe as the curve—that is to say, the net, though covering the top of the arch and opposite side of the pipe, need not reach down to the ground on the side where the operations are performed, but should fall gradually lower as it approaches the last working screen, from which, up to the trammel, it should be close and entire. Wild-fowl never attempt to escape by the outlet thus left, but always make for the opposite side, where the net reaches quite to the ground all the way along the pipe, and should be perfectly secure. From the curve to the trammel the net covers everything, and is simply secured to a row of small hooks tacked to a narrow boarding run along the lower part of the iron framework on each side of the upper end of the pipe.

It would appear, from some of the earliest accounts which can be traced, that at the mouth of the pipe of an old-fashioned decoy a drop-net was used, after the manner of a portcullis; so that when the fowl had been enticed a short distance within the pipe the net was suddenly dropped, and the fowl thus, at once, enclosed.[1] Modern experience has taught us that no portcullis is necessary, and that by forming the ditch upon a curve, the mouth of the pipe may be left quite open.; when, on the fowler showing himself at the entrance, as soon as the birds are decoyed within the pipe, they are deluded by the curve; and, instead of beating a retreat, follow up the ditch, as if assured of finding a means of escape at the other end.

On the *convex* side of the curve, extending from the mouth

to about thirty or forty yards alongside the pipe, are a number of screens (in some places termed 'shootings') rustically constructed, by arranging layers of green or dried reeds, perpendicularly, in a wooden frame, made for the purpose. They are each about six feet in height by eight, ten, and twelve in breadth, the two nearest the mouth of the pipe being from fourteen to twenty feet in breadth, and sometimes much more, particularly if the entrance to the pipe is very broad. From twelve to fifteen of the narrowest of these screens have to be judiciously placed along the bank of the pipe, in oblique positions (*see illustration*), each screen standing separately from the other; the whole, when in their proper positions, forming a perfect zigzag, and leaving narrow outlets of about two feet between each, which are all joined at the bottom, with tiny screens or leaping-bars, about eighteen inches high, for the dog; the spaces between the tops of the leaping-bars and the ground being filled up with short reeds, so as to complete the zigzag, and make the whole appear like one piece of fencing. Through these apertures the fowler shows himself, when advisable, after having enticed the birds a sufficient distance up the pipe to make sure of capturing them.

A great deal depends on the proper distribution and adjustment of the screens, for it is behind them that the decoyman has to perform his part, and there, in silence, and by signs, direct the movements of his only helpmates—the decoy-ducks and dog. In original decoys it appears there were no reed screens, but simply growing osiers: the invention of the screens is of more modern date.[1] In addition to the screens placed in zigzag position on the outer side of the pipe there are back-screens of the same height, but of wider proportions, placed in line to form a fence outside the zigzags, or working-screens, so as to protect the fowler from view when he has occasion to return to the mouth of the pipe to cut off the retreat of birds within it. This fencing extends only from the pipe entrance to the last working screen.

The illustration at the head of this chapter, though of necessity but a bird's-eye view, represents the decoy-pipe and screens, with the fowler in active operation of decoy. The dark figure kneeling behind the outer-screens is the decoyman's assistant, awaiting a signal from the fowler to rush forward to the entrance of the pipe, when, by merely showing himself and waving his hand, the fowl become alarmed, their retreat is cut off, and they are driven to the extreme end, into the tunnel-net, and captured.

Such is the decoy-pipe, up which it is the fowler's art to entice the birds, and finally drive them into the trammel, from which there is no escape. There are generally six or eight pipes to a perfectly planned decoy, each bearing towards a different point of the compass; but the curves must all be on the same axis, or they would be left-handed, and puzzle both dog and decoyer in their operations.

———————

[1] Lubbock describes the decoy-pipe as sixteen or eighteen inches in depth, which is too much. Many fowl would dive and beat a retreat in such a depth of water.

[1] 'And at the top and entrance must he nets to *let down* by the man that is to attend it, when he seeth the ducks all entered in, by which means they become taken.'—*Blome.*

[1] 'The place where these decoy-ducks entice them must not be very broad, and set on both sides with osiers.'—*Blome.*

CHAPTER IX

THE DECOY-DUCKS

'The devil would never have had such numbers, had he not used some as decoys to ensnare others.'—*Government of the Tongue.*

'If you give any credit to this juggling rascal, you are worse than simple widgins, and will be drawn into the net by this decoy-duck, this tame cheater.'—*Beaumont and Fletcher's Fair Maid of the Inn*, act iv. sc. 1.

EQUALLY indispensable to assist the fowler in his operations, and as appurtenant to the decoy itself, are the decoy-ducks. Their constant presence on the pond attracts the attention of wild-fowl which may chance to be flying high in the air in that direction, and induces them the more readily to drop their flight, and yield to the enticements offered; the presence of a number of their own tribe being a sufficient guarantee of the supposed safety of the retreat. And when once a flight of wildfowl have tasted the sweets of the decoy, and been allowed to remain there a few hours without being disturbed, they are almost certain to return again on the next or another day; this, then, is the first step gained by the decoy-man, for the next time they come, if a fitting opportunity offers, he calls his decoy-ducks to the mouth of the pipe, whereby he allures the strangers on another step; as they follow the others and approach—*catervatim*—the mouth of the pipe, where they find some tail-corn drifting on the surface, on which they feed in company with the decoy-ducks, and by such enticements they are induced to return daily to the decoy, and to follow the decoy-ducks in their movements, step by step, until at last they go a step too far and find themselves within the fowler's trammel.

It is a mistake to suppose that the decoy-ducks perform any *cunning* part; they only do that which is most natural to them, viz. go where food awaits them, and for that reason they obey the call of the decoyer, and swim up the pipe to which they are invited, the wild ones following them. Blome erroneously attributes their capture to the subtilty of the decoy-ducks.[1]

The number of decoy-ducks required for a pond in full employment is from twenty to fifty, according to the season. If many and large flights visit the pond, then the more decoy-ducks there are the better, particularly if the frost be very severe, because the large numbers keep together, and prevent the pond from freezing.

The breed of the decoy-duck (*Anas allector*) is not altogether of the wild species, but about three-quarters wild, or rather a cross between a thorough-bred wild-duck and a half-bred mallard. It is not absolutely necessary they should be of the peculiar species alluded to, though such birds are most useful to the decoyer. They should be reared within the precincts of the decoy, trained to respond to the decoyer's whistle, by going directly from any part of the pond to either of the decoy-pipes, at the mouth of which they should receive their daily food. Wild-ducks which go to decoys are more likely to follow birds of their own nature, whose habits are more in accordance with their own, than the common tame duck. The difference in colour between the decoy-fowl and the wild ones is immaterial, though brown and white are generally preferred.

It is sometimes found necessary to pinion some of the decoy-ducks, but such a proceeding is seldom resorted to. Others, which are entirely of the wild species, hatched and reared near by, are permitted to range at liberty and fly to adjacent marshes. These are termed 'wandering decoy-ducks,' and frequently return to the pond accompanied by large numbers of wild ones, and it would appear that in original decoys none but wandering decoy-ducks were employed;[1] but it would be folly at the present day to rely much on wandering decoy-ducks, which of all others would be most likely to be shot when away from the protection of the decoy.

When there are more widgeon on the coast than ducks it is not unusual, after taking some at the decoy, to pinion a few pairs, and turn them off with the decoy-ducks, when their peculiar whistle attracts others which may chance to fly over, and induces them to alight in the pond, but it is not desirable at any time to have pinioned fowls in the decoy, because wild birds are shy of associating with them.[2]

There must always be several pairs of proper decoy-ducks constantly in the pond, and they must not be over-fed at any time during the day, for fear of being too sleepy and lazy to answer the decoyman's whistle, in case he requires their services. On the other hand, they must not be too much under-fed, or they would respond too eagerly to his call, and fail to act the steady part he expects of them. Their best meal should be given them at dusk in the evening, as soon as the wild-fowl (if any in the decoy) have left for their nightly perambulations. Wandering decoy-ducks should always be greeted with food on their return to the pond. Well-trained decoy-ducks, under proper management, may be brought by the gentle whistle of the decoyman from one side of the decoy to the other at any moment, and at a steady swimming pace, which is the most likely to induce the wild, birds to follow them.

The whistle of the decoyman should be soft and low, never harsh and shrill; and so accustomed will the decoy-ducks become to a call of the kind, that the slightest note will not fail to attract their attention, and bring them to the pipe at which they are required.

It is highly important that the fowler should always feed the decoy-ducks himself, that they may become thoroughly familiarised with his voice; and they may also be trained to turn back to the open water, after going about half-way up the pipe with the wild birds. This, however, is a very easy though immaterial part of the proceeding; for if once they are driven into the tunnel-net and huddled together with the captured, they will be shy of going so far up the pipe another time.

Very noisy decoy-ducks are undesirable, though they should always respond *vivâ voce* to the fowler's whistle, which they seldom fail to do, well knowing that whenever they hear it, and from whichever pipe it comes, there is sure to be food awaiting them.

When the weather is frosty, and there is fear of the pond being frozen over, corn should be freely scattered upon the surface at night, about the entrance to the pipe, in order to induce the decoy-ducks to resort there and keep the water open. Tail-corn, hemp-seed, or any light grain, is the proper food to use at the decoy.

There are generally a few wild birds which return year after year, as if by instinct, to the same decoy, but which are too old and cunning to be taken; these are called 'leading-birds,' and are a great acquisition to a decoy, frequently bringing with them large flights of companions, early in the season, which fall easy victims to the stratagems of the decoyer.

———————

[1] 'I shall now speak of decoys, by which means great store of ducks and teal are drawn into a snare, and that by the subtilty of a few of their own kind, which from the egg are trained up to come to hand for the same purpose'—*Blome's Gentleman's Recreations.*

[1] 'These decoy-ducks fly abroad, and light into the company of wild ones; and being become acquainted with them by their allurements, do draw them into the decoy-place, where they become a prey.'—*Blome.*

[2] 'Of the coy-ducks, some fly forth and bring home with them wild ones to the pool; others have the outmost joynt or pinion of their wings cut off, so that they cannot fly, but abide always in the pool.'—*Willughby's Ornithology.* By Ray.

CHAPTER X

THE PIPER

'Tho' gay and winning in my gait,
  I'm deadly as the viper:
Follow me, and, sure as fate,
  You'll have to pay the piper.'—THE AUTHOR.

A DOG trained to the decoy is called a 'piper,' and is the most effectual instrument used by the fowler in this occupation. Thus we find that no legitimate sport can be successfully employed in connection with taking wild birds, and more especially water-fowl, without the aid of one or more of those noble animals which serve mankind with more true sincerity than any other living creature of the animal kind on the face of the earth. It is the very nature of the dog to be faithful to his master, regardless of all consequences to himself. If he appears unfaithful, his heart is aching because his endeavours fail to please. The dog forgives his master any injury, and in return for kindnesses shown him will lay down his life for his master's sake. Kindness in training a dog always succeeds, but whipping and cruelty break the spirit, spoil the dog, and leave him always in fear of the whip, whereby he performs his part with timidity, consequently with less satisfaction either to himself or his master.

The part a piper has to perform at a decoy is as remarkable as it is amusing, and has been the subject of much curious speculation. Without the assistance of a piper the efforts of the decoyman are generally unavailing. It is natural enough for those who are strangers to the art to imagine that the dog by some means or other drives the birds within the meshes of the fowler's net; but, in fact, it is the very reverse—the dog actually entices, either by winning ways or by exciting an antipathy towards himself, large numbers of wild-fowl to follow him up a ditch of water covered over with a net, when their retreat is then cut off by the sudden appearance of the fowler or his assistant from behind the screens; the dog soon after running round to his master's heels, wagging his tail at the successful issue of his performances, and all the while perfectly understanding that the object is to secure the birds! What instinct! what sagacity! what intelligence!

The breed or pedigree of a piper is not altogether material, though apparently peculiar to itself. The nearer the dog resembles a fox in size, figure, and colour, the better; and, indeed, a cross between a fox and a dog is the identical result required. Such animals make the very best pipers that can be had—inheriting as they do a share of that cunning so essentially valuable in a good piper. But in absence of such it is best that the dog be of a reddish-brown or red-and-white colour. It must be full of vivacity, very active, and the more playful the better, but perfectly mute. If the dog barks every bird will quit the decoy-pipe and decline to follow him.

There is a breed of dogs, erroneously said to be mongrels, which bear a very strong resemblance to the fox. They have heads, noses, and ears just like those of a fox; and their size and colour, together with the texture of their hair, are all thoroughly vulpine. They are, besides, very lively and frolicsome little animals; but are extremely rare in this country, though not very uncommon in France; and they are of far greater value than many would suppose. A dog of this breed and colour, when carefully trained, is a treasure to the decoyer, and the very keystone to his success.

The piper is taught to skip round in front of the screens, under the direction of the decoyer, who stands behind them, and conveys all his instructions by signal, and very frequently by the movement of the finger alone. The dog is first put through a small aperture, or over a leap, at the mouth of the decoy-pipe; he then runs briskly round in front of the screen, and directly before the birds, apparently regardless of their presence, but in reality regarding their captivity above all things. He, seemingly, takes no notice of them—though there be hundreds—beyond pricking up his ears and wagging his tail; he then hastens round to his master, who must not omit to reward him for his pains with a small bit of cheese or other sweet morsel. He is then directed to skip over the next leap, and run round in front of the next screen, after which he is again rewarded with another piece of cheese; and away he goes to the next, and the next, and so on; the wild-fowl all the while watching his movements apparently with aversion or curiosity, and swimming up the pipe in pursuit of him, whilst the playful deceiver is thus decoying his victims into the fatal snare. It must not be supposed that the dog swims; he never goes into the water, but simply runs along the narrow bank, purposely left between the screens and the water.[1] The dog has also another duty to perform: when the wild-fowl are reluctant to leave the bank and follow the enticements of the decoy-ducks, the fowler starts him suddenly upon the birds from behind a screen, when they scramble into the water and immediately face the dog with the most inquiring and braggadocio curiosity; but beyond that temporary alarm nothing more serious occurs, except that it is a practice which generally succeeds, the wildfowl being then induced to follow the rude intruder's enticements, and sometimes in less than five minutes the whole paddling, which just before appeared so sluggish as they sat basking on the bank, are decoyed up the pipe.

As soon as the dog has done his part and arrived at the last working-screen, on a signal from his master, he squats down behind it, not daring to move, except under directions, or until he finds himself released by the complete capture of the birds.

There are many speculations as to the influence the dog has upon the birds in enticing them up the pipe. It has been stated by some that he is made use of to rouse the lethargic and sleepy habits of the birds; by another,[2] that the wild-fowl, not choosing to be interrupted, advance towards the contemptible little animal that they may drive it away. But this can scarcely be the correct notion; there must be some other strong and almost irresistible attraction, or pugnacious desire, which induces the birds to follow him up the pipe. Everyone knows that when a strange dog suddenly enters a field in which a flock of sheep are grazing, at first they appear much alarmed at the intrusion, and muster in a closely-packed flock and face the dog, staring at him with curious and suspicious inquiry; but if the dog moves off or turns tail upon the flock, they advance towards him, and appear to watch his movements with intense interest and threatening attitude. The attraction is still greater with cows and oxen, which not only watch the dog, but follow him about the meadow, when he has suddenly intruded upon their privacy. The behaviour of wild-fowl towards the dog appears very similar to those of sheep and oxen when suddenly surprised by the appearance of such an animal among them; and whatever may be the secret of the attraction, it is evidently a curious instinct, which has powerful effect on the feathered tribe, or they would not so easily rush on to certain destruction in a narrow ditch, covered over with a net, and up which, in the absence of enticement, they would specially avoid proceeding.

After attentive observations of dog and ducks during the operations of decoy, I am disposed to believe that the birds follow or pursue the dog with a desire and intention to punish him; that they have a notion he is a fox (an animal which instinct teaches them is one of their greatest enemies), and that they muster in a closely-packed company with a numerical courage, and resolve on attacking him, particularly when he seems such a coward as to keep showing himself one instant and running away the next. They are thus constantly inspired with new ardour and greater aversion, and so rush on in pursuit of the contemptible little animal, their false courage inducing them to follow him up regardless of the snare which is spread over their heads.

It would seem also that curiosity has something to do with it, in leading the birds on to a pitch that makes them gaze with feelings so strong on the playful movements of the dog, as he jumps or runs from behind the screens, now appearing for a few moments and then vanishing. But whether this be aversion or curiosity, or both, or some other more powerful instinct, which draws the birds on with apparently magnetic influence, we must leave to the decision of those who have made the instincts of birds and animals a special branch of their studies, merely remarking that the subject is well worthy of deep thought and attentive consideration.

The piper should, whilst very young, be trained with much care and patience to play around and about the screens, under the silent directions of his master, and to be perfectly mute during these operations; the more active he is in his movements to and fro, behind and before the screens, the better, because the more likely to excite the curiosity of the wild-fowl. And in training a dog for the decoy it will be well, to use neither violence nor severe chastisement, for it is not by such treatment that the dog can be taught, but only by kind and encouraging language, gentle correction, and prompt reward. Mr. Richardson, in his book on 'The Dog,' observes: 'In training your dogs *keep your temper*; never correct the dog in vengeance for your own irritation; gentleness does far more than violence will ever effect; and a dog that requires the latter treatment had better be got rid of: he will ever be a nuisance.' We cordially endorse these views, and recommend them to the particular attention of those who may be training a dog for the decoy, or indeed for any other purpose.

When the birds appear sluggish and indifferent to the allurements of the dog, a red pocket-handkerchief is sometimes tied about his neck, and he is sent round the same screen several times in succession, in order thereby the more to arouse the curiosity of the birds.

In the absence of a dog a ferret is sometimes used with equal success, and answers the same purpose, except that it is not sufficiently nimble in its movements, and has to be led by a string fastened to its neck and passed over the top of the screens. Wild-fowl seem to entertain the same uncontrollable feelings towards the ferret as towards the dog, and will swim up the pipe in pursuit of it.

---

[1] 'The whelp in compassing the hedges [screens] ought always to keep his tail directed towards the pool; his head towards the pipe,'—*Willughby's Ornithology*. By Ray.

[2] Pennant.

CHAPTER XI

THE ART OF CAPTURING WILD-FOWL BY DECOY

'And as a skilful fowler birds employs,
Which by their well-known voice and treach'rous noise
Allure their fellows, and invite to share
Their fate, entangled in the viscous snare.'

Trans. from the Latin of VANIERE, b. xv.

WE have now arrived at the most interesting part of the proceedings—the *modus operandi* at the decoy. Having endeavoured to explain by separate descriptions the Pond, the Pipes, the Decoy-ducks, and the Piper, before going minutely into the details of the art it may facilitate our explanation by stating, theoretically, the science of capturing wild-fowl by decoy:—

The retired situation of the pond, the quietude of the surrounding country, the fresh water, and the presence of live fowl upon it, are sufficient, in this instance, to decoy the aërial travellers to make their first false step, when they are cordially welcomed with the wooing notes of the decoy-ducks; and, in language peculiarly their own, those pleasant occupants of the pond tell the hungry strangers flattering tales of abundant food and a safe retreat within that fair domain.

Soon as the fowler discovers the arrival of the strangers, he takes careful note of wind and weather; and, with a basket of tail-corn slung across his shoulder, proceeds cautiously to the weathermost pipe, and, unseen by the birds, scatters freely a few handfuls of the food upon the surface of the water, whistling softly to his decoy-ducks, which never fail to respond to the call; when the strangers, seeing and hearing the others undisturbedly feeding upon the floating grain, follow their new companions, and join greedily in the repast. They soon become bosom friends, swimming and quacking happily together hither and thither about the water; but they part company at twilight, the strangers not venturing to trust their precious lives there all night, nor caring to deprive themselves of their customary evening visit to some near or distant fens.

The next day the same strangers again appear upon the decoy, the attractions and enticements of the previous day having made such a favourable impression upon them that,

'Like simple youths, when lured by woman's charms,'

they cannot resist the temptation to call again as they pass over in their morning flight. This time they follow their pleasant companions readily, and without the least suspicion, to the mouth of the pipe, where the decoyman has just scattered some more food; but some of it is up a suspicious-looking ditch, which, on glancing at, they doubt, and decline following their kind enticers farther. Whilst curiously looking about them, and regarding their benefactors with surprise at the incautious manner in which they proceed up the suspicious ditch, they are at first slightly startled at the sudden appearance of a new object, in the shape of a playful dog, which appears on the bank a moment at the mouth of the pipe, and then vanishes. Again it appears! when every head and neck is stretched out, apparently in pleasing amazement. Again and again the playful animal appears! Their curiosity knows no bounds; the attraction is irresistible. They forget the suspicious appearance of the ditch; their whole attention is fixed upon the infatuating little creature upon the bank; and, as if their curiosity must be gratified, they proceed up the pipe a little way—

—'In vain the ditch,
Wide-gaping, threatens death.'

They pause, and again the curious little animal appears; when, just as they are beginning to feel suspicious of their safety, he again appears—wicked tempter!—and they advance a little farther. His movements are quicker and quicker. They have nearly discovered that he is simply a little red and white animal: their curiosity is well-nigh gratified: they are just thinking of beating a retreat, when, the fowler appears on the bank, directly in the very path by which they entered the ditch, and intended returning. Their alarm is great; but there yet seems one chance of escape: they imagine one route is as good as another, and think of getting out the other way: they turn the corner, following the ditch, and, too late, discover that retreat is impossible. Helter-skelter, in wild affright, they rush from the presence of the fowler, up the pipe, and into the tunnel-net; from which they never return!

Such is but a glimpse of the *theory* of decoy, as viewed from the watery stage *in front* of the screens. It will now be our purpose to enter fully and practically into the performances *behind* them.

The proceedings of the decoyer behind the screens are simply artful, though deeply interesting; but few amateurs have ever been fortunate enough to obtain permission to accompany the fowler through the whole of his stratagems, success depending so very much upon the caution and quiet of his performances. His only companions, during operations, are one assistant, a dog, and a few decoy-ducks. With these, and no others, the decoyman proceeds to put in force his curious art; and he must not be interrupted, nor must the attention of dog or ducks be diverted from the one object in view. There are many reasons why he should be as much by himself as possible when in the act of enticing the wild-fowl up the pipe—more particularly, that of not exciting the suspicion of the birds; which are so very susceptible of noise, motion, and smell, that the decoyer himself approaches not an inch nearer than is absolutely necessary, and is obliged to carry a piece of burning peat or turf in front of him, that the acute nasal organs of the wild birds may not detect the presence of a human being so close at hand; for

'Birds, like joy, are full of fear.'

So essential is it for the decoyer to observe all these rules of caution, that no success can be expected upon the least infringement or carelessness of operation; and, whatever the duties of his calling, he must never venture on the windward side of the birds without a brand of turf. Sound and motion, as well as effluvia, each travel like electricity to the eyes, ears, and nostrils of the vigilant species of wild-fowl; and the careless decoyer who presumes to act regardless of precaution will have the mortification of seeing every wild-fowl leave the water on detection of his presence behind the screens. Besides, too, the more birds there may be in the decoy, the more watchful they will be; consequently, the greater is the caution required.

All the fowler's observations are made by peeping through small apertures in the reed-screens; to facilitate which, short pieces of stick, pointed at one end, are generally stuck in every screen, so that, by gently thrusting one of such pieces between the reeds, a temporary peep-hole is made, which closes of itself on withdrawing the stick.

The decoyer, on discovering that he has a good number of birds upon the water, and time of day, weather, and other circumstances being favourable, proceeds in the following manner to decoy them up the pipe:—

Having provided himself with a piece of lighted turf, and thrown some soft corn upon the water at the entrance to the pipe, he whistles his decoy-ducks; and, as they approach, anxiously peeps to see if the wild ones follow, which, if all is favourable, they are sure to do. He then carefully watches their movements through an aperture of the wide screen at the entrance to the pipe, and probably finds that, though the tame birds have come several yards up the pipe after the corn, the others are unwilling to follow. He therefore directs his dog, by a wave of the hand, to run round the first working screen, and jump over the first little leaping-screen at the mouth of the pipe; and whilst the dog is gone on his errand, which occupies but a few seconds, the decoyer continues watching the birds, when he probably finds they make towards the dog, which returns to his master, at the next screen, where he is directly rewarded with a bit of cheese; and, by another signal of the hand, the dog is directed round the next working screen, and over the next leap; the decoyer all the while taking careful notice of the movements of his intended captives, and studying all their actions and deportment; and as they swim up the pipe faster or slower, he regulates his own movements and those of the dog, which he continues sending round screen after screen, in the same manner as the firsts rewarding him each time with the usual mouthful of cheese: and thus, by such apparently simple performances as those of a little dog appearing on the bank of the pipe a moment here and another there, skipping over a low fence and then vanishing, the fowler succeeds in enticing the birds a sufficient distance to admit of cutting off their retreat.

When thus far successful, he signals to his assistant, who is quietly waiting behind a back screen near the mouth of the pipe [see illustration, *ante*, page 52], and who then immediately comes forward, shows himself between one of the apertures of the working-screens, and takes off his cap or gently waves his hand; which is all that is necessary to urge the birds on farther up the pipe.

They are then all hurry-scurry, fright, and alarm; and not venturing to turn back, because of the presence of the fowler and his assistant—both of whom now show themselves on the bank of the pipe—and being unable to fly higher than the top of the arched netting, the birds follow the course of the pipe, in the hope to find an outlet at the other end, the fowler continuing to urge them on, by simply waving his hand as he walks along the bank outside the pipe, until they reach the tail-end of the fatal tunnel, from which there is no escape.

The decoyer then unhooks the tunnel-net, and by simply twisting or making a turn in it they are all safely secured. He then drags it to a grass-plat, and taking them out one by one, the murderous process of neck-breaking commences, it being indispensably necessary that the decoyer and his assistant should be expert in that unenviable performance, and despatch his victims with all possible precision,[1] being careful to avoid knocking them on the head, because they are more marketable when killed in a clean manner, without bruising their bodies or ruffling their feathers. They are then tossed one upon another, into a large basket or wooden crate, made for the purpose, and so carried away to market.

Wild-fowl (especially teal) sometimes, without any other enticement, follow the decoy-ducks far enough up the pipe to suit the decoyer's purpose, and they need not follow very far; a short distance will often suffice. The instant he finds them within control, and they appear reluctant to follow farther, he signals to his assistant to show himself in front of the entrance, and cut off their retreat. The tame fowl, after swimming about halfway up the pipe, return again, passing the decoyman and his assistant without fear, to the open water.

It is only when the enticements of the decoy-ducks are ineffectual to lead their wild companions on to destruction (and it is not very often they lure them farther than the entrance to the pipe) that the artifices of the dog are called into requisition, that sprightly deceiver being far more alluring than the feathered seducers, and this, the most curious part of the performance, seldom fails to succeed, though the seeds and tame ducks may be of no avail.

There is sometimes great uncertainty attending the decoyer's proceedings. A suspicion of alarm arises, for which the fowler is quite unable to account, when, although there be hundreds of birds upon the pond, not one can be taken; they seem to defy his efforts, and this though time of day, weather, and other circumstances are favourable.

Wild-fowl seem particularly quick in detecting the presence of a stranger behind the screens, and when so not a bird will pipe.

I may mention one instance which occurred at a decoy

belonging to a friend of mine. A visitor was admitted to witness the operations of taking some wild-ducks, which had been regularly using the pond during several days. The weather being bitterly cold, he was wrapped in a seal-skin overcoat, the effluvium from which was supposed to be sufficiently destroyed by carrying in his hand a piece of burning turf. He kept side by side with the decoyer, who tried his utmost to entice the ducks up the pipe; but no, they ventured as far as the entrance, and would go no farther. He then left the decoy, in company with the fowler, and took off the seal-skin coat and put on one of the fowler's jackets. Half an hour later, the decoyer again proceeded, with his visitor so attired, to make another attempt upon the ducks, and directly succeeded in taking every bird.

Other instances of similar tendency might be brought forward, all proving beyond doubt the acuteness of the nasal organs of the feathered occupants of the water. The fowler should, therefore, be particularly guarded against strong scents, and never approach a decoy-pipe with such about him. It is usual to keep a dress for the purpose; gray or light brown coloured garments are best adapted for the decoy.

The decoyer is also cautious, in his operations at the pipe, not to expose himself to the wild-fowl which may be upon the broad water, and to prevent this the reed-screens are so ingeniously placed that he can easily avoid doing so. The birds are supposed to have been enticed far enough up the pipe to ensure their capture when arrived at that screen where, owing to the curve in the pipe, nothing can be seen of their deluded companions by those remaining in the pool.[1]

The best time of day for taking wild-fowl at the decoy is about one or two o'clock, and the best weather, cold, with wind and frost. Wild-fowl sometimes alight in decoys on moonlight nights, more particularly when led there by wandering decoy-ducks. But it is only by broad daylight that the decoyer practises his subtleties; all attempts by moonlight would be fruitless.

The general season for working the decoy is from the end of October to February.

It must not be supposed that the whole of the birds in the decoy are taken at once; there are generally several drifts, or separate enticements, before a whole paddling can be secured. As many as five or six dozen have been taken at a single haul, which is considered a large number, and as many as an ordinary tunnel-net will hold. When there are very large numbers of fowl in the pond, the decoyer keeps at his art during the whole day, gradually thinning the numbers by a few dozens at every distinct enticement.

In whatever part of the decoy the wild-fowl may be, the fowler has means of discovering them, by peeping through some one or other of the reed-screens, and thus he is able to reckon them up, observe their movements, and discover whether they are 'banked' or otherwise; and if there are only a small number present, and it be not late in the season, the fowler will not disturb them, because he may fairly expect them to return another day, when the chances are much in favour of their being accompanied by a more numerous retinue. Such is often the *prestige* of the decoyer.

———

[1] The fowlers of the island of St. Kilda kill a solan goose with great alertness, by dislocating a certain joint of the neck very near the head. The lower part of the neck of the solan goose is much larger than the upper, and adapted to the purpose by which the bird obtains its food; so that, in the absence of skill, it would be difficult and tedious to kill them.—*Vide* Macaulay's 'History of St. Kilda.' Also, *post*, 'Fowling in St. Kilda.'

[1] 'The whole art consists in this, that the birds within the pipes may see the fowler, those in the pool not seeing him. So, those only seeing him, these, notwithstanding, often enter the pipes; and so sometimes, besides those the fowler drives before him, there are others taken the second or third time.'— *Willughby's Ornithology.* By Ray.

CHAPTER XII

THE ART OF CAPTURING WILD-FOWL BY DECOY—continued.

'Aucupari gratiam alicujus assentabiuncula.'—PLINY.

THERE are many considerations to be regarded by the fowler before he proceeds to put in force the means at hand for working the decoy-pipe. It is not at all times and on every opportunity that it would be judicious to attempt taking wildfowl in the decoy, though the water may be well covered; and an unsuccessful attempt may do much injury. The fowler has to consider, first, the species of fowl which have come to visit the decoy; if they are teal, he will probably try them at once, if ducks, he will take an early opportunity in the course of the day, but before doing so he will have to decide if the wind be favourable and the weather suitable. If the birds appear restless or otherwise suspicious, which may generally be known by their movements in the decoy, or if they keep in the centre, far away from the bank, they are supposed to be too wary to be enticed, and must be left in quiet possession of the waters two or three days, until they approach the bank fearlessly, and associate freely with the decoy-ducks.

He will also have to consider if the season of the year be early, mid-season, or late. If early, there are generally so many young birds among them that the fowler may resort at once to his manœuvres with decoy-ducks and dog, and if he is a good hand at his business he will generally succeed with the first flight, During mid-season he acts cautiously, and only attempts his stratagems when tolerably sanguine of good success. Later in the season the fowler's best skill is required, as the birds become exceedingly vigilant. Large numbers are not then often expected, and the decoyer has to practise his artifices upon small flights, but always with extreme caution, whilst the weather continues 'open,' as the term is, in appliance to cold weather without ice; but if the weather is very severe, and the decoy-pipe and entrance be kept clear of ice, there is seldom any difficulty in taking such fowl as happen to use the pond. During open weather the dog is the most useful means at hand for enticing the birds, but in severe weather the seeds and decoy-ducks are more serviceable.

If the fowler finds a 'goodly muster' soon after dawn of day—the time at which they generally arrive in the decoy after feeding on the marshes all night—he proceeds at once to put his plans in operation, but if the birds are unwilling to pipe, he awaits the more favourable hours of one and two in the day.

Wild-fowl do not generally spend their whole time on the waters of the decoy, but bask on the banks of the pond, where they also sit and sleep with their heads under their wings. It is always easier to take fresh arrivals of fowl than those which have been in a decoy several times before, and had a peep of suspicion at the entrance to either of the pipes; the latter birds are extremely wary.

As a general rule, wild-ducks prefer the leewardmost water of a decoy, but they like swimming with breasts to windward, particularly in strong winds and rain, the reason of which is, that the wind does not spread their feathers when in that position, but rather assists in keeping them close. An experienced fowler, with good decoy-ducks at command, generally succeeds in bringing wild ones across the pool to the pipe, and then, if time of day and other circumstances are favourable, he is rewarded for his pains by taking the whole paddling, however large it may be, though not all in one haul but in many. It is generally good policy not to be too greedy in capturing every bird, but rather to spare the last dozen or two, which, on leaving the decoy at twilight, unconscious of what has become of their comrades, may very probably act as leaders to other flights on an early occasion, and return to the decoy with hundreds of companions.

Notwithstanding what has been stated as to attempting to capture wild-fowl soon after their arrival in the decoy, experience tells us that if they can be allowed to remain undisturbed the first four or five days, they become familiarised with the place, and so much accustomed to the company and habits of the tame-fowl that the decoyer, taking advantage of a favourable time of day, and when the wind suits, may capture them without difficulty, though not so if he has before made attempts upon the same birds and his stratagems have failed. These experiences may be well worthy the decoyer's consideration-, but looking at the risk of a strong westerly wind rising before next day and sweeping them all away (and it must not be forgotten that it is by changes of wind that the movements of wild-fowl are chiefly regulated), or their being unexpectedly disturbed at the decoy, and so frightened as never again to return, besides the chance of their taking a liking to some other decoy, with various other casualties, it may be fairly questioned whether the fowler should not take a hint from the old adage, 'No time like the present,' and do his best on the first favourable opportunity, particularly if the flight be a large one; but if there are only a few, certainly the wiser course will be to wait a few days, because the few may return some fine morning with large numbers added to their little band; and it is the very nature of wild-fowl to follow their leaders, whether soaring high in the air, skimming the surface, or swimming on the water.

Sometimes wild-fowl will be found so suspicious of the security of their chosen resting-place in the decoy as to take up their quarters in close column in the centre of the pool, and there remain during the greater part of the day. When such is the case it is useless to attempt decoying them; they are best left to themselves, and in a few days will probably become less wary, and finally an easy prey.

There is no opportunity so favourable for decoying wildfowl as during a steady, or even a strong, breeze blowing directly down the pipe. They may sometimes be taken in calm weather, but he must be a skilful decoyer who succeeds on such occasions in taking any other fowl than teal.

Many decoyers prefer working their pipes with a *side wind*, and they sometimes do so with better success than directly in the wind's eye. When a side wind is chosen, the decoyer selects a pipe where he can conduct his operations from the leewardmost side, which he may do even more properly than with a current directly down the pipe. His operations are never performed from the inner circle, but always on the outer side of the curve of the pipe, therefore it would seem perfectly correct for the fowler to choose a side wind, particularly when taken into consideration that the pipe is formed nearly upon a semicircle, and the fowler's position is on the outer side of the curve. When following the dog up the pipe, wild-fowl always keep on the opposite side to that on which the screens are placed.

It is quite possible for the decoyer to take birds without

the aid of manual assistance, but not with so much certainty, because of having to return back unobservedly and silently from the last working-screen to the mouth of the pipe, during which the most valuable moments are lost, as in all probability the fowl are rapidly swimming back to the entrance of the pipe, the attractions of the dog having ceased, and unless the fowler is very quick it will be too late to stop them.

The decoyer should always approach the pipes with caution, especially on making his first round in the morning. It is not very unusual to find a few volunteers, particularly ducks, which have come into the pipe of their own accord, and far enough to be secured without any enticements. On a morning after a moonlight night wild-ducks are frequently found in the decoy-pipes, and sometimes fast asleep.

When the birds are 'banked' at the mouth of any one of the pipes, and the wind happens to be favourable for working that pipe, if they fail to move from the bank on being invited by the decoy-ducks, the fowler need not hesitate to pop the dog quietly among them, for which purpose there must be a small aperture through the bottom of each of the long screens at the mouths of the different pipes. Immediately on an intrusion of this kind by the dog the birds scamper off the bank into the water, and before they have had time to be alarmed the dog has vanished, and on re-appearing just inside the pipe the fowl are generally irresistibly enticed to pursue the intruder. This proceeding is constantly resorted to by decoyers, and generally with success.

It is always a good stratagem to scatter a little refuse corn or seeds into the windward pipes when wild-fowl are in the decoy, whether it be the intention of the fowler to operate that day or not, and more especially if the corn can be so directed as to drift directly towards the birds, which, after harmlessly feeding upon it on the open water, will be the more likely to take it eagerly in another place at another time. The tame birds, however, should always be signalled towards the pipe into which the seeds are thrown.

In frosty weather the decoy should be kept free of ice, and in very severe weather, when it is no longer possible to keep the ice out of the pond, the pipes and entrance must be cleared once or twice a day, and there is then less art in enticing the fowl up the deceitful stream, as they are sure to rest in and about the open water, and will feed greedily on the grain scattered up the pipe. The performances of breaking and clearing away the ice must be done before daylight in the morning, and for this purpose iron crooks attached to long staves will be found very useful. All hammering and other noisy operations necessary at the decoy must be performed at night during the absence of the birds, and the ice-breaking must be regulated according to the wind, so as to keep those pipes open which, regarding such circumstances, are most favourable for working. The 'rising' of the decoy, as it is termed, takes place at twilight, when the wild-fowl leave to take their evening flight to the marshes or places of nightly resort.

A few ducks and mallards usually visit decoys about July and August, but no experienced fowler would take them or allow them to be disturbed at such times; generally speaking, they are birds bred in the neighbourhood, and should be fed and encouraged to resort to the decoy as much as possible, for if spared they would probably, at a later period of the season, be the means of leading thousands of others to the decoy.

Before the customary decoy season commences for taking ducks, widgeon, and such like, there is generally good practice with teal, which visit the decoys about the first week in September, and often afford excellent sport to the fowler; with considerable remuneration. They come into the decoy in small broods, and are the least difficult to take of any of the wildfowl species. If the decoy-ducks fail to entice them into the pipe, the dog, if properly trained and directed, never fails to excite their curiosity, and lure them on up the decoy-pipe. Teal are as well worth taking as any wild-fowl that flies, and when plump and fat, as they generally are in early season, there are none of the duck tribe more delicious eating.

The Decoy plunderer.

There is sometimes a separate pipe for teal at decoys, and not unfrequently a separate pond, and when so, it is always called 'the teal pipe,' or 'the teal pond.' In the same manner there is often a widgeon pipe kept exclusively for widgeon.

The Essex decoys are still famous for their supplies of teal. A few years ago, a spring of four hundred visited a small pond at Mersea, in Essex, the greater number of which were taken within a few hours. Lubbock mentions an instance which occurred at a Norfolk decoy of 'two hundred and twenty teal being taken at once.'

The first flight of wild-fowl from the Netherlands may

be expected about the beginning of October, and if easterly winds prevail, large flights generally arrive, but if there be no easterly wind about this time, or but little, they come in small numbers only. The principal flight of wild-fowl from foreign shores and northern latitudes does not generally arrive until the severe weather sets in with north-east wind, when, in proportion to the severity of the season, they come in greater or less numbers and varieties.

The decoy is exposed to many plunderings and interruptions, which are sometimes beyond the fowler's control, though some of the marauders may be kept at bay. The boldest thief of all is the Fox, and the most mischievous, because he takes the decoy-ducks, it being seldom that he succeeds in capturing a wild one; and when once Reynard has discovered a retreat so favourable for his purpose, he notes the basking-place of the decoy-ducks, and then his cunning seldom fails him, particularly when sharpened with hunger. Whenever an intruder of this kind is found to practise his depredations at the decoy, the most sportsmanlike manner of being rid of the annoyance is to give notice of his doings to the nearest master of a pack of foxhounds.

Otters are also great annoyances to the decoyer. Though the food of these animals is chiefly fish, they nevertheless so disturb a decoy that no success can be expected if there be an otter's lair anywhere on the banks of the waters. The quietude of the place would seem to mark it as the chosen resort of the otter; and should one find its way within the bounds of the decoy, no wild-fowl will settle there until it is removed. It is not only the plunges of the animal when in pursuit of fish that disturb the fowl, but its stealthy creepings to and fro along the banks of the pond, and the sudden appearance of its grisly head above water—perhaps close upon the entrance to the pipe. Whenever an otter is found to visit a decoy it should be trapped as soon as possible.

Stoats, weasels, beavers, and water-rats are likewise constant annoyances—

    'Among the sportive tenants of the lake
      Wide havoc water-rats and beavers make'—[1]

and at the proper seasons for trapping and killing these vermin they should be kept down: with a little trouble and a few years' experience, the banks and surrounding hedges of the decoy may be tolerably cleared of such fatal marplots.

The falcon and moor-buzzard used formerly to be a great nuisance and constant interruption to the decoyer, though of late years the species have become so scarce, that very little disturbance now arises from any rapacious birds. But none of the feathered tribe cause the wild-fowler so much annoyance as the heron. It is not the stalkings and walkings of this majestic bird on the banks of the decoy, at which the wild-fowl take affright, but the unmistakable signal of alarm which it gives on extending its powerful wings to leave the scene of suspected security. This bird is particularly objectionable at the decoy; its senses of hearing, smelling, and seeing at long distances are so extremely acute, that its ever-watchful nature is almost certain to detect the presence or approach of man, especially in still weather; and when the wild-fowl at a decoy are quite unconscious of danger it sometimes raises an alarm, and instantly every bird leaves the pond.

There is yet another interruption to which the decoyer is liable, and which sometimes baffles all his efforts; it is no other than the presence of a voracious pike—

'The pike arrests the fowl with hungry jaws,
And to the bottom of the river draws;
Nay, as a boy in the smooth current swims,
His teeth he fixes in their tender limbs'—[2]

and who would expect wild-fowl to swim at ease over the head of such an ugly customer? As to ducklings, a pike makes but a mouthful of such delicious morsels. It is by no means unusual, particularly at mid-day, for a pike to be lying near the surface of the water at the very entrance to the decoy-pipe; and the angler and troller tell us that it is the nature and habit of the pike to make use of fleet ditches and rills for the purposes of spawning and lying in ambush for its prey. No wonder, then, that the pipe of a decoy should be a favourite haunt of this savage and greedy fish. If the decoy be kept entirely clear of pike and jack, it will be the better for the successful issue of the decoyer's art.

There is one species of the duck tribe which has hitherto baffled all the efforts of capture of the most practised decoyers. The pochard, or dun-bird, which is a constant frequenter of decoys, much to the annoyance of the fowler, is by nature so gifted with cunning that it defies his skill, and eludes capture by diving, and so passing by the decoyman regains the open water. But the ingenuity of our forefathers long since discovered a very successful method of taking these artful intruders by means of nets and poles, the ingenious proceedings relating to which will be treated of in subsequent chapters.

Coots are also exceedingly cunning; they may sometimes be enticed a considerable distance up the pipe and then insist on returning. But when the weather is very severe and there is much ice in the decoy, coots are compelled to keep in the clear open water at the mouth of the pipe; they are then sometimes taken, after a little time and humouring.

Wild-ducks, teal, and widgeon are the only species caught in large numbers in decoys; though many a pair of pintail-ducks, scoters, and others less gregarious, are sometimes taken with the species above named. Of late years, however, widgeon appear to have been very shy of decoys, and keep to the saltwater rivers and oozes, where they afford the finest sport to the punt-gunner of any wild-fowl on the coast. Brent and other wild-geese never use decoys.

----

[1] Trans. from 'Vaniere,' book xv.

[2] Ibid.

CHAPTER XIII

THE LAW OF DECOYS

A DECOY for taking wild-fowl is an enterprise of advantage to the proprietor, maintained at considerable expense, and in the nature of a trade of profit; there is therefore the same reason why a man should be recompensed in damages for wilful injury to his decoy or wilful disturbance thereof, or interruption in the operations connected therewith, as for injury or damage to him in any other trade, or in any other lawful enjoyment of his land. And accordingly we find that, although decoys are not the subject of any special statutory enactment, they are protected at common law.

And there is a distinction in law between an ancient and a modern decoy. If, by long usage and enjoyment, a decoy becomes established without interruption by the owners of adjacent lands, the occupier is so far protected in the free exercise, profit, and enjoyment of it, that an action would lie against anyone who injured the decoy, by firing off guns very near to it, or who made other wilful disturbance so as to frighten the wild-fowl resorting there, and cause them to fly away and forsake the decoy, and this although the disturbance be committed on the offender's own land.

A decoy established during twenty years, without interruption by the proprietor of adjoining lands or others, becomes a privileged place, and the proprietor acquires a right to command the accustomed quietude necessary for the successful operations of his art. But in the case of a recently established decoy, which may not have acquired any long or uninterrupted quietude of enjoyment, it is lawful to fire off a gun or shoot from one's own land at wild-fowl which may be apparently going direct to the pond, and at the time very near to the same.

Though a man can have no property in wild-fowl when they are flying abroad, yet he has when they are in his decoy, and they constitute a well-known article of food: he must not therefore be wilfully disturbed or hindered by other men in his operations of capturing them at his decoy.

If a man wilfully or maliciously frighten wild-fowl away from, or prevent their resorting to, a decoy, that is actionable.

The remedy is by action on the case when the injury has been committed *outside* the decoy, but by action of trespass when committed *within* the decoy-grounds.

In the year 1706 (Trinity Term 5th Anne) an important case was decided as to the rights of decoy-owners, and the remedy for injuries by interruption and disturbance in the enjoyment thereof, which case has ever since been recognised as the leading authority upon the subject The case alluded to is *Keeble* v. *Hickeringall.*[1] The plaintiff was lord of a manor, and had a decoy for wild-fowl. The defendant had also made a decoy on his own ground, next adjoining, and only a short distance from the other. The defendant went with his gun to the head of his neighbour's pond, and, by shooting several times, frightened away a number of ducks.

The facts, as appearing upon the record, were: that the plaintiff was possessed of a certain close of land, and in that close he had a *vivarium* (decoy) to which divers wild-fowl used to resort, and the plaintiff had at his own cost procured divers decoy-ducks, nets, machines, and other engines for the decoying and taking of wild-fowl, and enjoyed the benefits of taking them; the defendant, knowing which, and intending to damnify the plaintiff in his *vivary*, and to frighten and drive away the wild-fowl accustomed to resort thither, and deprive him of his profit, did, on the 8th of November, go to the head of the said pond and *vivary*, and discharge six guns laden with gunpowder, and with the noise and stink of the gunpowder did drive away the wild-fowl then being in the pond, and on the 11th and 12th of November the defendant, with design to damnify the plaintiff and frighten away the wild-fowl, did place himself with a gun charged with gunpowder near the *vivary*, and there did discharge the said gun several times against the said decoy-pond, whereby the wild-fowl were frightened away, and did forsake the said pond, &c. The defendant pleaded 'Not Guilty.' At the trial a verdict was found for the plaintiff, with damages 20*l.*

Sir James Montague (Solicitor-General) afterwards moved the Court in Banco on behalf of the defendant in arrest of judgment, on the grounds (among others), that the Declaration disclosed no good cause of action, that the plaintiff could have no possessory property in any wild-fowl but those which he had captured, that if plaintiff had such possessory property yet the defendant might shoot them on his own ground, and that it was not found that the defendant went on plaintiff's ground; and the learned counsel in the course of his argument stated, that decoys were not of any long standing, and he urged that it was against the law of the land to allure wild-fowl and take them there in such large numbers. Raymond, for the plaintiff, in the course of his argument, said he hoped the Court did know what a decoy was, though when Bracton wrote decoys were not known.

The case was twice argued before the Court of King's Bench, first in Hilary Term, 5 Anne, and afterwards in Easter Term, 5 Anne. The arguments are best reported in Holt's Reports, pp. 14 and 17. Holt, C. J., delivered the judgment of the Court in favour of the plaintiff, and said that, although the action was new in its instance, it was not new in the reason or principle of it; for, first, this using or making a decoy for taking wild-fowl is lawful; secondly, this employment of his ground to that use is profitable to the plaintiff, as are the skill and management of that employment. As to the first, every man that hath a property may employ it for pleasure and profit, as for allowing and procuring ducks to come to his pond. To learn the trade of seducing other ducks to come there in order to be taken is not prohibited either by the law of the land or the moral law; but it is as lawful to use art to seduce them, to catch them, and destroy them for the use of mankind, as to kill and destroy wildfowl or tame cattle. Then when a man uses his art or his skill to take them, to sell and dispose of for his profit, this is his trade, and he that hinders another in his trade or livelihood is liable to an action for so hindering him. And when we know that of long time in the kingdom these artificial contrivances of decoy-ponds and decoy-ducks have been used for enticing into those ponds wild-fowl, in order to be taken for the profit of the owner of the pond, who is at the expense of servants, engines, and other management, whereby the markets of the nation may be furnished, there is great reason to give encouragement thereunto, that the people who are so instrumental, by their skill and industry, so to furnish the markets, should reap the benefit and have their right of action. But, in short, that which is the true reason is, that this action is not brought to recover damage for the loss of the fowl, but for the disturbance; as in 2 Cro. R. 604, *Dawney* v.

Dee.

In a subsequent case—*Carrington* v. *Taylor*[1]—which was an action on the case for disturbing the plantiff's ancient decoy at Beaumont-cum-Moze, in Essex, it appeared that the defendant in part earned his living by wild-fowl-shooting; and the only proof of disturbance to the decoy was, that, being in his boat in an open creek, he first fired his fowling-piece within about a quarter of a mile of the plaintiff's decoy, when two or three hundred wild-fowl came out. Defendant afterwards approached nearer, and fired again at wild-fowl on the wing, at a distance of about two hundred yards and upwards from the pond, when he killed several widgeon, and immediately on the report of the gun four or five hundred wild-fowl took flight from the decoy; but it did not appear that he fired into the decoy. Evidence of the antiquity of the decoy, and plaintiff's right to the same, having been shown, Macdonald, Chief Baron, held that an ancient decoy was protected at law as Well as ancient lights or the enjoyment of a watercourse, and left the evidence upon the question as to the alleged wilful disturbance to the jury, who found a verdict for the plaintiff, with forty shillings damages. A motion Was afterwards made to set aside the verdict, as being against law and evidence; the defendant, it was argued, having a right to shoot at wild-fowl in an open creek or arm of the sea, where the tide ebbed and flowed, and not having gone upon the plaintiff's land nor fired into the decoy. The Court, however, refused to grant a rule, stating that they saw no reason for disturbing the verdict in point of law: and Le Blanc, J., referred to the case of *Keeble* v. *Hicker-ingall*, above stated, which he said had been followed by one or two others, within his own remembrance, on the Norfolk Circuit. And the Court observed that the evidence was proper to be left to the jury, who had decided upon it.[1]

The statute 9th Anne, cap. 25, prohibited the taking of wild-fowl by 'hayes tunnels or other nets' between July 1 and September 1, under a penalty of 5s. for every bird; and the subsequent statute of 10th Geo. II. cap. 32, extended that prohibition to the intervening time between June 1 and October 1. But those statutes had reference more particularly to a destructive system, formerly prevalent in this country, of taking wild-fowl by driving them into nets during the moulting season. The art of capturing wild-fowl by decoy, however, fell within the pale of those enactments, and the decoy season was regulated accordingly. Both those statutes are repealed by 1 Wm. IV. cap. 32, which also prohibits under certain restrictions the taking of wild-fowls' eggs.

And by the Wild Birds Protection Act 1872,[1] the taking of any wild-fowl or fen-bird between March 15 and August 1 in any year is prohibited.

[1] Holt's Eep. 14, 17, 19; 11 Mod. Rep. 74 and 130; 11 East, 574; 3 Salk, 9.

[1] 11 East, 571; 2 Camp, 258.

[1] The law does not recognise any property whatever in rooks, therefore no action lies for maliciously firing off guns so near to a rookery as to frighten the birds, and deter them from resorting to and breeding in the plaintiff's trees. And so in a case where the plaintiff was possessed of a close of land with trees growing thereon, to which rooks had been used to resort and to settle, and build nests and rear their young in the trees, by reason whereof plaintiff had been used to kill and take the rooks and the young thereof, and great profit and advantage had accrued to him, and the defendant, wrongfully and maliciously intending to injure the plaintiff, and alarm and drive away the rooks, and cause them to forsake the trees of the plaintiff, wrongfully and injuriously caused guns loaded with gunpowder to be discharged near the plaintiff's close, and thereby disturbed and drove away the rooks, whereby the plaintiff was prevented from killing the rooks, and taking the young thereof. Plea not guilty. Held, on motion in arrest of judgment, that this action was not maintainable, insomuch as rooks were a species of birds *feræ naturæ*, destructive in their

habits, not known as an article Of food, or alleged so to be, and not protected by any Act of Parliament, and the plaintiff could not therefore have any property in them, or show any right to have them resort to his trees.—Hannam *v.* Mockett, 2 B. & C. 934; 4 D. & R. 518.

[1] 35 & 36 Vic. cap. 78, and see *infra*, 'Laws affecting Wild-fowl and Fenbirds.'

CHAPTER XIV

THE POCHARD OR DUN-BIRD

(Fuligula ferina.)

'Tho' the wild-duck and widgeon may peril their lives,
When lured in decoy by the pranks of an ape!
More crafty the pochard, which cunningly dives,
And beats under water a certain escape.'

THE AUTHOR.

THE pochard or dun-bird is by nature one of the most artful wild-fowl in existence. The flight-pond, With its ponderous apparatus, was specially invented for the purpose of capturing these birds; their cunning being such that they elude the vigilance of the most practised decoyer. Pochards are fond of visiting decoys, and often frequent them in large numbers; they may sometimes be enticed a considerable distance up the pipe in company with Widgeon; but, notwithstanding such enticement, they are not to be taken in a decoy-pipe. When danger is apparent they instantly dive, and return to the open water by the route they entered, though beneath the surface. Other wild-fowl in their company may be captured—every one of them; but not a single dun-bird. Instances have occurred where an occasional straggler, with less cunning than his fellows, has been hurried up the decoy-pipe, *en masse*, with numbers of widgeon; but it is, nevertheless, a rare occurrence to take a pochard in the decoy-pipe.

As a species, the dun-bird is very abundant, the immense flights which used to visit our coast being of almost incredible extent; and it was nothing unusual, during favourable seasons, for several acres of inland water to be literally covered with them, as closely packed as possible for them to sit.

When suspecting danger, and on a small decoy, it is sometimes a difficult matter to induce them to take wing; but on large open waters and tidal rivers they are remarkably wary of the presence of human form. In decoys they will sometimes suffer themselves to be driven like sheep from one end of the pond to the other, rather than take wing—-so suspicious are they of the enemy. It is the nature of dun-birds to seek their food at inland waters, and when once a favourable feeding-place is discovered, they frequent it as much by night as by day. They dive with great facility, and feed on the richest fare of the lake, the juicy roots of the herbage which grows at the very bottom, and which they tear up with their powerful beaks. The flesh of the dun-bird is esteemed a great delicacy; and when plump and fat—which is invariably the case with inland fed dun-birds—they are equal in flavour to the celebrated American canvas-back duck, which they closely resemble in their habits and in the colour of their plumage. The dun-bird, however, is not so large as the canvas-back.

Another remarkable circumstance connected with the habits of the dun-bird, as well as others of the *Anatidæ*, is, that the whole night is generally spent in diving for food; during which operation they are widely scattered over the surface, more than half the flight being sometimes under water at the same time. An experienced punter seldom shoots at dun-birds by night: he knows they are dispersed over a large space, and that only very few could be killed at a shot. The dun-bird may be known at night by its note—a faint whistle slightly resembling the widgeon; but a little experience will soon teach the fowler to distinguish it from widgeon, and, indeed, from all other wild-fowl.

The best time for obtaining a favourable shot at pochards is at dawn of day, when they have just completed their midnight labours, and, with appetites fully appeased, are mustering in party previous to taking flight for their daily quarters: they require hard hitting, their feathers being thick and close. Pochards often stay all night in the decoy, when they go through the same exertions as just mentioned—sitting scattered all over the pond, as many at the bottom as on the top, and never failing to pipe to their companions every time they rise to the surface. They are generally considered a great nuisance to the decoyer, unless he has a dun-bird net and other flight-pond apparatus for taking them. They are also selfish and pugnacious towards duck and teal, often preventing such birds from going up the decoy-pipe in obedience to the decoyer's enticements, particularly if there be any sunken grains of corn at the mouth of the pipe, in which case the dun-birds will usurp possession, and not allow other fowl to come near until they have devoured all the spoil at the bottom of the water. They are, nevertheless, excellent purveyors for other wild-fowl during the severest part of winter, when they are indefatigable in their exertions in diving in deep water and bringing up to the surface abundant supplies of water-herbage, weeds, and other *lens palustris*, the roots of which having been eaten by the dun-birds, the refuse is then picked over by wild ducks and widgeon. When actively engaged in diving for their food, dun-birds generally keep in scattered doppings, within circles of about thirty or forty yards' circumference.

Dun-birds are much in the habit of alighting in decoys at night, when they are aware that good feeding is to be had there, and have been dopping about the sea-coast during the day. They fly in a much. more irregular body than the generality of wild-fowl: no straight or diverged line marks their course, but they proceed through the air in one closely-packed body, making a loud hissing noise with their short wings, which they use with very rapid stroke.

CHAPTER XV

THE FLIGHT-POND

'But you know
Strange fowl light upon neighbouring ponds.'—
SHAKESPEARE.

IT is very remarkable that the proceedings and contrivances connected with the flight-pond should hitherto have been so cursorily passed over as to excite but little attention from the multifarious writers upon sporting literature; yet so it is. The means employed at the flight-pond are no less ingenious and interesting (though totally different) than those of the decoy.

It is also worthy of observation that, notwithstanding the numerous decoys which were formerly used in various parts of Norfolk, and the abundance of dun-birds, but few traces can be found of flight-ponds having been employed in that county; indeed, they have seldom been met with in any other counties than Essex and Suffolk, which seem always to have been favourite localities with that particular species of wild-fowl.

During many years after decoys were invented no means could be discovered for taking the large flights of pochards which daily arid constantly frequented the decoys, to the vexation and annoyance of many an indefatigable fowler, who, day after day, raked his brain in vain to discover, by some ingenuity, a means of capturing them. The fowler saw them come and go to and from the waters of the decoy with impudent independence; they seemed to defy his efforts and ridicule his eagerness to take them. This state of things continued for many years after decoys were employed with considerable success and profit, and it is evident that the flight-pond was not known untij. long after decoys had been used for taking all other species of wildfowl frequenting inland waters.

The author has been unable to trace any other original allusions to flight-ponds than those few scanty notices referred to in the introduction, from which it must have been impossible for any novice to arrive at the faintest idea of the true principles, upon which the flight-pond was constructed, much less of the fowler's contrivances for taking the birds.

Besides a very attractive and formerly well-conducted flight-pond at Mersea, in Essex, which the author has been in the habit of visiting, he is also familiarly acquainted with another on the banks of the Stour, at Brantham, in Suffolk, where thousands of dun-birds have been captured. But, as the

Great Eastern line of railway intrudes within a few yards of the very grounds of this pond, the chances of decoy in that retired and picturesque locality are now nearly entirely destroyed. The Brantham pond was used both as a flight-pond and decoy. It had but three decoy-pipes—east, west, and north; the whole of the south and south-west sides being occupied with the poles and apparatus for taking dun-birds. But not a vestige now remains of the fowler's pipes, poles, nets, and machinery: what was formerly the dun-bird yard is now a cultivated field; and carp, tench, eels, and moor-fowl are the almost sole occupants of the deep waters of this once-renowned decoy and flight-pond. So favourably situated is this pond as a receptacle for wild-fowl, that to the present day (notwithstanding the railroad) a winter never passes but numbers of birds visit it, more or less, according to the severity or mildness of the season, in little trips of from two to twenty, when they (or some of them) are generally shot by the venerable and worthy old cottager who inhabits the decoy-house on the farm.

Before proceeding to explain the somewhat cumbrous machinery employed for taking dun-birds at the flight-pond, it is well worth while to inquire into the reasons which must have suggested so successful a trap. The dun-bird, it is well known, cannot rise suddenly in the air as a wild-duck; but, in consequence of its legs being so far back and its wings so short, it skims the surface, and proceeds many yards at an exceeding low flight ere it can make an ascent, and so gradually rise higher and higher in the air as the distance increases from the spot whence it first took flight. The formation of the dunbird is adapted by nature for diving and holding itself under water, but it is ill-suited for rising quickly or making a rapid or very lengthened course in the air. With these facts daily before him, the inventor must have felt pretty certain of the success of his project on small decoy-ponds, when he first put his rustic machinery into operation, whereby he was enabled to spring a lofty net from the brink of the pond and intercept the tardy flight of those birds as they prepared to leave it.

The apparatus for taking dun-birds at the flight-pond consists of a net about 50 yards in length by about 18 in depth, which by means of two stout poles, 50 yards apart, and heavily weighted at the lower ends, is suddenly poised high in the air in the face of the birds as they are leaving the pond; when, on striking against the net *en masse*, they drop down into narrow fens or crates, provided for their reception at the foo! of the net, from which they cannot rise. Hundreds of dun-birds are taken at a drop in this manner at the flight-pond.

A flight-pond, as far as regards the pool itself and the sequestered spot chosen for its cultivation, is similar to a decoy, but requires no tributary ditches, pipes, nor decoy-ducks for the purpose of assisting its operations. The very design of the flight-pond is to take a species of wild-fowl by nature too artful to be captured in the decoy, for which purpose the contrivances employed are admirably adapted. A decoy may be used in part as a flight-pond; but it is not always desirable that the two proceedings should be combined, because one requires a space clear of trees and obstructions; the other should be sheltered. When the pond is used for both purposes it is usual to have but one or two decoy-pipes, the rest of the space being required for working the dun-bird nets; so that when the fowler has practised his artifices upon such birds as may be taken in the decoy-pipe, he then enacts another part upon those which will not pipe, and, by means of the flight-net and apparatus, often takes every bird which may be upon the water. It is very rarely, however, that any but pochards and their species are taken in the flight-net; a wild-duck, widgeon, or teal has sufficient power of wing to soar suddenly high in the air, and avoid the net spread to capture it.

The spot selected for a flight-pond should be similarly situated to that of a decoy—a quiet and retired locality near the most favourite haunts of the aquatic tribe, and not far from the sea-coast. The planting, however, should be rather differently arranged, and the surrounding grounds and banks laid out in the following manner:—

The trees and underwood about the flight-pond must be in accordance with the number of posts, poles, and nets to be employed. In a complete flight-pond, used exclusively for capturing dun-birds, there must be posts and poles to suit the wind from at least four quarters; which, for the purpose of aiding our explanation, we will suppose to be east, west, north, and south.

It is not necessary that the pond should be an exact square; a circular space answers nearly the same purpose. But let us, for present elucidation, imagine a pond seventy or eighty yards square, which is about the best and most suitable size for a flight-pond. At each of the four corners as many trees, and as much underwood, should be planted as can be, so as not to interfere with the fowler's operations; and the taller the trees, and nearer they stand to the brink of the pond, the better. With the planting so arranged, there will be the four sides of the pond clear and open, which is the intention desired. These open spaces should command an extent of grass plat or tolerably level surface of sixty yards' frontage to the water, by thirty yards' breadth of back-ground. This is termed the dun-bird yard, beyond the boundaries of which the back-ground may be planted with trees and copse, so as to give the whole place a quiet appearance.

It is usual to throw up an embankment a few feet above the level of the water at each frontage, whereby a greater elevation is given to the posts and poles. The embankment also answers admirably as a screen to the fowler and his preliminary operations; and wherever requisite reed-screens must be placed, that no glimpse of the fowler or his movements may be had by the birds upon the pond.

The arrangement of the dun-bird pond under explanation would give four frontages; consequently four distinct dun-bird yards and four nets, requiring four sets of posts and poles. It will be sufficient for our purpose to explain the method of planting the posts and arranging the poles for one of the yards, all the others being planned in a precisely similar manner.

The main posts, or those to which the but-end of each pole is attached, are twin-posts, and must be of stout and solid substance, firmly fixed in the ground, and capable of bearing the great strain to be put upon them. They must be twelve feet in height, though planted on the top of the embankment, about ten yards from the brink of the water, and about fifty yards apart, according to the space of frontage and length of net. Each of the twin-posts must also be provided with a crossbar called the 'trammel-bar,' by which the poles are kept in upright position after they have risen perpendicularly. In the back-ground, at the opposite corners of the dun-bird yard, are placed two crotched posts of less substance, about fifty feet from the twin-posts, and parallel with them; these must be fifteen feet in height, and made with a crotch at the top, wherein to receive the upper end of the poles when fastened down ready for being used. Central in distance between these and the twin-posts are two other crotched posts,, one to each pole, which are merely to ease the others, and receive a share of the weight of the poles when resting upon them; they are also provided with a short piece of line and two iron staples, or a cleat, for the purpose of tying down the poles, so as to prevent their flying up when not in use.

Exactly central between the two outer crotched posts, or those farthest from the water's edge, is another post, called the 'trigger-post,' the use of which will be explained presently.

Two extra posts are required for the purpose of conducting a line for steadying the ascent of the poles. These are generally placed in the plantation, about equidistant from the twin-posts and the outer crotches.

The posts (nine in all), so arranged, are ready for the reception of the two poles, the but-end of each of which turns upon its axis, at the top of the twin-posts, where the libration is preserved by a very simple machinery, consisting of an iron pivot and trammel, by means of which, and a box of iron weights, the pole is forced up in the air, into a perpendicular position. The poles, so weighted and arranged, are then ready for reception of the net, which is simply laced to them, commencing at the top, and extending as far down as may be considered necessary, but never quite down to the lower end of the poles.

The net is in form a simple parallelogram, and extends from one pole to the other, covering the whole quadrilateral space between the posts.

The steadying-ropes and lines being arranged, all is ready for action. The trigger-post, before mentioned as standing exactly central between the two outer crotched posts, is the commanding position, as that where the fowler places himself; and, just before shooting the net, every fastening is cast off, except those connected with the poles at the outer crotches, from which a line with a noose is attached, leading to the trigger-post; when, by suddenly drawing a ring-bolt, the weighted boxes on the lower end of the poles force them up, carrying the net with them. At the top of each pole a ship's block, or sheave, is attached, through which a small rope is rove, in connection with corresponding sheaves in the extra posts before mentioned, the object of the rope being to steady the ascent of the poles; for, if they were permitted to fly up too suddenly, they would jump off the twin-posts, tearing away the trammels, and carrying destruction with them wherever they fell, and probably endangering the lives of the fowler and his assistants. By means of the lines and sheaves, the poles are drawn down again, the lines hove taut upon the sheaves, and secured until required for further service.

The poles are each sixty feet in length, twelve inches diameter at the base, by three and a half inches at the top. The length depends in some respects on the position in which they stand, and whether on level ground or on an embankment raised above the surface of the water. The lengths stated are for posts placed upon an embankment about five feet above the level.

The dimensions of the net are fifty yards in length, by eighteen in depth; or, if one yard less than the space between the poles, it is found to stand better. The net should be made upon a three-inch mesh, and the finer the twine the better, so long as it is strong enough for the work. About the ordinary-sized twine used for fishermen's peter-nets answers best. A three-quarter-inch rope is required for the top of the net.

The greatest caution is necessary in adjusting the weights, which are placed in strong wooden boxes, and swung upon the lower ends of the poles. If over-weighted, the poles cannot be properly regulated in their ascent; and if under-weigh ted, they will not ascend at all. The best plan is to try them well before attempting to use them for catching fowl: six cwt. will be about the quantum for each pole; and if the weights are in half-cwt. iron pieces, with handles, they will be found very convenient.

A number of small pens are arranged on the embankment, extending along the whole frontage between the net and the water, in line with the twin-posts; and some of them are placed immediately beneath the bottom part of the net. These pens may be formed of reed-screens, about three feet in height, by two and three feet square; and, by means of a few projections of wooden spikes at the lower part, may be stuck in the ground with facility; or the pens may be simply small wooden crates, temporarily arranged in the front line of the net. They should be of various shapes, placed in different positions, so as to form triangular or any other enclosures most likely to keep the birds from getting out.

With four dun-bird yards, upon the same plan as the one explained, extending along each side of the pond, the fowler is prepared to capture dun-birds, whichever direction they take on leaving the pond; and, bearing in mind that they generally rise to windward, he would naturally employ the poles in that quarter. Two nets will be found sufficient, as they may be unlaced from one set of poles and transferred to others.

The fowler never attempts to capture dun-birds on their first arrival: he has to watch them when they leave, at flight-time, and take careful observation of the route they take, that he may know which poles and net to make use of. They generally leave, night after night, by the same route.

When the wind is fair for taking the birds, and the nets are fixed in the right quarter, the fowler waits not for twilight, but proceeds at any hour of the day to put his plans in operation.

The crotches which support the poles and nets, when lashed down, keep the net well up from the ground, and out of the way of hares, rabbits, and pheasants, which may inhabit the surrounding locality.

When the nets and poles are not in actual use, the fowler removes most of the weights from the boxes, or takes them entirely off the poles, so as to ease the strain and prevent mischief.

CHAPTER XVI

METHOD OF CAPTURING DUN-BIRDS AT THE FLIGHT-POND.

'And urge them forth in wild affright,
While Hubert stands, with ready net
Carefully o'er each entrance set,
To intercept them in their flight.'

Annals of Sporting, vol. ii.

THE above illustration, though of necessity upon a very small scale, is intended to represent a flight-pond with four flight-nets and four decoy-pipes. Three of the flight-nets are supposed to be lashed down, the other is in actual operation, being sketched at the moment of capturing a large flight of pochards, consisting of several hundred. It will be observed that a few of the leading birds are permitted to pass over the top of the net, such being good policy on the part of the fowler, whereby he is the better enabled to intercept the main bulk of the flight. The birds remaining on the water at a distance from the captured are the decoy-fowl. When it is considered that the illustration is supposed to exhibit a space of nearly fifty acres, allowance will be made by the reader for the mere bird's-eye view of the spot.

The poles and nets being fixed according to the arrangements stated in the last chapter, and resting upon the crotched posts, the lashings at the middle posts are cast off, and the only remaining ties are at the trigger-post, where the whole machinery of poles and nets is held down by an iron pin, with a ring at the end, large enough to receive a man's hand when required, for the purpose of suddenly drawing it out and releasing the net, in order that it may fly up in the air, and stop the birds in their attempts to leave the pond.

Besides the two assistants whom the fowler requires to attend the steadying ropes, he sometimes finds it necessary to employ one or two others, termed 'flushers,' who station themselves on the opposite side of the pond to that on which the fowler works the nets, and on a signal being given suddenly show themselves, and thus drive the dun-birds forward, causing them to take wing, and fly over the yard where the snare is spread to meet them. The fowler always requires assistance of this kind when working his nets at any other time during the day than flight-time, as at that hour they are sure to leave the pond without being driven, and he may sometimes dispense with the assistance of the flushers, though it is not advisable to do so, for if the birds have the smallest suspicion of anything going forward at one end of the pond they will leave it by the other, unless driven in a contrary direction.

The same practice prevails at the flight-pond as at the decoy with reference to the manœuvre of permitting small trips of birds to remain for days and even weeks at the pond without attempting to capture or molest them in any way, the object of delay being that the numbers may accumulate to a large flight, and, indeed, this has been proved beyond doubt to be the essence of godd skill I the fowler, by delaying his performances a few days, is frequently rewarded ten and twenty-fold by the small trips returning to the pond with thousands of followers. Upon occasions of this kind, when such large numbers are expected to be taken, the fowler has several attendants near by to assist in the neck-breaking, which follows immediately after the drop or capture of a number of dun-birds.

The actual performance of flushing the birds, and raising the net to intercept their flight, is as follows:—

When the fowler proceeds to put his poles and nets in operation, and intends trying his skill upon a flight of dun-birds, having engaged a sufficient number of assistants, and looked well to his net and the machinery connected with it, he generally, if an experienced hand, performs the most critical offices himself; but first he places two of his best helpmates, one at each of the posts in the back-ground, where the falls of the steadying-ropes are conducted, and from which posts ropes are fixed, and led through sheaves at the extreme upper ends of the poless. The fowler then stations himself at the trigger-post, from which he gives his orders by signal; and having a commanding view of the water, looks out sharply for the birds on their being flushed from the pond, when, as soon as they have all taken wing, he draws the ring-bolt, and the net being thus set free, it instantly begins to rise. The duty of the assistants then is to steady its ascent, and regulate its rise in accordance with the flight of the birds and the directions of the fowler; slower or faster as it may happen, so that the net may intercept them in their flight on attempting to leave the pond, causing them to strike heavily against it, and drop headlong into the small diagonal and triangular enclosures (or pens, as they are termed), from which dun-birds cannot rise or take wing, but are secured as quickly as possible by the fowler and his assistants, and their necks broken with all due dexterity. The object of the pens is very apparent, for if there were none such the birds would run about the yard and escape; and if they were permitted to drop upon open ground they would flutter and scramble away, and many would take wing before the fowler could reach them to perform his 'Jack Ketch' duty; but when once the pochards fall within these pens they cannot get out, though there be no covering at the top; the form of the pochard, with its short wings and legs so far behind, precluding the possibility of its rising from so confined a space; besides which, when the flight is large, they fall into the pens in such numbers, and are so buried *en masse*, that more than half are suffocated, or nearly so, ere they come to the hands of the break-neck assistant. It would seem to be a very simple and easy art, though by no means a pleasing one to contemplate, to break the slender neck of a pochard; but it is not at all so simple as may be imagined, and requires some considerable practice and experience to perform it skilfully and expeditiously. It is done by wringing the head round with the thumb and forefingers of the right hand, and then bending it sharply, meeting the action with the left hand, by a sudden jerk; but the two hands must act simultaneously, or the operation cannot be successfully performed.

Every fowler, whether a punter or decoyman, should become familiar with this apparently cruel proceeding; else, after taking a goodly number of birds at the flight or decoy-pond, or making a good shot at a paddling of wild-ducks, he will find it a difficult matter to kill them with sufficient expedition, if at the decoy; and if in a gunning-punt he will lose half his winged and wounded birds by wasting much time in knocking them on the head after capture, instead of breaking their necks, every moment being of importance on such occasions. A wild-duck is hard to kill, even after capture in inexperienced hands, and however derogatory it may seem to the general reader for a sportsman to become proficient in so cold-blooded a proceeding, it is nevertheless necessary that he should understand the readiest means of finishing his captives with least suffering.

It would scarcely be credited by some men, inexperienced, that there is occasionally very great difficulty in driving a flight of dun-birds from a decoy-pond: they are sometimes so obstinate as to persist in remaining there; and, notwithstanding the hallooing and clamour of the flushers, they will, if they have the smallest suspicion of the fowler's intentions towards them, permit a gun to be fired near them rather than take wing: and sometimes when they have used the pond several days in perfect security, and suddenly find themselves in a state of apprehension, they will swim rapidly in a body round and round the pond with such velocity as to cause the water to stir like a whirlpool. Sometimes the flushers, whose duty it is, at a given signal, to put the birds up, have to get into a boat and row towards them, when, by waving their hats and otherwise alarming the birds, they may be compelled to leave by the apparently open route, where they are cunningly intercepted by the fowler in the manner before stated. Drawing the bolt at the critical juncture and regulating the rise of the net require discretion and good judgment, and the sole attention of the men who stand by it. The fowler, especially, must watch narrowly for the first rising from the water; and, in general, it is advisable to allow the first few leaders to go over the net, and then to strike boldly at the body of the flight, which always follow, or attempt to follow, in the track of their leaders, but which, if the operations be successfully conducted, rush headlong against the net, and drop into the pens below by hundreds. (*See illustration* at page 91.)

To give some idea of the immense flights of dun-birds which used to be taken in the flight-nets at Mersea and Gold-hanger, in Essex, the body of birds has there been known to be so great, that when their flight has been attempted to be intercepted they have actually been heavier in a body than the ponderous boxes of weights placed at the lower ends of the poles, and the consequence has been, that the birds have borne down the net, and partly spoilt the fowler's drop; but such is a rare occurrence, and cannot happen if the balance-boxes are judiciously weighted.

It is by no means unusual, when the fowler has been a little too slow in liberating the net, for the birds to strike before it has attained its proper perpendicular position; and, as the bolt is never drawn until they have actually risen from the water, it follows, as a matter of course, that the net would meet them in their flight, and thus cause them to fall the more suddenly into the pens. Dun-birds rise so slowly that this precaution has always been found necessary, and the bolt is never drawn until the birds have fairly taken wing; and when the number has been so great that their weight has for a moment prevented the net from rising to its perpendicular position, the author's own experience has been, that the birds, notwithstanding, fall pell-mell into the pens below; and he never knew an instance where the net was pressed down to its extreme bearings by the weight and numbers of the flight, though he has good authority for believing such a case to have actually occurred; but then the balance-boxes were not sufficiently weighted.

At these same decoys (Mersea and Goldhanger) the capture of dun-birds, on one or two occasions within present memory, has been so great at a drop that a waggon and four horses were required to' remove them from the yard; and they have fallen in such heaps on striking the net that many of those at the bottom of the pens were taken up dead, apparently crushed or stifled by the pressure of those above.

To give a further illustration of the countless numbers of dun-birds which sometimes used to assemble on the Essex flight-ponds, it is a fact, that the birds have been known to resort in flights so numerous as to cover apparently almost every available space of water on the pond.

There is also this peculiarity about dun-birds—when hard pressed they invariably appear obstinate, and are difficult to drive in the direction required; but when unsuspecting, and not so pressed, the fowler will find that, by keeping at a distance and using caution, they may be driven, either by night or day, as easily and as closely packed as a flock of sheep. From five to six hundred dun-birds at a 'drop' was formerly considered but a moderate capture; and to break the neck of every bird in that number would occupy three experienced men but twenty minutes.

If the pond is to be used conjointly as a decoy and flight-pond, the decoy-pipes must be at one end and the dun-bird yard at the other. The latter must be free from obstructions of trees and underwood, so as to leave a clear outlet for the dun-birds when on wing; and the remaining part of the surrounding grounds, where the decoy-pipes are, should be well and thickly planted, so that the only route by which dun-birds can leave the water shall be by the open space purposely cleared of trees and obstructions; or the pond may be provided with four decoy-pipes and four flight-nets, as in the illustration at page 91. If the pond be circular in form, then the planting would be similar in shape to a horse-shoe, the outlet or implanted space being used as the dun-bird yard, and laid down with grass turf.

CHAPTER XVII

WILD-FOWL SHOOTING

. . . .'And oh, the joy!

The passion which lit up his brow, to con

The feats of slight and cunning skill by which

Their haunts were neared.'—*The Fowler.* By Delta.

THERE are so many varieties in the sport of wild-fowl shooting that it is necessary to arrange them under distinct heads, with the observations applicable to each particular branch. But, as some of the remarks may be applied in general terms to every branch, it is the author's purpose to endeavour to impress upon the young wild-fowler a few indispensable injunctions, by attending strictly to which he may be the better capable of pursuing the sport successfully, and may not meet with so many disappointments as he must expect by disregarding them.

An English sportsman of the present day, on walking across a stubble with a double-barrelled gun on his arm, and springing a covey of partridges within range, finds no great difficulty in bringing down a bird with each barrel; still less on springing pheasants from a cover, to knock them down with unerring precision, the chief secret of success being, to acquire a habit of holding the gun straight and steady—an art so readily acquired at the present day, that a really bad shot is a personage seldom to be met with. It is therefore somewhat curious to note the ideas which prevailed so late as the sixteenth century with regard to the fowling-piece, and which in those days was quite of secondary consideration compared with other methods of fowling.[1]

There is not one word in Markham, under this head, as to shooting birds as they fly, such being an art considered at that age next to an impossibility; though he gives special instructions as to killing many birds at a shot rather than 'striving to shoote at a single fowle.'

There can be no difficulty at the present day in finding game in a well-preserved cover, and still less to flush it within range. And in a stubble or turnip field, with the services of a well-trained pointer or setter, the game may be found and approached without difficulty. But what a contrast to wild-fowl sitting on a large open river, on a lake, or on the sea! The sportsman must remember that there is neither stubble, turnip-tops, cover, nor ambush of any kind to screen the birds from view, or himself from their quick and watchful eyes. He surveys them at a distance, deliberately feeding on the fatness of the abundant productions of the oozy bed, as if conscious of their security: or, it may be, he observes a large gaggle of wild-geese sitting far out at sea, and garrulously revelling in their unapproachable position: the birds by nature taught that there is no hiding-place at sea when danger threatens, and that their escape must be by flight. To approach wild-fowl at such times, and in such situations, and get within deadly range, is therefore an art only to be acquired by much experience, labour, and perseverance; but we shall endeavour to show that such is to be done, and that the art, when well understood, as far excels all other branches of shooting as fox-hunting excels donkey-racing.[1]

The essence of enjoyment in shooting consists in searching for, finding, and approaching the game; persevering against difficulties, and struggling with obstacles apparently insurmountable; and not in walking into closely-stocked covers, banging right and left at pheasants with gun-barrels heated to danger, and filling bags and pockets with tame game. Such is not pure sport in the estimation of the author, but undignified slaughter; the poor victims have no chance of escape, rising as they do within a few yards of the gun: so that the veriest novice could not fail to do much execution with a double-barrelled gun and plenty of ammunition. Without discouraging those who may nevertheless think differently, I must say that I never could see any real sport in a *battue*.

The pursuit of wild-fowl shooting is a sport totally distinct from others, and the diversion is altogether so far superior to many other objects of the sportsman's gun, that it is to be preferred to the best pheasant and partridge shooting in the land, and it is only treated with indifference by those who have never thoroughly entered into it and shared in the varieties of the diversion: let them once do so, and they will know how to appreciate and enjoy it. As with many other sports, one successful day would leave such pleasing impressions upon the mind of those previously unacquainted with the sport as to make them esteem, if not prefer, it all the rest of their lives. The sport of a *battue* on a game-preserve cannot, in the opinion of many sportsmen, be put in comparison with the pursuit of water-fowl shooting; the one offers little or no variety beyond firing as rapidly as a gun can be loaded at birds which have been fed and familiarised with the human form until they have become almost as tame as common poultry, whilst the other, from being directed to birds not only *feræ naturæ*, but so wild as to be difficult of access, requires skill and energy to bring to bag; besides which the sport abounds with variety, incident, and excitement, and must be acknowledged by true-bred sportsmen to have by far the greater claim to the name of sport. For instance, it is no mean accomplishment to be able to approach within gun-shot of wild-fowl by daylight on *open waters*; and yet that is but one of the numerous branches of the sport now under consideration. The pursuit of wild-ducks and teal, on moors, fens, and bogs, where there is ample cover, is another branch affording excessively good sport, and in this the pleasant uncertainty and sudden surprises add much to the enjoyment. Then there is coasts-shooting (or 'shore gunning,' as it is not inaptly termed) both by night and day. Flight-shooting at eve and morning twilight, punting by daylight, moonlight, and starlight, under sail, and otherwise—these, and various other methods of pursuing the captivating sport, have each their claims to recommendation, and will be treated separately in these pages. Besides which, there are the many different species of wild-fowl, many of which require special consideration, and form subjects of distinct remark in a work devoted exclusively to the sport of wild-fowling.

The English sportsman will find there is no branch in the art of shooting that requires so much skill, practice, and hardy endurance as wild-fowl shooting, not on account of any difficulty in killing when once within range, but because of the cunning of the birds, and the difficulty of getting at them on the wide, open expanse of water, ooze, or savanna where they resort. It is not simply to pull a trigger and bring down with unerring aim a well-fed duck and mallard at a double shot; but to understand their habits, migrations, and instincts, and know how to approach them.[1]

Previously to the invention of gunning-punts, the method of shooting wild-fowl by night in the neighbourhood of broad tidal rivers was as follows:—One or two men would proceed down the river on the ebb tide, or at low-water, in a small flat-bottomed boat, creeping stealthily and noiselessly along the stream as close to the bank of the ooze as possible, anxiously listening all the while for their tell-tale notes. As the tide rose the boat rose, and, guided by the sounds aforesaid, the shooters made for the nearest approach they could obtain from the leewardmost position. The wild-fowl might then be discovered feeding in the puddles or on the grassy substances of the ooze, and the fowler would proceed, without showing himself, to get as near them as practicable, by rowing or sculling the boat up the nearest rill, the banks of which effectually screened him from view 5 and with a little ordinary precaution, and by occasionally raising his head to peep over the bank, he could easily discover when within range. A stout crotched stick was then stuck in the mud on the bank of the rill; and thus a rest was at once formed on which to place the barrel of the gun—a rather formidable weapon, of great length of barrel, and carrying from two to four ounces of shot, A steady and deliberate aim might thus be taken, and a vast number killed at a single discharge. Thousands of wild-fowl have been shot in this manner, and there are many old punters still living who, previous to the inyention of punt-guns, obtained annually a very comfortable winter's maintenance for themselves and families by this apparently rustic system of wild-fowl shooting.

Immediately after the gun was fired, the gunner or his assistant had to put on *splashers*[2] and proceed over the ooze in pursuit of the wounded, and to gather up the dead birds, the result of the charge. A winged bird on the ooze generally gives fine chase, and a man must be careful not to fall or the consequences may be serious—not simply a roll in the mud, but a chance as to being able to get upon the legs again on so soft and miry a foundation. The only practicable method of getting up from a fall on the ooze is by rolling over on the back, so as to draw the arms out of the mud, and then by placing one foot with the splasher firmly and flatly on the ooze, at the same time pressing both hands on the knee of the leg so raised, and giving a cautious but determined spring, a man may succeed in again bringing himself to his legs. But it is useless to attempt getting up by resting the hands on the mud, as one would do on hard ground: the arms only sink deeper and deeper, and if the mud be very rotten the fallen individual finds it impossible to rise in that manner, and by kneeling it would be just as difficult. Care should be taken not to fall, for the least that can result from it is, a thorough wetting and an unpleasant bedaubing with mud, to say nothing of the risk of not being able to get up at all, as in some oozy beds with which I am familiar the mud is so soft and deep that I believe it impossible for any man on falling to rise again without assistance.

The *Stalking-horse* was also another means employed by

the 'ancient gunner' for approaching wild-geese on the open moors:—

'One underneath his horse, to get a shoot, doth stalk;
Another over dykes upon his stilts doth walk.'[1]

The practice was simply that of making use of a live horse or cow as a screen, by leading or driving it leisurely towards the birds, when, if both horse and gunner performed their part judiciously, they got within range; the geese taking no notice of the animal when *apparently* unaccompanied by any human being. It is a well-known fact that wild geese are never intimidated by the presence of horses and cattle, those birds being often seen feeding within a few yards of the animals on open moors.

The stalking-horse was sometimes partly covered with a rug or cloth extending well down below the hocks, the better to protect the gunner from exposure. But the proceeding of stalking wild-fowl in the open country did not often succeed without extraordinary skill and caution, the watchful and suspicious nature of the birds often detecting the imposition long before the gunner Was able to get within deadly range.

The inhabitants of foreign countries, for centuries past, have been accustomed to employ stalking-horses for the purpose of approaching wild-fowl. Trained oxen were used by the Spaniards,[1] and to this day stalking-horses are in use in some districts, both in England and on the Continent.

Artificial Stalking-horses were sometimes employed, where the fowler was unable to provide himself with a living one.[2] These were sometimes made of canvas stuffed with straw, being shaped and proportioned as nearly as possible in resemblance to a horse, with its head down, as if grazing on the herbage, and light and portable so that the fowler could lift and move it with one hand. Artificial cows are still used in various parts of France, and sometimes with remarkable success.[3]

The stalking-horse, both living and artificial, was constantly employed by the ancient fowler, and whether for approaching wild-fowl on the open moor or by the brink of the water.

The artificial figures were painted and fitted with switch-tails, so as to resemble as nearly as might be the living animal, and they were sometimes made after the form and figure of horned cattle, deer, or such animals as the fowl were most accustomed to in the neighbourhood.

Shrubs, bushes, artificial trees, mock-fences, and such like contrivances[4] were also employed with some sort of success; regard being had, at all times, to the figures and forms most common in the particular locality, so as to awaken least suspicion to the birds. When this latter class of stalking appara-1 us was employed, it was usual to place them near the haunts of the fowl a long time beforehand, or move them by the gentlest possible means, else the device would be detected. And it would appear that these devices were found fitter for excursions in early morning or twilight than broad daylight, the natural watchfulness of the birds frequently enabling them to detect the imposition being practised upon them.

Artificial Decoy-ducks.—Wooden and gutta-percha decoy or dummy ducks are now used With great success on small lakes and private waters as decoys for wild-fowl passing over in their flight. Some of these are admirable imitations of living ducks. They are anchored at the spot required by means of a cord and stone or lump of metal. When used for decoying birds within gun-shot the wooden ones are to be preferred; for although the gutta-percha are more buoyant, being hollow, yet if a shot penetrates the gutta-percha, they fill and sink, and are thereby rendered useless. In America almost every species of wild-duck is shot over these wooden decoys, which in that country are generally made of cedar, and shaped and painted so as to represent the various species that frequent the American lakes.

The modern wild-fowler should not be disheartened at disappointments, nor should he repine at *blank* days. It is these which make him relish the more successful ones, for, if he were always sure of success, the excitement and true sportsman-like feeling would be considerably diminished. The uncertainty attendant upon the sport enkindles a desire for success, and induces a man to exert himself the more strenuously.

Some branches of the sport are truly rather hazardous to

careless individuals, but in all sporting pursuits there is more or less of that character, much of which may be avoided by skill and caution.

The young sportsman should always take care of himself, his health and comfort being of more importance than all the birds in the land, and if much exposed to the weather, as of necessity he will be, in pursuing the sport vigorously, the greater precautions are necessary. Warm clothing and good living are indispensable requisites to the man who goes wildfowl shooting, and, above all things, he should keep his feet and body warm and dry.

Leather water-boots are to be preferred to india-rubber; the latter, from not being porous, are cold and uncomfortable, if they become damp inside they remain so; whereas leather, from its porousness, absorbs dampness, and becomes dry in a very short time, and by having the boots dressed over two or three times a week with neat's-foot oil and tallow, in about equal proportions, they are rendered impervious to wet, the leather is preserved, and the boots are kept black and pliable. Worsted gloves are to be preferred to leather for punting, because it is impossible sometimes to avoid getting the hands wet at that pursuit, and by simply wringing the worsted glove it may be directly put on again, and will keep the hand warm, notwithstanding its being a little damp, but a leathern glove shrinks, becomes cold to the hand, and uncomfortable.

The punter should wear a white flannel jacket similar to those worn by journeymen carpenters, than which there is no more comfortable or convenient dress for rowing or punting. It is short, and therefore does not drag about the boat or become damp and disagreeable, but fits the punter closely, and is warm and convenient in every way. He may wear as many under-garments as he pleases, but the flannel jacket should be outside them all, and it is, besides, a colour which wild-fowl least suspect. He will most likely take with him a pilot-cloth jacket or an oil-skin, in case of rain or having to sit about without exercise, and this, being pulled off and rolled up when punting at birds, makes a convenient cushion for the chest, and indeed answers both the purposes required. The punter will find that working the paddles over the sides of the punt soon chafes holes through the under part of the jacket-arms, and as there is no means of preventing the chafing, the question arises, which is the best way of meeting it? The answer is, by wearing something not expensive, and which can be easily replaced with a new sleeve-piece. The flannel jacket is therefore just the thing.

Notwithstanding the numerous perils and difficulties attending the various branches of wild-fowl shooting, they are materially preponderated on the other side by the excessive pleasure attached to so fascinating and varied a sport, and although the whole routine of wild-fowl shooting abounds with uncertainties and disappointments, it is, nevertheless, intermixed with many agreeably sudden and unexpected surprises, in which the indefatigable sportsman delights, and thus have the disappointments of the day previous been entirely dispelled by the success of the day following.

Can anyone imagine a more vexatious occurrence than this: After lying one night upwards of half an hour stretched upon the floor of my punt, having heard a number of widgeon not far off, when, as they were so scattered, I found a difficulty in getting at their company, or finding a sufficient number together to make it worth while firing the punt-gun, well knowing by the noises they made that a very large flight was near by. The night was calm and the water smooth, the air keen and frosty; the movements of the paddles had therefore to be conducted with the greatest caution, particularly as several stragglers were swimming about within fifteen yards of my punt, calling and piping to their companions with the pretty 'Wheoh! wheoh!' when, fancying I had discovered the direction of their position, with all the caution of which I was possessed I carefully directed the punt towards them, but, most unfortunately, one of my paddles struck against a piece of ice. The slight concussion made sufficient noise to alarm the whole company, which instantly rose in the air directly over my head, and I had the mortification to observe that it consisted of several hundred birds.

But the sportsman must not vex himself with such

occurrences, whether on the water or on land, for a vexed man generally misses his next shot, through being flurried or overanxious. He should remember that the best and oldest sportsmen meet with the same crosses. Neither should a young sportsman ever vex himself at missing an occasional fair shot. The old sportsman does the same sometimes; he should, therefore, keep himself cool and in good nerve.

The movements of wild-fowl depend very much upon the wind, and the sportsman should pay particular attention to its variations. A strong easterly wind, in the month of October, never fails to bring with it to this country a goodly sprinkling of wild-fowl, and it should always be the endeavour of an ardent fowler to be prepared for them with punt and gun on their first arrival. At no other time will they sit the sportsman so well as after a long flight across the sea, when they first alight in strange waters, on the coast, and inland lakes and rivers, where they find abundance of food, and lucky is the man who falls in with a flight at such a time; if he have but a good gun, and be tolerably well skilled in its use, he may be sure of splendid success. Sometimes, however, the birds are not in good condition on their first arrival, particularly if the weather be very severe, but the October birds are invariably fat and heavy.

———————

[1] Markham observes; 'The next engine to these is the gun or fowling-piece, which is a generall engine, and may serve for any fowle, great or little, whatsoever; for it hath no respect at what it striketh, being within the levell. And of the fowling-piece you shall understand that to be the best which is of the longest barrell, as five foote and a halfe or sixe foote, and the boare indifferent, as somewhat under Harquebush, for these hold the best charges, and carry the farthest level. . . . As for the shape or manner of it, 'tis better it be a fire-locke or snap-haunce than a cocke or tricker, for it is safer and better for carriage, readier for use, and keepes the powder dryer in all weathers, whereas the blowing of a coale is many times the losse of the thing aymed at.'

[1] The author of 'Sport and its Pleasures' remarks:—' It must, indeed, he glorious sport—that of wild-fowl shooting—to those who have the health and stamina to endure weather the most severe, fatigue and excitement the most intense.'—P. 100.

[1] 'If shooting could speake she would accuse England of unkindnesse and slouthfullnesse: of unkindnesse towards her because she, being left to a little blind use, lacks her best maintainor, which is cunning; of slouthfullnesse towarde theyr

owne selfe, because they are content with that which aptnesse and use doth graunt them in shooting, and will seeke for no knowledge as other noble common-wealthes have done.'— '*Toxophilvs: The Schoole or Partitions of Shooting, contained in two bookes.*' (Black letter.) By Roger Ascham. A.D. 1589.

[2] Also termed 'mud pattens.' Thin boards, about 18 inches square, lashed under the soles of the boots, for the purpose of preventing the wearer from sinking into the mud when walking on the ooze. They are also sometimes made in a similar manner to the snow-shoes used for treading the snow-clad surface of Northern countries.

[1] Drayton.

[1] Alonzo d'Espinas.

[2] Of artificial stalking-horses Markham remarks: 'Now forasmuch as these stalking Horses, or Horses to stalke withall, are not ever in readinesse, and at the best aske a good expence of time to bee brought to their best perfection; as also in that every poore man or other, which taketh delight in this exercise, is either not master of a Horse, or if he had one, yet wanteth fit meanes to keep him: and yet nevertheless this practise of Fowling must or should bee the greatest part of his maintenance.'—*Hunger's Prevention.*

[3] *Vide* 'Aviceptologie Française.' Par C. Kresz Aîné: 1854.

Tit. la Vache artificielle.

[4] *Vide* 'Aviceptologie.' Tit. la Hutte ambulante. See also Blome's 'Gentleman's Recreations,' &c.

CHAPTER XVIII

THE WILD-FOWL SHOOTER'S DOG

'But the poor dog, in life the firmest friend,
 The first to welcome, foremost to defend,
 Whose honest heart is still his master's own,
 Who labours, fights, lives, breathes for him alone.'—
BYRON.

THE wild-fowl shooter who practises his sport on the land requires the services of a dog specially trained to the pursuit, one that will 'keep to heel' whenever required, that will neither chase nor 'give tongue,' but obey its master's signs and directions at all times, whether spoken or merely indicated by a wave of the hand. It must always possess a fine courage, and be ready and willing to dash into the water after a winged fowl in cold weather if required.

The best-bred dog for the purpose is the curly-coated retriever. Newfoundland dogs are used for this sport by many wild-fowl shooters,[1] but generally speaking they are too large; it being often necessary to take the dog across a river or bay in a boat, when the wet and dirt they sometimes bring with them, after having been overboard, or running about dykes and marshes, make it very disagreeable to the sportsman or other occupants of the boat. The curly-coated retriever, from the nature of his skin, is far less dirty, and, when carefully trained to the sport, is the best breed of dog that can be had for the purpose.

It is not desirable that the dog should be very large, particularly if in the locality of muddy savannas, because the lighter the weight of the animal, the quicker and more readily will he be enabled to walk over the rotten surface in pursuit of winged or wounded birds.

The dog intended to be trained for wild-fowl shooting should commence a course of instruction when about ten months of age, and the first thing to be taught is, to fetch and carry, and, in imparting this instruction, kindness and patience are the best preceptors, and will be found to do more in the way of bringing the dog under control than blows. The spike-collar, recommended by some professed dog-breakers, should not on any account be used; it inflicts unnecessary torture, and, as General Hutchinson very properly remarks in his excellent treatise on dog-breaking, 'it is a brutal instrument, which none but the most ignorant or unthinking would employ.'

Sambo

The wild-fowler's retriever must be trained to fetch from the water in the *summer* time, and the training continued through the autumn; it would spoil the animal's courage to attempt training it to the pursuit in winter. But, after a course of careful and judicious instruction, a well-bred and high-couraged dog never refuses the water, though ever so cold. Retrieving by land may be taught at any season, with the aid of a stuffed glove at first, and afterwards a stuffed bird-skin; but in no instance should hard substances be employed in the education of a retriever.

These animals delight in bringing birds in their mouths, and everything depends on the first lessons they receive in this practice, as to their ever being of good service to the sportsman; for if they become 'hard-mouthed' through injudicious training, and lacerate the birds they retrieve, such dogs are useless, and if left to themselves would very soon eat every bird they could get hold of. They must be taught to fetch and deliver the birds at the sportsman's feet; and the more they are practised when young, the more useful and valuable will they be in after years. The engraving opposite is a portrait of the author's favourite dog 'Sambo' in the act of retrieving a mallard.

By keeping the dog strictly to heel when walking along the shore, or beside dykes and rivulets, it will very soon acquire the art of watching where the bird falls, so as to go, on its master's signal, straight to the spot.[1]

It is very useful to teach a dog to retrieve the wounded before picking up the dead wild-fowl. The faithful and valuable creature, whose portrait is given on the opposite page, used to do this as if by instinct; and it was a rare occurrence indeed with the author to lose a winged or wounded bird when 'Sambo' was with him.[1]

The wild-fowl shooter's dog must be well fed, or it cannot stand the cold and hardy endurance necessarily encountered, in the pursuit. But it is a mistake to keep it in a warm room at night; such nursing destroys the constitution of a dog exposed to such severe hardships and risks of weather as wild-fowl shooting incurs. It should have a dry and clean bed of straw, in a stable where a horse is kept (dogs are fond of the society of horses). If in an outhouse or kennel, the floor must be boarded and raised above the ground; bricked floors, or exposure to the cold earth, bring on rheumatic pains in the limbs, and unfit a dog for work long before old age would do as much.

When wild-fowl shooting in the fens or moors, the dog must be perfectly mute; his services will seldom be needed, except to fetch birds which fall in the water or on the opposite side of dykes and rivulets. Wounded wild-fowl, when on the water, are very trying to the skill and patience of a dog; and it must be a clever animal indeed that is able to capture a winged Brent goose in a sea-way. Some dogs will dive and follow the birds under water; but a Brent goose which has merely had one of its pinions, or the outer joint of its wing, shot away leads a dog a trying chase, as it rises and falls at every moment on the crest of the heaviest surfs, or disappears in the trough of the sea.

The services of a dog are not required on board a shooting yacht; on the contrary, such an animal is an unnecessary incumbrance, always in the way; and the work required can generally be better performed by one of the crew in the yacht's boat, or with the cripple-net. It is, besides, cruel and unfeeling treatment to put a dog overboard in frosty weather, and then receive it again upon deck—wet and cold—with no space for the poor brute to ran about and dry itself; the shooting yacht is no place for dogs.

———

[1] In America Newfoundland dogs are in common use with the wild-fowl shooters of Chesapeake Bay.—*The Dog and the Sportsman.* By J. S. Skinner.

[1] General Hutchinson, in his admirable work on dog-breaking, says: 'A really good water-retriever is a scarce and valuable animal. . . . He should be perfectly mute; of a patient disposition, though active in the pursuit of birds; of so hardy a constitution as not to mind the severest cold—therefore no coddling, while he is young, near a fire—and possess what many are deficient in, viz., a good nose, consequently, a cross that will improve his nose, yet not decrease his steadiness, is the great desideratum in breeding. He should swim rapidly, for wild-fowl that are only winged will frequently escape from the quickest dog if they have plenty of sea-room and deep water.'—P. 52 (4th edition).

[1] General Hutchinson remarks as to this accomplishment in a retriever: 'This a knowing old dog will often do of his own accord; hut you must not attempt to teach a young one this useful habit until you are satisfied that there is no risk of making him blink his birds. You can then call him off when he is swimming towards dead birds, and signal to him to follow those that are fluttering away. If the water is not too deep, rush in yourself; and set him a good example by actively pursuing the runaways; and until all the cripples that can be recovered are safely bagged, do not let him lift one of those killed outright. If very intelligent he will before long perceive the advantage of the system, or at least find it the more exciting method, and adhere to it without obliging you to continue your aquatic excursions.'—*General Hutchinson on Dog-breaking*, p. 305 (4th edition).

CHAPTER XIX

THE LANGUAGE OF WILD-FOWL

'I shall not ask Jean Jacques Rousseau
If birds confabulate or no:
'Tis clear that they were always able
To hold discourse—at least, in fable.'—COWPER.

A GOOD ear for ornithological sounds is as necessary to the midnight sportsman as the natural musical ear is to the most accomplished harpist. He must be as familiar with the different calls and confabulations of the various species of wild-fowl as the fair warbler alluded to is with the popular airs of the day; and but little success can be expected unless he is so gifted.

The language of wild-fowl is instructive and pleasing alike to the ears of both sportsman and naturalist—to the one for the advice it gives him as to the species, as well as the whereabouts of their talkative assemblages, and to the other for the opportunity afforded of contemplating, from lessons of life, the beautiful perfections of Nature, so exquisitely revealed even in the simple and apparently unmeaning noises of the feathered tribe; but which, in reality, express to their species the unmistakable language of the heart—its love, hatred, wants, sympathies, doubts, and alarms—and all by sounds so sharp and short, yet too distinct and expressive to be misunderstood by those for whom intended; though to human ear a jumble of inexplicable similarities. No alphabet or vocabulary of words, no grammar or syntactical lessons, form any part of the education of the feathered tribes. Nature is their sole instructor; and by Nature they are gifted with a language and power of expression, to which they resort in all their wants, their passions, and their pains:

'Or in soft cooings tell their amorous tale.'

The faintest croak is full of meaning, and instantly obeyed by those which hear it. Who has not heard and seen the mother of her brood suddenly utter a strange, and to human ear unmeaning, croak? when, young and powerless as her fledglings may be, they instantly take heed; and, each turning one of their tiny eyes up towards the sky, as directed by their mother, they behold the threatening attitude of a hovering hawk, which their ever-watchful parent by that single note had given them to understand, once and for ever, was a dangerous enemy; and, though the first and only occasion in their fleeting lives that they may hear the warning, it is never forgotten.

The wild-duck, when suspicious as to the security of her brood, and whilst danger threatens, gives a warning that is instantly obeyed, and every duckling disappears from the surface. Let those who imagine there is no meaning in the language of the feathered tribe recall to memory such sharp intelligence in fledglings but a few days old, and wonder more and more how instinct should so early have taught the young their parent language.

So the old bird calls her young, encourages, cautions, and consoles them, all by different notes, as distinct, and even more so, than can be expressed by multitude of words in human language.

What is it that teaches the chicken to turn from a wasp or bee with a shudder of alarm and note of warning? The same instinct which tells the chicken it may itself be stung induces it to caution its companions to avoid the threatening pain. What is it that makes the captive bird, when rudely grasped, utter a shriek of anguish, too palpable for the veriest child to mistake for any other passion? Is it not the same instinct by which all living creatures (of which mankind is but one) express their feelings when in captivity or pain? A chicken may be nursed and fondled by human hand in the presence of its mother; but let it be ill-used, and utter only one note of pain, and the mother rushes instantly to its rescue, in fretful attitude, and with fierce expression.

Who, then, can reflect on facts and scenes like these, and say there is no meaning in the language of birds? Who would not rather exclaim with Aristophanes:—

> 'One question answer in the fewest words,
> What sort of life is it among the birds?'

With what remarkable instinct does the parent bird of such species as are hatched on the ground, and run almost as soon as out of the shell, attempt, by various stratagems, to draw the attention of any intruding living creature, likely to trample upon or injure her young, to some object apart from the immediate spot where her tiny brood may be, But in no fowl are those artifices more palpable than in the lapwing. When the human plunderer is farthest from her young she is most clamorous, and endeavours to impress him with an idea that he is very near them, whilst she is all the while enticing him away; though, when he actually approaches near those about whom she seemed so earnest in her fears lest they should be injured, she is silent; thus endeavouring, by a careless indifference, to lead the intruder to suppose he is nowhere near the objects of her solicitude. The curlew, and some other fen-birds which make their nests and hatch their young on the ground, perform similar artifices to those of the lapwing.

Every wild-fowler, from the practised sportsman to the decoyman's wring-neck, is more or less familiar with the *ordinary* notes of the species duck, widgeon, geese, and such like. He knows the trumpet-like noise of a gaggle of wild geese, resembling at a distance the rich tone of a pack of foxhounds in full cry; the sonorous and saucy 'Quack! quack!' of the wild duck; the soft but attractive 'Wheow! wheow!' of the widgeon; the sharp and wailing whistle of the plover; the shrill but mournful cry of the curlew; the simple 'Peewit!' of the lapwing; and the 'Frank!' warning of the majestic heron. With these and many others a practised wild-fowler becomes so easily acquainted that a mistake of species cannot well be made; but it is with other signs and expressions in bird-language that the master of the art has to do before he can become an adept at evening and midnight sport; for, whilst the ordinary notes above-mentioned reveal the species, others less vociferous reveal their actions, their movements, and suspicions.

Pliny says most birds cry and sing as they fly; yet some there are, contrariwise, that in their flight are always silent.[1] It is asserted by ancient writers, and confirmed by subsequent authorities, that sea-fowl appear to have some presentiment of tempestuous weather; and when they anticipate a gale they assemble together, and are. very clamorous.[2]

The fowlers of St. Kilda are so well skilled in the different accents of the solan goose, or gannet, that they instantly understand, through the different modulations of the voices of those birds, whether they are actuated by fear or hope: and so those fowlers regulate their movements accordingly, creeping stealthily over the rocks, and gradually drawing nearer towards the birds, whilst no alarm-note is given. And it would appear that the success of the St. Kildan fowler depends very much upon his familiarity with their notes. When free from all suspicion, and unconscious of danger, the note of the solan goose is 'Grog! grog!' and so long as the fowler hears no other note he is assured the birds are not suspecting him; but if he hears their watchword—'Birr! birr!'—he instantly desists, and remains as quiet and motionless as possible, because he knows it is the warning-note of the sentinel, which, in that one sound, informs all its companions of the suspected approach of an enemy. Generally, after lying still a few minutes, the words of assurance, 'Grog! grog!' are repeated; and then the fowler resumes his movements.[1]

The warning given by a sentry wild-fowl, of whatever species, seems to strike through every ear of the assemblage with electrical precision, and this though numbering many hundreds: in an instant heads are up, ears searching, eyes piercing, and all from the effects of the sentry's single note; then, if the suspicions are confirmed by further noise or movement of the enemy, the whole flight simultaneously takes wing, and the bungling fowler's chance is gone.

An experienced decoyman can always tell, by the talk of the birds, when they are thinking of leaving the pond for an excursion out to sea or to feed on the savannas. Just before twilight the debate is opened by wild ducks, the clamour of the female being loudest and most incessant; this is continued some ten or twenty minutes, as if they were arranging a rendezvous at some distant fen; and when all is decided, they quietly leave the decoy, in small and separate teams of from ten to twenty or more, according to the extent of their numbers.

The decoyman also knows, by the talk of his tame ducks, when any fresh arrivals have alighted on the water. From being constantly the unobserved inspector of their privacy, and the eavesdropper of their confabulations, he is familiar with their habits and instincts and with many of their notes, and needs no second hint to tell him when the moor-buzzard, their deadly foe, is hovering about the decoy; nor when the fox, the water-rat, or other enemy, is detected lurking on the banks of the pond.

So the punter must become acquainted with the language of wild-fowl, and be able to know, by the talk of the birds, when he is suspected, whether he may approach them without exciting suspicion, and when they have thrown off their alarm. It may require years of experience to become familiar with such signs and expressions; but when once learnt, the punter reaps his reward in the extra success attending his exertions.

The notes of the different species of water-fowl are so clear, yet so expressive, that the human ear soon becomes familiar with them; and it is from the fact of there being nothing artificial in the tone, that the precise sameness of the note—

though it be seldom from the same throat as that which taught the fowler to know it—is nevertheless so faithful that the sound, when once learnt, was never known to be forgotten or mistaken. It is because of this clearness of expression that the memory retains the firmer impression.

An experienced punter would no more mistake the talk of a widgeon at night for any other fowl than a higgler would mistake the talk of a turkey for a game-cock. Thus he knows, when they keep up a continuous confabulation, they are not suspecting danger; but when heard only at intervals, it is an indication of restlessness and suspicion. If a warning-note be given, and all is silent immediately afterwards, the punter rests on his oars, nor moves a limb until they open concert again, by which he is assured of their having thrown off that one suspicion.

Some sportsmen can produce an accurate imitation of the call notes of fen-birds, particularly of the plover and curlew, which a good mimic can turn to useful account, by enticing stray birds to draw near to his call, when he stops their flight with a charge of shot, fired from some place of concealment. But to acquire the art is no easy task. Practice, a good ear, and familiarity with the notes of the birds are the best instructors. It is a very old artifice, and prior to the invention of guns and shooting was probably considered an acquisition to a fowler. Chaucer says, 'Lo! the birde is begyled with the merry voice of the fowler's whistel, when it is closed in your nette.'

Artificial bird-calls[1] are also sometimes used for the same purpose; but it is always difficult to obtain one to the true key, and unless a very faithful imitation of the natural note of the bird can be produced, they are worse than useless.[1]

I knew an old sportsman who had all his life-time been accustomed to fen-shooting; and, on occasionally accompanying him, have been much amused at the clever manner in which he *called* plovers and curlews within range of his gun, simply by the mimic cry of their notes, but without any artificial bird-call.

All water-fowl which seek their food at night, such as ducks, widgeon, geese, and the like, are very clamorous whilst feeding: it is their perpetual loquacity that enables them to keep together.

---

[1] 'Sine voce non volant multæ aut e contrario semper in volatu silent.'—Lib. x. cap. xxxviii. s. 113.

[2] 'Tempestatem futuram præcognoscunt, et cum vident

eam imminere vociferant atque clamant.'—*Glantvilla.*

[1] *Vide* 'History of St. Kilda.' By Rev. Kenneth Macauley.

[1] 'But if you cannot attain to it by your industry, you must then buy a *bird-call*, of which there are several sorts, and easy to be framed, some of wood, some of horn, some of cane, and the like.'—*Cox on Fowling,* A.D. 1686.

[1] 'Now forasmuch as this art is a little hard and curious, and that no words in writing can express the true sound thereof, or show the motions, ordering, or sounds which must proceed from the lippes, tongue, and breaths, it is meet that he which is studious and would be skilfull in this Art, do goe into the fields where these birds do haunt, and there marking their notes, chirps, and whistles, practise as near as he can to counterfeit the same, till he be growne to that exquisite perfectnesse therein that he may perceive the Birds to gather about him.'—*Markham's Whole Art of Fowling,* A.D. 1655.

CHAPTER XX

THE FLIGHT OF WILD-FOWL AND FEN BIRDS

'And now, their route design'd, their leaders chose,
Their tribes adjusted, clean'd their vigorous wings,
And many a circle, many a short essay,
"Wheel'd round and round, in congregation full
The figur'd flight ascends, and riding
high The aerial billows, mixes with the clouds.'—
THOMSON.

No less curious in point of interest, and instructive in the art of fowling, are the volitations (or acts and powers of flying) of wild-fowl. The fowler should make himself as familiarly acquainted with these as with their language, that he may be able the more readily to distinguish their species, though at a long distance, soaring high in the air, each having a manner and method of flight peculiar to itself. 'Expandunt alas pendentesque raro intervallo quatiunt, aliae crebrius, sed et primas dumtaxat pinnas.'[2]

It is not within our province to discuss the 'auguries of birds' beyond a few remarks thereon touching the flight of wild-fowl. Modern sailors, however, even at the present day, regard certain auguries with the same respect as did the ancient mariners of Greece upwards of two thousand years ago, in reference to which Aristophanes remarks—

'Προερε τ ι s ἐ ì τ ῶ ν ρ ν θ ω ν
μ α ν τ ε υ ο μ έ ν π ε ρ ì τ ο ῦ π λ ο ῦ,
Νυνὶμπλε χ ε ι μ ν σ τ α ι . ν υ νὶπ λ ε
kέρ δos π έ σ τ α ι .'

Some of the accounts which have reached us as to the auguries of birds are undoubtedly fabulous; yet there are many very truthful signs to be noted from their flight and habits, especially those of sea-fowl,[1] some of which will be referred to in other parts of these pages, more particularly under the head, 'Wild-fowl Shooting under Sail.'

Water-fowl, of whatever species, when flying high in the air, always appear bent on some determined aim or destination, of which they are careful not to lose sight.

Wild-swans fly in strong flight, with their necks straight forward and their feet straight backward, as remarked in the 'Glantvilla de Rerum Proprietatibus:'—'Volant autem cygni silvestres volatu forti collis extensis, et pedibus ad posterius applicatis.'

These large heavy-bodied birds, on rising from the water, have not the power to ascend perpendicularly in the air: on the contrary, they flap along the water, beating the surface with their wings, some 50 or 60 yards, before they are able to suspend their bodies more than a couple of feet or so above the level.

The novice would be surprised, as well as amused, on coming within range of a herd of wild-swans on a calm day, at the crackling, snapping noise they make on rising from the water, as if every bone in the wings of the whole herd were being snapped asunder, and quite as loud and distinct. The noise, however, is produced by their large expanded wings striking the water and the pinions of their companions as they flap, flap along together, with outstretched necks, in their efforts to gain sufficient balancing power to rise in the air: it is not to be heard when the swans are fairly suspended above the surface, but only at the time of taking wing.

The velocity with which wild-swans fly *down* wind is very great: but their progress to windward is slow. In calm weather they pursue a steady course of flight, sometimes ranging in angular form like that of wild-geese, but always close together, generally in line, one behind the other.

That magnificent bird the albatross, weighing from 19 to 20 pounds, is another instance of the violent exertion required by birds of large proportions on rising from the water. The albatross, like the wild swan, stretches out its neck, and seemingly runs along the water with its gloriously expanded wings, measuring from tip to tip from ten to twelve feet, skimming the surface to the distance of 100 yards or more before it can obtain sufficient velocity to overcome the force of gravitation and launch itself into the air. But when once fairly upon its wings, the power and ease of its flight are very striking. And so, on alighting upon land at the end of a swoop, the momentum of the body is carried on after its feet have touched the ground, until it sometimes turns a complete somersault in its endeavour to balance itself and gain a firm footing.

Wild-geese are known by the catenarian figure in which they fly—precisely as if linked together, or strung on a line, and hence they are spoken of by the fowler as a 'skein' of geese; and whether they soar higher or lower in the air, the same link-like discipline is observed, though they are often changing their leaders and altering their figure: 'Colla imponunt præcedentibus, fessos duces ad terga recipiunt.'[1] But whatever the changes, the wedge-like order of flight is preserved: sometimes the rank is in form a long-shaped wedge, then a narrow one, then a broad, and so on, all the changes being effected in perfect order, as if the birds were linked together.

They always fly with outstretched necks and in. the conical order above stated, as if instinct had taught them that such a form encountered least resistance on passing through the air. Pliny compares their manner of flight to a pointed squadron;

and the stem of a vessel at sea.[2]

Ducks also fly in similar form, with heads and necks stretched straight out, in line with their bodies, and may be distinguished from widgeon by the steadier and greater regularity of their movements in the air; and when within range of gun-shot the brown of the ducks' feathers may be distinctly discerned. Ducks, when bent on long flights, do not all move through the air at the same altitude, but some much higher than others; and large flights generally seem to have a break in the centre, and present a figure very much resembling the outline of North and South America as it appears on the map. When flying near the surface of land or water they are sometimes in a confused mass.

Widgeon sometimes fly with much regularity, following so closely one upon another—though not so strictly in figure as ducks and geese—that it is one of the peculiarities by which they may be distinguished. Their movements on the wing are quicker than ducks, and the size of their bodies being smaller and their necks shorter, it is not difficult for the wild-fowler to distinguish their species. Wigdeon, when in flight, always keep up their call-note; ducks fly in silence.

Dun-birds (or pochards) are gifted with wonderful powers of diving, as they obtain their food from the bottom of the water: consequently they have very short, but strong and stiffly formed wings, which they use under water like the fins of a fish, and when they fly it is with great exertion, and by a very rapid movement of the wings, causing a noisy twittering in the air. They may be known in flight by these appearances, and by the shortness of their pinions and heavy-looking bodies, and especially by their flying in a closely-packed lump, and not in line or figure, as widgeon and duck.[1]

The flight of shovellers is very similar to dun-birds; but they generally fly low in the air, and never in large doppings.

Teal may be known by their small size: their method of flight very much resembles the widgeon, and, when in large springs, they fly either in single line or in triangular form.

Coots fly in a similar manner to moorhens, but swifter, carrying their heads straight out and their legs hanging down, the reason of which is that their wings are placed so near their necks that the centre of gravity is not correctly balanced; the distinction of flight between the coot and moorhen being, that the latter carries its head erect when on wing, the other as stated above.

The heron flies with slow and lazy-looking flight, having its long legs thrown straight out in line with its body, as if they formed part of its tail, and carries its head and neck the very opposite to that of round-beaked fowl; instead of stretching it out forward, the heron gracefully curves the neck, and throws its head upon its back when flying through the air, in the same manner as a stag when charging a fence.[1] All waders such as stalk with long shanks, when they fly stretch out their legs at length beyond their tails.[2]

The curlew is best known on the wing by its long beak: in flight it is powerful; but the movements of its wings are rapid.

The snipe is known by its swift and graceful movements in the air, and the immense power of its stroke of wing, its zigzag dartings, and the circular route of its flight.

The grey and golden plover fly with a similar stroke of the wing to that of the snipe, but steadier; and just before alighting they droop their wings, with apparently lazy or enfeebled effort. They do not present that rapid zigzag movement so peculiar to the snipe, though many of their motions in the air resemble them.

The lapwing may be distinguished in flight by the rounded shape of its wings, and the steady regularity of the short flapping strokes which it makes with them; also by the black colour of its wings and the whiteness of its body, by its turnings and tumblings, and by its well-known note, 'Pee-wit!'

A fling of oxbirds is known by the singular and beautiful appearance those birds present in the air; the grace, swiftness, and compactness of their flight—the wing of every bird in the fling apparently (though not in reality) touching those of its nearest companions, and yet preserving the mass entire as if linked together in one broad sheet, dark on the upper-side but of silvery whiteness on the under; in which compact form the sportive little band dart and rush through the air with wonderful rapidity, now skimming along within a few inches of the surface of the water, and then rising some 20 or 50 yards high in the air, and turning *en masse* in the most perfect and compact rank, and tipping up edgewise the broad-sheet of the whole fling, and so exposing at the same instant, with incomparable grace and beauty, the silvery under-side of the wings and bodies of every bird in the fling, and presenting the appearance of a cloud of frosted silver. The flight of a large cloud of oxbirds on a bright winter's day is a marvellous feat of order and instinct, and one of the most interesting and beautiful sights that can be witnessed in the volitations of birds.

Everyone is familiar with the hovering motion of the seagull, totally different to that of other sea-fowl; it seldom appears bent on any determined aim, but wheels about in the air as if indifferent to locality, and seldom making a long flight either over sea or land. It should be remembered that none of the duck and diver species are capable of hovering in the air without any motion of the wings; whilst, on the contrary, gannets, sea-gulls, terns, petrels, and others, may be easily distinguished at long distances by their hovering flight, and the easy and leisure-like strokes they make with their wings. In all birds that dive under water the wings are small in proportion to the size and weight of their bodies, consequently when they fly, the motion of their wings is rapid and laboured, and they fly in a straight or direct line, never suddenly changing their course at angles, but only in long curves; and when they alight on the water they drop with a splash.[1]

A little experience will also teach the wild-fowl-shooter to distinguish the different species of wild-fowl when *swimming* on the water, though at a considerable distance.

Swans and geese are always distinguishable on the water from other wild-fowl by their size.

Ducks may be known on the water from widgeon, teal, and other species by their larger size and longer necks, and by the brown-coloured feathers of the female, and bright colours of the mallards. Widgeon look blacker upon the water and smaller than ducks.

Coots are known by the regularly-scattered extent of their coverts and the wide space of water they occupy; shovellers by their movements—constantly diving and disappearing from the surface.

Sea-gulls, which look dark by moonlight, and are often mistaken for wild-fowl by a novice, may be readily distinguished by their tails sticking up higher than their heads.

Divers of the merganser and colymbus species swim with their tails low, and their heads and breasts boldly erect.

Such are among a few of the readiest means by which the

different species of water-fowl may be known when flying in the air or swimming on the water at a long distance from the sportsman.

---

[2] Pliny, lib. x. cap. xxxviii. s. 111.

[1] 'The sea-gulls are considered as ominous. When they appear in the fields, a storm from the south-east generally follows; and when the storm begins to abate, they fly back to the shore.'—*Sir John Sinclair's Statistical Account of Scotland.*

[1] Pliny, lib. x. cap. 23, s. 63.

[2] 'Liburnicarum more rostrato impetu feruntur, facilius ita findentes aera quam si recta fronte impellerent.'—*Ibid.*

[1] 'In most genera of swimming birds both purposes are combined, and the wing is just so far reduced in size and stiffened in texture, as to make it workable as a fin under water, whilst it is just large enough to sustain the weight of the bird in flight. . . . It is a necessary consequence of the area of the wing being so reduced, in proportion to the size of the bird, that great muscular power must be used in working

it, otherwise the force of gravity could not be overcome at all.'—*The Reign of Law*. By his Grace the Duke of Argyll (5th edition), p. 148.

[1] 'Few persons have any idea of the force expended in the action of ordinary flight. The pulsations of the wings in most birds are so rapid that they cannot be counted. Even the heron seldom flaps its wings at a rate of less than from 120 to 130 strokes in a minute. This is counting only the downward strokes, preparatory to each one of which there must be an upward stroke also; so that there are from 240 to 300 separate movements per minute. Yet the heron is remarkable for its slow and heavy flight, and it is difficult to believe, until one has timed the pulsations with a watch, that they have a rapidity approaching to two in a second.'—*The Reign of Law*. By the Duke of Argyll (5th edition), p. 133.

[2] 'Longipedes porrectis ad caudam cruribus volant.'—*Pliny*, lib. xi. cap. 47.

[1] The Duke of Argyll observes, in his interesting work:[1] 'It is remarkable that the Force which seems so adverse—the Force of Gravitation, drawing down all bodies to the earth—is the very force which is the principal one concerned in flight, and without which flight would be impossible. It is curious how completely this has been forgotten in almost all human attempts to navigate the air. Birds are not lighter than the

air, but immensely heavier. If they were lighter than the air, they might float, but they could not fly. This is the difference between a bird and a balloon. A balloon rises because it is lighter than the air, and floats upon it. Consequently, it is incapable of being directed, because it possesses in itself no active force enabling it to resist the currents of the air in which it is immersed, and because, if it had such a force, it would have no fulcrum or resisting medium against which to exert it. It becomes, as it were, part of the atmosphere, and must go with it where it goes. No bird is ever for an instant of time lighter than the air in which it flies; but being, on the contrary, always greatly heavier, it keeps possession of a force capable of supplying momentum, and therefore capable of overcoming any lesser force, such as the ordinary resistance of the atmosphere, and even of heavy gales of wind.'

---

[1] 'The Reign of Law' (5th edition), p. 130.

CHAPTER XXI

THE GUNNING-PUNT

'Behold his punt now ride the restless wave,
  A little speck, scarce scanned from off the shore.'—T.
HUGHES.

A BOAT, for the purpose of carrying one individual sportsman
with a punt-gun, ammunition-box, shoulder-gun, and
other requisites for punting, should be just large enough to
be safe and serviceable, but nothing more. The smaller the
appearance of the boat on the water, the greater will be the
punter's chance of success, the more convenient it will be to
manage, the quicker he can make up to birds, and the less will
be the exertion necessary to propel it.

The size of a wild-fowling punt, however, must be in some
proportion to the size of gun intended to be used, and also in
proportion to the height and weight of the punter himself.

The most useful-sized punt-gun for general purposes is that
carrying about half-a-pound of shot at a charge; and as there
are more punt-guns in use on the coast of that size than any
other, the recommendation would seem to be confirmed.

A punt to carry a gun of the description stated, with a man of ten or eleven stone weight, should be of about the following dimensions:—

Length over all	7 feet.
Breadth amidships	2 feet 10 inches.
Ditto, ditto, at bottom	2 feet 8 inches.
Depth at bows	4 inches.
Ditto at stern	8 inches.

A boat of this description may be built either with a flat bottom or a flat floor, the distinction being, that the one which is 'flat-bottomed' is perfectly flat as the bottom of a box, the other, which is 'flat-floored,' is built more like the bottom of a skiff, *i.e.*, clench-built, and the sides do not commence from an angle, as in a flat-bottomed boat, but are round as a whale-boat, though it is a great desideratum to maintain the floor throughout as flat as it consistently can be, with due regard to shape; and, when ingeniously constructed, such is by far the best form of punt that can be used.

Col. Hawker condemns all round-bottomed punts, such as are used at Southampton and Itchen ferry, as on a bad construction, and gives as a reason that they have unsteady bearings.

Now, without disputing the colonel's assertion as to the Southampton and Itchen ferry gunning-punts, it is insisted that the reason of round-bottomed punts having unsteady bearings is because they are *too* round at the bottom. If they be constructed with a long flat floor—as flat as it is possible to make a clench-built punt—they will be safer and even steadier than a flat-bottomed punt.

The punt under consideration should be built with a spring in her bottom, fore and aft, of from 1| to 2 inches; or in other words, the bottom of the punt, as taken in a line from stem to stern, should form a section of a circle, and this, whether a flat or round-bottomed; the object of which is, that in going into very shallow water, when the bottom of the boat grazes the mud, it may nevertheless be pushed ahead many yards farther; whilst a boat without any spring in her bottom would be set fast. This is sometimes a great consideration, when punting to birds on the ooze, as the tide flows towards them, when the success of a shot may depend on the chance of being able to push the punt a few yards farther ahead.

The fore-part of the punt from stem to cross-piece should be covered over with a very thin scantling of deal, as lightly as possible, so as to add no more to the weight forward than absolutely necessary, because of the heavy gun which has to be placed there.

The cross-piece alluded to is placed just abaft the scantling, and marks the balance for tipping the gun.

The covered part of the punt may be finished off abaft the scantling with a semicircle, if the punter attaches any regard to appearances; and the edge should then be completed with a neat semicircular piece, rising an inch and a-half or two inches from the scantling-deck, which affords a sufficient screen to the punter when making up to birds.

Another cross-piece of light wood should be placed athwart the gunwale, about 2 1/2 or 3 feet from the stem, before the scantling is put on; this is for the purpose of fixing the rest for the outer end of the barrel. The rest should be a simple copper screw, with a small semicircular crotch in which to receive the barrel.

It should be made in connection with a female screw, attached to the fore cross-piece; and the male screw should be of sufficient length to raise or lower the elevation of the muzzle end of the gun from one to two inches.

As to the position of the chock or strong-piece, to which is attached the necessary apparatus for checking the force of the recoil, it must depend entirely on the means intended to be employed. If the patent spiral recoil-spring is used, the interior of the punt must be fitted accordingly. But if the strain is to be thrown upon the stem-piece, the builder must take care to fix the same strong enough to receive it.

The fore-parts of gunning-punts are sometimes left quite

open, and without any scantling or fore-deck; but, when so constructed, they require to be rather deeper at the bows than the dimensions before stated.

The gunning-punt may be built entirely of fir, or the upper strakes which are above water may be of fir, and the lower ones of elm; if all fir, the boat will be so much the lighter and more buoyant. A gunning-punt should never be built of oak; it is too heavy for the purpose. Many punters express astonishment that Colonel Hawker should have recommended such a material: during the latter days of the colonel's sporting career, however, he appears to have given the preference to elm and fir.

The only objection to clench-built gunning-punts with round bottoms is, that in a breeze the ripples on the water make a trickling noise against the planks of the punt when rapidly propelled, called, in nautical language, 'tell-tales;'[1] that is to say, the noise tells the helmsman of a breeze springing up.

The author once heard an objection raised to clench-built punts, the punter stating that but for the 'tell-tales' he could have heard the birds feeding, and so discovered their whereabouts; whereas the noise of the water rippling against his clench-built punt not only precluded him from so doing, but frightened the birds and caused them to take wing. But the statement appears scarcely feasible, because, by resting a moment on the paddles, the 'tell-tales' become silent, and they certainly cannot be heard by birds beyond forty or fifty yards' range. I have never found the smallest inconvenience myself from the 'tell-tales.'

It is desirable that there should be no farther projection of the stem of the punt beyond the muzzle of the gun than is absolutely necessary; and this depends in a great measure on the form and construction of the punt, and may be materially provided against by continuing the floor as flat and far forward as practicable, so that it may be more buoyant under the heavy weight of the gun-metal, which depresses the head of an ordinary punt. The muzzle of the gun should never extend beyond the stem of the boat.

It is a considerable protection to the bows of a punt to affix a piece of thin sheet-copper round the stem, and a foot or two along the water-streaks, when accustomed to move much among shell-ice; but it is well to dispense with it when not required, so as to maintain the bow as light and buoyant as possible.

Rounded wooden thowls should be used: iron or copper or fixed rowlocks are one and all objectionable in a gunning-punt, and more especially those heavy prominent projections which were attached to Colonel Hawker's punts, and which used to stick up above the gunwales as very conspicuous objects. There is nothing more suitable or lighter and more convenient than small, round-shaped, wooden thowls, such as may be shipped and unshipped at pleasure.

The punting tyro should not venture in a narrow or crank punt; such is dangerous at all times, more especially under unskilful management. The broader and flatter the punt at the bottom, so much the safer it will be, and the less will be the draught of water. The tyro is recommended to use a flat-bottomed punt at first, as such is not so liable to get out of trim as a round-bottomed one, and thus alter the range of the gun; round-bottomed punts are more apt to vary, from slight causes of misplacement in the interior, and require a more experienced hand to regulate their bearings, and manage them under the different changes of position.

A punt may be the more graceful and pleasing to the eye when sharp and narrow at the bows, but grace and elegance must not be too much regarded by the boat-builder in this respect; because the weight of the gun-metal is of necessity so heavy, that it cannot be carried so far forward in the punt as it ought to be, if the boat is sharp and narrow at the bows.

Particular attention should be paid to the outside of gunning-punts; they must be kept clean and free from any discolourings or stains. The best colour for the exterior of a punt is dusky white; or, a shade of light green may be intermixed with the white lead: a very little lamp-black stirred into the white paint makes a good invisible colour for a punt intended for night-work. No varnish or shining material should be used in the paint, but the duller and deader the colour (though snowy white) the better. The interior of the punt may be a light buff, or straw colour, or any other which suits the fancy, so long as it be not gay or attractive. But, after all, a great deal of the good or ill success attending the sport depends not so much on the punt as the skill of the punter.

There is a slight difference in the form and build of gunning-punts at various places round the coast; for instance:—

The *Hampshire gunning-punts* have round sterns, and are short and narrow, the usual length being but fourteen feet, and the breadth at gunwales from two feet six inches to two feet eight inches, according to the size and strength of the punter. The recoil of the gun in the Hampshire punt is received by a rope breeching, rove through a strong wooden knee, firmly fixed across the bottom planks of the punt, a little in advance of the gun's balance; and this method is also adopted in some other localities, as the strongest place in the punt on which to throw the force of the recoil, though it may well be doubted whether the stem is not the best place through which to reeve the breechings and receive the strain.

The *gunning-punts of the Eastern Coast* are of considerable reputation, particularly those in the neighbourhood of Maldon in Essex, the form of which is much in favour with those who resort to the pursuit of punting in winter as a means of subsistence.

The form of the Maldon gunning-punt is very similar to a coffin; simply flat-bottomed, with nearly upright sides, formed of two broad strakes. The usual length is sixteen and a-half to seventeen feet, and the breadth two feet eight inches to two feet ten inches. They are very handy for setting to birds, because of the narrowness of their form, enabling the punter to use his arms freely, and, by means of the paddles, with considerable effect; but they are easily upset, and require very great care on the part of the occupant in all his movements. They have strong gunwales and cross-piece, and are the least costly of any gunning-punt that can be built. When intended for an extra large gun, they are built in proportion—longer and wider—as may be required.

In loading the gun (if a muzzle-loader) whilst afloat in one of these punts, it is usual to row ashore, or lash the punt alongside a larger vessel.

Two-Handed Gunning-Punts.

Two-handed gunning-punts, or those constructed to carry two persons, are seldom used at the present day. Many years ago, when the birds were less persecuted than now, two-handed punts were commonly used. But they have too formidable an appearance on the water to allow of much success; and although manned by two persons, they make slower progress through the water, and are much more sluggish to propel, than single-handed punts. One man sits or kneels at the stern, in a cramped and uncomfortable position, and sculls with an oar, whilst the other lies down to attend the gun; and if his arms are long enough to reach across the boat (which must of necessity be much wider than a single-handed punt), he assists with the paddles in propelling the boat towards the birds.

Among other objections to two-handed gunning-punts is that of the difficulty of preserving the proper elevation of the punt-gun; any slight movement by the man at the stern, such as leaning back in the boat, may tip up the outer end of the punt, and so alter the elevation of the gun that on firing at birds sitting on the water the shots will all fly over their heads.

The advantages of two-handed gunning-punts are, that they are enabled to carry a larger punt-gun than others; sometimes a full-sized stanchion-gun, which throws from one and a-half to two pounds of shot at a charge, making fearful destruction among large numbers of wild-fowl; and when loaded with mould-shot, they sweep the water from sixty to one hundred and twenty yards, spreading terrible slaughter among the feathered tribe all the way.

The gun is generally fitted so that it may be 'tipped' with the facility of a smaller one: and flying shots are often made, just as the birds rise from the water, the man at the helm turning the boat skilfully with his oar in the direction taken by the birds when rising in the air. There is but little success to be had in these days with two-handed gunning-punts. He who would kill wild-fowl by daylight must go in a single-handed punt, unless he uses a sail.

———————

[1] This must not be confounded with 'tell-tale,' a portable mariner's compass.

CHAPTER XXII

PUNT-GUNS

'Praise in old time the sage Prometheus won,
Who stole ethereal radiance from the sun;
But greater he whose bold invention strove
To emulate the fiery bolts of Jove.'

Translation by MILTON.

IMPROVEMENTS have gone to such an extent of late years in guns of every description, that there is now no difficulty in obtaining a sound and useful gun for any purpose required, and whether a breech or muzzle loader. If the fowler wishes to become acquainted with the arts and contrivances of fitting and stocking, or even casting and making, a gun, there are several treatises to be consulted on the subject, which is one upon which it is not the purpose of the author of this work to treat. It will therefore only be necessary to make a few remarks on what is considered, from practical experience, to be the most useful sort of gun, and the best, safest, and most convenient methods of fitting, placing, and elevating it for the punt, and those also regarding the stanchion-gun for the shooting-yacht.

And first, of the *punt-gun:* Unquestionably a breech-loading punt-gun is to be preferred to a muzzle-loading one, because of the inconvenience in the latter of having to shift to the aft-part of the punt so heavy a piece of artillery, for the purpose of reloading; to say nothing of the danger of capsizing the punt during the operation, unless great caution be used. Moreover, the breech-loading punt-gun may be reloaded in less than a minute, and without moving or altering its position on the head of the punt. Whereas a muzzle-loading punt-gun can scarcely be shifted, reloaded, replaced in its proper position, and capped, in less than ten minutes, unless a very light gun; and with a heavy muzzle-loading punt-gun and light punt it is necessary, for safety's sake, to row ashore for the purpose of reloading.

As to the size and weight of a punt-gun, whether breech or muzzle loading, it should be no heavier than necessary, but of sufficient size and weight to carry three-quarters of a pound of shot, if intended for wild-goose shooting or for use on the open coast; but if required merely for duck and widgeon, and for the general purposes of inland sport, a gun carrying half-a-pound of shot will be found most suitable.

It is very desirable that the lock of a punt-gun should be safe and secure, or accidents of the most lamentable nature may occur (as they have done, to the author's own knowledge), and the punt-gun should never be shifted about, or taken to or from the punt, with a cap on the nipple. It is also indispensably necessary that the lock should be protected from the weather and ill effects of salt-water, by an oil-skin or painted canvas coating, lined with thick flannel, which should be kept over the lock at all times, except when actually punting or setting to birds.

Elevation of the Punt-gun,

The success or failure of the punter's expeditions depends mainly on this important consideration; for it must be obvious to everyone that, unless the punt-gun be placed in a position bearing accurately upon the object fired at, the shot will be ineffective. Now, it would seem an easy matter to place a gun, whether heavy or not, in such a position upon the head of a punt as to sweep the water of every living thing in line with the muzzle from 60 to 100 yards range. It is, however, by no means so simple a matter as many would suppose.

In the first place, the punter must remember that his gun is not so light and handy a weapon as to be capable of being moved about with the facility of a shoulder-piece; and when he is lying flat on his chest on the floor of the punt, working his way towards a number of wild-fowl, he cannot (or ought not) then shift his gun, nor can he, in an ordinary way, alter the elevation, but must fire it from the position in which it is placed; and unless he has previously ascertained the correct elevation, such is more likely to be too high or too low than to be *exactly* right, as it must be, or he will not hit his birds.

A punt-gun, to be strictly in its proper and most effective position, should lie so as to bear point blank upon the object fired at eighty yards from the punt; and, if the punt be of proper form and depth, as already described (p. 120), the strong or effective shot will range from sixty to one hundred yards, killing everything in its track within that distance; and, when once so elevated, the punter should be careful to keep the gun always in that position. The slightest alteration makes material difference—*i.e.*, if the muzzle of the gun be raised ever so little, the shot will strike the water at too great a distance; and probably the effective shot will all strike out of range, whilst only a few loose and weak grains will hit the object. On the other hand, if the muzzle be ever so slightly depressed from the ascertained elevation, the shot will strike nearer the punt, killing only those birds that are very near, whilst many others, which may be farther off, but within range, will escape unhurt. And an alteration in the elevation may arise from a very slight cause—either from raising the muzzle of the gun or the breech, or, *vice versâ*, from depressing either; or it may arise from altering the trim of the punt—*i.e.*, by putting heavier weight in the fore or aft part, such as changing the position of the ammunition-box from its proper place in the stern to the fore-part of the punt. Moving the position of the body a little farther forward or aft will also alter the elevation;

or, if the punt be leaky, the water which gets in may disturb the equilibrium. And, if the gun be drawn farther inboard, or pushed farther out, the same consequences must obviously ensue.

It will thus be seen that a slight cause of the kind may so far alter the trim of the punt, and consequently the elevation of the gun, as to completely disappoint the punter's expectations when he shoots. It therefore becomes highly important to see carefully to the correct bearings of the gun; for sometimes an unconscious movement may do ail the mischief; and more especially if the punt be a light or small one. A heavier or lighter one than that for which the gun is elevated will generally incur the same result; and it is too late to discover this error when making up to birds, because of the difficulty of being able to find the exact elevation at such a time, and the danger of disturbing the birds by moving or exposing oneself in the punt. An experienced punter knows whether his gun is in the right position or not the moment he lies down and runs his eye along the barrel in line with the water, which he always does, or ought to do, on all occasions before going in pursuit of wild-fowl. And if he finds it not in correct position, he raises or lowers the muzzle or trims the boat until he obtains the proper elevation.

It has been the author's endeavour to explain the system of elevation somewhat minutely, though at the risk of being tedious, because of its great importance in the art of using the punt-gun successfully. Some of the difficulties suggested may, however, be obviated by the use of a small copper screw, with a crotch or rest for the barrel of the gun to lie in, by means of which the outer or muzzle end of the gun may be raised or depressed at pleasure; and such is a convenient means of adjusting the elevation of the punt-gun (*ante*, page 122).

The author has seen inexperienced hands fire within fatal range of numbers of wild-fowl without killing a bird, because of the gun not lying at a proper elevation; and he has seen others fire at wild geese successfully, whilst with the same gun, in the same position, they fired at widgeon without a shot touching them. It was because of the gun lying a little too high. The geese being larger birds sat higher on the water, and received the shot, whilst the widgeon being so much smaller, and sitting very low on the surface, the strong shot all flew over their heads.

But a gun, when *correctly* elevated for ordinary purposes, *ought* to be in such a position as to kill both geese and widgeon with equal facility sitting on the water; but before shooting at swans the muzzle should be slightly elevated, and the same for waders, such as herons and curlews, which stand on the mud above the ordinary elevation of a punt-gun.

The punt-gun should be placed a little to the right of the punt, that the shooter may place his shoulder firmly to the stock on taking aim without having to shift his body on one side or the other, or alter the trim of the punt in any way.

Gun-breechings and Recoil-springs.

And now as to the means of checking the recoil of the punt-gun. There are several different methods of accomplishing this operation, the most ancient of which is by means of a strong iron pin fitted into a stout cross-piece of wood, the latter built into the punt a little forward of the midships. The iron pin is in the form of a crotch at the upper part, in which to receive the stock-end of the gun; the stem of the crotch being fitted into an iron socket, and a cross-bolt or shifting pin run through the upper ends of the crotch and the stock of the gun, it is thus firmly secured; and the stem of the crotch fitting easily into the socket, the gun may be worked as if on a pivot. But this old-fashioned plan is the worst of all, and the most dangerous, it being an error to confine the gun so that it cannot be relieved in recoil. And the danger of tearing the cross-piece from the punt is great; the jar occasioned by the recoil when the gun is confined is also very serious; besides which, it throws up the muzzle, and not infrequently seriously injures the face or shoulder of the punter. Worse than all, a gun so confined shoots very inaccurately, and has to be laid at a high elevation, because, when fired at an object in line, it throws the shot below it.

The most simple contrivance of all for relieving the jerk of the recoil is by means of rope-breechings; and there are two or three methods of employing them. One is by passing a rope, of proper size, through the stem of the punt, and securing it on both sides of the barrel of the gun: on the one side by a loop or eye hooked over the headed side of the iron cross-bolt, which passes through that part of the gun-stock which incases the outside of the barrel, and by a couple of hitches on the other end of the cross-bolt. This is as good and simple a plan as any, the length and elasticity of the breechings easing the recoil without jarring the punt or straining anything but the rope; and the gun shoots accurately.

Another plan is that of securing the two ends of the rope to a chock or cross-piece inside the punt, by simply reeving them through holes in the chock, and making knots in the ends to prevent their being drawn back; a loop of the rope is thus formed, which falls into a groove in the stock cut to receive it. For this purpose the rope must be larger than that used for the gun-breechings last described; and the more elastic the rope the easier will be the jerk of the recoil. This plan, though neater, is not so good as the other, as the gun is more confined and has less room for recoil-play.

Another method frequently adopted in open punts, or those having their fore-bows uncovered, is by reeving a rope through a ring firmly bolted to the stem-piece, and leading it aft on each side of the barrel; securing it to the cross-bolt by two loops, or by a loop on one side and a hitch on the other. This is a very good plan, as the extra length of the rope gives ample room for recoil-play.

Either of these plans is very simple, and is recommended as safe, serviceable, and inexpensive. But the best plan of all is Colonel Hawker's invention of a steel spiral recoil-spring, to make use of which it is necessary for a plug to be cast with the gun-barrel, the recoil-spring and its fittings being separately cast, and on being secured by shifting bolts, or otherwise, to a strong chock, the barrel is attached to the recoil apparatus by the iron plug before alluded to; when the whole force of the recoil is, by means of the patent apparatus, thrown directly upon the spiral spring, and the barrel having sufficient play, it works with remarkable facility, no perceptible jerk or inconvenience being felt on placing the shoulder to the stock of the gun when firing it. The apparatus being necessarily composed of iron or gun-metal, it adds slightly to the weight in the fore-part of the punt; but the same apparatus answers equally well for the shooting yacht or sailing punt. The patent spiral recoil-spring and apparatus, as adapted to the punt and shooting yacht, though exquisitely simple, is one of Colonel Hawker's best and most useful inventions.

The punter intending to fit a punt-gun with the spiral recoil-spring should have the punt built purposely to receive the fittings, and the boat-builder will find the difficulties of his task much simplified if he has the gun and fittings by his side whilst building the pun.

A punt-gun of moderate dimensions may be used without any breechings, provided the shooter has sufficient courage to fire it, a thickly padded cushion being all that is necessary to place to the shoulder; but I cannot recommend anyone to fire a gun loaded with half a pound of shot and upwards without gun-breechings wherewith to ease the recoil, though I have seen it done by placing the but-end just *under* the arm, and nipping it close between the arm and ribs, and in that manner allowing the stock to pass *beneath* the shoulder on the gun recoiling.

CHAPTER XXIII

MANAGEMENT OF THE PUNT-GUN

'Come, come! Mr. Gunner!
Prythee, Mr. Gunner,
A little more powder
Your shot doth require.
Eire! Gunner, fire! do, do!'—*Suffolk Ditty.*

EVERY man who uses a punt and gun for wild-fowl shooting should carry an ammunition-box, which should be made to fit into a place assigned to it in the stern of the punt, whereby it assists, when containing ammunition, in counterpoising the fore-part of the punt against the weight of the large gun. The interior of the ammunition-box may be fitted, according to the punter's fancy, so as to contain his breech-loading cartridges and other apparatus: or, if a muzzle-loader, all the necessary requisites of powder, shot of various sizes, gun-charger, oakum for wadding, extra caps, priming-tunnel, and whatever else the sportsman may consider essential to his complete equipment. The box must be perfectly tight and water-proof, and the powder should be kept in flasks or canisters. The punt-gun ought always to be loaded with coarse-grain or battle powder, and for any gun carrying over four ounces at a charge, cannon-powder, the grains of which are about the size of tare seed, is best. It is a great mistake to load the punt-gun with fine-grain powder; it does not shoot so well with it as with the other, and if laid by a few days, it is highly probable the gun will not go off at all, or, if it does, it will hang fire. Fine-grain powder is very susceptible to changes of atmosphere, particularly when taken out on salt-water, and soon loses much of its force; it is also very liable to stick to the sides of the barrel of a large gun when loading, unless deposited at once and directly in the chamber of the gun. Glazed powder is not desirable; on the contrary, the other is to be preferred, because of its greater purity.

There is no difficulty in loading with the battle powder, for by tossing a charge in at the muzzle, and then raising the barrel slightly, the powder rolls down to the chamber afc once, rattling against the inside of the barrel as it descends, and thereby assuring the sportsman that it does not stick to the cylinder.

In addition to the ammunition-box, which must contain the requisites already enumerated, and many others which from the peculiar construction of the gun may be found necessary, a loading-rod must form part of the equipment of a muzzle-loader, and must be fitted with a good strong spiral-worm made of copper for drawing the charge or wiping out the barrel.

On loading the punt-gun, if it be a breech-loader, no difficulty will be encountered if the sportsman load it according to the special instructions of the inventor. But a muzzle-loader requires careful handling when loaded in the punt, or both gun and gunner may topple overboard. To load a muzzle-loader when afloat in the punt, first cast off the lashings and gun breechings, and carefully slide the but-end of the gun to the stern of the punt, bring the ammunition-box forward, so as to have it handy, let the muzzle of the gun be slightly elevated, resting on the cross-piece of the punt or on the midships of the gunnel, take the loading-rod, and if at all wet wipe it carefully with a bit of oakum, then take a small handful of oakum and roll it on to the spiral-worm of the loading-rod, with this well wipe the interior of the barrel, and the gun will shoot all the better if you take a second piece of oakum and wipe out the barrel a second time. This done, take the *charger*, which should be made of copper or tin, a simple tube of conical form, the small end fitting easily into the muzzle of the gun, but the base sufficiently large to prevent more than half the tube entering the barrel, carefully measure a charge of cannon powder, pouring it directly from the canister into the charger, toss it immediately into the barrel, raise the muzzle, and it will all roll rattling down into the chamber of the gun, without the aid of a loading-spoon or any such useless incumbrance. Then take another handful of oakum, clean and dry, roll it firmly into a ball, thrust it into the barrel, and ram it home on the powder, then load with shot in precisely the same manner, except that the oakum wadding placed over the shot should consist of only half the quantity of that used for the powder.

Having loaded the barrel with powder and shot, carefully slide the gun back again into its berth, and secure it to the breechings. Then, if it goes with copper tubes instead of gun-caps, there is nothing else to do but merely slip in the tube and all is ready for action; but with a percussion nipple a little more remains to be done. The gun being charged with cannon powder, and the nipple carefully wiped, some fine-grain gunpowder must be drilled into the nipple, by means of a tiny copper or brass tube made for the purpose, and the nipple being filled and capped, the percussion gun is then ready for action.

Oakum is recommended[1] for loading the punt-gun, as far preferable to, and more reliable than, cut or punched wads. Wads cut with a punch answer admirably for small guns, and of course no sportsman would use anything else; but they are not desirable either for punt or stanchion guns.

The wadding placed over a charge of powder which is to scatter from 1/2 lb. to 1 1/2 lb. of shot should be a tough and solid substance, and the larger the bore the thicker must be the wad. Throughout my experience I have never seen anything so well suited to the purpose as a ball of oakum, which, when rammed over the powder, remains firmer than any punched wad yet invented; and I have always found my guns throw the shot sharper and more compact with an oakum wad than with anything else. There is another advantage, in the event of having occasion to draw the charge from the barrel. The spiral-worm will take firm hold of the oakum wad, because of the stringy nature of the material; and be it ever so firmly embedded in the barrel, it may be drawn out, which is not the case with a punched wad—the latter being often very difficult to draw from large guns, generally coming out bit by bit, and finally mixing its dusty substance among the charge.

It may be very desirable to give the young sportsman a caution as to drawing a charge of powder from a punt-gun with a spiral-worm made of *steel* or *iron*, instead of copper. In screwing it into the powder wadding, if of steel or iron, he must be cautious; for if the worm goes through the wad into the powder, and comes in contact with any hard or brittle substance or with the inside of the barrel, it may explode the powder and blow him instantly into eternity. And here, again, is another important advantage in the oakum wadding, which may be drawn out without screwing the worm entirely through it, though such could not be done with punched wadding.

It is very seldom, however, that the powder wadding has to be drawn from the punt-gun; the most that is required is the shot wadding, which it often becomes necessary to draw for the purpose of changing the shot for larger or smaller, according to the size of the birds the punter may happen to meet with. But the young sportsman is recommended to avoid drawing a charge of powder from the barrel, it being more prudent to fire it off.

The sportsman must pay due regard to the size of his shot, for if too small it only wounds, and kills nothing outright; but if too large, the pellets fly at random, and not sufficiently compact in form. The size of shot must therefore be regulated in accordance with the magnitude of the gun and size of the birds fired at.

The author found that the best-sized shot for the general purposes of punting were BB. and AA. But when expressly in pursuit of wild-geese, with the stanchion gun, he used S.S.G. (15 to the oz.) or S.S.S.G. (17 to the oz), and for swans L.G. (of these there are only 5 1/2 pellets to the oz.). S.G. there are eleven. For the punt-gun, by night, he used No. 1, or single B.'s.

If the punt-gun (muzzle-loader) be loaded with shot cartridges, an oakum wadding should be put over the powder just the same, though it need not be quite so large as for loose shot.

Firing the Punt-Gun.

'Come, come! my brave boys!—
Though rarely well done—
Show them the way
You, fire the great gun!'—*Suffolk Ditty.*

The shoulder of the punter should always be placed firmly against the stock of the punt-gun on firing, but he must be cautious that his feet do not press horizontally against any part of the punt, or any unyielding substance offering resistance to his feet, because the gun, though carefully breeched, will not admit of being too closely confined, and must be allowed a little space for recoil; for, although it be secured with rope breechings, there is generally sufficient back-force to push away the prostrate punter, who, with no resistance against his feet, glides harmlessly back; whilst, if his feet were pressing against the stretcher or any other fixture, the kick of the gun would probably break his collar-bone, and this notwithstanding that the gun be secured with stout rope breechings.[1]

Tipping the Punt-Gun.

By tipping the punt-gun is meant pressing upon the stock or but-end, and thus elevating the muzzle for the purpose of firing at wild-fowl on the wing. This proceeding becomes necessary when the birds are wild, and rise before the punter has succeeded in getting fairly within range for a sitting shot, but not too far for a flying shot. Birds may be killed at a greater distance when on the wing than when sitting on the water with their wings closed. Now, from the peculiar position of the punter (lying flat on his stomach), it is obvious that tipping the gun and taking a flying shot is no very simple task, but one that requires tact and skill. Young hands frequently miss these shots, because they do not aim high enough or shoot soon enough, and thus the whole charge passes harmlessly beneath the birds.

The punter must be careful of his shoulder in making flying shots with a large punt-gun, or he will assuredly do himself a serious injury; and he must also take care that his gun does not fall overboard from the force of the recoil. It is an awkward position from which to shoot with a heavy gun, though with caution and practice it may be safely performed. And it is highly important for every punter to understand it, as many of the best shots are sometimes made by putting up the birds and tipping the gun.[2]

It will thus be seen that the punt-gun must be balanced with nice precision, or it cannot be tipped. But the equilibrium may be sufficiently maintained without placing the gun in such a ticklish position that the slightest touch would throw up the muzzle; indeed, that would be highly erroneous: it should rest on the cross-piece, so that a moderate pressure—say, of four or five pounds weight—will tip it up, or just so that when the gun flies back in recoil from a horizontal shot it may not lose its equilibrium and throw up the muzzle, contrary to the intention of the punter.

Punt-gun triggers often have a short bit of string attached to them, that the hand may not be injured by the trigger when the gun recoils. But, as a general rule, small punt-guns are fired without the string; and, when so, it is safest to put all the fingers before the trigger at the time of pulling it. Neither punt nor stanchion gun should have guards over the trigger, because of the danger attending such on the recoil of the gun in bruising, and sometimes severely lacerating, the hands and fingers if incautiously placed within the guard when pulling the trigger.

The Stanchion-Gun.

'Hear his proud thunder floating on the tide! Mark the dread fiat of the death-winged shower!'—T. HUGHES.

A gun carrying from a pound to a pound and a half of shot at a charge must of necessity be a formidable weapon, and no one should attempt fitting one to a shooting-yacht unless experienced in the manner of using large guns; the necessary appendages for their safe management, with the requisite equipment for handling, loading, and firing them, being totally different to those employed for small guns.

The barrel of a stanchion-gun capable of carrying such a charge is generally about eight feet in length, and the interior or bore of the barrel one inch and a half in diameter. A gun of such proportions is much too large for punting; and the only proper place for using such is aboard a shooting-yacht, where, with a proper equipment, it may sometimes be employed with immense success on the large gaggles of wild-geese which annually visit our coast. Stanchion-guns of this magnitude are of comparatively modern invention, and many improvements have been made in them of late years, so that they may now be used on board shooting-yachts with the facility of a shoulder-piece; and with care and attention may be kept in as perfect order, and as bright and clean, as the most fastidious sportsman can desire, and this, too, though in daily use upon the salt water.

During the last ten or fifteen years improvements in breech-loading guns of all kinds have been very considerable, so that there is now no difficulty in obtaining a safe and perfect breech-loading gun of any required size, either for the gunning-punt or the shooting-yacht.[1]

The patent plug and spiral recoil-spring before alluded to is a valuable and indispensable appendage to the stanchion-gun, and is one of Colonel Hawker's best contrivances. It is a great improvement on the cumbrous machinery which was used previous to that invention, called the 'grasshopper-spring'—a rude and unsightly construction, made of steel gig-springs, and bearing some resemblance in shape to the legs of a grasshopper, whence its name—but which, since Colonel Hawker's neat and perfect invention of the spiral recoil-spring, has been wholly cast aside.

---

[1] Col. Hawker, after all his experience, also fonnd that for waddings for punt-guns there was nothing like the best picked oakum.

[1] A small gun, loaded with only two drachms of powder, will break a man's collar-bone if fired straight up in the air from the top of his shoulder, the man standing upon hard ground. Accidents of this kind frequently occur at rook-shooting parties, through firing from positions directly beneath the birds.

[2] One of the most satisfactory shots I ever made in this manner was at two pairs of black geese, which I had punted to, and when within range found they sat so awkwardly that it was impossible to kill more than a pair at a shot; so I frightened them up, tipped my gun, and knocked down all four.

[1] The '*Mont Storm' principle* of breech-loading appears to be one of the best and safest for a print or stanchion gun. I have not had an opportunity of trying one of these guns, but I have more than once seen and carefully examined one belonging to Mr. Charles Phelps, of No. 3 Rood Lane, London.

CHAPTER XXIV

PUNTING BY DAYLIGHT

'Wary they gaze—our boat in silence glides,
The slow-moved paddles steal along the sides.'

ALEXANDER WILSON.

IN punting for wild-fowl the sport is pursued with a punt-gun in a small boat termed a gunning-punt.[2] One of the rudiments of the art is that of propelling the punt ahead by means of a pair of paddles when in deep water, and in shallow water it is sometimes pushed ahead with the assistance of a pole, termed a 'setting pole;' in the absence of which an oar answers the purpose of the latter. The punter, when using either paddles or setting pole, lies prostrate on the floor of the punt, upon his chest or stomach, the gun being placed at a proper elevation on the fore-part of the punt, and in that position he approaches and shoots the birds, either as they sit upon the water, or just at the moment of their taking wing.

A considerable deal of practice is necessary before a man can become a proficient in this, *la crème de la crème* of the sport of wild-fowl shooting. Colonel Hawker, speaking of the art of punting, says it is 'least understood of any sport in existence;' and certainly at the time when the Colonel wrote punting was in its infancy.

When once a man has made himself master of the art, and become familiarised with the habits of wild-fowl, there is no sport more captivating and exciting than punting by daylight.

In this, as in all other branches of the sport, the punter must ever bear in mind that wild-fowl are remarkably keen of sight and acute of hearing, and he must conduct his movements accordingly.

When roving about the water in pursuit of sport, the punter uses a short pair of sculls, sitting with his back to the prow, as in an ordinary rowing boat. But when in the immediate expectation of finding birds, he shifts his position and faces the other way, either sitting or kneeling upon the floor-cushion, and by back strokes with the sculls propels the punt ahead.

Directly the punter discovers any birds, if within reasonable distance, he lies down at once, unships his oars, and proceeds to approach them through the assistance of the paddles. If in deep water, he will confine himself to the use of these alone for the purpose of 'setting up' to the birds, but in shallow water he generally resorts to the *setting-pole, i.e.,* a small pole about eight or ten feet in length, shod at the lower end with an iron ferrule or a lump of lead, so as to assist it in sinking to the bottom. If the setting-pole have a forked end, it will be found useful in pinning down wounded birds by their necks, when pursuing them on the ooze. When the punter requires one or both hands inside the punt for the purpose of steadying the gun and pulling the trigger or otherwise, he need not take in the paddles at the moment, but may leave them hanging over the sides of the boat.

The young punter will find it no easy task to work his punt ahead in the wind's eye, with a pair of hand-paddles, whilst lying flat upon his stomach. The pursuit will try his arms severely at first; for it is downright hard work, much more so than rowing, on account of the prostrate position in which the punter has to perform his operations. It is usual to be provided with an extra jacket and a cushion, on which to rest the chest and stomach. The extra jacket will often be found useful when obliged to sit about in the cold, waiting the flow of tide, also in case of snow or rain and such like casualties. If the punter can afford to be luxurious, an air-cushion of proper size and proportion will be found a great comfort to lie upon on the floor of the punt when setting to birds.

The paddles used for the purpose of punting are about 2 J feet in length by four or five inches in breadth: they are of the form and substance of oar-blades, rounded at the top for handles, slightly forked at the bottom, and connected together by a string or small cord, which is secured through a little hole bored in the top of the handles; the object of the cord being to prevent their drifting away when dropped in the water alongside the punt at the time of using the hand for pulling the trigger.

The frontispiece engraving is intended to represent a scene of one of the author's best shots by daylight. It occurred at about eight o'clock one morning in the month of January, during a snow-storm, when the birds appeared particularly tame: the scene is therefore termed 'the day for ducks.' The punter has just fired half-a-pound of shot among a paddling of wild-ducks, killing twenty-nine and wounding twenty-two and upwards, making fifty-one at a shot—the number captured on the occasion.

On pulling the fatal trigger a cloud of smoke immediately rises before the shooter, through which he dimly sees hundreds of ducks flying off in line, with here and there a victim mortally wounded dropping dead from the team, whilst the echo of the murderous artillery resounds afar across the freezing waters. On the smoke clearing off he beholds, as it were, a pathway of dead and dying ducks, extending a long distance in line with the position of his gun. At first sight this line of slaughter appears compact and unbroken, but on approaching to collect the victims of his charge, one by one there emerges from the dead and dying, some less severely struck, winged and wounded birds, which make off as best they can, fluttering and struggling in the water; and thus the imaginary pathway soon becomes a broken and scattered extent of dead, dying, and disabled victims.[1]

When these heavy shots are made the punter seldom recovers all his wounded birds; from ten to twenty of those which are slightly wounded generally contrive to get so far away from the scene whilst the punter is gathering those nearest him, that they entirely elude his grasp, more especially if there be much floating ice, as there generally is when wild-fowl are numerous, and assemble in such large flights as to admit of these wonderful shots being made.

It must be borne in mind that it is only from the punt that such large numbers as here enumerated can be killed at a shot. If the same gun, loaded in precisely similar manner, were fired at equal distance from the deck of a shooting-yacht, or any more elevated position, at the same number of birds, probably less than half the number would be killed; and this will be immediately apparent to anyone who will give himself a few moments' reflection. A gun, large or small, fired point-blank at any object, as from the deck of a yacht, can only throw the shot within a limited space, because the course of the shot must go (allowing for gravitation) in direct line with the barrel; and consequently, if a stanchion-gun be fired from the yacht at birds sixty yards off, probably some of the shot kills or wounds every bird which may be sitting within a circular space of three or four feet, or even more, and the remainder of the shot are then buried under water within the same circular space. But, on the contrary, when the gun is placed on the head of a punt only a few inches above the surface of the water, and in line with any objects which may be sitting on that surface within a certain distance, the destruction which follows a discharge from so formidable a weapon must be very extensive, as the shot riddles every living thing within its track upon the surface of the water.

It requires considerable experience ere a man can adjust a punt-gun with that accuracy which is necessary to make his shot tell to the greatest advantage. If the elevation be in the least degree too high or too low, though he may kill a good many birds at a shot, still he does not destroy so many as he might do if capable of adjusting the gun upon the head of the punt with that scientific nicety which is requisite for directing the full force of the charge in its most effective course.

In illustration of this, let anyone fire a gun from his shoulder, whilst standing upright, at (say) twenty pigeons feeding on the ground, at forty or fifty yards distance, as closely huddled together as may be, then let him try his skill at the same distance and same number of pigeons by firing from a level of a few inches from the ground, and he will find the shot tell with nearly double effect as it sweeps the level of the surface.

It is a mistake, however, to place the gun too low; for instance, if the head of the punt were only two or three inches above the surface, the gun might then be placed at an elevation of only four inches from the actual level of the water, which would not be high enough for an effective shot, and though many birds might be killed at a discharge, nevertheless, in no proportion to the numbers which otherwise would be from an elevation two or three inches higher; nearly half the strong shot would be thrown under water in the one case, whilst, in the other, almost every shot in the barrel would be thrown directly at the objects—that is to say, birds would be killed sitting upon the water within line of the shot from sixty yards to one hundred and twenty and upwards. A little experience and practice, which are always the best instructors, will enable the young punter to understand this—a very important secret of success in the art of killing large numbers of wild-fowl at a shot, and he must remember that large shot kill at farther distances than small. But for very long ranges cartridges are particularly recommended, and they may now be had to fit punt-guns of every size. Cartridges are not desirable for night punting, but for daylight sport, both for stanchion and punt guns, they are very effective.

It is necessary that a punter should be a good oarsman; for, if he be ardent in the pursuit, he will frequently have to row many miles during the day, and often against wind and tide, which will try his strength and courage as well as his skill; if not accustomed to small rowing boats, he ought not to venture in a gunning-punt.

Strength of arm is indispensable for punting; the muscles of the wrist and arm are severely tried, and the longer the punter's arms the more useful they will be found for the purpose, and the less will be the exertion required.

The tyro will find that those punters who pursue the sport as a precarious means of subsistence are very reluctant to instruct a novice, and he may be assured the 'old hands' will not impart their best tactics, though paid ever so liberally. There are many boatmen who profess to understand the sport, but in reality know next to nothing about it, and this is the case in every wild-fowling district. Men who have punts and guns go out daily without success, though probably firing away as much (or more) powder and shot as the most successful; their guns not being properly placed, or their method of punting being erroneous, is the cause of their ill-success.

Every punter should carry a small shoulder-gun in his boat, and if a double-barrelled one so much the better; it will be found an almost indispensable part of the equipment of a gunning-punt, not only for the purpose of despatching strong wounded birds, but in a variety of ways; for instance, suppose a pair or three birds are seen swimming on the water at no great distance, and offering apparently a fair chance to the punter, he will scarcely think it worth while to discharge his punt-gun at any less number than two or three pair, although it may be truly said that the smaller the number the better the chance of getting near them. The best way would seem to be then, on such an occasion, to lie down and punt in the usual way, getting as close to them as possible, and working in their direction with the paddles until they actually take wing. There is then ample time and opportunity for an active man to raise himself quickly to his knees, seize the shoulder-gun, and kill a pair with certainty. I have shot many pairs and single birds of the web-footed species in this manner.

During windy weather, and when the birds are very unsettled and unapproachable, I have sometimes succeeded, by way of last resource, by lying down and allowing the punt to drive from windward to leeward towards the birds; but this cannot properly be done unless the punt be furnished with a rudder and yoke lines; the latter must be of sufficient length to reach the hands of the punter as he lies prostrate in the boat.

It not unfrequently happens that two or more punters are attracted to the same spot, especially when a large flight of wild-fowl is collected in one particular place upon the ooze, and the punters are awaiting the flow of tide, so that they may be able to get at them with their punts just as the water reaches the birds' legs; then, as is usual in such cases, the two or three punters proceed in company as close as they can; and, according to the rules of punting, it matters not who was first there, since, if there be more birds than can be killed with one gun at a shot, the others have a right to join in the attempt and share the success. On such an event it is always agreed between them, before they commence operations, as to who shall give the signal for firing, which usually consists of two words—'Ready!' and 'Fire!' The moment the first word is uttered fingers must be put to the trigger, and at the utterance of the second, which should follow after a moment's pause, triggers must be pulled. When 'setting 'to birds side by side with other punters, care should be taken to keep the punts as level and regular as possible in line with the objects ahead—never allowing the punt to swerve from her course, but constantly pointing 'right ahead,' with the gun bearing straight upon the birds; the punter is then ready for any emergency should they take wing, and it become necessary to tip the gun and take a flying shot.

It is always preferable for a punter to approach birds alone by daylight, it being very seldom that two or more in company succeed in the daytime, unless the weather be very severe. But at night it is better for punters to go in company for two important reasons: First, that there is less danger of accidentally shooting each other; and, secondly, that the noise arising from the report of two or three guns discharged at one and the same instant disturbs the surrounding waters no more than one gun; but if the punters are scattered in various directions about the waters, the danger of their shooting each other is much greater, the banging more frequent, and the birds more restless, consequently they spoil each other's sport.

The punter is equally liable to disappointment by day as by night, especially when the water is rough, so as to cause the boat to float unsteadily. It is then very difficult to shoot with certainty from the punt, because the muzzle of the gun must rise and fall with the waves; and, as the slightest deviation from the regulated level position of the gun will entirely alter the range of the shot, it would seem the height of indiscretion to fire the punt-gun under such circumstances at birds sitting upon the water; the chances being that the shot will either strike the water before reaching the birds, which would be the case if the fore-part of the punt fell into a wave, and *vice versa* as regards the aft-part, in which case the shot would fly over their heads.

The only method whereby success can be expected at such times is to get as close to the birds as possible, but to reserve the charge until they are fairly on the wing, when a well-directed shot will often do splendid execution, and kill even more than a discharge at the same number sitting in smooth water.

The punter should be cautious never to allow an over-eagerness to lead him into danger, but at ail times to regard personal safety as the first consideration; and this is a trial which will frequently be put to the test in those who pursue the sport energetically. The punter should never leave his boat a moment without making it fast or easting out the anchor. Young sportsmen have lost their lives in this way; others may do the same when anxious to recover wounded birds within a few inches of their grasp, they step out of the punt on to a sand or mud bank by the water-side, and in their eagerness to secure their prize neglect to carry out the anchor; in the next moment their punt has drifted away, and they are left as hapless mortals on a barren ooze or island far removed from human assistance, where the tide will rush upon them in a few hours, and their fate must then be inevitably dreadful.

The punter should not only be cautious to anchor his boat in an available spot, but take care to see that the cable is properly made fast; and when the tide is rising he must watch his boat, and be cautious not to wander so far away, or be gone so long, that on returning the boat cannot be regained. He must be doubly cautious at night, for then the danger is considerably greater, but in foggy weather worse than at any time. It is strongly urged upon the punter never, under any circumstances, to go out of sight of his punt in a fog when away from the mainland. Let him know the locality ever so well, if once he turns about, after being out of sight of any landmark, he becomes bewildered and finally lost.

It is a wise precaution to be provided with a pocket-compass when wild-fowling on open waters during foggy weather; but such is never a desirable time for punting, because objects look so much larger on the water during fogs than in clear weather.

The punter may dress himself in any fashion he pleases, though the colour of his hat and jacket, as a general rule, should be white, especially in frosty weather, or when there is ice upon the water or snow on the ground. As to disguising the punt, a practice by no means uncommon, it answers best in rivers and inland waters. There are various suggestions; but none are better than strewing small boughs of trees about the punt, or distributing a few tufts of grass and rushes upon it, or anything of like verdure to that growing in the locality frequented by the birds. The most complete disguise of the kind in winter is drift ice and snow; but these, as well as all other weighty substances, placed on the head of a punt, require care in adjustment, or they incur danger to the punter, by rendering his frail little craft less steady; and the elevation of the gun is very likely to be disarranged by the process. When the boat is artfully disguised the punter is generally rewarded with success. It is, however, a practice seldom resorted to, except when the birds have become very wild, and shown themselves awake to all other stratagems on the part of the punter.

The sportsman who would be successful at the pursuit of punting by daylight must be very watchful during the seasons when wild-fowl are expected, for they sometimes arrive suddenly, and leave equally so. Thousands of birds may be in a particular locality on one day, and gone the next. The punter should not put off his excursion till the following day, but go at once, if the weather be suitable. There are no chances equal to those which may be had on the very first arrival from distant shores of large flights of wild-fowl. They are then, generally, exceedingly tired and hungry, and lucky is the punter who falls in with them at such a time.

The easterly winds of November never fail to bring numbers of wild-fowl to our shores: and as soon as the wind abates, and the water becomes sufficiently smooth, the sportsman should launch his punt and proceed to their haunts, when, if he understands his business, he may be certain of success. After several days' strong east wind, during the winter months, with severe frost and snow, thousands of wild-fowl throng our shores, and abundance of sport may be had; but it is advisable, immediately, to make use of the opportunity; because, if the wind changes to the west, in all probability they will take themselves off and fly out to sea.

The remarks made as to proceeding at once and without delay to the haunts of wild-fowl on their first arrival relate more particularly to public waters, such as are free to anyone.

In private lakes or wild-fowl preserves it is better to allow the birds to rest undisturbed a few days, when they become reconciled to the place; and though they may leave it at the hour of evening flight, they return again in the morning, sometimes bringing hundreds of followers with them.

It would be better for the sport in general if public waters could be protected in a similar manner, so as to allow the birds to settle; but, in the absence of such protection, the first man who advances upon a newly-arrived flight of wild-fowl has the best chance, and this whether they be geese, ducks, widgeon, or indeed almost any description of wild-fowl.

To be successful in wild-fowl shooting, the sportsman must be an early riser: the best chances of all, with the punt and gun, are to be met with at dawn of day; and the same observations apply to wild-fowl with the shoulder-gun on marshes and freshes; because, as the birds only go to such places at evening, so they leave them at morning twilight. Everyone who desires to follow up the sport effectively should rise before daylight, and, if a punter, should proceed in his punt to the feeding-haunts of the birds, taking care to place himself as much in the shade as possible. If the weather be tranquil, and the surface of the water unruffled, the cautious punter will, long before daybreak, be listening for the garrulous notes of the water-fowl—the well-known 'whe-oh' of the widgeon, the 'quack' of the mallard, and the clattering cackle of the geese; and when discovered he will watch the sky for the first dawn of morning, and as soon as signs of such are to be detected in the horizon, he will place himself and punt in such a position that the birds may be betwixt the dawn and the boat; then, if there be. high land in the rear, and a bright dawn before him, the birds may be seen at a long distance on the glittering surface, whilst the punt, from being in the opposite shade, cannot be detected until close upon them. None but those who have been on the water at such a time, tried the experiment, and seen its effect, can tell the advantage of such a position. When thoroughly understood, this method of punting is wonderfully successful, except on cloudy mornings, or when the water is too much ruffled by the wind. The same observations apply to punting by evening twilight. In frosty weather the western sky often exhibits a luminous appearance for an hour and upwards after sunset; when so, and there are wild-fowl on the waters, it affords golden opportunities to punters.

> 'For thy dark cloud, with umbered lower,
> That hung o'er cliff, and lake, and tower,
> Thou gleam'st against the western ray
> Ten thousand lines of brighter ray.'

I have made as many as four excellent shots with my punt-gun, during the short space of *one hour*, whilst rowing homewards, with a bright western sky 'right ahead.'

On looking towards the light, objects may be detected at a

long distance; but on looking back, all looks dark and dreary, and it would be difficult to discover in that direction a small object on the water, unless very close.

From the foregoing remarks, the tyro will see the necessity of attending to the changes of wind, tide, and weather, and also to the hours of twilight: the movements and demeanour of wild-fowl depend so much on these, that he is particularly recommended to observe them.

A Fall on the Ooze.

Allusion has already been made (page 100) to the occasional necessity of making use of splashers or mud pattens, for the purpose of walking upon the ooze to collect dead and wounded birds after firing the punt-gun; but I have yet to speak of the dangerous consequences attending a fall on the ooze, of the difficulty of again recovering one's footing on a substance so soft and rotten;[1] and in explaining the perils of 'ooze ranging,' probably I cannot do better than lay before my readers particulars of an adventure which occurred some few years ago, when I rescued a man, probably, from a horrible death.

On returning home up a river on the eastern coast, in a shooting-punt, my attention was arrested by distant cries for help, when I immediately pulled in the direction whence the sound proceeded, which, as I drew nearer, appeared louder and more imploring. On approaching the spot by a creek, the first thing I saw was a punt without its occupant; there were gun, pea-jacket, oars, paddles, &c, but no splashers, and I therefore concluded the owner was somewhere upon the ooze; so, putting on my own splashers, I walked on the ooze in the direction of the cries, to which I had already cheerily responded at the very top of my voice, when I soon discovered a man floundering in the mud, who told me in most touching tones of despair that he had fallen into a bog and could not get out, the mud being too rotten to permit him to get upon his feet. On coming closer to the spot I saw at once his perilous predicament, and assured him help was at hand; but such a scene presented itself to my gaze as I never before beheld, and at which I could not refrain from laughing. There he lay, in a soft, bumby-like bed of mud, wallowing in the mire, smothered and bedaubed from head to foot with black soil, and bearing but little resemblance to a human being, but in reality a great fat man, with features obscured by the mud; and who said he had been chasing a 'winged widgeon,' and in stooping to catch it toppled headlong into the bog, from which he found it impossible to extricate himself: the more he struggled to get up, the deeper he sank in the mud. Before I could render the man any assistance I found it necessary to return to one of the punts and fetch the bottom-boards; and having carefully placed the same on the bog in front of the luckless individual, by their aid and that of an oar I assisted him to his legs. By no other available means could I have got him out, so soft and rotten was the ooze at that particular spot. Half an hour afterwards the tide flowed over it.

———————

[2] *Supra*, page 120.—The Gunning-punt.

[1] Not wishing to make these pages the medium for chronicling his own successes, the author merely mentions the numbers killed on the occasion alluded to for the purpose of explaining the engraving; he will therefore, in subsequent pages, carefully refrain from anything like a record of the numbers which from time to time it has been his good fortune to kill at a shot. Keeping strictly within the bounds of facts occurring under his own immediate observation, it may be stated, in round numbers, that from sixty to one hundred widgeon have often been stopped, by the single discharge of a large punt-gun.

[1] These perilous gulphs are also very common in some parts of France, where they are termed *mortes*.

CHAPTER XXV.

WILD-FOWLING IN DRIFT-ICE

. . . . 'Yea, even the fowl—

That through the polar summer-months could see

A beauty in Spitzbergen's naked isles,

Or on the drifted ice-bergs seek a home—

Even they had fled, on southern wing, in search

Of less inclement shores.'—*The Fowler.*

DURING hard winters, and when the frost is so severe that the navigation of some of the salt-water rivers about our coast is temporarily impeded by ice, wild-fowl are always abundant. The inland ponds and lakes are frozen over, the surface of the earth is thickly coated with snow, and the only resorts for the web-footed species, when thus shut out from their more inland haunts, are the salt-water estuaries, bays, and rivers on the coast, where the force of the tide breaks up the ice, and drives it up and down with every current. Rushing and crushing masses, capped with crystallised snow, float about the waters, and form themselves into solid substances and pyramidal icebergs, some in positions curious and beautiful to behold, with edges upwards, sloping, or askant, and graced with sparkling clusters of transparent icicles; whilst here and there are little arctic-like islands of solid ice, drifting to and fro, the white-clad surfaces of which are here and there chequered with little spots of black. These black spots, the practised fowler well knows, though at the distance of a mile and upwards, are the very objects of his pursuit. There they sit, huddled together like chickens crowding beneath their mother's wings. But it is not to the icebergs alone that the wild-fowler's attention is drawn on occasions such as these: wherever his eyes turn, wild-fowl may be seen in restless movement, some flying in little trips, others in large flights, hovering over the frozen element or darting off in every direction, the whole bay abounding with wild-fowl life.

There is, then, no lack of sport for those who have the courage and hardihood to expose themselves to such trying severities of weather. At every dip of the oar-blades the ice congeals thicker and thicker upon them, and the oars eventually become so heavy that it is necessary every now and then to knock them one against the other, to throw off the burthen of ice they gather: and this is no overdrawn picture of wild-fowling in England during severe weather, but the result of my own personal experiences. It is but a few years ago since similar severities attended my pursuits on the eastern coast, when every dash of spray which chanced to fall upon the punt, or indeed upon any part of my attire, down to the worsted gloves upon my hands, froze into ice before it could be wiped away.

More than ordinary caution is necessary in the navigation of a gunning-punt when proceeding upon this diversion under such circumstances, and amidst so many surrounding perils. So frail a bark may at any moment be crushed when moving amongst solid blocks of ice in a tide-way; and it is sometimes the height of imprudence to venture in a gunning-punt among such obstructions. Wind, tide, and time of day have each to be regarded, ere the punter launches his boat and ventures on his perilous sport. But when familiar with the locality and the effect of changes bf wind and tide, the experienced punter may venture, for then is the time to make marvellous shots, and fill his boat with wild-fowl in a few hours.

When the rivers are blocked with ice in this manner, it is only at certain intervals of tide that prudence admits of the punter's launching on the frigid surface; and it is necessary to watch carefully the direction taken by the drift-ice, the largest and heaviest pieces of which move off with the first rush of the ebb, and drive to the most leeward part of the waters. When the tide has run off the ooze, and the current is then confined to the channel, there is less danger of venturing, but the punter must choose a fitting opportunity, and 'shove off' as clear of the icebergs as he can. The best chances will probably offer at an hour or so before low water, when the channel is usually clearer than at any other time. But it is advisable to contrive, either by land-carriage or otherwise, to get the punt round to windward of the ice, where there is generally open water; and, in fact, that is where the largest numbers of birds will be found.

The chief danger to be avoided is that of being set fast between two floating icebergs, which would crush a punt as if a mere bandbox. The punter assuredly finds, in severe seasons, that by far the greater skill is required to keep clear of obstructions than to kill the wild-fowl, which often float past him, upon the drifting ice, within gun-shot; but, from his perilous position, or the impossibility of recovering the birds after killing' them, he is often induced to reserve the fire of his big gun for a more fitting opportunity. But he may often make excellent shots with his shoulder-gun when driving down the current among ice-floes.

It is a very good plan, when the waters are so blockaded, to look out for a space in a small tributary or bight which may be clear of ice; and, by lying in ambush a short time, there is every probability of a shot offering, from the numbers of fowl which are constantly drifting past in the main channel. After shooting, the punter must not be too eager in attempting to recover his birds if they are amidst drift-ice; and it will be useless to attempt getting any but the dead ones, and sometimes not half of those. One by one the wounded birds will disappear, the rushing and crushing masses of ice scattering and running completely over them. The dead ones which drift away make food for the crows, which are always eagerly watching upon the oozes and icebergs for such prey. The wounded, after hard struggles and perilous encounters with the ice, at last reach the shore, to combat with further difficulties, and become the lawful prizes of those who are fortunate enough to be first on the spot with a dog and small gun, wherewith to salute them with a *coup-de-grâce*, and secure them.

The costume of the wild-fowler when seeking his sport among the drift-ice should be white, and the gunning-punt of the same colour, so as to resemble a block of ice. The birds will sometimes suffer a punter so attired to approach within range, if he silently drift down with the current; but if he attempt to work against it, they suspect him and fly; for they seem to know that blocks of ice never run against the current.

The punter should attentively mark the commencement of a thaw after a long frost, and proceed at once on such an occasion to the open waters. It is a fine opportunity; the birds then feed upon the soft substances of the ooze very greedily, and may be approached, under ordinary precautions, almost with certainty. Some of the best shots I have ever made with the punt-gun have been on the first breath of a morning-thaw.

The round-bottomed punt before described is preferable to the flat-bottomed for moving amongst drift-ice; because, by listing the boat on one side, slightly below her bearings, the other side rises to the ice, and allows it to pass beneath the bottom; and, if accidentally hemmed in between two icebergs, the round-bottomed punt is far the less likely of the two to be crushed.

In windy weather the punter should be cautious of venturing among drift-ice, more especially on a lee-shore; the punt is very liable to be stove in or seriously damaged by the hard frozen substances driving against it; and it is almost impossible to extricate a punt, under ordinary circumstances, from among the iron grasp of a drift of ice-floes on a lee-shore.

Should the punter accidentally find himself beset, and there is no fear of immediate danger, he should remain quiet a few hours, until the tide turns, when he may stand a chance of getting out: and it is his only chance; for, if the ice be left on the ooze by the receding tide, he must be left also; his position then becomes by no means an envious one, it being impossible to conjecture upon what sort of a landing the punt will rest. If across a rill or hollow, such must be an extremely perilous position both for the punt and its occupant.

The punter will find the same, or greater, difficulty in

returning home from an excursion among the ice, as that which he encountered on setting out; and unless he can return up the channel in advance of the ice, it will be of no use to make the attempt; he had better row ashore in the open water to windward of the ice, and walk home afoot, though it should be ten miles distance.

To attempt forcing a passage at night-time through heavy drift-ice would be next to madness: no one at all conscious of the risk would incur it.

Whilst the punt is employed during such severe frosts, the sides and bottom are very liable to become corroded with ice. This must be looked to, and the ice carefully removed or it will alter the trim of the punt, and, consequently, the range of the gun. But on no account should it be knocked off with force; such a proceeding assuredly makes the punt leaky, as the sportsman will find, to his discomfort, on the first thaw.

Both the inside and outside of the gunning-punt must be kept clear of ice and snow, or the bearings of the gun will require to be regulated afresh on every occasion of using it.

Gunning-punts should be carried ashore and placed under cover, when not in use, during sharp weather. If exposed to frost and snow, they soon fall out of trim; and this is of more importance than many would suppose. A punter who is careless about his boat will frequently have the mortification of finding his gun lying at wrong range: when such is the case, as a natural result, he may as well stay ashore, for he will kill nothing until the range and level of the gun are re-adjusted.

The dangers encountered by punters in drift-ice claim special attention. In my own experience I never knew of a punter losing his life in the ice, but I have seen men in most perilous positions, surrounded by inextricable masses of floating ice. Experienced persons, however, are extremely cautious not to incur such risks.

I remember once seeing a recklessly adventurous young punter in such a position that it seemed quite a miracle his punt was not crushed to atoms between the floating masses, and he buried alive beneath its freezing influence. This man had very indiscreetly gone out on a windy day—far too much so for punting; when, besides, the drif-ice is rendered doubly dangerous from the additional force which the wind gives to its movements. The tide rose rapidly, and rushed like a torrent up the river, bringing with it acres of floating ice, which soon surrounded the incautious punter, who in a short time found himself quite beset, and totally unable to extricate himself from its crushing grasp. During several hours he remained in that helpless position, standing erect in the punt, and waving signals of distress to people ashore. The force of the current drove his boat many miles up the river, and thus assisted in binding it more firmly than ever in the grasp of the ice. Whilst in this critical position, the alarm of his friends ashore as to his safety became intense, and, the tide being then shortly about to ebb, it was feared the consequences would inevitably prove fatal; the wind also continuing heavy, it seemed next to an impossibility to release or render him any assistance. At length an admirable scheme was suggested by a gentleman ashore; this was, to fly a kite over the unfortunate man, and drop him a string, by means of which a rope might be conveyed to him. The suggestion proved quite practicable, and the plan entirely successful. The adventurous punter gladly hauled on the kite-string until he caught the rope, which he made fast to the stern of his punt; he then sat down in the fore-part, and was thus dragged ashore over the ice, amidst the general rejoicings of a whole village of spectators.

This same reckless individual was, a few years afterwards, shot in the leg, whilst incautiously hauling his punt ashore, with the gun lying upon it at full-cock. The jar occasioned by dragging the punt over some shingle up the beach caused the hammer to fall, and the charge blew his right leg almost to atoms. A peasant saw the melancholy accident; but before medical aid could be procured, or the poor fellow taken to a house, he bled to death.

Facts such as these tend to show, more truthfully than anything the author can urge, how cautious sportsmen should be of themselves and their weapons, not only when wild-fowling among drift-ice, but indeed at all times, and they teach us that personal safety should always be regarded as the first duty of the sportsman.

_____

CHAPTER XXVI

THE SAILING-PUNT

'The boat goes tilting on the waves,

  The waves go tilting by:

There clips the cluck, her back she laves;

  O'erhead the sea-gulls fly.'—H. G. DANA.

THE advantages of the sailing-punt for the purposes of wildfowl shooting are peculiar. If all the punters in any particular locality used sailing-punts, the wild-fowl would become very shy of them, and it would be easier to approach them in a rowing-punt, which is, to all intents and purposes, the more eligible boat. But as rowing-punts abound in every wild-fowling locality, and sailing-punts are few and far between, it often happens, as I can testify from personal experience, that more success is obtained by making up to birds under sail than by paddling towards them. The birds become accustomed to persecution from one particular form of craft, and do not suspect a novelty, and thus, frequently, a march is stolen upon them. With a light wind and smooth water, the rapidity with which a properly rigged sailing-punt skims over the surface is astonishing; even whilst the birds are in the act of taking wing the little craft may be run in many yards nearer upon them, and thus a highly effective shot may sometimes be made.

The sailing-punt enables the wild-fowl shooter to obviate a great deal of the hard work which he must of necessity encounter in a rowing-punt, and affords him a pleasant and satisfactory means of enjoying the sport of wild-fowl shooting, particularly in mild weather; but in severe seasons the punter will find no great difficulty in making up to wild-fowl in a rowing-punt by aid of the hand-paddies alone.

The young wild-fowler, however, must observe that it is not every punt which can be sailed; a boat of peculiar and special construction is required for the purpose, for so surely as an inexperienced hand attempts sailing an ordinary rowing-punt, such as is commonly used for wild-fowling, so surely will he capsize it. Of all the forms of gunning boats, the punt is the least safe under sail and the least manageable. A boat must be built specially for the purpose of carrying sail; and it may be so constructed as to be capable of being used either as a sailing or rowing punt, so that a strong man with long arms may propel it with paddles nearly as fast as an ordinary rowing-punt. Such is precisely the description of boat recommended by the author, who, after trying several forms, used one many years, and found it not only a most comfortable but serviceable boat for the purpose, and it looked no larger on the water than an ordinary rowing-punt.

The length of the sailing-punt from stem to stern should not exceed eighteen feet (if it be intended also for rowing and paddling,) and the extreme breadth amidships three feet three inches, gradually tapering from the midship section towards the stern, and finishing with a perpendicular stern-piece; the forepart of the punt should also taper gradually from the midship section to an upright stem-piece. The depth forward should be four and a half to five inches, and aft eight inches. It must be built with a keelson extending about three inches below the floor at the stern, and gradually lessening to one inch at the bows, so as to answer the purpose of a keel. This and all the floor strakes should be of elm, all the others of red pine. The form of the floor must be as flat as it is possible to build a keel-bottomed boat, and as near like that of a whale-boat as can be, with stem and stern-post alike, sharp at each end. The bow should be fine at the entrance, though by no means hollow, but maintaining the full flat floor, as far as consistent, towards the stem, because of the pressure upon it from the weight of the gun. The sides of the punt should be carefully formed, rounding gracefully as a whale-boat, and the quarter full and bur-thensome, though tapering to a stem of similar form to the stern.

The object of maintaining the floor as flat and long as possible is not only for buoyancy and easy draught of water, but for stability under sail.

The fore-part of the punt should be covered over with a thin but water-tight scantling, very slightly arched, so that neither rain nor spray may rest upon it.

The depth of the punt amidships, and up to the cross-piece which terminates the covered head, should be six inches; and about two inches of the scantling should be placed edgeways across the punt, abaft the covered head, so as to screen the punter from view when taking aim at the birds.

Neither water-decks nor wash-strakes are required for the sailing-punt, because no reasonable man would venture to set sail in so frail a bark in rough water.

The mast must be a shifting one, so that it may be readily shipped and unshipped at pleasure, a small light spar, about the size of a mop-handle, and from four to five feet in height.

The mast-stepping hole may be made either through the scantling in front of the screen-piece or just abaft it, and a little towards the left side, so as to be clear of the balance-rest on which the punt-gun lies. Neither shrouds nor stays should be fitted to the mast; either would make it dangerous; because, should a heavy squall strike the sail, it is better for the little mast to 'go by the board,' carrying all sail along with it, than to capsize the boat, which would be the result under such circumstances if the mast were confined. It is preferable, therefore, to select a slender mast that has not sufficient substance to overturn the punt. Never mind its bending in a strong breeze; the carrying away of a mast now and then is far less to be regarded than the upsetting of a punt. The punt's mast must be fitted at the top with a small metal sheave for the halliards, which, after being led through the sheave-hole, are attached to an iron or copper traveller, sliding up and down the mast, and a thumb cleat being tacked on to the lower part of the mast, just above the punt's deck, all is ready for making fast the halliards whenever the sail is hoisted. The sail should be of lateen or settee shape, and made of very light duck or white calico.[1] It is unnecessary to give the exact dimensions of the sail, as these must be in proportion to the stability of the punt, but, as a general rule, the lateen-yard for spreading the sail may be fifteen feet for a punt of the size and length described. It would be advisable for a beginner to set only a small sail at first, and then increase it as he becomes accustomed to the boat. The tack of the sail should be hooked on to a small copper ring about two feet in advance of the mast, on the weather side, or it may be hooked to the lower part of the mast. The main-sheet should lead through a thimble or sheave at the stern, and be carried forward to a cleat somewhere amidships, so as to be near at hand when the punter is lying down in the boat.

The rudder bands must also be sufficiently long to enable the sportsman to steer his craft with the greatest precision when lying at full length on the floor of the punt, as in that position he has to take aim and shoot.

A small cushion will be found very convenient, and a great comfort to the punter in the sailing as well as in the rowing punt, or a life-buoy may be carried instead, which will answer the same purpose. And if a little dry straw or fern be strewn upon the floor of the punt, such will make it more comfortable for the punter.

The form of the sailing-punt described is graceful and buoyant, and, when unincumbered with gun and other weighty substances, may be rowed with the ease and rapidity of a wager-boat. It is intended to carry one person only, as having two occupants of a punt is at all times a great impediment to success in wild-fowl shooting.

The sailing-punt should be painted a dusky-white colour, and the sail ought always to be kept clean and of snowy whiteness.

No other ballast will be required than that of the punter himself (who is virtually *the ballast*), the punt-gun, ammunition-box, and other accoutrements, all of which must be placed in exact position, so as to trim the boat to a nicety. The punter need not lie down until he finds the birds, but as soon as found he should stretch himself flat on the floor, and be cautious not to move a limb above board as he approaches within range. If the sail be of light material and fairly proportioned, the punt will be quite safe in smooth water in experienced hands. But *one* sail only should be used, and that the lateen before mentioned. The rapidity with which a little boat of this kind skims along 'on a reach' is astonishing; and the young sportsman will often be agreeably surprised at the easy and unsuspecting manner in which it may be run up to wild-fowl in a steady breeze: and if a shot cannot always be obtained before they take wing, by luffing the punt whilst they are rising, in the same manner as with a yacht or sailing-boat, an excellent flying-shot may frequently be made,

The sailing-punt should not be taken into rough water. Independently of the danger, no sport could be had, it being impossible to shoot with any certainty whilst the punt is rising and pitching in the waves, to say nothing of the danger of its getting filled with water or swamped. The sailing-punt can only be used in smooth water, the few inches it sits above the surface rendering it unsafe under any other circumstances. When it is desirable to go after wild-fowl in water too rough for a punt, the sloop-rigged sailing-*boat*, to be hereinafter described, will be the proper craft to venture in. It is not the strength of the wind which produces the danger; for if the water be smooth, and the punt built according to the directions here laid down (with keelson and long flat floor), sail may be carried fearlessly in an ordinary and even a stiff breeze. But the inexperienced are warned against the peril of carrying sail on a punt with a heavy gun on the bows, in any but smooth water. The effect of venturing into rough water with a long, low craft, and pressing her ahead under sail, would be to drive her bows under water, which the weight of the gun on the head of the punt would considerably facilitate; the danger is therefore obvious.

And if the punter moved forward to lower the sail, his extra weight thrown suddenly upon the bows would, in such a case, inevitably send the punt under water head first; and, independently of such a glaring indiscretion, it is impossible in a heavy sea to prevent the water from flying over the gunwales of the punt when under sail. Therefore, once more, the wild-fowler is cautioned *not to venture into rough water with the sailing-punt;* for a sportsman's life is supposed to be of more value than that of a duck.

———————

[1] A small sketch of a sailing-punt, fitted with lateen sail, may he seen in the engraving of 'The Day for Ducks' (see the Frontispiece).

CHAPTER XXVII

NIGHT-PUNTING

'Loud were their clamouring tongues as when
The clanging sea-fowl leave the fen;
And, with their cries discordant mixed,
Grumbled and yelled the pipes betwixt.'—SIR W. SCOTT.

NIGHT is, undoubtedly, the best time for wild-fowl shooting with the punt and gun: then it is that the punter may steal upon his birds unseen and unsuspected: but even this branch of the art requires much practice and experience in order to become a proficient. The midnight punter must be familiar with the different notes, calls, and clamours of the aquatic tribe; for by those sounds, and those alone, he will have to be guided as to the spot to which his efforts must be directed; and when wild-fowl are abundant, as is always the case in hard winters, he will sometimes find himself so surrounded and be-wildered. with fheir noises as to be in absolute doubt which way to steer. Experience will soon teach him that the stragglers are loudest and most clamorous, and the assembly quietest when on the feed or ('all a guzzle').

In all cases, he must direct his movements according to the positions of light and shade; that is to say, he must keep his punt on the shady side of the moon, and when he lies down in the punt to paddle towards the birds he must advance upon them with the moon shining in his face.[1] By this means the birds are brought immediately beneath the light of the moon, and can be distinctly seen upon the water by the punter, who, from his being in the opposite direction, is with his boat invisible to the birds, or, at any rate, but very indistinctly seen, so long as he keeps in the position indicated.

The movements of the punter must also be regulated according to the wind, for it is generally a useless task to attempt punting to leeward upon wild-fowl. A side, or slanting, wind may suit, though the best plan is to work directly in the wind's eye, and, if possible, with a favourable loom at command.

The clanging noises made by large numbers of wild-fowl at night are very apt to lead a tyro-punter to suppose himself within shot, and induce him to fire out of range. Experience, however, will soon remedy this common error.

The punter should always bear in mind that wild-fowl, whether sleeping or feeding, have sentinels watching, and in waking they change places: 'Vigilias ordinant et in vigilando vices mutat.'[1] So that the slightest noise or movement is instantly detected, and by a single note of warning communicated to all the others. Therefore, if the oars squeak, they should be muffled.

There is no better time for night-punting than clear moonlight nights, with a gentle breeze, provided it blows in such a direction as to enable the punter to face both moon and wind on 'setting' to birds.

If there be ever so little moonlight, it will be found of great assistance to the punter. He can then find the birds the more readily, on approaching within hearing of their notes, by bringing his punt to bear upon the gleams of light thrown across the water by the moon; and if at any time he discover a number of birds on the outer or wrong side of the moon (as he frequently will), he should not be tempted to set towards them, but must row in a contrary direction, and work his course so as to bring them into the proper light, between the punt and moon; and this must be done by the punter who hopes for success, though it may occupy half an hour's rowing to accomplish. It is so utterly useless to attempt setting up to birds in any other manner that the punter had better return home, and go to bed, if too lazy or careless to take the trouble to row the roundabout course necessary for bringing them into bearing with the moonlight.

For this diversion widgeon afford the best sport of all. Wild-ducks, on the contrary, seek the land, and creep as closely in-shore as the tide will carry them, so as to render their position almost impenetrable to the punter; for although he may distinctly hear the 'quacking' of the mallards, he cannot see them. It then becomes necessary to be guided by sounds and experience, and to shoot by guess.

There is no better opportunity for killing wild-fowl, whether in large companies or small, than when on their 'last legs,' as it is termed—*i.e.* when the flowing tide has covered with water every particle of the ooze, except perhaps a small mound, around which they crowd and cringe, delaying to take wing until fairly lifted from their legs by the tide. Such are among the most desirable opportunities that can be had: the birds are then so closely packed together, that very large numbers may be killed at a shot.

Anyone accustomed to the navigation of large rivers by night knows, that during a breeze the ripple darkens the surface of the water where deep,' or clear of growing seaweeds; the oozes also, when the tide is out, look very black by night, but the shallows show a silvery whiteness: and, as the tide gradually flows over the ooze, and around the legs of the birds, though in total obscurity until the tide reached them, they are then visibly exposed as so many live, dark objects on the 'white water,' as it is termed by wild-fowl shooters. It then becomes the punter's duty to wait, in the deep or dark water, until there is sufficient depth beneath the white surface to enable him to approach, with his punt, within range of the birds.

So white does the water show on the black ooze, on first

covering it, that birds may sometimes be distinctly seen within range, though there be no moon at all: but, in the absence of the moon, there must be *very* bright starlight; and on such nights none but experienced punters stand the remotest chance of success. They are first attracted near the spot by the voices of the birds; and, after waiting until the tide reveals the secret of their whereabouts by flowing around them, the punter cautiously approaches.

During starlight, when there is no moon, the punter shoots directly he is able to distinguish the birds, for they cannot be seen out of range on such nights; the punter has, therefore, to use extra vigilance and discretion in the nightly diversion under any but a moonlight sky.

Colonel Hawker speaks of bright starlight as 'best of all' for punting; but my own experience teaches me differently. Stars alone do not give sufficient light; and it is only by the merest chance that the punter is enabled to make a good shot by such light. I am, therefore, disposed to prefer moonlight, and the brighter the moon, in my opinion, the better is the punter's chance, especially with a gentle breeze sufficient to ripple the deep water.

Another opportunity for night-punting is at the 'ground-ebb'—*i.e.* just as the tide is leaving the mud, when the shallow water looks white in the breeze, whilst the deep is dark. But, as a rule, it is not a wise plan to go on a punting excursion by night on an ebb-tide. There is so much risk of being left on the mud by the receding waters, that, unless the punter is uncommonly well acquainted with the creeks and channels of the locality, he will wish himself at home. However easy it may be to step out of the punt and launch it a few yards over the mud, it is no easy or pleasant task to have to launch a distance of a hundred yards or more, which will sometimes be found necessary, on the least act of carelessness or negligence on the part of the punter.

Another disadvantage attending night-punting on the ground-ebb is, that the drain of water sets from the ooze, and against the punter, as he proceeds to work up to birds on the mud; whilst it is just the contrary on the white water of a flood-tide, which helps the punt along with considerable sway, and when by the aid of the paddles the punter is quickly upon the birds.

It is sometimes desirable to lie in ambush, at night with punt and gun; and this may happen when wild-ducks are heard near by, and a small stream of fresh water is known to flow into the salt water in. that particular locality; when by proceeding, with the punt, early in the evening, to the mouth of the stream, and getting as much in the loom or shade of the land as possible, and waiting the flow of tide, a very profitable shot may often be made.

Wild-ducks are particularly fond of these freshwater

rivulets, and generally contrive to find them out, be they ever so few and far between. On these occasions, as on almost every other, the midnight punter should shoot *from* the shore, and, if possible, always avoid shooting *inland*.

When it so happens, as it will occasionally, that, from the cloudy state of the atmosphere, it becomes difficult to adhere firmly to the rules as to punting towards the light of the moon, because of the uncertainty of its rays, occasioned by passing clouds, or, it may be, the wind is blowing from an unfavourable quarter; the punter should then, on such occasions, look around him, and choose the best loom or background he can, wherefrom to advance. If there be a shade from the land or a tall tree, he should directly make for it, and advance to the birds from that position; or, in the absence of a cast of shade from land or tree, a dark cloud will be the best and only remaining substitute. The punter should bear in mind never to advance upon birds from a light into a shady position, because it is invariably useless, as they are thereby enabled to discern his punt and all his movements long before he can see them.

When setting up to birds at night, the punter should carefully attend to their noises; for he may be sure they do not suspect him whilst they continue 'in charm;' but the instant they are silent he should be very guarded, and rest awhile on his paddles, when, if all be quiet, they will probably 'open concert' again. Whenever the birds are suddenly silent as the punter approaches, he may be sure they have detected the movements of an enemy, and are suspecting his designs.

It is very rarely that wild-fowl move about much at night. When once settled at their feeding-places, if undisturbed, they generally remain there till daylight next morning.

On calm nights, the punter, as he approaches them, will frequently hear most distinctly the clatter of the wild-ducks' bills whilst busily feeding and dabbling in the water, and this may sometimes be heard at a distance of eighty yards and upwards. The clatter cannot be mistaken for any other sound by anyone who has ever listened to it attentively. When the noise is very distinctly heard, the sportsman may generally conclude he is close enough to fire; but it is advisable to take other circumstances into consideration before pulling trigger, and always to be *quite sure* that the moving objects he is about to shoot at are assuredly birds.

In a work of this kind, whilst describing the pleasures of any particular branch of our sport, it is necessary to make special allusion to the perils; the young punter is, therefore, *most earnestly* cautioned against the dangers of going out of sight of his punt at night, whenever it becomes desirable to traverse the ooze in splashers, or otherwise in pursuit of winged birds. Unless bright moonlight, it is better to pick up those only which are killed, or so severely wounded as to be unable to flutter away; the slightly wounded birds he had better leave until the tide sets them afloat, so that he can row after them; or he had best abandon them altogether. At any rate, he should always avoid wandering on the ooze at night, far away from the punt, because of the great difficulty of finding the way back, and the danger of becoming bewildered, when the tide may flow so rapidly round the punt that it cannot be safely regained; and then the consequences to the punter are fearful to contemplate, as, unless help be at hand, his fate would seem to be inevitable.[1]

The punter should remember that time goes fleetly when he is ardently pursuing winged birds on the ooze, and, in his eagerness to recover them, he must not risk his personal safety; for the tide admits of no delay, and sometimes proves a subtle and overwhelming foe.

Another danger which attends the punter who walks the ooze at night is, the risk of encountering holes and rotten places, which abound in some oozes and savannas, and over which it is unsafe to walk even by daylight, though in splashers, the soil being so soft that it will scarcely bear a duck. The perils of venturing over such ground have already been referred to in a previous chapter.

It is useless to go on a punting excursion on rough windy nights; for, if the moon be ever so bright, the birds cannot be seen until close upon them, because of the ripples upon the water. The more successful proceeding, on a windy, moonlight night, would be to go in a small sailing boat with a swivel gun.

---

[1] See the engraving 'Anxious Moments,' which faces p. 166.

[1] Glantvilla.

[1] It is but a few years ago since two unfortunate youths lost their lives in this way, at Brightlingsea, in Essex. They had anchored their boat by the bank-side of the ooze, and, having provided themselves with splashers, which they lashed to their feet in the usual manner, proceeded to their calling—that of collecting periwinkles, when they wandered a long distance from their boat, and, a fog coming on, they became quite bewildered: after wading and groping about several hours in most painful alarm, endeavouring to find their boat, but without success, they cried in vain for help, which unfortunately was not at hand; but their heartrending cries were heard at a long distance. The feelings of the poor boys can be better imagined than described, as grim death was constantly before them, and gradually drawing nearer and

nearer, in the hideous form of an ugly tide, rapidly encircling their bodies, rising higher and higher towards their heads, and finally swallowing them up, and launching them into eternity. The poor boys were both drowned before a boat could approach them. A more appalling or more horrible death can scarcely be imagined.

CHAPTER XXVIII

NIGHT-PUNTING—continued.

'Now when the stars

Slowly decrease, and the faint glimm'ring light
First trembles in the east, we hasten forth
To seek the rushing river's wandering wave;
The doubtful gloom shall favour our approach.'

Fowling: A Poem, book v. p. 137.

NIGHT-PUNTING, when once well learnt, is the most satisfactory of any branch of the sport. When wind, tide, and moon are favourable to the pursuit, and there are wild-fowl on the waters, an experienced punter is invariably more or less successful.

There is no time of night or day more suitable for punting than the first hour of daybreak. The punter should proceed to the most favoured haunts of the birds some little while beforehand; and soon as the first day dawn appears, he may cautiously move his punt ahead by the back strokes of his oars, going directly in face of the dawn, when, from the light thrown upon the water by the opening sky, he will the more readily detect any birds which may be upon the water, though a long distance ahead; and, being in the shade himself, golden opportunities frequently occur, whereby to repay the early riser for his energy and perseverance.

During severe frost, the midnight punter will find no lack of sport in saltwater bays and rivers. Wild-fowl are compelled to seek their food in the saline feeding-grounds at such a time; and widgeon and duck, for the most part, stay all night in such places rather than take their flight inland, where nought but hard ground, ice, and disappointment await them.

The midnight sportsman must be equally watchful with his ears by night as with his eyes by day; indeed, he will require the best services of both those organs during moonlight; for it would be a useless night excursion to sit with the back in the direction from which sport is anticipated, to say nothing of the inconvenience of constantly turning round to see if there be anything ahead. The motion of both man and boat is too often discovered by the birds long before the sportsman is aware they are in sight; and he could scarcely expect to find wildfowl in the aft-track of his boat, although there may be chances of such both to the right and left.

The engraving opposite will convey to the reader a notion of the art of night-punting, with the manner of approaching wild-fowl by moonlight. The two punters, it will be observed, are advancing with the birds in full view, whilst the men in the punts are in the loom, and consequently not seen or suspected by the hundreds of widgeon which are busily engaged feeding in the white water on the brink of the ooze. The punters are approaching steadily, cautiously, and with apparently exquisite precision, and probably each reckoning on the numbers that will fall to his lot. Such are 'anxious moments 'to the punter, because, in the event of any unexpected noise, as the report of a gun at a distance, the bark of a dog, or other alarm, the whole 'company 'would instantly take flight, and the punter's chances would then be gone.

———'Now is the time!

Closer they join, nor will the glowing light
Admit of more delay.'

It is altogether a useless attempt to punt at wild-fowl on moonlight nights in any other position than that already explained. The moon must be 'bearing on;' that is, shining either directly or crosswise towards the punter's face when he lies down to paddle towards them; and until he thoroughly understands this most essential part of the proceedings attending night-punting he had better remain at home, for the perils of proceeding in an opposite direction may be serious.

The danger alluded to cannot be more truthfully exhibited to the reader than by narrating to him one of the most perilous and providential escapes ever recorded in the annals of punting, which will remain indelibly impressed upon the author's memory as long as he lives, as it will also, probably, upon the memories of all concerned in it.

It was a bright, moonlight night, fine and frosty, and as calm and inviting as any wild-fowler could desire—a night such as to be resisted by no lover of the sport; when I ventured, as I was frequently in the habit of doing, clown a certain river on the eastern coast, famous for its thousands of wild-fowl in hard winters. I had proceeded about a mile in my punt, with large gun, loaded, capped, and ready for action, and was watching, listening, and anxiously waiting a chance for discharging the contents of the barrel, when I suddenly encountered two fellow-punters, both of whom were personally known to me; and as they appeared to be bound for the same bay as myself it was suggested that it would be better for the whole three to keep together and shoot in company, sharing the result of good or ill success, as is usual on such occasions. After reconnoitring' in and about the bay some little time, the widgeon's familiar note 'whe-oh,' 'wheow' was distinctly heard, and we proceeded cautiously to the shade of a grove near by, in which position a loom was obtained, whence we proposed to advance in trio upon the birds. Having thus carefully taken up our positions, we lay down in the punts and commenced 'setting' in the direction of the sound before mentioned, when, clouds passing at the time, the moon became partially obscured, and the light on the water was less bright. Still we cautiously proceeded, I in the middle punt, and my companions one on each side. Nearer and nearer we seemed to be drawing to the sound, when suddenly, upon the water about a hundred and fifty yards in front of us, a dark object was descried, which was at once supposed to be the very objects of our pursuit, a company of widgeon, and therefore we gradually drew towards them: my companions having invested in me the honour of giving the signal to fire, as we were now apparently within range, they began to grow impatient to pull trigger, but, as we approached I began to suspect the dark object was not in reality a company of widgeon at all. One of the men whispered that we ought to fire; I replied, 'No, not yet. I should like to see the birds separate a little; they appear all in lump, and I am not sure that they are birds at all.'

Anxious Moments

331

'But I am certain they are, though,' replied one of the men; 'don't you hear the noise they are making?'

A few seconds elapsed, and one of my companions grew more and more impatient, suggesting that we were getting too close, and unless we shot directly they would fly. I was that instant about to give the signal, 'Ready!' 'fire!' when the moon peeped from behind the clouds, and suddenly a veil was lifted, as if by some guardian angel, which enabled me instantly to distinguish that the object at which we had been punting, and at which my companions had been so eager to shoot, was not a company of widgeon, but *a man in a punt!* The moment the discovery was made, one of the men rose to his knees and warned us not to fire, at the same time calling out, 'Good heavens! man, who are you? Had the moon remained behind those clouds but another instant, you would have been blown to atoms!'

We then pulled alongside the strange punt, and found it contained no other than a young clergyman from a neighbouring village, who, having been disappointed of success in his daylight excursions, had chosen a moonlight night for his diversion, in the hope of meeting with better success. The reverend sportsman was unacquainted with the ordinary regulations of night-punting, consequently was pursuing the sound of the birds in a wrong direction, by which he exposed himself to great danger, without the chance of obtaining a shot, and, in consequence, was probably nearer being blown suddenly into eternity than ever before in his life. It was truly a most providential escape; and though we were all heartily thankful for having reserved our fire, we severely and unsparingly reprimanded him for venturing on midnight punting before being properly instructed in the art. On hearing of the imminent peril from which he had just emerged, he appeared to feel sincerely grateful for his providential escape, which probably formed a subject of deep reflection for him on returning home, if it did not also give him a useful hint in preparing his sermon for the ensuing Sunday. The danger he actually escaped may be somewhat imagined by the reader when informed that three punt-guns, each carrying half-a-pound and upwards of shot, primed, capped, and cocked, had been bearing fully upon him for several minutes, and latterly at no greater distance than fifty or sixty yards; and which, but for the favoured light of the moon at that perilous instant, would all have been discharged point-blank at him, the consequences of which are fearful to contemplate. We ourselves were exposed to the risk of *his* fire—had we not discovered him as we did—punting as he was directly in-shore, instead of out-shore; it would, on such a night, have been impossible to have seen a punt under the shade of the land. As a proof of this, here were three experienced punters working out-shore, with the moon 'full on,' as it is termed, and yet mistaking a man and punt for a company of widgeon;

but who would think of finding anyone so rash as to proceed in a way directly contrary to the rules of night-punting? This was probably what put my companions so completely off their guard, and made them think the dark object could be nothing else than a company of wild-fowl, consequently they were eager to shoot and secure as many as they could.[1]

It is very desirable that punters, on going out in dark nights, should hold a consultation before embarking, and each decide on the particular locality he will proceed to, by which means many accidents might be avoided.

One or two instances have come under my notice in which night-puntmen have felt so jealous of a 'gentleman gunner,' as they term him, as to endeavour to frighten him from pursuing his sport at night, by pretending that he was going in a wrong direction at the birds, and was in danger of being shot. But such tricks are easily detected by anyone understanding the pursuit, and the jealous feeling of those who would gladly persuade him to keep at home at night, that they may have the better chance of success themselves, cannot always be concealed.

A tyro desirous of learning the mysteries of night-punting should go out frequently in company with an experienced hand, though it may be difficult sometimes to find one who would undertake to instruct a novice. But the sight and offer of silver are sometimes irresistible with native punters, who pursue the sport as a means of maintenance. When once night-punting is properly understood, there is no fear of incurring risk on a moonlight night; but the oldest and best of punt men. amongst others, incur more or less risk of another's fire on dark and cloudy nights: and if the ardent wild-fowler value his life and limbs, he will not grope about on dark nights in pursuit of his sport.

There can be no doubt but night-punting is an extremely hazardous undertaking to the uninitiated. I remember many years ago two accidents occurring in one season on the same river, and to men living in the same parish. It was a very severe winter and there were abundance of wild-fowl; the inviting prospects of sport had induced several inexperienced individuals to provide themselves with punts and guns; and so long as they confined their operations to the sport by daylight all was well, but on venturing upon night-punting without having first been out with those familiar with the sport, two serious accidents occurred within a few weeks of each other.

One man, a shoemaker, who would have done far wiser to have 'stuck to his last,' was groping about on a cloudy night amidst a number of widgeon, whose constant 'whe-oh!' 'wheow!' so bewildered him, that he knew not in which direction to pursue them until a dark moving object attracted his attention, which he immediately supposed to he the identical company of birds from which the noise proceeded;

and not imagining for one moment that it could be anything else, he levelled his punt-gun and deliberately pulled the trigger! At the same instant, the shrieks of a man in the point-blank direction of his gun convinced him he had been mistaken in supposing the dark moving object to have been a knob of widgeon, and, on pulling alongside, found his unfortunate victim, an experienced punt-man, in great agony, with three shots in his wrist and arm.

Fortunately the sufferer's punt was of rather thicker material than the ordinary class of gunning-punts, and the shot had not penetrated quite through the side-planks. The punter had, the moment before, been setting up to some widgeon, and it was whilst in the very act that the shoemaker fired the luckless shot. Had the sufferer's head or any part of his body been above the sides of the punt, there is little doubt but the shot would have proved fatal. Enough mischief had, however, been done to the arm and wrist to deprive him of its use during a period extending over many months.

The other accident occurred a few weeks later, under precisely similar circumstances, except that the two performers were both inexperienced, and were punting one at the other, muzzle to muzzle, each supposing the other to be a little knob of wild-fowl. One man fired, and luckily but *one* grain of shot took effect, though that a most lamentable and ill-fated one— it entered the other's right eye, and forever closed it. During several subsequent weeks it was feared he would die, until a skilful surgeon succeeded in extracting the shot; the man's life was saved, but the eye entirely lost.

These are facts which have come under my own immediate observation; let them act as warnings to those who may have a relish for the infatuating sport of night-punting not to venture until thoroughly instructed in the art, and never to shoot until *quite* certain the object aimed at is in *reality* a species of the feathered tribe.

Since the publication of the last edition of this work, a punter named Ward was tried and convicted at the Suffolk Assizes, 1871, before Cockburn, Lord Chief Justice, of unlawfully and maliciously wounding a fellow-punter named Chatten.

It appeared that Ward, the prisoner, and Chatten, the prosecutor, were fishermen, and both were in the habit of going out in punts to shoot wild-fowl in a creek on the river Aide, in Suffolk. The prosecutor was lying with his face downwards in the punt, extending his arms over the sides, and propelling the boat with a pair of short paddles, so as to avoid as much as possible being seen by the birds on the water. On the evening in question, in the month of January, the prosecutor had been out in this way, but finding no birds about, he determined to return; and having put out his arm, was using one of the paddles to slew the punt round, when he heard the report of a gun, and at the same moment was struck by shots in the arm and eye, the effect of which was seriously to injure his arm, and so to damage his eye as to render its total extraction necessary a few days after. The night was light and no birds were about, and it was proved at the trial that the prisoner was jealous of persons pursuing wild-fowl at that spot, and had threatened to shoot, though persons might be between him and the birds; the suggestion of the prosecution being, that the prisoner intended to disable the prosecutor. On the other hand, it was proved that the prisoner had at once come forward to say that he had fired the shot, and that the prosecutor would not have been hit if he had not suddenly turned round, and he was proved to be on good terms with the prosecutor, and was given a high character for humanity and good conduct, and it was urged that it was accidental, or at most that he had only intended to frighten the prosecutor. The Chief Justice, leaving the question of intent to the jury, told them that on the latter hypothesis they might find the prisoner guilty of unlawfully wounding. The jury so found, and, on a case being stated for the opinion of the Court for Crown Cases reserved, the conviction was affirmed.[1]

¹ The substance of this adventure was first published by the author, as a warning to wild-fowl shooters, in the 'Sporting Review,' vol. xxxv. 1856.

¹ The Queen *v.* Ward, 41 L. J. M. C. 69; S. C. 36 J. P. 453.

CHAPTER XXIX

WILD-FOWL SHOOTING IN SCOTLAND

'The air was clirkifc with the fowlis
    That cam with yammeris and with yowlis,
    With shrykking, screeking, skrymming scowlis,
    And meikle noyis and showtes.'—DUNBAR.

WILD-FOWL shooting, in many of its branches, may be abundantly enjoyed in various parts of the Highlands of Scotland and about the coast, bays, and rivers of that interesting country. The sailor sportsman will find ample use for his stanchion-gun, the punter for his less ponderous artillery, and the pedestrian sportsman, with dog and shoulder gun, may sometimes meet with as good sport of the kind there as in England. Wild-fowl always prefer the nether to the mountainous countries; but from the more northerly position of Scotland, and the attractions her bays, lochs, and lakes, there are generally plenty of wild-fowl in that country, particularly during mild seasons.

Numbers of wild-fowl are annually bred in many of the Scottish lakes, more especially those which communicate with the sea, and are interspersed with small islands and impenetrable beds of swamps and rushes.

Loch Lomond has long been famed as a favourite resort of wild-fowl of every variety: the advantages offered by the Peat Island render that locality one of the strongholds of water-fowl, flat and extensive as if is, and abounding with morasses, among which wild-fowl love to dwell, whilst the quietude and wild character of the spot tend to invite the repose of migratory fowl as they pass over from northern countries. In many parts of the island alluded to the water is shallow, and with grassy margins and muddy bottom it offers to water-fowl the fairest indulgence with abundance of food. But, notwithstanding such advantages, punting is but little practised in the immediate locality of the lakes and lochs, the comparative smallness of the numbers of birds with those which visit the sea-coast and shores of the island, combined with the inaccessible nature of the locality, being always considered obstacles to the successful issue of such a diversion.

The Cromarty Frith, the Tay, and a few other places on both sides of the coast, are, however, much frequented by wildfowl of every variety, and are well known as favourite districts for wild-fowl shooting, and affording every facility for punting and shooting with the sailing yacht. The more general method of wild-fowl shooting among the lakes and lochs of Scotland is, by stalking the birds from some temporary ambuscade, which may generally be found among the rocks and cliffs of the Scottish waters. In some parts a hut is erected on a raft, and moored within range of their haunts, in which the sportsman hides and shoots the birds when they alight upon the water.

A high-couraged and well-trained retriever is always a necessary companion to the sportsman who pursues this diversion under such circumstances.

If authority were wanting in support of our own experience as to the abundance of wild-fowl in the sea-lochs as also in the fresh-water lakes of Scotland, we could not refer to higher than that of Mr. St. John, from whose well-known and interesting works it is perfectly clear that wild-fowl in every variety are abundant in Scotland, and that excellent shooting may be had in those parts.[1] Moreover, the birds arrive there earlier than in England.

Waders also are found in great plenty around and about most of the bays and lochs. Brent-geese, however, are not partial to Scotland, though sometimes pretty numerous in some parts. Large companies of widgeon may sometimes be seen day after day in the same waters, and though they might be easily approached with a punt and large gun, they are not nearly so often disturbed by such artillery as in English waters. The sport is pursued chiefly by stalking them from behind rocks and projecting cliffs in the daytime, and by flight-shooting in the evening.

The flight-shooting in Scotland is remarkably good, particularly when the birds are plentiful at sea, There, as in England, they come inland at twilight to the fields and meadows to feed; not in large flights, but in little trips of from three or four to a dozen or more. Mr. St. John says he considers the Loch of Spynie (a fresh-water lake and private property) to be about the best loch in the north for wild-fowl shooting, but strictly preserved. Its situation is excellent; and being for the most part shallow, and covered with grass, rushes, and tall reeds, it is well adapted for sheltering and feeding all sorts of wild-fowl, which resort there in incredible numbers, and of every kind from the swan to the teal. And he says the widgeon in this loch are remarkably fine, and more abundant than any other wild-fowl.[2]

---

[1] See Mr. St. John's works, 'Wild Sports and Natural History of the Highlands,' 1846; 'A Tour in Sutherlandshire,' 1849; 'Natural History and Sport in Moray,' 1863.

[2] 'A Tour in Sutherlandshire.' By Charles St. John, Esq. 1849.

CHAPTER XXX

WILD-GOOSE SHOOTING

'In this late dearth of wit, when Jose and Jack
Were hunger-hit for want of fowl and sack,
His noblenesse found out this happy meanes
To mend their dyet with these wild-goose scenes.'

Epigram on Wild-goose Chase.

THE subject of wild-goose shooting has already been partially discussed in this treatise, under the different heads of punting; and it will also be generally treated under the title, 'Wild-fowl Shooting under Sail;' but there are many incidents connected with the sport which require special notice under distinct heads, to which the attention of the sporting tyro is invited before he ventures on this attractive branch of our diversion.

In former days wild-goose shooting was held in higher estimation than the pursuit of any other species of water-fowl, apparently for the quaint and logical reasons stated below.[1]

The BRENT GOOSE (*Anser Brenta*) is the smallest, most abundant, and most delicate for the table, of the whole species of wild-geese. It is more familiarly known in some districts on the English coast as the 'black-goose,' and it affords the fairest sport of any of its tribe. The large gaggles of brentgeese which in severe winters are sometimes seen off the east and south-east coasts of this country are truly astonishing. In some parts of France and Ireland they are also in some seasons very numerous off various parts of those coasts. They are also abundant in Hudson's Bay, Greenland, Spitzbergen, and other northern countries,[2] whither they resort in their migrations: 'Simili anseres quoque olores ratione commeant sed horum volatus cernitur.'[3]

But notwithstanding that they are generally more numerous on some parts of the eastern coast of England than elsewhere, they are not partial to the North Sea, and are seldom seen in such numbers on the coast north of Essex as on that and more southern parts.

Be the winter mild or severe, there are always some of the species about the south-eastern coast; and in very severe winters they assemble in countless numbers, making a trumpet-like noise as they fly through the air, which, when heard at a distance, resembles the deep tone of a pack of harriers in full cry.

The brent-goose differs from the ordinary grey-lag, and several other of the goose species, as regards its habits, in some important particulars, inasmuch as it never feeds on fresh-water herbage, nor flies far inland, nor alights in fresh-water;

but its tastes are exclusively salmons. The brent-goose never resorts to green fields nor meadows, though it is occasionally met with in salt-marshes, which are watered by every tide. The favourite haunts and feeding-grounds of brent-geese are the muddy flats and green oozes of large saline rivers, salt-water lakes, and sheltered bays, to which they resort as soon as the receding tide leaves them a resting-place for their feet. They generally take their stand on that part of the ooze which is most open and unapproachable by creeks or rills; and there, if undisturbed, they feed greedily until the next tide fairly lifts them from their legs, when, if by daylight, they fly out to sea beyond the coast, except in very rough weather, at which time they seek for shelter in the rivers and inland arms of the sea.

Brent-geese are eagerly pursued by the wild-fowl shooter with yacht and swivel-gun; they also afford splendid sport to the punter. They are generally very wary; though sometimes, and on certain occasions, they are quite the reverse, and may be approached without difficulty. We allude more especially to their habits just before a storm or gale,[1] when instinct seems to warn them to make the best of their time; for on such occasions a whole gaggle may frequently be surprised by the wild-fowler, who finds half the number with their heads under their wings. And the same *after* a gale, particularly if it has lasted two or three days without intermission: they then become so hungry, that when feeding they may be easily approached under ordinary precautions, and after their appetites are appeased they are so glad of rest, that a still better opportunity generally awaits the punter.

The best means of pursuing wild-geese, and that which affords the finest sport, is by the shooting-yacht or sailing-boat, with stanchion-gun. But as that sport will be fully treated of in subsequent pages under those heads, it is unnecessary to enter upon them here.

Black-geese are well worthy of pursuit, and, in the opinion of most epicures, are the finest flavoured wild-fowl that is brought to table. They have a thick coating of feathers, and require hard-hitting to bring them clown. The winged and wounded offer excellent chances to young sportsmen with shoulder-guns; but a more amusing chase can be had by pursuing them in a small boat: this is called the 'cripple chase,' of which we shall speak presently more at large.

During a strong wind and spring tide they are seldom to be approached; at such times they sit more dispersed about the water, and in a more sunken form of attitude; they are then more vigilant than at other times. When the weather is very rough they seek a refuge within harbour, though always reluctant to do so; taking care to quit it before nightfall, and to betake themselves to the stormy sea rather than abide in inland waters at night.

The punter's best chances at brent-geese are just before sunset; then, if they are feeding on the ooze, and it so happens that there is sufficient water for the punter to get at them, he may, with skill, be almost sure of a shot: they feed very greedily about that time, apparently anxious to fill their crops before taking their flight out to sea. An opportunity of the kind is termed by the local puntmen taking a shot when they are all 'a-guzzle.'

Another very favourable opportunity for obtaining a shot with the punt-gun at brent-geese is just at the *ground-ebb*, when they are eagerly seeking their food on the first portion of ooze that may be uncovered by the receding tide. The punter should make up to them briskly, but with extreme caution in all his movements, as they are always watchful, and their suspicions soon aroused.

Wounded black-geese are sometimes difficult to capture, and lead their pursuers a spirited chase. When wounded they make for the tideway or the heaviest sea that is near by; they dive boldly at first, but eventually become exhausted, and resign themselves to fate after being closely pursued.[1]

Brent-geese also afford good sport to the coast or shore-gunner, especially in thick weather, when they always fly low in the air, and appear bewildered, sometimes coming close to the land. The sportsman should conceal himself behind some embankment, temporary or otherwise; and in the absence of such, or a screen of any sort to protect him from view, he should lie down upon his back on the beach, keeping himself perfectly still, when in all probability the whole gaggle may come within easy range, mistaking his live carcase for a bundle of sea-weed: he should then rise suddenly to his legs, when they will immediately turn, and, in their haste to avoid the human form, present him a chance of killing two or three pair at a shot; but he will find some difficulty in recovering those which are not killed; for when pursued by a dog black-geese dive and elude him, and it must be a clever animal to catch a winged goose in deep water. When the weather is very windy they fly low, and hover about the coast in large gaggles, frequently passing within fair shot of the beach-gunner. They appear to observe strict discipline in their order of flight, sometimes flying in a breast-like line, with all the regularity of a troop of soldiers in marching order, at other times they fly in angular lines; but there is not generally so much regularity in large gaggles as small ones. They are known when on the wing by their black-looking bodies and white rumps.

Latham mentions that wild-geese are sometimes attacked by falcons, when, notwithstanding the rapacity and spirit of the bird of prey, the wild-goose generally comes off victoriously.[1]

Pliny also alludes to the attack upon large water-fowl by rapacious birds, and states that, after seizing upon their prey, they are sometimes not able to wield it, but are drawn under water by the aquatic fowl, and so drowned.[2]

———————

[1] 'What prayse soeuer is geuon to shooting, the goose may challenge the best part in it. How well doth she make a man fare at his table: Howeasely doth she make a man lye in his bed: How fitte euen as her fethers be only for shooting, so be her quilles fit only for wryting.'—*Toxophilvs* (*back letter*). By Eoger Ascham. 1589.

[2] Sir Leopold McClintock mentions that he shot some brent-geese in Levesquo Harbour, Bellot Straits.—' Narrative of the Fate of Sir John Franklin,' p. 184. By Captain McClintock, E.N. 1859.

[3] Pliny, lib. x. cap. xxiii.

[1] 'When they do make a gaggling in the air more than usual, or seem to tight, being over-greedy at their meat, expect then cold and winterly weather.'—*Wills-ford's Nature's Secrets*.

[1] Pennant says brent-geese 'cannot dive' (*vide* 'Arctic Zoology,' vol. ii.p. 552), an error which I am very much surprised to find made by that author; but probably he was more of a naturalist than a sportsman. I would fain say *I wish they could not dive;* if it were so I should have been spared many a half-hour's trying cripple chase in pursuit of them.

[1] 'While these hawks here mentioned be remaining with us in the heart of England, they doe prey upon divers and sundry sorts of fowls, as brants (brentgeese), wild-geese, &c.; but they are, especially the passenger-soar-falcons or the young hawgards, of great metal and spirit that, for want of understanding their own harme, doe venture upon such unwealdy prey, who, notwithstanding, will afterwards learn to know their own error, and, by being brusht and bearen by those shrewd opponents, will desist, and leave oif to meddle with them any more.'—*Latham's Falconry*, A.D. 1658.

[2] 'Sæpe et aquilæ ipsse non tolerantes pondus ad prehensum una mergnntur.'—*Lib*. x. cap. iii.

CHAPTER XXXI

THE GREY-LAG GOOSE

*(*Anser palustris.*)*

'But, for the water-fowl the air's too dry;
The geese find out there's no grass in the sky,
And say a common's needful for their health.'

Translation from ARISTOPHANES.

THIS species is said to be the origin of the tame goose, which, truly, it very much resembles. It also claims to be the veritable species which saved the Capitol: and according to Ovid, tame-geese, which were probably a species of the grey-lag, were sometimes kept as house-dogs by the ancient cottagers.[1]

The grey-lag is the largest of the wild-goose species which visits our shores. It is seldom seen in company with any other than those of its own species—-though a solitary grey-lag is only to be met with when wounded.

The grey-lag goose is very strong on the wing, and, notwithstanding its heavy body, flies at a rapid rate. When moving about the coast, up rivers, and in bays, its flight is low;

but when flying over land, or on a migratory tour, it flies very high. In severe winters they visit our shores in large gaggles; but if the season continues very mild, they do not come so far south.

On first arriving in strange waters, they are generally so tame that there is no difficulty in obtaining access to them with punt and gun; but they afterwards become extremely shy, and the utmost skill of the sportsman in attempting to approach them is sometimes unavailing. When first driven by a stormy sea to seek shelter inland, they select some large salt-water river or sheltered bay; and when a party of grey-geese have found temporary security in such waters, they frequently use it the whole winter season, returning at different intervals during every day; if it be an extensive plain of ooze, they often spend the whole day there, and as soon as the customary hour of evening flight arrives they soar high in the air and fly many miles inland, in search of green fields and meadows; and when once good feeding, in a safe retreat, has been discovered, they use it nightly, if undisturbed.

When on a long flight they are generally sufficiently high in the air to be out of the range of an ordinary gun; but a good marksman may sometimes bring one down with a rifle. Their movements are very interesting, flying always in catenarian order, as if linked together, and hanging by the same thread— sometimes in one figure and sometimes in another. The most general one is wedge-like or angular, with one bird as a leader, the others forming in two perfect lines, following just as if fixed on a string. When changing their course in the air or their leader, they seem to endeavour as much as possible to preserve intact the apparent connecting link of their party. And thus, wedge-like, by little and little they spread broader and broader behind, bearing a great length besides with them, by which means also they gather more wind to bear them up and urge them forward.[1]

They often alight, just before dusk, in fields of green wheat, on the blades of which they feed with much relish, always taking up their position in the most central part of the field, and seldom within range of an ordinary shoulder-gun. But they are not always secure in their rural position on the farmers fields; indeed, most farmers in the flat counties are familiar with the habits of grey-geese, and often contrive, on being honoured with a visit by those birds, to stalk and kill one or more of the gaggle with a small shoulder-piece. Cunning sportsmen have sometimes stopped six or eight of these noble birds at a shot, when a gaggle has been unsuspectingly busy feeding in open fields or meadows.

Whilst feeding in small fields they are generally perfectly mute; but when disturbed, their cackling is exceedingly loud and noisy: their note is a clangulous sort of call, sounding like 'haunk! hawnc!'

They are also particularly fond of frequenting flooded moors and large water-meadows; indeed, they spend the greater part of their time at such places, more especially by night. In such positions it is very difficult to get at them; and it is seldom they are killed in open countries. But if a place of concealment can be made, or found, near their haunts, or in the line of their flight on leaving the moor, the sportsman may be sure of success. They present so large a mark that it is very easy to bring them down when within range; and their flight, on first taking wing, is but a few feet above the ground: they have not sufficient power of wing to ascend in any other manner, but are obliged to proceed over some considerable space before rising high in the air.

I have sometimes found, after a heavy gale from the east, and when snow and sleet have accompanied it, that among the thousands of wild-fowl of numerous varieties which have been driven for shelter to the inland waters, none of the birds would sit the punter so well as the grey-geese; and though large numbers of duck and widgeon may have been sitting near them on the ooze, and taken alarm before the fowler could approach, the grey-geese have unconcernedly maintained their position and received the charge.

A young grey-goose makes a very delicious dish for the table, and the old birds are pretty good eating, but not to be compared with brent-geese.

Grey-geese are often to be met with off the sea-coast by daylight, when they offer fair chances to the yachter who happens to be equipped with a swivel-gun. But they always fly to the inland feeding haunts at or before twilight, where they remain until next morning. In some seasons they arrive in the western part of Scotland and in the neighbourhood of the Cromarty Frith as early as August, and visit the farmer's oat-fields in those parts, when, if not disturbed, they sometimes remain there the greater part of the day, doing much mischief to the crop. They also breed in the wilds of Sutherlandshire.[1]

The grey-lag has very wide geographical range: it summers as far north as Iceland, and is found in more or less abundance in various parts of Europe, Asia, Africa, and America.

----

[1] 'Unicus anser erat minima custodia villæ.'

[1] 'A tergo sensim dilatante se cuneo porrigitur agmen largeque impellenti præbetur anræ.'—*Pliny*, lib. x. cap. 23. And *vide ante*—'The flight of wild-fowl,' chapter xx.

[1] 'A Tour in Sutherlandshire.' By Charles St. John, Esq.

CHAPTER XXXII

THE BERNICLE GOOSE

*(*Anser Bernicla.*)*

'The   Scottish   barnacle,   if   I   might   choose,
That of a worme doth waxe a winged goose.'

HALL'S *Virgidemiarum.*

'Like   your   Scotch   barnacle—now   a   block,
  Instantly a worm, and presently a great goose.'—
MARSTON.

> 'The barnacles with them, which
> wheresoe'er they breed—
>   On trees, or rotten ships—yet to my fens
> for feed
>   Continually they come, and chief abode
> do make,
>   And very hardly forc'd my plenty to
> forsake.'—DRAYTON.

THESE birds were formerly much more numerous on the coast than they are now; they used to be met with on the plains and savannas of most of the northern counties bordering on both the eastern and western coasts of England, and on the western coast of Ireland they were very abundant. They spend their days at sea, near sandy shores and banks, and their nights inland, on fens and moors, as is the habit with some other of the wild goose species.[1] They visit us in greater or less numbers, according to the season. Bernicle geese have powerful means of flight, and keep together in line in the air, after the manner of other wild-geese. Different to the grey-lag in some respects, they are very sociable in their habits, both among their own and other species.

The sportsman, however, will find them shy and difficult of access. The best and most successful means of approaching them is under sail, when they may, with large shot, be killed at a considerable distance if fired at on the wing, and it is not very often that a sitting shot will be obtained at a gaggle of barnacles.

A ridiculous notion once prevailed that this bird was not produced from an egg, but from a shell or crustaceum which grew on wood long immersed in salt water, and that the gosling was hatched from this shell without the warmth of the parent bird's body setting upon it. This ignorant delusion arose from the circumstance that these birds are frequently seen at sea swimming near and among pieces of decayed wood covered with barnacles, containing downy or fringed spawn of fish, which were fabulously supposed to be goslings. Another notion was prevalent to the effect that they grew on trees, and were hatched by the warmth of the sun. In the 'Cosmographe and description of Albion,' prefixed to the history and chronicles of Scotland of Hector Boece, the author takes pains to contradict an assertion as to 'claik geis' (barnacle geese) growing on trees, and then proceeds with a lengthened statement, to the effect that he has sailed through the seas where these birds are bred, and finds, by 'gret experience,' that 'the nature of the seis is mair relevant cans of thair procreationn than ony uthir thing.' He then goes on to state that trees being cast into the sea, in process of time become worm-eaten,' and in the small boris and hollis thereof growis small wormis; first thay schaw their heid and feit, and last of all thay schaw their plumis and wingis; finaly, quwhen thay ar cumin to the just mesure and quantite of geis, thay fle in the aire as othir fowlis dois.' We quote from the translation of old Bellenden.

According to ancient tradition, which is asserted to have been notably proved in the year 1490, in the presence of many people at the castle of Petslego, a large tree was said to have been brought by alluvion and flux of the sea to land; and on dividing it with a saw there appeared 'a multitude of worms thrawing thaim self out of sindry hollis of this tre. Sum of thaim war rude, as they war hot new schapin; sum had baith heid, feit, and wingis, hot they had na fedderis; sum of thaim war perfit schapin fowlis.'

The chronicles alluded to also record the circumstance of other trees being washed ashore, and found to be covered with goslings; also of a ship which had lain four years at anchor, and on being brought to Leith and examined, all the planks were worm-eaten, 'and the hollis thairof full of geis.'

The ludicrously incredible narratives of some other early writers upon the subject of the barnacle are equally amusing.

In 'Grerarde's Herbal, or History of Plants,' written about the time of Elizabeth, a similar doctrine is attempted to be upheld.[1]

The manner in which that author concludes his assertions tends much to show that there were, even in those days, many persons who were sceptical of his doctrine; he adds, 'If any doubt, may it please them to repair unto me, and I shall satisfie them by the testimonie of good witnesses.'

An authority of no less distinction than Hollinshecl says he saw with his own eyes the feathers of these barnacles hanging out of the shell at least two inches.

Dr. Wm. Bulleyn, who wrote in the year 1552, alludes to the subject, but evidently with cautious and reluctant credulity. He says, 'There be also barnacles whiche hath a strange generacion, as Gresnerus saith, which never laie egges, as the people of the north partes of Scotlande knoweth, and because it should seme incredible to many I will geve none occasion to any either to mocke or to maruell.'[1]

Willughby was less credulous than other ornithologists who wrote in that century; he makes some strong remarks upon those who had asserted such fabulous stories respecting the barnacle.[2]

Another author, who wrote in the following century, also makes allusion to the singularly delusive notion, and attributes the solution of the story to the Dutch.[3]

Those who may wish to inquire into the natural existence of the barnacle as a curious species of shell-fish will find an interesting account of it in an amusing little work called 'The Seaside Book,' by W. H. Harvey, M.D., 1857 (fourth edition), wherein the author states it to belong to the class of animals called *Cirrhipoda*, which combine the characters of Crustacea and mollusca.

---

[1] Markham, speaking of the haunts and habits of wild-geese,

says: 'The wild goose and barnacle delight not in water above their sounding, for when they cannot conveniently come to the bottom to suck upon the ouze, or fatnesse of the water, they presently depart thence, and seeke more shallow places; also, these two sorts of fowle, the wild-goose and barnacle, are infinitely delighted with greenewinter come, as the blades of wheate or rye; and, therefore, they are ever, for the most part, to be found where any such graine is sowne, especially where the ends of the lands are much drowned, or have much water standing about them, wherein they may bath and padell themselves after their feeding.'—*Hunger's Prevention.*

[1] 'There is a small island in Lancashire called "The Pile of Fonlders," on the west side of the entrance into Morecambe Bay, about fifteen miles south of Ulverston, where are found the broken pieces of old and bruised ships, also the trunks and bodies, with the branches of old and rotten trees cast up there likewise; wherein is found a certain spume or froth, that in time breedeth unto certain shells, in shape like those of the muskle, but sharper pointed, and of a whiter colour, wherein is contained a thing in form like a lace of silke, finely woven, as it were, together; one end whereof is fastened into the inside of the shell, even as the fish of oisters and muskles are; the other end is made fast unto the belly of a rude masse or lump, which in time cometh to the shape and form of a

bird: when it is perfectly formed, the shell gapeth open, and the first thing that appeareth is the aforesaid lace or string; next come the legs of the bird hanging out; and as it groweth greater, it openeth the shell by degrees, till at length it is all come forth and hangeth only by the bill. In short space after, it cometh to full maturatie, and falleth into the sea, where it gathereth feathers and groweth to a fowl bigger than a mallard and lesser than a goose, which the people in Lancashire call by no other name than a tree-goose; which place aforesaid, and all those parts adjoining, do so much abound therewith, that one of the best is bought for three pence.'

[1] 'The Book of Simples,' fol. lxxij.

[2] 'But that all these stories are false and fabulous, I am confidently *persuaded*. Neither do there want sufficient arguments to induce the lovers of truth to be of our opinion, and to convince the gainsayers. For in the whole *genus* of birds (excepting the phœnix, whose reputed original is without doubt fabulous) there is not any one example of equivocal or spontaneous generation. . . . . Those shells in which they affirm these birds to be bred, and to come forth by a strange *metamorphosis*, do most certainly contain an animal of their own kind, and not transmutable into any other thing.'

[3] 'To finish this Treatise of Sea Plants, let me bring this admirable tale of untruth to your consideration, that whatsoever hath formerly beene related concerning the breeding of those Barnackles, to be from shels growing on trees, &e., is utterly erroneous, their breeding and hatching being found out by the *Dutch* and others in their navigations to the northward, as that third of the *Dutch* in anno 1536 doth declare.'—*Parkinson's Theatrum Botanicum*, p. 1306. London: 1640. Folio.

CHAPTER XXXIII

THE BEAN-GOOSE

*(*Anser ferus.*)*

'But this I know, that thou art very fine,
Seasoned with sage, with onions and port wine.'

SOUTHEY'S *Lines to a Goose.*

THE species termed the 'common wild-goose' is generally abundant in this country in winter, but its movements are much in keeping with the weather. When too severe in the north of England, these birds proceed towards the south. Wild-geese appear to be guided by a very reliable almanack; and, as Shakespeare wrote in years gone by,

'Winter's not gone yet if the wild-geese fly that way.'

The habits of the bean-goose are nearly identical with those of the grey-lag; they fly out to sea by day and inland by night, feeding on growing corn, young clover, turnip-tops, or almost any green cultivated substance. In early spring they alight in green bean-fields, where they feed heartily, sometimes doing considerable injury to the plant. They are also to be

365

met with, occasionally, on green moors and plains, but they are at all times wary, and will tax the sportsman's cunning to get at them. The clamour of their gabbling and cackling may sometimes be heard at a long distance. These also fly in wedge-like form and catenarian figures when in large gaggles. A small number fly in a straight line, one behind the other. When the wind is high, and accompanied by snow and sleet, they fly low in the air; the shore-gunner may then often bring them down by watching on the beach, standing perfectly still. They then sometimes fly so near as to give him a fine chance of a shot.

THE WHITE-FRONTED OR LAUGHING GOOSE (*Anas albifrons*), also termed the 'bar-goose,' from the dark-coloured bars across the breast, is a bird of beautiful plumage, but of inferior value as an edible one, not even so good as the grey-goose. In size it is a little larger than the brent, but not so large as the grey-goose. It is a regular winter visitant to the British Isles, though in numbers more or less, according as the winter is severe or mild. They are strong on the wing, moving through the air in single and angular line of flight. They are difficult birds to kill, being generally wild and unapproachable, and requiring hard hitting to bring them down, so thickly coated are they with feathers.

The sportsman who would kill them should use large shot, and reserve his fire until they take wing.

366

These birds do not proceed so far inland as grey-geese, and seldom alight in corn-fields, their favourite resorts being fens, marshes, and rivers near the sea-coast, where they are often shot by puntmen, though more frequently by means of a swivel-gun and small sailing vessel.[1]

THE PINK-FOOTED GOOSE (*Anser phœnicopus*) is a very beautiful bird, and has been the subject of much discussion of late years among naturalists and ornithologists.

The sportsman will invariably find these birds so wary, that it is difficult to get within range; they appear remarkably watchful, and are awake to every suspicious movement or noise on the part of human being. The punter's best skill is required, and the sailing sportsman must use his best cunning, to get at them. They are not very abundant, but in sharp winters there are generally a few killed on the coast.

---

[1] Col. Hawker speaks of these birds as quite unknown to the gunners of the Hampshire coast till the year 1830, and adds that he has seen none there since. The inference to be drawn from Col. Hawker's assertion would therefore seem to

be, that it is only in the severest winters they visit the *south* coast. My own experience of wild-fowling does not carry me back so far as 1830, but so long as I have felt interested in the sport I have, every winter, met with some of these birds on the eastern coast.

CHAPTER XXXIV

THE SOLAN GOOSE

*(*Pelecanus Bassanus.*)*

'I'm one of those who in Basse Isle,
Where *Bear* did govern longest while,
Lost all my eggs and goslings too;
Eor Bear did make the De'el to do.'

The Bream of the Solan Goose.

THE solan goose or gannet is a fine and beautiful bird: and although not in very high esteem by the modern apician, is extremely curious and interesting in its habits, and, being familiar to the wild-fowl shooter as a peculiar species of the wild-goose tribe, we are not disposed to pass it over unnoticed.

Several small islands in the north of Scotland, especially those of the Hebrides, are favourite resorts of these birds during the breeding season. The Bass Rock, at the mouth of the Firth of Forth, is also notorious as swarming with them;[1] so also Ailsa Craig, on the west, by the Firth of Clyde. They range themselves upon the ledges and *helds* of the rocks in irregular ranks; and so, studded from top to bottom, the most inacessible parts sometimes appear literally alive with solan geese. The Bass Rock, which has been alluded to by authors of travel as the 'solitary giant of the deep,' strikes the beholder with an amazement he never forgets as he gazes for the first time in his life upon the wild and stupendous scene,[2] not the structure of human hand, but the work of Nature, in one of its grandest and most majestic forms.[3]

The solan goose is also well known in northern countries, and is common on the coast of Labrador and in the Gulf of St. Lawrence.[1]

When seen at a distance, in the air, a casual observer would be very likely to mistake a solan goose for a large sea-gull, which it very much resembles both in colour and flight; but, on a closer view, the goose may be clearly distinguished from the gull by its long neck, large head, and black feathers at the points of its wings.

The solan goose is by no means gregarious, though these birds follow each other in flight, in apparently regular succession, keeping at a respectful distance, in order that one may not interrupt the operations of the other, their means of subsistence being such as to render their efforts more successful without companionship.

The manner in which the solan goose obtains its food is

remarkable and, it would appear, very precarious.

The bird is by nature gifted with very powerful wings, also a large, bright, piercing eye, and strong sharp-pointed beak. It flies leisurely over the sea, generally following the shoals of pilchards and herrings, or such other fish as swim near the surface or occasionally show themselves above water. Upon these the gannet keeps a watchful eye, and pounces from its exalted position in the air with astonishing velocity, sometimes like a heavy stone falling from the clouds, and seldom missing its victim, a herring, pilchard, small mullet, sprat, or some such fish. The gannet darts down perpendicularly as a falling stone, though not in a headlong position, as a hawk, but so as to strike the water heavily with its breast, at the same instant that it secures the fish between the vice-like mandibles of its beak:

     . . . . 'Lo! gannets huge,
And ospreys plunging from their cloudy height
With leaden fall precipitate, the waves
Cleave with dashing breast, and labouring rise,
Talons and beak o'erloaded!'[2]

Most people who have been at sea, or lived near the sea-coast, are familiar with the habits of the gannet, and its dextrous performances upon surface-fish.[1]

A cruel method of taking these birds is commonly resorted to by the sea-fishers of the north; it is by fixing a fresh herring or a pilchard to a piece of board, which has a small weight underneath, to sink it a little below the surface of the sea. The gannet, unconscious of the trap, pounces upon the plank, and, striking at the fish with its usual force, either thrusts its bill completely through the board, or breaks its neck or breastbone, thus falling an easy victim to the fishers,[2] who dress it for table in the same manner as an ordinary goose; and when on long voyages, and short of fresh meat, an old gannet is eaten by sailors with very much relish. Young ones used to be sold in Edinburgh and other north-country towns at 1*s.* 8*d.* each, and were esteemed a favourite dish when roasted and served up as wild-goose. Old gannets partake too much of the flavour of hsh to be palatable to the modern gourmand.

There is no doubt but that, during the ages of archery, these birds afforded the ancient toxophilite excellent sport, and it appears arrows of a peculiar form were used specially for shooting wild-geese and other large fowl.[3] See further, as to the habits of the solan goose, *supra* ' The Language of Wildfowl,' and as to capturing solan geese in the island of St. Kilda, *infra* 'Fowling in St. Kilda.'

----

[1] 'None of the birds are permanent occupants of the island,

but visitors for purposes of procreation only, staying there for a few weeks, in lodgings as it were, and until their young ones can take wing along with them.'—*Harvey on the Generation of Animals:* 1651. *Vide* also 'The Bass Rock and its History.' By Professor Fleming and others.

² *Vide* 'Rocks and Rivers.' By John Colquhoun, Esq.

³ There is the following amusing reference to solan geese in 'The Cosmographe and Description of Albion,' prefixed to the 'History and Chronicles of Scotland 'of Hector Boece: 'In it' [the Bass Rock] 'ar incredible noumer of Soland Geis; nocht unlik to thir fowlis, that Plineus callis See Ernis; and ar sene in na part of Albion, hot in this crag and Ailsay. At thair first cumin, quhilkis in the spring of the yeir, they gadder sa gret noumer of treis and stikkis to big thair nestis, that the samin micht be sufficient fewell to the keparis of the castell, howbeit thay had na uthir provision, and thocht the keparis tak fra thir fowlis thir stikkis and treis, yit thay tak litil indingnation thairof, bot bringis haistilie agane als many fra uthir placis quhair thay fie. Thay nuris thair birdis with maist deligat fische; tor, thocht they have ane fische in thair mouth, aboue the seas, quhair thay fie, yit gif they se ane uthir bettir, thay lat the first fal, and doukas, with ane fellon stoure, in the see, and bringis haistilie up the fische that thay last saw; and thoucht this fische be reft fra hir be the keparis of the castell, scho takkis litill indingnation, hot fleis incontinent for

ane uthir. Thir keparis of the castell forsaid, takis the young geis fra thaim with litill impediment; thus cumis gret proffet yeirlie to the lord of the said castell.'—P. xxxvij.

Martin in his 'Account of the Scottish Western Isles,' mentions that the Steward of St. Kilda found an arrow, besides other strange items, in a solan goose's nest: the former doubtless had fallen from her wounded body.—*Vide* 'Hansard's Archery,' p. 408.

[1] 'The Birds of Canada.' By Dr. A. M. Ross (2nd edition): 1872.

[2] Gisborne's 'Walks in a Eorest.'

[1] 'I seem's though I see her, with wrath in each quill,
Like a Chancery lawyer, a filin' her bill,
An' grindin' her talents ez sharp ez all nater,
To pounce like a writ on the hack o' the traitor.'

The Biglow Papers.

[2] Macaulay's 'History of St. Kilda;' Goldsmith's 'Animated Nature,' &c.

[3] 'For geese or other large birds they (the arrow) should be double-forked, sharp, and strong, to cut a wing or a neck clean off. The blow from a common shaft rarely inflicts a wound

sufficient to bringdown the game at once; notwithstanding she be hurt or shot through, she will fly off and die in another place.'—*La Maison Bustique, Liebault.* A.D. 1620.

CHAPTER XXXV.

THE HERON

'Lo! at this siege, the Hern,
Upon the bank of some small purling brook,
Observant stands to take his scaly prize,
Himself another's game: for mark, behind
The wily falconer creeps; his grazing horse
Conceals the treacherous foe, and on his fist
The unhooded falcon sits: with eager eyes
She meditates her prey.

.   .   .   .

Unhappy bird, our father's prime delight!

Who fenced thine eyry[1] round with sacred laws.'—
SOMERVILE.

IT is a great mistake to imagine that this noble species of
water-fowl has become nearly extinct in this country. It is true
there are now but few heronries in England, compared with
what there were many years ago, but there are nevertheless
plenty of herons; and it would seem that these birds have given

preference to exclusive solitude of late years, for the purpose of building their nests, hatching and rearing their young, rather than to assemble in those ancient heronries which used to be regarded as objects of considerable attraction.

The days have long passed away since the heron had place in chivalry, when, among our ancient customs, was one of swearing an oath upon the dead body of a heron, and whereby many a gallant knight has, in years long passed, plighted his troth to his 'ladye faire,' as the most solemn and honourable manner of assuring her of his fidelity.

The heron was formerly esteemed one of the daintiest luxuries of the dinner-table, and stood at the head of the game course on every festive occasion.[2]

According to the prices of wild-fowl assessed by the Mayor of London, in the time of Edward I., the cost of a heron was 1*s.* 4*d.*, and of an egret, or dwarf heron, 1*s.* 6*d.*, which are among the very highest assessed prices of water-fowl in those days.[1] By the same authority the price of a mallard was assessed at 3*d.*, a teal 2*d.*, and so on.

This apicianic preference to the heron was not confined to English taste alone, hut extended to continental choice as well. They were so greatly in esteem a century ago that higher prices were paid for them than for any other wild-fowl; thus maintaining, through centuries, the character of choice and preference which had been awarded them by the ancient epicure.

The heron was also distinguished as the noblest quarry for the falconer—

> 'And the slow heron down shall fall,
> To feed my fairest fair withal.'[2]

The method of capturing herons by the art of falconry, as practised in former days, was a highly animating diversion. Ladies not only accompanied the falconers in pursuit of the heron, but took active part in the recreation, and often excelled them in skill.[3]

The time of day generally chosen for the pursuit was noontide, because at that hour herons were supposed to be well gorged with fish, and consequently unable to fly so swiftly as at other times; and if pursued in a hungry condition, the hawk seldom succeeded in striking its quarry. The rapacious bird generally attempts to soar above its prey, well knowing the difficulty of attacking a heron from any other than an uppermost position; the heron, equally conscious of this advantage, soars higher and higher, and it appears, that when overtaken and overpowered, turns its head upon its back, and strikes at the enemy with its bill, sometimes transfixing the hawk at a blow.

> 'As when a cast of faulcons make their flight
> At an herneshaw,[4] that lies aloft on wing,

The whiles they strike at him with heedlesse might,

The wary fowle his bill doth backward wring.'[5]

Herons have, undoubtedly, a decided antipathy to birds of prey; and when attacked in their flight high in the air by the hawk, they struggle fiercely with him for the uppermost place.[6]

A full-grown heron is capable of inflicting a severe wound with its beak, which is a very powerful weapon of defence. When the heron is captured by the hawk, and has reached the ground, it is the custom with Indian falconers to rush forward to the scene of the struggle, and plunge the heron's beak into the earth, when, by holding its legs and wings, a small hawk is enabled to kill it.[1]

Falconry is still a highly popular recreation in many parts of India, more particularly in the territory of Scinde. It has also long been a favourite sport amongst the Persians. It was a custom with the nobility of Mingrelia, when they had taken herons by falconry, to cut off the scapular feathers of the bird for the purpose of making heron-tufts for bonnets, and after such disfiguration the birds were set at liberty.[2]

'Nor mighty princes now disdain to wear
Thy waving crest, the mark of high command,
With gold, and pearl, and brilliant gems adorned.'[3]

Sir John Chardin relates an interesting anecdote as to a

heron-tuft, set with jewels, being presented by the King Abas to Luarzab, King of Georgia, on surrender of the latter, during the Georgian war. 'This is an ensign of royalty,' said Abas; 'and it is my pleasure you should always wear it upon your head, that people may know ye to be king.' The author of the anecdote then proceeds to relate how Abas afterwards treacherously commanded one of his guards to rob Luarzab of the tuft, in order that he might have apparent cause of offence against Luarzab for losing it, and under cloak of that false accusation pretend to justify his desire to put him to death.

The pinions of the heron were also worn in the hats and bonnets of the highest in the land as trophies of valour and distinction.

> 'As glossy as a heron's wing
> Upon the turban of a king.'[4]

The statute 19 Hen. VII. cap. 11, prohibited the taking of herons in this country, except by hawking, or with the long bow, upon pain of forfeiture of 6s. 8d. for every bird taken contrary to that statute. It also restrained the taking of young herons out of their nests, on land belonging to other persons (except with the licence of the owner of such land), under a penalty of 10s. for every bird so taken.

Herons were thus, during many years, protected by statute; but the game act of Geo. IV. has repealed all the statutes which specially prohibited the destruction of these birds, their young and eggs, except under certain restrictions.[1]

There is something peculiarly majestic and interesting in the heron, and it is amusing to watch this bird in its lonely habits, standing as it does sometimes an hour at a time, in apparently motionless position, at the brink of the water, whilst the tide continually washes its silvery feet, and unsuspecting little fish and eels swim boldly beneath the shadow of its graceful form, when they are instantly detected by the keen eyes of the bird, as it strikes with piercing and unerring precision at the intruders, rarely, if ever, failing to secure the slippery victim.

It is the habit of the heron to place itself at the extreme point of some soft-soil promontory washed by every tide, and there to stand, sometimes until the water fairly reaches its feathers, when it either retreats a few steps, or flies, or marches to some other spot. But the water must be clear, or it is no place for the heron. And this is one of the most striking characteristics of this bird; for wherever the water has become polluted or cloudy, so that the heron is unable to see its prey through the liquid element, it leaves that locality and seeks one better adapted to its habits-, and affording the facilities of clear water for the exercise of its skill in obtaining its food. Neither does the heron like rocky coasts or hard soil, because of the risk it incurs of injury or pain to its bill on striking it against hard substances at eels and other fish which may be near the bottom; it rather prefers muddy flats and the oozy beds of tidal rivers, in some of which, on the eastern coast, and more especially the rivers Stour, Orwell, and Deben, these birds are to this day abundantly numerous.

It being the habit of the heron to seek for solitude and loneliness, it is naturally a shy bird and wary of the human form. So in building its nest it generally seeks some tall tree in the loneliest part of a large and quiet wood; if undisturbed, it returns year by year for the same purpose to the same tree. Generally after a time other herons come, and the nests increase in number year by year until quite an extensive heronry is formed.

The habits of the heron in this respect are the very opposite to those of the rook, which seeks to establish its rookery as near as may be to human habitation.

One of the most ancient heronries in Norfolk is at Wolferton, in a large wood there on the estate of His Royal Highness the Prince of Wales. Another of large and considerable importance in the same county is at Didlington Park, the seat of W. A. Tyssen Amhurst, Esquire; which appears to have been formed upwards of sixty years ago, when a sedge of herons, which had previously been in the habit of building their nests and rearing their young among the sedges and sallows of the Fens at Felt well and Hockwold, shifted their quarters to a grove of lofty fir-trees at Didlington, where they have ever since continued to resort, and under the care and preservation of the proprietor a considerable number of herons are every year hatched and reared there.

Herons forsake their haunts if fired at by night from beneath trees on which they build or roost. They are open to any fair challenge by day, but decidedly averse to such midnight attacks. They are extremely watchful birds, and are at all times an annoyance to the wild-fowler, frequently giving alarm long before any other birds which may be near them have detected the smallest sign of suspicion.[1]

They are also great enemies to the decoyer, and sometimes, when he has just commenced his artifices upon a paddling of freshly arrived wild-ducks, some suspicious heron which may happen to be near the pipe of the decoy causes every bird to leave the water, by stretching its long neck and giving a sonorous warning 'frank!' as it rises from the water's edge, spreading its huge wings, and alarming every bird within the pond. And it is the same whether pursuing the sport of wild-fowl catching at the decoy, or shooting on the open waters and oozes with punt and gun; whenever the warning note of the heron is heard, up go the heads of all the wild-fowl near about him, and they are thus made acquainted with the enemy's approach. The lives of many hundreds of wild-fowl have been saved by this keen detective of the waters. When standing erect, what with its long legs, long neck, and tapering body, the heron can see the approach of the enemy at a considerable distance; and when wild-fowl are feeding near this bird, they always appear to rely on it for a signal in case of danger. The curlew also frequently enacts a similar part when feeding with other birds.

When once a heron has found food at any particular place it is almost certain to return to it again, and probably nearly every day, if undisturbed. The quietest way of getting rid of the nuisance at the decoy is, to bait a large fish-hook with a small live roach or eel, and place it at the water's edge, near the feeding-place of the heron, securing the hook by means of a strong line to a stake or branch.

'There o'er the shallow water's bed
His baited hooks at eve he spread.

. . . . .

And e'en the heron's crested pride
By the frail slender line is ta'en.'[1]

The heron will swallow the bait if a live and fresh one, and thus become an easy capture to the decoyman. But the hook must be baited with a *live* fish: the heron will not touch a dead one. Giles Jacob also gives directions for taking the heron with a baited fish-hook.[2] This plan is far better than shooting it, because of the quietness of the proceeding; and although a time for shooting the heron might be chosen when there are no wild-fowl in the pool, the report of the gun disturbs the decoy-ducks, and resounds to the marshes in the locality. The other is, besides, the most effectual, because it is sometimes difficult to get within gun-shot of a heron, even under cover of decoy-screens and brushwood; and to make the other plan more certain, two or three hooks might be baited and placed in different places on the banks of the decoy.

When herons are restless and constantly on the wing, moving to and fro in the locality of their feeding haunts, it presages stormy weather.[1]

'The hern by soaring shows tempestuous showers.'[2]

The heron offers a fair mark for the rifle-shot as it stands motionless on the bank at the brink of the water, watching for eels or other prey which may unsuspectingly approach within gaze of its piercing eye. And the heron does not seem to regard an ordinary-sized rowing-boat with that suspicion it does a gunning-punt; therefore, if the sportsman wishes to kill a heron in a sportsmanlike manner, the rifle and shooting canoe are his proper equipments. And just after harvest, in August and September, when small fish and tiny eels are abundant in the salt-water rivers and bays where oozes abound, herons are plentiful; and at that season there are numbers of egrittes, which may be instantly distinguished from the old birds by their whiter plumage.

When within range of the shot-barrels, they are very simple shots for the merest tyro, presenting a mark so large as to render it almost impossible to miss them except wilfully. They do not require hard hitting; a slight blow will bring them down.

A winged heron requires careful handling; it is a savage bird, and will attack dog or man, striking very fiercely and sharply with its strong pointed bill. Let the sportsman beware!

Cranes were also, in former times, highly esteemed as articles of food—

'The crane, the fesant, the pecocke, and curlewe,
The partriche, plover, bittorn, and heronsewe,
Seasoned so well in licour redolent,
That the hall is full of pleasant smell and scent'—[3]

but are now judged to have forsaken this island.[4] They were formerly as common as the heron.[5]

A most improbable assumption once prevailed that the crane, when on duty as the sentry of its herd, held a stone within its talons, the object of which was supposed to be (according to the reasoning of Aristotle), that standing throughout the watch on one leg, if the sentry crane chanced to fall asleep unintentionally, the stone would immediately fail from its talons, and rouse the sleepy bird to its sense of duty. 'Vigil lapillum. inter pedes tenet, ut si forsitan surrepserit somnus, casu lapidis excitetur.'

The same thing is asserted by Pliny, who says, 'Exeubias habent nocturnis temporibus lapillum pede sustinentes qui laxatus somno et dee id ens indiligentiam coarguat.'[1]

It is also said that cranes used to assemble together before migrating from our coasts, and thus, as if a proclamation had been circulated among the species fixing a day and hour for the occasion of taking their departure, they rise high in the air in one entire herd; and having performed a few circumvolutions, dart off in apparently determined flight.[2] The habits of cranes, in this respect, are similar to those of wild swans (*infra* ' Wild-Swan Shooting').

---

[1] No one was permitted to shoot within 600 yards of an eyry or heronry under heavy penalties.

[2] 'At principall feestes. Item, it is thought in likewyse that *hearonsewys* be bought for my lorde's owne mees, so they be at xijd. a pece.'—*Northumberland Household Book, temp. Henry VIII.*

'Cranys and herons schulle be enarmed with lardrons of swyne, and rostyd, and etyn wyth gyngynyr.'—*Ancient Cookery*, A.D. 1381.

[1] *Vide* 'Liber Albus Grildhallse,' introd. p. xxxiij.

[2] Cotton.

[3] Strntt's 'Sports and Pastimes,' p. 26.

[4] Herneshaw (heronshaw) is a full-grown heron.

[5] Spencer's 'Fairie Queen.'

[6] 'The heron or hernesew is a fowl that liveth about waters, and yet she doth so abhorre raine and tempests, that she seeketh to avoid them by flying on high. She hath her nest in very loftie trees, and sheweth, as it were, a natural hatred against the gosse hawk and other kinde of hawks; and so likewise doth the hawk seek her destruction continually. When they fight above in the aire, they labour both especially for this one thing—that the one might ascend and be above the other. Now, if the hawk getteth the upper place, he overthroweth and vanquished the heron with a marvellous earnest flight.'— *Speculum Mundi, or a Glasse Representing the Face of the World*, By John Swan, M.A., late Student of Trin. Coll. Camb. 1635: p. 400.

[1] *Vide* 'Falconry in the Valley of the Indus.' By Lieut. R. F. Burton: 1852.

[2] *Vide* 'Travels in Persia and the East Indies.' By Sir Jno. Chardin: 1643.

[3] Somervile's 'Field Sports.'

[4] Moore's 'Lalla Rookh.'

[1] Herons are not included in the Wild Birds' Protection Act, 1872, nor in the Sea Birds' Protection Act, 1869; *infra* 'Laws affecting Wild-fowl, Sea-Fowl, and Fen-birds.'

[1] 'The herrons gaif ayne vyilcl skreech as the kylhed bene in fyir, guhilk gart the quhais [curlews] for fieyitnes [fright] fle far fra hame.'—*The Complaynt of Scotland*, A.D. 1548.

[1] 'Annals of Sporting.'

[2] *Vide* 'The Compleat Sportsman.' By Giles Jacob: 1740.

[1] Willsford's 'Nature's Secrets.'

[2] Drayton.

[3] Barclay's 'Egloges.' A.D. 1570.

[4] Pennant's 'British Zoology.'

[5] 'Northumberland Household Book.'

[1] Pliny, lib. x. cap. 23.

[2] 'Abiturse congregantur in loca certa comitatseque sic ut nulla generis sui relinquatur nisi captiva et serva ecu lege preedicta die recedeunt.'—*Pliny*, lib. x. cap. 23.

CHAPTER XXXVI

WILD-SWAN SHOOTING

——'Majestic swan
Or heavy goose—with many a fowl beside
Of lesser size and note, who, when the world
Has sunk to rest, beneath the moonbeam dash
The sparkling tide.'—*Fowling: a Poem.* A.D. 1808.

THE wild-swan (*Cygnus ferus*), the largest and most majestic of the wild-fowl species, is at all times a bird of considerable attraction to every wild-fowl shooter. The sport of wild-swan shooting, however, is so rare in this country, that probably there are not many English sportsmen who have taken any frequent or considerable part in the diversion. In some localities the killing of a wild-swan is looked upon as a notable performance, and although no very difficult task to accomplish by a properly equipped sportsman, it is, nevertheless, no every-day adventure, even in our sharpest winters.

A severe winter seldom passes without our being visited by some of the wild-swan species from northern latitudes; but they generally remain off the coast, at sea, until a heavy gale compels them to seek less turbulent quarters. They then fly over-land, and alight in the largest tidal river in the neighbourhood, or the one that is least affected by ice, and there they remain until the gale subsides and the sea becomes smoother.

Wild-Swan Shooting by moonlight.

The punter should watch for the first abatement of the gale, and proceed in his punt as soon as the weather permits, and endeavour to get the first shot. They are generally strangers to punts and punters on their first arrival in European waters, and may be approached under the most ordinary precautions.

On the arrival of wild-swans in a public river, they are such conspicuous objects, and are so great an attraction, that every wild-fowler in the neighbourhood is on the *qui vive* to shoot them, and the midnight punter will often be surprised, on approaching a herd of swans which may have arrived during the fury of a gale on the previous day, to find that two or three other punters are bent on the same pursuit.

The engraving opposite is designed by the author in representation of a scene which occurred during a hard winter, on the evening succeeding a heavy gale on the eastern coast, when a herd of wild-swans sought refuge in the river Stour, and were assailed in the evening, under the favourable auspices of a calm moonlight night, with the charges of two punt-guns of heavy calibre. Neither of the punters was aware of the presence of the other, some large blocks of ice intervening between them; butboth gunners being within range and 'ready,' on the discharge of my gun, which killed three of the birds as they sat upon the water, the other punter had ample time for tipping his gun, and by a flying shot he killed one and winged another.

Wild-swans soon learn to shun the presence of a punter, and generally, after being once or twice fired at, they become the wildest and most wary birds upon the waters.

There is a distinction between the tame swan and the hooper, or wild-swan, with which most wild-fowlers are familiar; for though difficult to be distinguished at a distance, when near enough to allow the colour of the head to be seen there can be no mistake. The skin, or soft substance above the upper mandible, is black in the tame swan, but bright yellow in the wild one.

The hooper may also be known from the tame swan, at a distance, by its note, the wild bird making a sort of hooping noise, which, after hearing it once, the fowler is not likely to forget. They are termed 'the peaceful monarchs of the lake,' from the contrast they bear with the mute swan (*Cygnus olov*), which attacks all other freshly arrived birds that venture within its reach.

The young hoopers, like other cygnets, are fawn-coloured, and do not attain that beautiful white plumage until two years of age; till that time they are classed as cygnets. The, skin, or soft substance before alluded to, is not so bright in colour in the cygnets as in swans. The wild cygnet exhibits a pale flesh-colour in the place of the bright yellow, and the tame swan has, besides, a protuberance just above the upper mandible.

It is only in the hardest winters that wild-swans visit our coasts and inland waters, and then there are frequently many tame swans among them, which, having found themselves frozen out of the lakes or ornamental waters where they were reared, take wing, soaring high in the air, and making direct for the sea-coast: when, should they chance to alight in the neighbourhood of punts and guns, they are almost certain to fall victims to the first gunner who goes in pursuit, and who, regardless of swan-marks, swan-herdsmen, and swan-laws, is only too proud to secure a specimen of the 'monarch of the waters.'

Many fabulous assertions have been set up by ancient writers as to the 'sweet singing' and musical notes said to be uttered by a dying swan. But this 'sweet singing' of the swan when dying has been repeatedly contradicted, as will be seen by the references below.[1]

The hoopers, or wild-swans, afford fine amusement, and try the punter's skill as much as any of the wild-fowl species. They are generally very wild and difficult of approach, but with caution and patience a fair shot may sometimes be made. The punter should always bear in mind that these large birds have not the power to rise suddenly in the air, but flap along the water, beating the surface with their immense wings, some thirty or fifty yards, before they are able to suspend their ponderous bodies above the level of the punter's gun.[2]

When punting to wild-swans, the sportsman should reserve his best strength till they take alarm, and seem to be preparing to fly, when at that instant, by putting on a bold spurt with his paddles, a few good strokes will take him several yards nearer; bat he must remember that they face about to windward before rising, and that it may, therefore, be necessary to turn the punt so as to keep the muzzle of the gun bearing upon them. It is always better to reserve the fire at swans until they commence their efforts to take wing; there is then just time enough to turn the punt, take aim, and fire whilst they are getting up.

If the swans be very wild and unapproachable, a successful shot may sometimes be made by adopting the well-known manœuvre of placing a few pieces of ice and snow upon the head of the punt, by way of disguise; but, as this alters the trim, and consequently the relative position of the gun, the punter must be careful to regulate the range accordingly, or put corresponding weight in the stern of the punt.

The author has generally found that the best and most successful means of shooting swans by daylight is by aid of the sailing-punt, so as to approach them under sail, on a slanting wind, taking care to luff up quickly into the eye of the wind the moment they attempt to rise, and reserving fire until the instant of their crossing the bows of the punt.

It sometimes happens, during severe frosts, that swans, in flying overland, present remarkably fair shots, and may be killed with small shoulder-guns. I have seen many a swan brought down with a charge of an ounce and a half of No. 4

shot.

Whenever an opportunity of the kind offers, and a swan, or herd of swans, is seen to be approaching in line with the sportsman, who has but a small gun, he should lie down and remain motionless until the birds are fairly over his head, then suddenly rise up, and, just as they are flying from him, send the charge after them; his mark should either be the head of one of the birds, or the under part of one of the wings. An experienced sportsman never shoots at wild-fowl of any kind when flying *towards him*, but always reserves his fire until they have passed, because the shot finds its way to the flesh of the bird when fired behind it, which it seldom does when fired at its breast.

The sportsman should not allow his dog to retrieve a wounded swan; for if not badly hit, a swan is more than a match for a large dog, and will assuredly give some hard strokes with its powerful wings ere it can be captured, and it is besides a very awkward bird for a dog to mouth,

When wild-swans are driven to our shores by the severity of winter, and find food and shelter in any lake or secluded locality where the tide ebbs and flows, they generally keep to it, if undisturbed, until late in the spring; dividing their time apparently between visits to the sea, the moors, and the lakes, spending more of their leisure at the lakes than elsewhere. But, from the incessant attempts of punters to approach them, they become so vigilant, that they often take wing as soon as approached within the distance of two or three hundred yards.

The author remembers an instance of a herd of wild-swans taking up their quarters, during a severe winter, in an extensive salt-water pool into which every tide ebbed and flowed. The pool was a branch of a large river, bounded on all sides by private property; and the swans—about thirty in all—were not permitted to be disturbed, but were fed and enticed by the 'Squire of the domain' to resort there, and take up a permanent abode. They remained long after the frost had gone, and the spring had so far advanced that the Squire congratulated himself on the valuable acquisition to his estate of an easily-acquired swannery. One fine morning, however, in the month of April, the whole herd of swans were observed to soar high in the air, where they performed most interesting circular evolutions higher and higher above the lake upon which they had for so many weeks enjoyed the good Squire's hospitality and protection. They continued hovering around in the manner described for several minutes, as if to take a last fond look and thank the Squire for his hospitality, and then sniffed the air, and dashed off, with noble flight, in that direction indicated by the compass as—due north.

Wild-swans which have been driven from their northern quarters by hard weather return in herds during the months of April and May. They are sometimes exposed to much persecution in northern countries during the moulting season, when they are unable to fly. They lose their feathers in August, and for a few weeks are quite without the power of flight: in this helpless condition they are pursued by the natives ashore and by sailors in boats, who run them down, chasing them to and fro until they are quite exhausted, and thus become captives.

In Kamtschatka wild-swans are so common, both in winter and summer, that at every entertainment given by the poorest person the table is graced with one or more of these noble fowls.

The Kamtschadales take them, in winter, with gins and nooses, and by various other devices which they employ, in such rivers as do not freeze; and in the season when swans are moulting they hunt them with dogs and kill them with clubs.[1]

In Iceland, also, these birds are objects chase when unable to fly. The natives then pursue them with dogs and active horses, capable of passing nimbly over the boggy soil and marshes where they resort, and they run so swiftly that a fast horse is required to overtake them. The greater numbers are caught in the chase by the dogs, which are taught to seize them by the neck; this causes them to lose their balance, when they become an easy prey.[2]

The flesh of the wild-swan is highly esteemed by the Icelanders (especially that of the young birds), insomuch so that, summer or winter, no entertainment is deemed complete without a swan.[3]

Mr. Lloyd, in his 'Scandinavian Adventures,'[4] gives an elaborate account of the great Government swan hunts, with an engraving showing the manner in which they are assailed during the moulting season at Malm6 by men in boats armed with clubs and sticks. Formerly the returns at these haunts were very great, as many as six hundred swans and upwards having been killed or taken alive in a single day; but at the present time, says our author, perhaps hardly a tithe of that number is captured.

Professor Yarrell gives some amusing particulars respecting the feeding of young swans of the year for the table, as still practised in the city of Norwich, by which it appears that the Town-clerk sends a note from the Town-hall to the public swan-herdsman, members of the Corporation, and others who have swans and swan-rights; and 'on the second Monday in August the cygnets are collected in a small stew, or pond, the number annually varying from fifty to seventy, many of them belonging to private individuals. They begin to feed immediately, being provided with as much barley as they can eat, and are usually ready for killing early in November. They vary in weight, some reaching to twenty-eight pounds. If kept beyond November, they begin to fall off, losing both flesh and fat, and the meat becomes darker in colour and stronger in flavour.'[1] A printed copy of the following lines is usually sent with each bird:—

TO ROAST A SWAN.

'Take three pounds of beef, beat fine in a mortar:
Put it into the Swan—that is, when you've canglit her.
Some pepper, salt, mace, some nutmeg, an onion,
Will heighten the flavour, in Gourmand's opinion.
Then tie it up tight with a small piece of tape,
That the gravy and other things may not escape.
A meal paste, rather stiff, should be laid on the breast,
And some whited-brown paper should cover the rest.
Fifteen minutes, at least, ere the Swan you take down,
Pull the paste off the bird, that the breast may get brown.'

THE GRAVY.

'To a gravy of beef, good and strong, I opine
You'll be right if you add half-a-pint of port-wine;
Pour this through the Swan—yes, quite through the belly;

Then serve the whole up with some hot currant-jelly.'

'N.B.—The swan must not be skinned.'

There is an ancient privilege granted by the Crown, of allowing certain individuals and public companies the right of keeping and breeding swans on public waters. In allowing such a privilege the Crown has always insisted on some particular swan-mark being specified and used, by which the birds are marked and known.

The swan-mark (*cigninota*) is either some letter, initials, chevron, annulet, crescent, or device, or more frequently some crest or arms having reference to that used by the party to whom the grant is made.[2] The swan-marks are cut on the upper mandible of the swan, by means of a small, sharp instrument used for the purpose, and in some instances a hot brand is used instead.

The officer anciently employed by the King as swan-herdsman was called *Magister deductus Cignorum*.

The Dyers' and Vintners' Companies of the City of London have long enjoyed the privilege granted them by the Crown of keeping, breeding, and preserving swans on the Thames, at any part of the river between London and Windsor, and some miles beyond the latter place, a privilege they still keep up; and they also continue the ancient custom of proceeding up the river, on a swan-voyage, with their friends and visitors, accompanied by the royal swan-herdsman, their own swan-herdsman, and assistants, on the first Monday of August in every year. They embark at Lambeth, in one or more large boats, the object of their voyage being to catch and mark all the cygnets, the property of their respective companies, which have been reared during the season; and they also renew any marks in old birds which may have become partially obliterated.

There are now about 700 swans on the Thames, some of which belong to the Queen, some to the Dyers' Company, and others to the Vintners'.

---

[1] 'Olorum morte narratur flebilis cantus, falsò ut arbitror aliquot experiments.'—*Pliny.*

'De eygni vero cantu suavissimo quem cum mendaciorum parente Grsecia jactare ausus es, ad Luciani Tribunal, apud quem aliquid novi dicas, statuo te.'—*Scaliger.*

'Cantandi studiosos esse jam communi sermone pervulgatum est. Ego, vero, fortasse neque alius.'—*ÆMilan.*

[2] See as to the 'Flight of Wild-Swans,' *supra* p. 115.

[1] 'History of Kamtschatka.' By James Grieve: 1764.

[2] *Vide* Daniel's 'Rural Sports,' vol. iii.

[3] *Ibid.*

[4] Vol. ii. p. 445. 1854.

[1] *Vide* Yarrell's 'British Birds,' vol. iii. p. 225.

[2] There is a very interesting and elaborate account in the third volume of Professor Yarrell's 'British Birds' (3rd edition) as to swan-marking, swanneries, and swan-herds, to which the reader is particularly referred for further information on this subject. And see also 'The Loseley Manuscripts.' By A. J. Kempe, Esq. London, 1835, 8vo.

CHAPTER XXXVII

SWAN LAWS

THROUGH centuries past there have been laws for the preservation of swans from the hands of the spoiler, most of which are still in force; so that it sometimes becomes necessary, in the event of swans becoming the subjects of litigation, to refer back to a very remote period, not only of the statute-book, but also to the law of prescription and prerogative, and some very early judicial decisions.

An important case affecting swans and swanneries was decided in the 34th of Elizabeth, which is well known as 'The Queen *versus* Lady Joan Young and Thos. Saunger.' It is also known as 'The Swan case,'[1] and otherwise as 'The case of the Abbotsbury Swans.' The result of the litigation in that case settled the law of swans upon a basis which has never been disturbed: it placed the rights and ownerships, with the laws affecting them, in so clear a light, that the case has ever since been a leading authority upon the subject.

A swan is a royal fowl, as whales and sturgeons are royal fish; and all those, the property whereof is not otherwise definable, when within the British dominions, belong to the Crown by virtue of its prerogative.[2]

A person may prescribe to have a game of swans within his manor, and he may prescribe that his swans may swim within the manor of another person; but a prescription to have all wild-swans which are *feræ naturæ*, and not marked, building their nests, breeding and frequenting within a particular creek, is not good.

Cygnets belong equally to the owner of the cock and the owner of the hen, and must be divided betwixt them. This was decided in a very old case—'Lord Strange *versus* Sir John Charlton'[1]—which is referred to by Sir Matthew Arundel in his judgment on 'The Swan case.'

A custom for the owner of land on which cygnets are hatched to have the *third* is good, and was adjudged reasonable, because if swans go upon a stranger's land he may chase them out; but if he suffer them to hatch there, it is a reasonable custom that he should have a third for the sufferance.[2]

All wild-swans (unmarked) which may be in any open waters, either public or private, belong to the Crown as royal fowls, except where there is a prescription to the contrary; and there are several instances on record in which grants have been given by the Crown of all swans within a certain district, or for a certain number of years. For instance, in Kot. Parliament, 30 Ed. III. part 2, No. 20, the King granted to C. W. all wild-swans unmarked, between Oxford and London, for seven years. In eodem Rot. an. 16 R. II. p. 1, No. 39, a similar grant of wild-swans unmarked, in the county of Cambridge, was made to B. Bereford, Knt. In eodem Rot. an. 1 H. IV. p. 9, No. 14, a grant was made to J. Fenn to survey and keep all wild-swans unmarked, 'ita quod de proficuo respondeat ad Scaccarium.' By which it appears, the Crown may make grants of wild-swans unmarked in any particular district,[3] though it is a privilege that has not been exercised for many years.

The swan-mark cannot be legally impressed without a grant or prescription. And where there is such grant he who has a right to the swan-mark may grant it over, or transfer it, by deed.

According to tradition, as well as the authority of Sir Edward Coke, it was formerly the law that he who stole a swan lawfully marked, in an open and common river, the same swan, or another, was hung in the house by the beak; and he who stole it, in recompense thereof, was obliged to give the owner so much wheat as would completely cover the bird, by putting and turning the corn over the head of the swan until it was entirely hidden in the wheat.[1]

It is felony to take swans that are lawfully marked, though they be at large.[2] And it is the same as to unmarked swans, if they are domesticated or kept in water near a dwelling-house, or on a manor or other private property.

A case of swan-stealing was tried before the late Baron Channell, at the Spring Assizes of the year 1859, at Reading. A prisoner named Lovejoy was convicted of stealing a swan, the property of the Wardens and Commonalty of the Mystery of Dyers. The charter of the company, granted in the reign of Queen Anne, was put in evidence to prove the title of the Dyers' Company, as alleged in the indictment, and the swan-marker proved the mark of the company. The learned judge held, upon the authority of Lord Hale,[3] that a swan, though at large, and a bird *feræ naturæ*, was, under certain circumstances, the subject of larceny, as in the present case—marked and pinioned; and the prisoner was sentenced to a short term of imprisonment.

Formerly, the punishment for stealing swans' eggs from the nest was imprisonment for a year and a clay, with a fine, at the will of the King.[4]

Persons not having the right of killing game upon any land, nor having permission from the person entitled to such right, are prohibited by statute from taking or destroying the nests or eggs of swans, under a penalty not exceeding 5*s*. for every egg.[5]

———————

¹ *Vide* 7 Co. Rep. p. 16.

² 'Stamf. Prerog.' 37 b; Plowd. 315; Bracton, lib. ii. cap. i. fol. 9.

¹ Year Book, 2 Richd. III. p. 15.

² *Ibid.* 'Strange *v.* Charlton.'

³ 'Reg. *v.* Lady Young,' 7 Rep. 18.

¹ 7 Co. Eep. 17.

² Dalt, c. 156.

³ *Vide* Hale's 'Pleas of the Crown,' vol. i. p. 511.

⁴ 11 Hen. VII. cap. xvii.

⁵ 1 & 2 Wm. IV. cap. xxxii. s. 24. See also, *infra*, 'Laws affecting Wild-fowl.'

CHAPTER XXXVIII

WILD-FOWL SHOOTING UNDER SAIL

> . . . . .'With fiery burst,
> The unexpected death invades the flock;
> Tumbling they lie, and beat the flashing waves,
> Whilst those remoter from the fatal range
> Of the swift shot, mount up on vig'rous wing,
> And wake the sleeping echoes as they fly.'
>
> *Fowling: a Poem*, book v.

WILD-FOWL shooting at sea in the depth of winter is supposed by some persons (and not without reason) to be so cold a sport that none but those who have been thoroughly accustomed to it, or who have lion-like constitutions, can endure it.

A man who enters spiritedly upon the sport of wild-fowl shooting in all its branches must, truly, be robust and strong in health and limb; but to enable him to partake of the pleasures of the diversion under sail, he will not require that muscular strength which is necessary for punting and many other branches of the pursuit. His constitution, however,

410

will be well tried in the shooting-yacht, and still more so in the open sailing-boat, if he exposes himself to severities of weather, which he must do if he expects to be successful. He who follows up the sport effectively will assuredly be exposed to rough weather on some occasions, winter cruising being far different to summer yachting; and the chances of encountering bad weather are at least two to one in the winter season as against those of the summer. The sea-going sportsman must, therefore, be prepared to face keen winds, snowstorms, and biting frosts.

In the opinion of all indolent sportsmen (if any such there be) there is no branch of the pursuit so agreeable as this; and, indeed, it may sometimes be indulged in with little exertion and very much pleasure. It is one which need not be pursued alone: the sportsman may invite to accompany him friends and amateurs, who, if they be well behaved and obedient to his injunctions when approaching birds, will be no hindrance to success; and the cripple-chase, which immediately succeeds an effectual shot, generally affords half an hour's amusement with plenty of sport for two or three shoulder-guns, and is excessively good fun for the yachtman's friends and *compagnons de voyage*.

The best position for using a swivel-gun on board a yacht is in the fore-part of the vessel, but in small yachts and such as are used for other purposes than wild-fowling the gun is generally fitted to a chock, placed on the top of the yacht's cuddy; the sportsman then stands below, just outside the gangway, and in that position, by aid of the swivel and recoil apparatus, he is enabled to shoot on the windward side of the sails, or indeed on either side, if the main-tack of the sail be triced up. It is usual, however, to shoot only on the windward side, particularly when the gun is placed abaft the mast.

The advantages of being able to work the gun in front of the mast are several. In the first place, the sportsman stands in a foremost position, and is several yards nearer the birds than when abaft the mast; he can shoot with equal facility from either bow, and very much quicker than in the other position, because he has not to guard against so many obstacles, as ropes and rigging, which are frequently in the way on taking aim or firing from the aft-cabin gangway. In the next place, it is seldom necessary for any of the crew to go in front of the gun when fitted for use over the bows of the yacht; whilst in the other position there is constantly some one or other of the crew obliged to go forward in advance of the gun, to attend to sails and ropes.

When the swivel-gun is fitted to the yacht with recoil-spring and other indispensable appendages,[1] it may be employed with the facility and certainty of a small shoulder-piece: a very little practice will soon make the newest tyro familiar with its action, and enable him to kill with tolerable success. The most difficult part he has to learn is to judge of distances: small objects on the open sea are so deceptive to the eye, that a good deal of practice is necessary before anyone can correctly judge of gun-shot range on the open water. It is laughable to see a novice at the sport squandering away powder and shot by banging at wild-geese 300, 400, and even 500 yards distant, and then wondering how it is he does not kill, attributing the fault to the gun, which he perhaps condemns as of 'no good.'

The stanchion-gun (if a muzzle-loading one) may be quickly and handily loaded aboard the shooting-yacht, and generally without unshipping it or casting off any of the tackle. It is of much importance that the gun should be carefully wiped out with a bit of oakum before reloading. Instructions for loading the punt-gun, which apply equally to the stanchion-gun, have already been given under the head 'Management of the Punt-gun' (*supra*, page 132).

It is usual to take a gunning-punt with the yacht when venturing to sea on a shooting excursion: it can be hauled on deck in rough weather, and during calms it is often found useful to the sportsman for going in pursuit of wild-fowl in shallow water and sheltered bays, where it would not be prudent, and is sometimes impracticable, to venture with the yacht. Opportunities of this kind are of daily occurrence during severe weather.

Mild winters are unfavourable alike for this branch of the

sport as others; for, besides the scarcity, the birds are generally more wary in mild weather than in severe, consequently the sportsman must not expect much sport with his swivel-gun, unless the winter sets in in good old-fashioned earnest.

The pursuit of wild-fowl shooting under sail, with yacht and swivel-gun, is chiefly directed to the gaggles of brent-geese which frequent various parts of the coast in winter; but with sailing-*boat* and swivel-gun the pursuit is generally confined to extensive inland waters, where small birds, as duck and widgeon, form the chief objects of the diversion; and the sailing-sportsman should make himself as familiar as possible with the habits of such birds under the various changes of wind and weather, which always more or less regulate their movements.

'As now the season comes, the fowler marks
Sagacious every change, and feeds his hopes
With signs predictive.'

In fine weather wild-fowl are generally watchful, sprightly, and difficult of access; in cloudy and threatening weather they are either drowsy and reluctant to rise from the water, or so busily engaged in feeding that they regard the sportsman's movements with far less concern and suspicion than during bright and open weather. On sunny days, immediately succeeding rough weather, storms, or a gale, wild-fowl are resting and sleeping during the day, and will sit to the sportsman with remarkable indifference. In very windy weather they are generally unsettled and difficult of approach; but in a moderate breeze the sportsman will often be able to come at them in smooth water, whilst he will find it no easy task in a heavy sea.

Whenever there are many wild-fowl about the coast, and the sportsman has been cruising about among their haunts at sea for several hours, without observing any, or but few, on the wing, he may rely upon it they are resting; and such is generally a faithful foreboding of the near approach of bad weather: instinct seems to warn the feathered occupants of the waters to obtain all the repose they can, previous to being tossed and driven to and fro in restless confusion during an impending gale. On such occasions the sportsman should make the best of his time, and obtain as many shots as he can; and then, without delay, seek a safe harbour for himself, his vessel, and crew.

During thick weather, when there is only little wind, with snow and sleet, sea-game may generally be bagged with good success; the birds are tamer in their habits, and do not fly so far on being disturbed as they do in clear fine weather. But the most golden opportunities are those of a few hours immediately preceding a gale, and also those immediately succeeding it; on both which occasions the sea-going sportsman will invariably find that, with ordinary precautions, access may be obtained to the wildest gaggles which frequent the coast.

Wild-geese and ducks prefer muddy flats and shallows, tideways, the margin of sea-banks, and the locality of surface floatage. Pochards, shovellers, and such like, when at sea, frequent sandy bottoms and deeper places than those of other fowl. A thorough knowledge of the coast or inland waters, or wherever else the sport may be engaged in, is of paramount importance to the sailor-sportsman; indeed, either he or one at least of his crew must be familiar with the locality.

Much of the success depends on the skill of the skipper or helmsman; it is, therefore, very desirable that the sportsman should engage the services of an efficient captain—one familiar with the arts and manœuvres of the sport. The yacht should always be well in hand, and the skipper's whole, undivided attention must be directed to the pursuit. He should lay his course at the birds with a free wind, so as to be enabled to fetch them on a 'full and by,' and thus have scope to make a powerful sweep on luffing up to them, and] so 'head' the birds as they rise to windward.

As the deadly range is being gained upon wild-fowl the sportsman should take care to have his gun in readiness; and he must avoid looking back at the helmsman to give instructions of any kind, more especially that of waving the hand, which would immediately put up every bird. Having given his directions long before approaching within range, the sportsman must rely entirely on the helmsman for his chances of obtaining a shot; and, regardless of the actions of any of those behind him, he should keep his attention mainly upon the birds pursued.

A well-trained crew will require no caution; as the yacht approaches the birds they keep their heads below the bulwarks, and avoid moving head or limb.

On putting up a flight of wild-fowl at sea, the route they take should be narrowly watched, their alight carefully noted, their species made out, and other things considered, previous to pursuing them. A powerful telescope is an indispensable requisite aboard a shooting yacht, and indeed for almost every branch of the sport as connected with boating.

When a gaggle of black geese is discovered at sea it should first be considered by the helmsman whether he can fetch to windward of them or not; for it is invariably found useless to attempt getting within range by running directly to leeward. The skipper should bear-away, or make two or three tacks in a contrary direction, until he finds he can fairly fetch them; then by reaching along at full sail, keep the yacht on such a tack that the birds may be under the lee-bow. The sails of the vessel hide the deck and its occupants from view, so that nothing can be seen stirring—the yacht all the while gaining rapidly and coming quickly upon them: the moment they rise, the helm should be put down to luff the yacht into the eye of the wind, for they are almost certain to rise to windward, and cross the bows of the yacht. Then is the critical moment (if within range) to pull trigger, when—

'Some lifeless fall, others, with flutt'ring wing,
Attempt, in vain, to rise again in air.'

By neglecting to put the helm down at the moment of the birds rising from the water, they will be found to be too far to windward—or, rather, abreast of the weather-shrouds—before the sportsman can shoot with the stanchion-gun; and then, of course, it is too late. The stanchion-gun should not be fired abaft the shrouds: independently of the difficulty of taking aim in a broadside position, there is danger of shooting away the yacht's rigging, besides other obstacles rendering such a proceeding imprudent. Almost everything depends on the helmsman aboard the shooting yacht: he must be constantly on the *qui vive*, and quick and skilful in luffing up in such, a manner as to cross the flight of the birds (see the engraving opposite). Wild-fowl are unconscious of the speed of a sailing-vessel, and are completely deceived by the rapidity with which it gains upon them after they have taken alarm and are preparing to fly away.

A Scientific Sitot at Brent Geese

Immediately after discharging the stanchion-gun at wild-geese or other fowl their line of flight should be long and carefully watched; many birds which are mortally wounded sometimes fly a long distance, as a mile and upwards, before dropping dead:[1] these are called 'droppers.' It is, therefore, usual for one at least of the crew to watch the skein as long as it can be seen, carefully observing the direction of their flight; and, on alighting, to mark, by aid of the compass, a buoy, or some land-mark, the spot where they go down; so as to be enabled to follow in their track, pick up the droppers, and endeavour to obtain another shot.

It is an excellent plan, in moderate weather, to work both punt and yacht at the same birds; or rather, to send a man round with punt and gun to make the best shot he can, the yachtsman meanwhile watching from a distance the punter's movements and those of the fowl. Having judiciously placed the yacht on the track which the wild-fowl would naturally take on rising, the sailing-sportsman may generally obtain a shot directly after the punter has fired. A person accustomed to note the route generally taken by wild-geese, and the manner in which they rise, will find no great difficulty in thus intercepting their flight, and adding considerably to the numbers killed by the punter.

There are some days when the fowler may be sailing about from morning till night amongst plenty of wild-fowl, and not meet with a single shot: every sailing sportsman can vouch for this, though but few can account for it. The day may appear most favourable; indeed, the identical occasion when one might hope and expect to bag a good number; and the sportsman finds, to his disappointment, quite the contrary, the birds being thoroughly fidgetty and unapproachable. Another time he may put to sea under less favourable auspices, and make from six to twelve excellent shots; but *twelve* shots, it should be observed, is an unusual number for one day's sport with the stanchion-gun: six may be fairly reckoned as a good day's sport. I have heard of sixteen being made, but probably more than half were random shots, and the result of such sport has generally been inferior to that of other sportsmen who expended their ammunition less freely.

The sailing sportsman must not be disappointed at 'blank days,' which he will encounter quite as often at sea as on land. Every wild-fowl shooter is exposed to similar disappointments, whether he pursue his diversion by land or water. Experience teaches, that the fewer and more select we make our shots, the more effective they are, and the more satisfactory the results; it should, nevertheless, be borne in mind that wild-fowl, contrary to game, are mere birds of passage, and though here today they may be gone to-morrow; therefore the old proverb may be well applied—Delay not till to-morrow what may be done to-day.' A wild-goose chase is seldom effective, but when so, the sportsman should make the most of it; and such considerations should influence everyone who pursues the sport of wild-goose shooting with stanchion-gun, at sea.

---

[1] *Supra*, p. 130.

[1] Captain T. Williamson says, 'If one be wounded, it always separates from the flock, and generally changes its course. I have known a goose to fly nearly four miles before it has dropped.'—*Oriental Field Sports*, A.D. 1807.

CHAPTER XXXIX

THE WILD-FOWLER IN A GALE

'With palaver and nonsense I'm not to be paid off;
I'm adrift, let it blow then great guns:

A gale, a fresh breeze, or the old ge'man's head off—
I takes life rough and smooth as it runs.'—DIBDIN.

IT is from no desire to make myself the hero of success and
perilous adventure that I am about to relate as briefly as
possible a stirring scene which happened to fall to my lot a
few years ago; but because it is my firm conviction that there
is not a better or livelier means of conveying to one's readers a
clear notion of this branch of the sport, with the enthusiasm,
enjoyment, and (more especially) dangers, which sometimes
attend wild-fowling adventures at sea, than by a faithful
narrative of individual experiences on trying occasions.

The wind had been blowing lightly from the south-east,
snow and sleet were falling with most dismal threatening, when
I embarked at eight o'clock one morning, in the early part of
the month of February, aboard a small shooting yacht of twelve

tons admeasurement. A sporting friend accompanied me, in addition to my crew, which consisted of one man and one boy! I firmly believe my friend wished himself ashore (though he did not say so) before he had been on board the yacht five minutes, so cold, wet, and dreary was the weather. As the clay advanced, the wind moderately increased, the snow and sleet ceased to fall, and my friend became more cheerful; but the sky still looked threatening—very threatening all around: it was freezing, but not severely. The breeze was just the thing for the yacht, which glided noiselessly, but rapidly, through the water, as a shooting yacht should do, and without dashing the spray about or making much disturbance at her bows.

After making in the course of the morning four or five very successful shots at Brent geese, much to the delight and amusement of my friend, who was a stranger to the sport, I observed that the sky wore a fiercer aspect, and therefore deemed it prudent to abandon the pursuit, and make sail for a safe harbour; when, soon after putting about, a very inviting shot at some widgeon which lay in our course tempted me to uncover the stanchion-gun once more, draw the large shot from the barrel, and substitute smaller. This done, I gave my friend the chances of the shot; and the birds really seemed so tame that we did as we liked with them, and put them up within beautiful range. My friend knocked down exactly a baker's dozen, every one of which we secured without difficulty.

The excitement of the sport had drawn attention from the coming gale, now rapidly bearing down upon us. I cast an eye to windward, and on seeing the white scud driving fiercely across the sea, and close upon us, I instantly gave directions to Hake in the jib, and set the spitfire! Haul down a pair of reefs in the mainsail, and make all snug!' But before these orders could be obeyed, such a squall came upon us as made our little vessel

'To shudder and pause like a frighted steed,
Then leap her cable's length.'

It was the first blast of the gale which a few hours previously had been predicted, from a familiar acquaintance with the habits of the fowl which had been so unusually tame and easy of access throughout the whole morning; and it now raged in right good earnest. We were about ten miles from the nearest harbour, and the wind lay 'right on end.' With such a prospect before us, and the sea increasing every minute, no time could be lost in preparing for a rough passage. A third reef was taken in the mainsail, the foresail close reefed, the deck cleared, stanchion-gun taken into the cabin, hatchways firmly secured, and every precaution taken for guarding against accidents, and preparing to meet the roughest weather. The sea now began to run tremendously high, as harder and harder blew the gale. The wind was bitterly keen; but cold was unheeded whilst the excitement lasted. We had a safe and sound little vessel to navigate, and nothing but good seamanship was required to manage her. But it was desperate work, as she pitched and plunged in the tumbling waves, dashing along and throwing clouds of spray over the whole deck, wetting everything and everybody aboard. So heavy was the gale, and so rough the sea, that it became each one's business to hold on as he best could; and from my critical position at the helm, I took the precaution to pass a lashing round my waist; a very necessary one it proved, indeed, as a few minutes later a big wave struck the little vessel abroad sides, and soused me from head to foot in my oilskin garments, and, but for the lashing, would inevitably have carried me over the taffrail. We were four long hours working our course to windward, which in fine weather had often been performed in less than half that time; consequently it was getting dusk before we weathered our point at the entrance to the harbour. Every rope had remained true to its berth during the whole struggle with wind and waves, although the severest strain had been put upon them; and so far fortunately, for had any of our principal ropes been unequal to the strain and given way, I could not have answered for the consequences in such a gale and heavy sea. Several large vessels were observed running for shelter in the harbour; and whilst rounding the point a fine schooner, with loss of foretopmast, passed us, as she was also making for a place of refuge. Her crew, which it appears had been watching our little craft for some time, as she laboured in the sea, gave us a hearty cheer, which was warmly responded to with our small united efforts. One reef was now shaken out of our mainsail, and we ran to leeward through the harbour at a rapid rate; it was quite dark before we came to anchor, after as desperate a pitch-and-tumble cruise in a winter's gale at sea as I ever experienced. As to my friend, who had been lashed to the bulwarks in the waist of the yacht, he seemed more dead than alive; and, notwithstanding the pleasure the sport afforded him in the morning, about which he had been quite in ecstasy, he now thought far less of its attractions after a taste of its disagreeables. Thus terminated a very trying adventure, after as good a day's sport with the stanchion-gun as I have ever had the pleasure to enjoy.

. . . . .

'Well may we pause to-day! may Eortune smile
As kindly on each fowler's gen'rous toils

As she has done on ours!'

The narrative above recorded is but a true picture of what the wild-fowler must sometimes expect if he follows up energetically the pursuit of wild-fowl shooting at sea.

CHAPTER XL

THE SHOOTING-YACHT

'Aye! at set of sun:

The breeze will freshen when the day is done.

My corslet—cloak—one hour, and we are gone!'—BYRON.

THE shooting-yacht is, comparatively speaking, a modern invention connected with the captivating diversion of wild-fowling. It affords a pleasant means of pursuing the sport, though by far the most costly. The pleasures connected with it are healthy and invigorating to those whose constitution enables them to bear the cold without inconvenience. And cold enough it is sometimes. I have found myself engaged heart and soul in the sport when every dash of spray congealed into ice before it could be wiped from the deck with the mop. But that is the best time of all for pursuing the sport of wildfowl shooting, because the weather is then so severe that it makes the birds tamer, though restless, and affords the sailing sportsman splendid amusement.

During the time when Colonel Hawker wrote the shooting-yacht was little used, but a large open sailing-boat, bearing no resemblance, and claming no place beside the splendid specimens of yachting architecture lately brought out for the purpose.

Many yachters, at the present day, who take their pleasure-cruises in summer, dismantle their yachts of the sunny-sky canvas as soon as the season is over, and substitute smaller sails, of stouter material; fit a chock, swivel, and recoiling apparatus on the bows of the yacht; and thus convert their summer cruiser into a winter sporting vessel. Others, whose yachts are too large for the purpose, keep a smaller one, which takes up the moorings of the larger as soon as the summer cruising ceases.

But the complete shooting-yacht is a great comfort, more especially to some sportsmen; and, as such vessels are not to be met with every day, it is purposed to give a description of one of modern construction, with its fittings and equipment.

In the first place, it should be borne in mind that the shooting-yacht must be adapted to sea-going purposes, because it is only at sea that the sport of wild-goose shooting can be thoroughly appreciated.

The vessel itself should be from fifteen to twenty tons

burthen O.M.—a fast-sailing, but stiff and burthensome vessel under canvas. It must be of easy draught of water, that the wild-fowler may be enabled to pursue his sport in shallows, and close to the shore, such being favourite places of resort with the aquatic species.

The yacht should be yawl-rigged, if the gun is to be worked from the cabin-hatchway, abaft the mast; but it may be cutter-rigged, if the gun be worked over the bows of the vessel; which latter method is the proper one.

The cabins of a perfect shooting-yacht are in the reverse positions to those of an ordinary pleasure-vessel; the sailors' cabin being sternmost, the state-cabin occupying all the forepart of the craft, and the sleeping-cabins the centre. There is also an open well, or fore-hatchway, in which the sportsman stands and manages the gun, which works on a pivot fitted directly in the centre of the fore-deck, between the bows, so that it can be used over either side of the vessel; and there should always be plenty of room abaft the gun, for the sportsman to move around and about it. The recoil-spring and apparatus, with swivel, should be so fitted that he may take aim and fire with equal effect from a broadside as across the bows of the vessel.

The skylights, hatchways, and other above-deck fittings should be constructed with all the neatness of a racing-yacht, nothing rising above the level of the bulwarks; and even they should be no higher than absolutely necessary, that the vessel may show no more of her hull, and present as small an appearance above water, as consistently may be.

The bottom of the yacht should be cased with copper or other metal, which should be of extra thickness at the bows, that it may not be damaged by coming in contact with ice, which most shooting-yachts are liable to encounter at some time or other during severe seasons.

There are conveniences on the decks of such a vessel as the one under explanation, for carrying two gunning-punts in such a manner that they are not seen above the level of the bulwarks; everything being snugly arranged, and with especial regard to the comfort of the wild-fowler, his friends, and crew.

The cost of a yacht of the description here attempted would be from 300*l.* to 500*l.*, according to material, workmanship, fittings, and other circumstances.

Three men will be sufficient to navigate a vessel of the kind; or two, and a good useful lad, if the yachtsman himself occasionally lends a hand, and which he would only be required to do now and then—for instance, if caught in a heavy gale, and having suddenly to reef sails. On such occasions no shooting could be done; and the gun should be well coated with tarpaulin, or placed below, in the cabin. If a very heavy sea comes on, the fore-hatchways must be put on and secured; in which case access may be obtained to the cabin from the aft-hatchway, and through one of the sleeping-cabins. So desperate a gale as to require all these precautions to be carried out would probably not occur more than once or twice in several years, with ordinary prudence; but, having more than once been in perilous predicaments myself, I have felt it worth while to give the caution.

The only other occasion when the yachtsman might be called on to take the helm or assist in tacking the vessel would be when one or two of his crew have manned the punts, or the yacht's gig (if she carries one), to go in quest of the wounded birds, just after firing the large gun. At such a time it is usual for the yacht to be laid-to; or, if wind and weather be favourable, the cripples are pursued with the yacht, despatched with the shoulder-gun, and picked up by means of a cripple-net, which is very similar to an angler's landing-net, attached to a long staff. The cripple-net forms part of the necessary equipment of a shooting-yacht, and is also an indispensable requisite to the shooting-*boat* hereinafter described.

Men who make wild-fowl shooting their business, in the season, proceed to sea in parties of three or four, in a small vessel of from ten to twenty tons, taking each a punt and gun with which to pursue their calling, and making simply a temporary habitation of the vessel. These men frequently endure great hardships, and remain at sea several clays at a time. They seldom put off in their punts by daylight, but watch the birds at morning and evening twilight, when they mark their whereabouts, and steal upon them whilst it is dark, often making a profitable return.

The wild-fowlers on the Eastern coast are, for the most part, a hardy, independent class. They usually employ themselves during summer as fishers or dredgers; and when winter sets in some of them pursue the more precarious calling of wild-fowl shooting as a means of maintenance.

As there is generally a good deal of gunpowder on board a shooting yacht, by way of caution everyone should be made acquainted with the place where it is deposited, directly he sets foot on deck, and all should be cautious in using pipes and cigars, never to lay them down carelessly. If in haste at any time, the best way is to throw them overboard at once, though only half-smoked. It is during hasty and excited moments that accidents generally occur.

It is usual to keep the guns loaded aboard the yacht (except they are breech-loaders), both punt-guns and others; but neither should be laid by or taken into the cabin until the caps are removed and a piece of tow or oakum placed over the nipples, and if a breech-loader, the cartridge withdrawn. No one on board should ever be allowed to stand or sit before the muzzle of a loaded gun; and whenever firearms are used in small open boats, the greater precaution is necessary, unless the muzzles are held pointing upwards, and the butt-ends resting on the floor of the boat. Small boats are more liable than large ones to sudden movements, as rolling and pitching; and a slight jerk will sometimes cause a gun to explode.

No sudden surprise should induce a man to forget that he holds in his hand a most dangerous and deadly weapon, and that the slightest carelessness may cause a fatal accident, which would embitter with sorrow the remainder of his days, and probably plunge his dearest relatives into the deepest grief; all of whom perhaps the moment before were gay and cheerful, their lives unclouded by regret, and bright with the fairest sunshine of happiness. I can picture to myself no sharper sting of remorse than to have hurried a fellow-creature into eternity through carelessness or incaution.

CHAPTER XLI

THE SHOOTING-BOAT

'But a far nobler spoil

Awaits him on the river; where the rocks

Aiding the roaring stream, it keeps at bay

The eager frost, and many a broken pool,

Half liquid and half solid, forms; the haunt,

Of all the kindred tribes that love to cleave

With glossy breast and paddling feet the flood.'

Fowling: a Poem, book v.

THERE is a highly agreeable and satisfactory means of pursuing the sport of wild-fowl shooting under sail, which is but one stage less in importance than that afforded by the shooting-yacht. It is that usually resorted to in large rivers and shallow bays, where the shooting-yacht is precluded from proceeding, because of drawing too much water. Thus the shooting-yacht and stanchion-gun are used for sea-going purposes, and the open sailing-boat, with gun of smaller proportions, for inland waters and shallows.

A boat for this purpose should be about twenty feet in length by seven feet beam; a shallow craft, with powerful bearings.

Stability is a great desideratum in a boat required for this diversion. It is not desirable that the boat should list on her side too much when under sail, as it interferes with the management of the stanchion-gun. A narrow deck-way of ten or twelve inches should be formed on each side of the boat, which should have no bulwarks, but the deck-way should be upon a level with the gunwales. The fore and aft part of the boat may also be partly covered in by a flush-deck, but in other respects it may be entirely open or partly covered in, so as to form a small cabin or cuddy.

A boat of this description will require several hundredweight of lead or iron ballast, which must be deposited with careful discretion beneath the platform.

The stanchion-gun should be fitted with chock and necessary recoiling apparatus upon the flush-deck at the bows, and must be placed so as to swing clear of the fore-stay, that a shot may be fired from either bow.

The best form of rig for this boat is the 'sloop rig,' by which the fore-stay, instead of being made fast to the stem, stands farther out at the extreme end of the standing bowsprit, thus giving more room for the sportsman to work the stanchion-gun clear of ropes, and enabling him to place it in a more advantageous position.[1]

A pair of sweeps[2] should form part of the equipment, so as to guard against calms; a cripple-net, for the purpose of picking up dead and wounded birds, should also be carried. It is desirable that a small punt should accompany the boat, to assist in recovering the strongest of the cripples.

The shooting-boat so fitted and equipped affords the wild-fowler a very pleasant and agreeable means of pursuing the sport.

The method of approaching birds with the shooting-boat is identical with that of the shooting-yacht already explained under the head 'Wild-fowl Shooting under Sail;' the same motionless silence must be observed, and the same skill is required on the part of the helmsman in luffing the instant the birds rise from the water, thus giving the sportsman— who should always station himself at the prow of a shooting-boat—the best possible chance of a shot.

The sportsman will require one man only (or a man and a boy) besides himself, to manage a boat of this description, provided he occasionally assists in hauling on a rope, taking in a sail, and such-like light duties: and there will be ample accommodation for two or three friends, who may provide themselves with small shoulder-guns, for the purpose of despatching winged birds in a cripple-chase.

The pursuit may also be followed in a boat of this kind on moonlight nights, if desirable; but it will be found far pleasanter by daylight. Open boats when used for wild-fowl shooting should be furnished with two or more strips of oilcloth lined with thick flannel, each about six feet in length by two in breadth, one edge of which should be tacked lengthwise on each side of the boat directly under the gunwales inside, in such a manner as to hang down, and form at all times a protection from wet and frost to the shoulder-guns, which, when not in actual use, should be placed beneath it. A covering of this kind should be tacked on the inside of all shooting-boats, whether used for rowing, punting, or sailing.

But for certain objections probably no better form of boat could be invented for traversing the shallow waters of inland bays and rivers, the resort of wild-fowl, than an American centre-board boat.[1] Such a craft, by reason of its great stability, would carry the stanchion-gun well. The keel might be lowered at pleasure, or when beating up the channel of a river, or in deep water; whilst the shallow form of the boat would enable the sportsman to go over almost any ooze or sand-bank with facility, where there was a depth of one foot or afoot and a half of water. There are, however, some awkward objections to the use of such boats for the stanchion-gun. In the first place, the mast of an American centre-board boat is placed in the bows, close to the stem; so that the gun could not be worked in the fore part of the boat; and as the centre-board case would be in the way of fixing the gun amidships, it is difficult to find a convenient place for working it with facility. In addition to which the mainsail of a centre-board boat of suitable size for wild-fowl shooting is fitted with a boom, which also would interfere with the free working of the stanchion-gun.

———————

[1] An engraving of a sloop-rigged shooting-boat under sail, and equipped with stanchion-gun, &c, is contained in my work, 'The Sailing Boat' (4th edition), p. 101.

[2] Long two-handed oars.

[1] See description and engravings of these boats in my work, 'The Sailing Boat' (4th edition), p. 80.

CHAPTER XLII

THE WILD-FOWL CANOE

' 'Tis now the fowler mans his little bark,
    Equipped with gun, and dog of sturdiest strain,
    Prepared to weather the relentless blast—
    To deal destruction 'mid the feathered train.'—T.
HUGHES.

THE canoe for wild-fowl-shooting is a small boat about twelve feet in length by three and a half in breadth, and about fifteen inches deep in the fore-part by ten inches in the aft. It is clench-built in a similar manner to a skiff, and with a keelson, but as flat in the floor as it is possible to make it, because of the occasional necessity of going into shallow water. The canoe is intended to carry two persons and a dog; it is used for the purpose of proceeding up the creeks and rills of tidal rivers and under the banks of oozes at low water; when, as the tide rises sufficiently high to bring the top rim of the bows of the canoe upon a level with the surface of the ooze, the sportsman may sometimes make a very successful shot.

He must be provided with a large fowling-piece of

proportions too heavy for lifting to the shoulder or firing in an ordinary way, but of such weight and dimensions as to require a rest on which to place the barrel when taking aim. A gun of this description generally carries about four ounces of shot at a charge, and should be loaded with No. 1 or single B's.

When the sportsman has discovered wild-fowl feeding on the savannas he places himself on his knees in the fore-part of the canoe, rests the barrel of the gun on the bow of the boat, whilst his companion cautiously sculls the canoe, with one oar, towards the birds. For this purpose a sculling rowlock is fitted to the centre of the stern-piece through which the oar is thrust; and the bows of the boat being higher than the stern, the movements of both men are concealed from view, and effective shots are sometimes made, particularly on moonlight nights.

When not actually approaching wild-fowl one person sits facing the prow, to look out for sport and give directions to the other, who rows the boat with a pair of sculls up creeks and rills, or wherever there may be a prospect of sport; and notwithstanding that it is an old-fashioned method of wild-fowl shooting, very *good* sport may sometimes be had with a boat of this description, particularly during sharp weather, when wild-fowl are generally more abundant. A dog is sometimes carried in the wild-fowl canoe, for the purpose of fetching the birds after a successful shot has been fired; but it is not always necessary that a dog should accompany the sportsman, the better plan being to carry a pair of splashers, which the sportsman or his boatman can put on and go upon the ooze to collect the dead and wounded birds; and such is the more usual course, and certainly the more humane, for it must be at a risk of serious constitutional injury to a dog to get very wet in sharp weather, and then be compelled to remain a long time in that miserable condition, without exercise, in a small open boat; to say nothing of the annoyance it occasions the occupants of the canoe, having a wet dog at their feet during the rest of the day.

The wild-fowl canoe will also be found useful for curlew shooting, as described under that head (*infra*, cap. LVII.); also plovers, oxbirds, sandpipers, and other frequenters of marshy lands intersected with tidal waters. Three persons may be occasionally accommodated in the canoe, one of whom may carry as large a shoulder-gun as he can manage, whilst another attends the great gun; the whole duty of the other must be to attend the canoe. It is a pleasant means of enjoying a day's wild-fowl shooting, and often highly satisfactory to ail parties, particularly those who do not venture on the more 'crack performances' of punting, with its difficulties, dangers, and laborious exertions. The canoe is an excellent cradle in which for a youth to take his first lessons in the famous sport of wild-fowl shooting; and if an experienced hand accompanies him., attends to the boat properly, and knows how to manage it, the young sportsman may soon learn sufficient of the habits of wild-fowl, the method of approaching them, and management of a boat, to enable him to try his hand at punting.

The canoe is also a useful boat for chasing cripple wild-fowl, the result of heavy charges from the punt and stanchion guns.

CHAPTER XLIII

THE CRIPPLE CHASE

'Sportsmen, be merciful in death,
Nor ever let your prey breathe out its life
In ling'ring agonies.'—*Fowling: a Poem*, book i.

THE cripple-chase follows immediately upon a successful shot with stanchion or punt gun. It is in fact nothing more than the chase of the winged and wounded, which, though unable to fly, contrive to elude their pursuers a long time, by diving, dodging, and swimming away. It would appear to be a wanton pursuit to chase disabled birds as the objects of sport; but, as one-third at least of those which are stopped by a discharge from the stanchion gun are only wounded, it becomes a matter of necessity, if the wild-fowler wishes to secure them, that he should pursue them by the best means that he can; and as a web-footed water-fowl, when only slightly wounded, is not so easily captured as many would suppose, a cripple-chase is not always attended with successful results.

Directly the cripples find themselves pursued they make for the deepest water at hand, and then, as an invariable rule, work

443

their course to *windward*, swimming off as fast as they can. As their pursuer gains upon them they evade him by incessant diving and dodging, frequently keeping up the chase some fifteen or twenty minutes, and only resigning themselves to fate when sheer exhaustion compels them. The cripple wild-duck shows great spirit and tenacity, much more so than the mallard, which may be captured with far less difficulty.

The ordinary method of pursuing a cripple wild-fowl is by rowing after it as fast as possible, following it up as closely as can be, striking it across the neck with the edge of one of the oar-blades, and thus, by blows and activity, tiring it out, so that it has no longer strength to dive, when the pursuer seizes it by the neck and takes it into his boat. He then goes in pursuit of another, and so on, one at a time, fairly tiring them out.

The cripple chase affords fine fun for young sailors and cabin-boys, and when it arises from a shot fired by a sportsman from his shooting yacht he generally sends his two youngest hands (two boys, if such are aboard) in the yacht's dingay, or a punt to capture the wounded birds: so that whilst it affords the boys infinite delight to chase the cripples, the yachtsman himself finds equal amusement in watching their proceedings from the yacht's deck.

The Cripple Chase

'Here it is!' and 'There it is!' are echoed simultaneously as the bird suddenly rises again to the surface, after diving beneath the boat; when, after a long chase of many minutes' close pursuit, its powers of diving gradually become weaker, and the exits from the surface are of shorter duration, until, at last, the poor victim, powerless from exhaustion, is secured.

A strong cripple sometimes leads its pursuers half-an-hour's chase before it can be taken, particularly in rough water.

The punter always goes in pursuit of his cripples before reloading; and if he has a small double-barrelled shoulder-piece with him, as every punter ought to have, he can, if he chooses, make short work of the cripple chase, and spare many of those helpless creatures the pain of wanton torture.

445

A good deal depends on the skill of the oarsman as to the time it takes to capture wounded birds. If two novices are put into a boat, they can no more capture a strong cripple-duck than they can fly; but it is, nevertheless, laughable to look on at their attempts: every now and then one or another 'catches a crab,'[1] and his heels fly up in the air in the most ludicrous manner, to the great amusement of those looking on. At another time, just as one stretches out his hand over the gunwale of the boat to grasp the bird, it 'shuts the door upon him,' by instantly disappearing beneath the surface, and remaining under water a minute or more; then when it again appears, to their astonishment, it is some fifty or sixty yards off; thus, again and again they make their useless attempts, until they tire themselves, and are obliged to abandon the chase to more skilful oarsmen.

The engraving opposite is intended as an illustration of the proceedings in a cripple chase after firing 1 1/2 lbs. shot from the stanchion-gun on board a sailing-yacht at a team of wild-ducks. The cripples are being pursued among some floes of drift-ice by three amateurs in a rowing-boat. Whilst the yacht is also engaged in picking up the dead birds, a small herd of wild-swans are observed passing over the yacht; and the stanchion-gun not being re-loaded, one of the sportsmen on board the yacht takes a pop at them with a shoulder-piece, bringing down a fine full-grown cygnet.

All web-footed birds, when first wounded, swim into deep water; then, if they are not pursued (as is often the case at night), they soon afterwards make for the lee-shore, the smarting pain of their wounds being irritated by the salt-water, and instinct seems to tell them that the pain can only be alleviated by rest ashore. Waders, such as curlews, plovers, and the like, always avoid the water when wounded, and make direct for the land.

I have often been surprised at the wonderful cunning and dexterity displayed by wounded wild-fowl, and the extraordinary manner in which they evade their pursuers by contriving to keep under water, particularly shovellers, duck, and widgeon. The mallard is not so expert at manoeuvring as the duck; the latter, when only winged or slightly wounded so as to be unable to fly, often puzzles the oldest and most experienced gunners. But if the water be calm and the surface smooth, by following up the wounded duck quickly and closely when it dives, it may generally be captured after a few minutes' chase; though, if there be a ripple upon the surface, the chances are fifty to one that it will escape, more especially if by the side of an ooze-bank, on which weeds grow under water: there will the wounded duck hide, holding itself under water a considerable time, then rising to the surface a moment to breathe and mark the course taken by its pursuers, showing nothing but its head above water; when down it goes again, gradually creeping farther and farther from the punter, who frequently gropes about in wild astonishment, and is at last obliged to abandon the pursuit.[1] I have found it a very good plan in shallow water to stir the bottom with one of the punt oars near the spot where the bird was last seen to dive; thus I have frequently brought wounded birds to the surface and captured them, after they had been hiding some minutes in the sea-weeds under water.

Wild-fowl having simply a pinion broken, swim with their bodies deeply buried in the water. These are the strongest cripples of all, and give the boldest chase.

The cripple-net, which is of similar form to an angler's landing-net but larger, and is provided with a longer staff, may always be employed in the pursuit of badly wounded birds, which, on feebly attempting to escape by diving, may be captured by the fowler with the cripple-net; he must use a little skill in aiming the net below the surface just at the moment the bird dives. A little practice will enable the fowler to use the cripple-net with considerable advantage. It is at all times desirable to capture cripple wild-fowl without firing at them, because of the advantage of securing them without filling their flesh with shot.

In the sharp winters of years gone by, wild-fowl were so abundant that the punter seldom used to think of taking much trouble about the cripple chase, but used merely to collect those only which were killed outright, or so severely wounded as to be unable to flutter away or make any but feeble attempts at diving. The cripples were permitted to hobble ashore, where they became the lawful prize of those who were fortunate enough to secure them.

---

¹ So called in nautical language; *i.e.* topples head over heels in the boat, in consequence of missing a stroke with the oar.

¹ It would seem that the late Lord Chancellor Erskine was very familiar with the difficulties of the cripple chase. He once humorously remarked in the House of Lords, in allusion to the frequent minorities of the Ministerial party in the year 1810, 'It reminds me strongly of shooting wild-fowl in a large lake; for, though you are fortunate enough to knock them down, it is extremely difficult to get them out.'—Vide *Parl, Deb*. 1810.

CHAPTER XLIV

WILD-DUCK SHOOTING

'Down close! the wild-ducks come, and darting down.
Throw up on every side the troubled wave,
Then gaily swim around with idle play.
With breath restrain'd, and palpitating heart,
I view their movements—.'—*Fowling: a Poem*, book V.

THE wild-duck (*Anas boschas*) is more eagerly pursued than any other species of wild-fowl; the decoyer, the punter, the shore-gunner, and the sailor-sportsman, one and all, are his constant persecutors. It is not, therefore, to be wondered at that wild-ducks, as well as others of the species wild-fowl, are the most timid birds of the feathered creation; their customary resorts by daylight being on the loneliest open waters, they are less familiar with the human form than land birds, and consequently more susceptible to alarm and more suspicious of the movements of their enemies.

Wild-duck shooting upon land requires the strictest silence, watchfulness, and precaution, together with the services of a dog specially trained to the pursuit.[1]

The wild-duck being common throughout every country in the universe, all sportsmen are more or less acquainted with its habits, and everyone with its flavour as a table luxury, though it cannot now be purchased at so cheap a rate as in centuries past, when a good mallard might be had for twopence.[2]

The flesh of the wild-duck is indisputably far superior to that of the tame duck; it is more delicate, juicy, and of finer flavour than the domestic fowl. The author of 'Sport and its Pleasures, Physical and Gastronomical,' quaintly remarks:— 'Wild-duck shooting is a first-rate sport, and wild-duck eating a most agreeable undertaking.'

It is the nature of wild-ducks to feed at night and rest during the day, preferring the quietest retreats at all times; and from secluded spots where they may be unobservedly watched they are often found in attitudes which might form very interesting studies both to the naturalist and the artist. Among many other of their peculiar and favourite postures when revelling in unsuspecting security, some may be seen with one of their legs comfortably thrust into the feathers of its side or tucked under its wing, as if to warm its slender toes, whilst others poke their heads beneath their wings, and a few act the part of sentries during the repose of their companions. In such interesting attitudes it would seem very relentless to disturb them, and far worse to take their innocent lives; but the sportsman is said to be cruel, hard-hearted, and eager, and has no room in his conscience for tender considerations about innocent birds. In reply to such aspersions of cruelty we would say, in the language of the unknown author of the spirited poem on Fowling—

. . . . 'And ye, who proudly boast

Of feelings delicate, and most refined,

Ye male or female *sensibilitists*,

Who shrink and shudder at the fowler's sport,

Yet from your doors unpitied, unreliev'd

Turn the poor vet'ran, whose best blood has stream'd

For your security so ill deserv'd,

Blush and he silent: blush again with shame

When you reflect upon the cruel cates

Your tables often yield, with which the Muse

Will not pollute her strain.'

The time of the departure of wild-ducks from the north is about the middle of October, and continues during a part of the following month; when the immense teams of ducks which migrate during that season, passing across the sea and over land, are most attractive and remarkable.

They are supposed to start on their extensive and distant

migrations at the customary hour of evening flight (sunset), and to continue their aerial course throughout the greater part of the night and sometimes during the next day. In the same manner they return in spring to their old quarters.

The habits of wild-ducks indicate a preference for lee-shores. They feed no farther from the land than necessary, so that they can reach the bottom with their bills without sinking their bodies, frequently turning themselves up endwise, in the same manner as tame ducks, when the water is a little too deep to enable them to reach the bottom in a sitting posture; their tails only thus sticking up above the surface, whilst they are busy with their heads and necks dabbling in the mud or weeds at the bottom.

In spring, when wild-ducks are seen in pairs, they sometimes dive for their food after the manner of dun birds and shovellers, but their exits from the surface are of much shorter duration than those of the other species alluded to. As it is only at that season of the year that wild-ducks ever feed by diving, it may be inferred that the objects of their deeper research are water insects, which are always abundant at that particular season.

It is by no means unusual in the early part of winter to find large suits of mallards unaccompanied by ducks. It would seem to be very ungallant on the part of the male birds to leave their companions behind them on the voyage of migration, but so it is—the mallards leave the north earlier than the ducks, which generally remain with their young until the severity of the frost compels them to proceed to a more southern climate.

Wild-ducks are generally very wary by daylight, particularly after having been once shot at. When pursued by the punter they swim fastly away, sitting in a sunken posture, with breasts and bodies deep in the water, and with necks well-doubled and heads down close upon their breasts; in running water they always sit with their breasts to the stream. A few moments before taking wing they lift their heads and rise buoyantly upon the surface; they then turn round head to wind, presenting a broadside to the punter, and, unless stopped by his shot, they instantly rise from the water. The critical moment for pulling trigger is (if near enough) just as they emerge from their sunken attitude and before they turn round head to windward, as that is the last movement before taking wing. Many sportsmen make it a rule to wait for the other opportunity before pulling trigger, and say the birds present at that instant the fairest mark for a shot; it may be they do so, but it is nevertheless decidedly wrong to wait for the broadside chance, unless the punter intends to fire at them on the wing, in which case he is perfectly correct to wait until the last moment, so as to get as near them as possible.

Although the objects appear larger on the water when their broadsides are presented to the punter, it is an indisputable fact that a less number can be killed when in that position than when swimming directly away with their tails towards the gun. This fact I have proved by experience over and over again; but I know several punters who always wait for the broadside chance.

One of the keystones to success in wild-fowl shooting is the art of being a correct judge of distances. Some punters reckon their range by the space of water between the birds and the punt; others never shoot until they can distinctly discern the eye of one or more of the birds; others wait until they can clearly distinguish the colour of the feathers—all which must be uncertain guides, and as some days are more cloudy than others, it would appear that the sportsman is often mistaken and misled by such means.

The only certain and really correct method of judging as to when within range, whilst lying flat on the floor of a punt, is from the bearing of the muzzle of the gun upon the object ahead. Let the gun be once laid in proper range upon the fore-part of the punt, and experience will show that as soon as the muzzle is found to cover the object, the trigger may be pulled with certain success. The punter should not wait for the broadside chance, nor for the colour of the feathers, as either of these may be too late; he should endeavour to get within range whilst the birds are swimming from him; such is the punter's most deadly chance.

Wild-duck shooting at night is often attended with considerable uncertainty (even though the punter may be within fifty yards' range of the birds), on account of their habit of feeding close in-shore among weeds and grasses; totally different to widgeon, which generally feed away from the shore on the green weed they tear up by its roots and other soft substances of the ooze, and the floating refuse of the tide. I have spent many a hour on a cold winter's night within forty and fifty yards of wild-ducks without being able to discover their exact whereabouts, the only guide being the 'quack!' of the mallards.

I have often shot entirely by guess without seeing a bird and killed two or three pair; and I have as frequently shot by guess without killing a single bird, but with the mortification of seeing some forty or fifty rise from the grass within a few feet of the spot where I had supposed them to be feeding.

If wild-fowl detect the least suspicious noise or movement of the enemy whilst they are feeding at night, a death-like stillness instantly prevails; when, if they discover no object near them, in a few moments they resume their dabblings. I have sometimes found it answer my purpose to endeavour to find them by making a slight noise, which causes them to stretch their necks, rear their heads, and look around. This manœuvre, however, requires more than ordinary precaution, or it will operate in the very reverse manner to that intended.

A keen wind and hard frost, with deep snow, are peculiarly favourable for wild-duck shooting, and indeed for wild-fowl shooting generally, though too much wind may interfere with the operations of the punter.

As a general rule, where the wild-duck finds food and quiet inland, it invariably returns. It. is, therefore, a frequently-successful means of obtaining a shot, to watch during the day for stray feathers and such-like signs at the water-side; and then by lying in ambush near the spot, about flight-time, the ducks will in all probability return, and offer a fine opportunity to the sportsman, who, if there be several birds, can take his time, and wait before pulling trigger until he gets them well together or in line.

If the sportsman finds they do not return on the first night of his lying in ambush, he should not be disheartened, but lie-by another night or two, as variation of wind or weather may have affected their movements, and induced them to seek temporary change of feeding-ground; but the *animus revertendi* to the old spot remains, and, sooner or later, the persevering sportsman will be rewarded for his pains.

> 'Down! down! a mallard comes; contain your arm,
> His breast with feathers arm'd no shot can harm.
> Assault him from behind, where less secure,
> He can the piercing message less endure.'[1]

The flight of a wild-mallard, as it suddenly rises from the

moor, presenting a fair shot to the unequipped sportsman, has many a time in my hearing, as probably also in that of many others, brought out the expression,' If I had but a gun! 'as the beautiful bird swept through the air within a few yards of the sportsman's form.

Wild-ducks are fond of resorting by night to large tidal rivers, when they feed so close in-shore that the punter who goes in pursuit of them incurs great risk of being shot by men who prowl about the shore at night, in search of any sort of water-fowl they can find. These men are called 'shore-gunners.' Many a time have I been disappointed of a shot, after lying a long time on the floor of my punt, endeavouring to find the whereabouts of a party of noisy ducks and mallards; and, when just in the act of pulling the trigger, have been startled by the sudden report of a gun from the shore, the shot of which have sometimes come far too near my head to be pleasant; then, directly afterwards, a dog bounds into the water, and, one by one, carries the wounded birds to his master ashore. Some of these men make almost as good a living at shore-gun shooting as a punter; their success is sometimes astonishing, when provided with a good dog and useful gun.

Their pursuits are not entirely confined to night-shooting. They make early excursions along the lee-shore, of a morning, at daybreak; and if there has been much execution done by the punters on the night previously, a vast number of winged and wounded birds are collected. A well-trained retriever is all that is required to find them. The author has known of instances where one man has secured from twelve to fifteen pair of winged and wounded widgeon and duck on a single morning's excursion without firing a shot. And if considered for a moment, this will not appear so very extraordinary; a punt-gun charged with three-quarters of a pound of shot, and fired at a company of widgeon or a paddling of ducks within range, makes terrible slaughter, in which numbers of wounded escape the grasp of the punter, more especially by night.

If I had but a Gun!

Wounded birds by instinct seek the shore, the influence of the salt water upon their wounds probably creating a smarting pain, which can only be alleviated by rest on land.

He who desires to become an efficient wild-fowl sportsman must be prepared to face disappointments without murmuring. He may be a fair shot, and well experienced; still, he will be liable to frequent disappointments, and in no branch of the sport will he find so many as in wild-duck shooting.

An occurrence as vexatious as any I ever met with in my sporting adventures happened one moonlight night, when the weather was severe and the birds were numerous. Having detected, by sound, a fine paddling of ducks feeding in a small bay, the shore of which was skirted by a thick copse, to the shade of the latter I proceeded in my punt. The birds were feeding in some grass on the shore; yet, although a bright night, I could not exactly discover where the bulk of them were. Several stray fowl could be observed, and had I fired anywhere into the grass, I believe my shot would have been fatal to several, so numerous were they; but, eager for the best chance, I waited a few minutes, hoping to make the desired discovery, when an old mallard actually marched within ten yards of my punt, and took alarm. Whilst acting with twofold caution when I found the birds so near, the mallard had 'twigged' my movements while in the act of stooping my head to avoid observation, and, on a signal from the sentry, a cloud of birds instantly rose in the air, the whole body of which were, the instant before, feeding unsuspectingly within range of my gun.

I was so vexed at the moment, and unprepared for the event, as to forget that I might have made a splendid flying shot; and when I found a double chance gone, I rose to my knees in the punt in still greater disappointment. The reader may judge of my unbounded regret when *another* flight immediately rose within a hundred yards' range of my gun. This latter team had evidently not discovered the cause of alarm, and would probably have remained on the marshes, thus enabling me to have satisfactorily appeased my first disappointment; but, as I naturally supposed all had left the bay, I unsuspectingly disturbed them by rising up in the punt; thus *three* excellent successive chances were one after another in a few moments entirely thrown away, partly by indiscretion, and partly by a too eager desire to grasp the horn of plenty.[1]

Flapper Shooting.

A 'flapper' is a young wild-duck in a state of immaturity, partly fledged, and consequently unable to soar in the air or to fly any distance.

It is very unsportsmanlike to go in quest of flappers, and no wild-fowl shooter with the pretensions of a sportsman will advocate the sport. It is a highly undignified proceeding to pursue them, young and helpless as they are, and affording no very choice relish to the epicure when bagged, for, whilst not full-favoured, they are not full-flavoured.

The pursuit is generally carried forward in a small boat, of easy draught of water, which one man rows amongst rushes, reeds, and sedges, by the river side, or wherever else they may grow. The 'sportsman' (if such he may be called) sits either at the prow or stem of the boat, it being immaterial which. The flappers are disturbed by the presence of the boat in their place of retreat, and, in great fright at the apparently threatening danger, make their very first attempt to fly, when a charge of shot is sent at them, and their untimely flight is stopped. They generally make such a sorry attempt at flying, and present so fair a mark to the wanton shooter, that it would seem impossible to miss them. A dog is generally taken in the boat in company with the idle adventurers, that a wounded bird may not escape in a bed of rushes, or evade its pursuers by diving or hiding.

The time of year for this pursuit is August. Flappers take wing about the first and second weeks of that month.

In France this diversion is termed 'halbran shooting'—a 'halbran' signifying a half-grown duck—and, as practised in that country, it is even more derogatory than flapper shooting in England. The halbran shooter first contrives to kill the parent birds. He then places a tame decoy-duck on the water, securing it by the leg to a stake thrust into the mud, within range of gun-shot. He then hides behind a tree or in other ambuscade, and watches an opportunity, which the halbrans soon afford him, by unsuspectingly approaching the decoy-bird, the incessant noise of which entices them to the spot. Every halbran in the pond may thus be killed in a very short time.

----

[1] 'This particular kind of sport requires more silence and prudent precaution than any other, of which the dog should, by unremitting perseverance, be made as perfectly sensible as his master.'—*The Sportsman's Cabinet, or Delineations of Dogs.* By 'A Veteran Sportsman.' 2 vols, quarto: 1803.

[2] 'Item: It is thought good that *mallardes* be boght onely for my Lordes own mees, so they be good, and boght for ijd. a pece.'—*Northum. Ho. H. Book, temp. Hen. VIII.*

[1] Pteryplegia.

[1] Having in this work related some of my most successful adventures, I have thought it only fair to give a specimen of the unsuccessful; and, indeed, I am not sure that the young sportsman may not derive as much instruction from the one as the other.

CHAPTER XLV

WIDGEON SHOOTING

'The wandering flocks, expelled from northern shores,
In varied forms pursue their trackless way,
Courting the genial aspect of the south,
Whilst iron Winter holds his despot sway.'—T. HUGHES.

THE widgeon (*Anas Penelope*) offers the fairest sport to the wild-fowl shooter of any bird that flies, but more to the punter than he who confines himself to the sport on shore: in winter, whether by night or day, widgeon may be found in large companies in quiet bays, rivers, and arms of the sea. The natural habits of the widgeon are not wild; indeed, no bird of the duck species is easier to tame: but when subject to frequent persecution by the sportsman, they acquire a watchful habit, and sometimes become the most difficult of all wild-fowl to approach successfully with punt and gun. Their favourite haunts are on the extensive oozes, grassy creeks, and muddy savannas of tidal bays and rivers, where every tide waters and refreshes those plains, and forces the vegetation of a green sea-weed with long stringy blades, causing it to grow luxuriantly on the putrescent but soft rich soil of the ooze. On the very roots of that weed the widgeon feeds and fattens.

These birds are highly esteemed for the table, as one of the most delicious of wild-fowl, and always find a ready demand and sale in the markets. In former clays they were considered only *second* to wild-duck, as appears by the prices paid for them.[1]

Widgeon are migratory as well as gregarious, and are generally very numerous about the coast and inland sea-waters in sharp weather, often remaining, at different intervals, the whole season in one particular locality where abundance of food is to be had; and, when so settled, all the persecution of the punters, both by night and day, will not induce them to leave it, though they thus become remarkably wary and difficult of access. A company of widgeon sometimes consists of several thousand birds, which, when flying in the air, resemble a large dark cloud, and when they have alighted on the surface they literally cover many acres of wafer—

'Their numbers being so great, the waters covering quite,
That, rais'd, the spacious air is darkened with their flight.'[1]

They become exceedingly watchful after frequent attempts on the part of the punter to approach them; but they are sometimes a little off their guard, and the indefatigable sportsman who may have made many unsuccessful attempts will, sooner or later, be rewarded for his pains with a highly remunerative shot, such as will amply compensate him for his perseverance. When, through a continuation of coarse weather such as during many days precludes the sportsman from following his pursuits, a few calm days succeed or intervene, then is a glorious opportunity for the punter, who, with his best skill, may generally succeed with the previously unapproachable widgeon. They form the chief diversion for the punter at night and afford him the fairest opportunity by day. The sportsman may also have fine sport with them under sail, either with shooting-yacht or sailing-boat. The sailing-punt is, in like manner, an excellent means by which to approach them by day. Many thousands of these beautiful little ducks generally arrive at various parts of the coast early in October; and if easterly winds prevail during the latter part of September, they come at that time. The male birds arrive first; and in early spring, when wild-fowl leave our shores for their northern migrations, the cocks are the first to go by themselves, the hens following a few weeks after.

Widgeon are considerably more abundant on the eastern coast than elsewhere, though they frequent the southern coast in great numbers.

The sportsman who pursues them by night with punt and gun will be guided to their whereabouts entirely by their notes—an interesting call, or whistle, sounding like the nondescript words 'Wheow!' or 'Wheoh!'—which, when once familiar to the ear, cannot be mistaken, no other wild-fowl making a similar noise. In foggy weather widgeon are always more silent than at any other time. In cold weather they sit very close together, and assemble in large companies. The widgeon is a bird that will not be driven, but takes to its wings on the first alarm, rising directly high in the air.

The sportsman who would be successful at the sport of widgeon shooting must make himself familiar with the natural habits of the birds. He should leave them to themselves in undisturbed seclusion a few days, occasionally moving near them with punt and gun, but without offering to disturb them; by such-like coaxings he will often be rewarded for his pains. And after long, unsuccessful persecution with a rowing-punt, he will frequently find an excursion in the sailing-punt, by way of change, an effectual means of getting at them; when he may run upon them, at an unguarded moment, in his frail little bark, with all the ease and precision he could possibly desire.

Much more upon the subject of widgeon shooting will be found under the different headings relating to punting and wildfowl shooting in its various branches.

Widgeon are sometimes taken in decoys which they frequent by daylight; but they generally fly to the oozes and muddy flats of some salt water bay or river at night, where they remain if undisturbed, calling and talking to each other in their pretty, innocent tones, all night long.

------

[1] 'Item, wegions for my lorde at principall feestes, and no other tyme, and at 7d. ob. the pece, except my lorde's commandment be otherwyse.'—*Northumb. Ho. Book.*

[1] Drayton.

CHAPTER XLVI

THE PINTAIL DUCK

(*Anas acuta.*)

'Quick flashing thunders roar along the flood,
And three lie prostrate, vomiting their blood!
The fourth aloft on whistling pinions soar'd;
One fatal glance the fiery thunders pour'd,
Prone drops the bird amid the dashing waves,
And the clear stream his glossy plumage laves.'

ALEXANDER WILSON.

THE pintail duck is one of the most beautiful and interesting of the cluck species. It is sometimes called the sea-pheasant, on account of its long-pointed tail and the delicate nature of its flesh. It is eagerly sought by the wild-fowler, as a choice bird for the table; indeed, it is considered by most epicures as the most delicious bird of the whole duck species; and its price in the London market would seem to bear out the assertion, it being seldom to be had except at what may be termed a 'fancy price.'

The pintail is of somewhat singular habits. It is rarely seen in any but small numbers; more frequently in pairs or parties of four or five. It is by no means unusual to find the pintail among a company of widgeon, or a team, or paddling, of the ordinary species of wild-duck. The pintail seeks shallow waters for its food; and, generally speaking, is much tamer when on the water than many other wild-fowl. When on wing, the flight of the pintail is very rapid. It may be readily distinguished on the water from other wild-fowl, though at a long distance, as it swims with graceful and interesting movements, frequently bowing its head and sometimes skimming the surface with its beak, carrying its tail high, and breast low and deeply imbedded in the water.

The pintail is an annual visitant to this country during the winter months, but it seeks more northern latitudes at other seasons of the year.[1]

Whenever the punter chances to find pintails by themselves, if he is cautious he may generally get within range. Unless they have been much persecuted they are usually careless of danger, and easily approachable. They are always looked upon by wild-fowl shooters as a great prize.

In my experience I never remember an instance in which, having found any of the pintail species on the water in my punting excursions, I was unable to get within range. On one occasion, now many years ago, during a heavy storm of snow and sleet, and when, notwithstanding all precautions as to keeping the lock covered, my punt-gun missed fire at a pair of pintails, they actually permitted me to re-cap my gun twice and snap down the hammer unsuccessfully without taking alarm. The powder had become damp from the sleet having penetrated the nipple, and I thus lost a very fair shot: and, as if to add to my misfortune, I had no shoulder-gun with me at the time, though I scarcely ever went without one. They made no attempt to fly until after the report of the second gun cap, when they rose from the water within fifty yards of the muzzle of the gun.

When in company with the common wild-duck, or with widgeon, they are not so tame, but appear to follow the movements of the party. I have often observed when pursuing a company of widgeon that the birds nearest me, or rather the rearmost of the alarmists, were pintails, and consequently the most certain to be killed, being the first to feel the effects of the shot.

A wounded pintail seldom dives; but if near the ooze will swim towards it with all possible despatch, and, having gained it, will make a great effort to escape by running—a performance for which it is much better adapted than the generality of the waddling species.

The haunts of the pintail are the open waters and grassy borders both of fresh and salt water rivers, broads, and lakes.

It is rarely met with on the open coast.

The pintail is found in most countries where other wildfowl resort, and, according to Mr. Baring-Gould, is abundant in Iceland.[1]

The *Golden-eye Duck* (*Fuligula Clangwla*), or Whistle wing, though not a choice bird for the table, is well known to all wild-fowl shooters as a regular visitant to this country, and not unfrequently found and shot among other wild-fowl, but never in large numbers. It is also sometimes taken at the decoy along with wild-ducks. When in this country it frequents broad sea-going rivers and bays, and is occasionally found in fresh inland waters in company with other wild-fowl. It is said to breed in Canada, building its nest in a tall dead tree, or in the top of a stub; it lays six or eight eggs of a greenish blue colour.[2]

---

[1] Several long-tailed ducks (sea-pheasants) were shot by one of McClintock's party in Bellot Straits. See 'Narrative of the Fate of Sir John Franklin,' p. 323. By Sir Leopold McClintock, R.N.

[1] 'Iceland; its Scenes and Sagas,' pp. 282, 827. By Sabine Baring-Gould, M.A. 1863.

[2] 'The Birds of Canada' (2nd edition), p. 104. By Dr. A. M. Ross. 1872.

CHAPTER XLVII

TEAL SHOOTING

'And near to them you see the lesser dibbling teal
  In bunches, with the first that fly from mere to mere,
As they above the rest were lords of earth and air.'

DRAYTON.

THEEE is no bird of the duck tribe more beautiful in plumage than the teal (*Anas crecca*), and, what cannot be said in general of fine-plumaged birds, its flesh is of surpassing excellence.[1] Teal always meet with a ready sale in the market; and, small as they are, from 5*s*. to 10*s*. per pair is often paid for them in seasons of scarcity. They afford sport to the fowler in almost every form: at the decoy, in the gunning-punt, under sail, and in the canoe. And to the land sportsman with dog and gun there is no better sport than teal shooting in the neighbourhood of fens, dykes, and fresh-water streams.

They are the tamest and apparently the silliest wild-fowl that flies; they are generally to be met with early in the season in small 'springs' of six or eight, apparently broods; and lucky is the punter who falls in with them; he may almost invariably kill every bird, for they sit nicely packed together; and if any of the party escape the first shot, they alight again at no great distance, when, by marking and following them up, the punter may generally obtain a second shot, and bag the whole 'spring.'

There is but one caution to be given to the punter when fortunate enough to meet with so great a prize as a spring of teal, which is, that, as they are easily approachable with ordinary precaution, he need not fire a random shot; but as soon as fairly within range, pull the trigger without hesitation, because they do not, like duck and widgeon, turn head to wind before rising, but spring from the water without any such warning the instant they take alarm.

In very dry weather, and also during long and hard frosts, teal leave their accustomed haunts and retire to rapid streams and small inland currents, upon which the frost has but little effect.

To the wild-fowler who pursues his sport ashore among fens and dykes teal sometimes afford excellent amusement; and here again the sportsman need never fire a random shot, for if the bird rises out of range it is almost certain to go down again at no great distance. He should mark the spot as carefully as he can, since they sometimes pitch, or pretend to do so, and rise again, skimming along over the stream some fifty or a hundred yards farther.

A slight blow will kill a teal; they generally offer a fair shot when they rise from a brook or dyke. If the sportsman happen to miss his shot, it is ten to one but the bird will pitch again close by, unless it be early in the morning, when on being disturbed they often fly directly away.

The teal feeds chiefly in fens and fresh-water pools and streams, which it seems at all times to prefer to salt water. No other wild-fowl scatter themselves so far inland as teal. They sometimes assemble in great numbers on decoys; but I have never seen more than fifty in a spring on open waters near the sea-coast. They are the earliest visitors of the season to the decoy, of any wild-fowl, and there are none which afford the decoyman so much satisfaction for his pains in practising his mysterious art upon them, nor which remunerate him better.

It is sometimes the practice of the fowler to delay his performances a few days when there are only a small spring of teal; this delay frequently proves highly judicious, for when undisturbed they assemble at decoys in great numbers. Instances have occurred at several of the Essex decoys where from two hundred to four hundred teal have been taken in one day.

The Garganey.

The garganey, or summer teal, is a bird of elegant proportions, a little larger than the other species, and with a longer neck, smaller bones, and lighter-coloured plumage.

The flesh of the garganey is quite equal to that of the common teal, and is considered by the gourmet to be superior. It is seldom found in this country during severe weather; but in the spring of the year a few of the garganey are generally found about the time wild-fowl migrate to other countries. Early in the winter season, and particularly if the weather continues mild, the garganey may occasionally be met with; but even in the mildest seasons they are scarce.

———————

[1] 'This bird, for the delicate taste of its flesh, and the wholesome nourishment it affords the body, doth deservedly challenge the first place among those of its kind.'— *Willughby.*

CHAPTER XLVIII

COOT SHOOTING

'The coot her jet wing loved to lave,
  Rock'd on the hosom of the sleepless wave.'

ROGERS' *Pleasures of Memory.*

THIS remarkable bird (*Fulica atra*) offers excellent sport to the fowler, sometimes taxing his skill, his patience, and his cunning to the utmost. They are more abundant at some places on the coast than any other species of water-fowl. In some localities they assemble in such large coverts as would appear almost incredible to those who have not seen them. To a certain extent, they are migratory; but many remain in this country throughout the year. Their numbers seem to increase tenfold in winter, and they always appear to prefer the eastern parts of England to all other districts. The coot has indeed many peculiarities.

'The coot, bald, else clean-black, that whiteness it doth bear
  Upon the forehead, star'd, the water hen doth wear,
Upon her little tail, in one small feather set.'[1]

Besides being very local in their habits, and making favourite resorts of some particular waters, they are scarcely ever to be seen in neighbouring waters, which may be within a few miles of their chosen haunts, though offering equal advantage as regards food and nesting. The river Stour, which ebbs and flows between the counties of Essex and Suffolk, and runs many miles inland, watering some of the fairest pastures of a luxuriant valley, some of the beauties of which have been so faithfully portrayed on canvas by the late talented artist Constable, was formerly a very favourite resort of coots; so much so, that the town of Manningtree, which stands on the south bank of the river, was quite renowned for its abundant supply of those birds. Before the invention of punt-guns coots were so numerous on that river,[2] that the gunners never thought of shooting at small numbers, but only at very large coverts; and then, not unless there was a chance of killing from a dozen to a score and upwards, which, with the guns at that time in use, was considered pretty good sport.

At the time of which we are now speaking the ordinary retail price of a pair of coots in that neighbourhood was sixpence, and the vendors sometimes found great difficulty in disposing of them even at that rate. The wild-fowl shooter who pursued the sport as a means of maintenance never thought of shooting at coots if any other fowl were near, or if there was the smallest chance of killing anything more saleable.

But notwithstanding that the coots were formerly thought of so little value in the vicinity of the Stour, in some other localities they were as eagerly sought as any other wild-fowl; for with some persons the coot is esteemed as superior to wild-duck. Although I cannot say I agree with those who hold that opinion, I *do* consider the coot, when dressed *à la Soyer*, a very wholesome and delicious bird.

The best manner of divesting the coot of the thick down in which it is encased, and which so tries the patience of the cook, is to put the bird, after it has been plucked, into scalding water, then, by taking some powdered resin in the hand and rubbing the skin of the coot, the down may be easily removed, leaving the skin as clean and delicate as that of a wild-duck. The stubbornness of the down on the body of the coot has induced some cooks to resort to the foolish plan of flaying the bird, a process which spoils it for cooking.

Among the signs and marvels of the age of superstition, the movements of the coot were anciently regarded as suggestive of certain changes in the weather; for instance, it was considered a sure sign of a strong tempest at sea when coots flew shrieking to the shore.[1]

It is also stated by an ancient authority[2] that coots are fond of pecking at the foam of the sea, and that by sprinkling it in places where they used to hunt these birds they were the more easily captured.

Another peculiarity of the coot is, that when flying in large coverts they are generally closely huddled together, but when on the water they sit widely scattered, and apparently in some sort of order, as they are for the most part nearly equidistant. When feeding or roosting on the ooze they are not so scattered. They run at a great pace, and a winged coot will outrun its pursuer, particularly if his feet be clogged with splashers.

It is considered a very good omen when a covert of coots have taken to any particular locality, as other birds always follow them; they are attractive to all kinds of wild-fowl, and therefore valuable as decoy-birds on ponds and inland waters.

It is very remarkable that duck, widgeon, and some other fowl appear to seek the company of coots; and there can be no doubt that one reason is, as Col. Hawker expresses it, that they are such good sentries to give alarm by day when the other fowl generally sleep.

Coots swim rapidly from the punter when suspicious of his intention; he must therefore put on his best strength if he expects to get within range; they are very cunning, and often rely much more on the power of their legs than their wings. I have often found, when punting to coots, that after swimming rapidly from the suspected punt, if there was a mud-bank near at hand, rather than take wing, they would creep upon the bank and run across the ooze at such a rate as to be out of range in a very short time, and when pursued they are so artful that they swim across creeks, and so endeavour to cut off the pursuit, being always reluctant to fly; wounded coots do the same, but a wounded duck or widgeon always makes for the water, depending entirely on its diving powers for hopes of escape. A winged coot, however, will elude its pursuers effectually by cunningly making for the bank, which if once gained the fowler has little chance of capturing it.

A wounded coot will also make a last effort to escape, when in the hands of the fowler, by scratching his hands, and burying its sharp talons in his flesh. The young fowler will do well to be cautious in handling live coots; no water-fowl is more tenacious of life, nor more vigilant and cunning in its habits.

Coots require hard hitting, and the sportsman must not expect to recover many unless he kills them. If there be any way of eluding his grasp the wounded coot will assuredly embrace it. As soon, as possible after firing the punt-gun, and before attempting to pick up a bird, the sportsman should seize his doiible-barrelied shoulder-gun, and give the *coup de grâce* to two of the strongest of his wounded victims just as they are making off.

It is easy to distinguish coots from other wild-fowl when on the water, though at a considerable distance, from the different position in which they sit to most other wild-fowl. The coot carries its head low, and thrown forward in a poking attitude, with tail sticking high above its body, and, as before observed, they sit scattered widely over a large space of water rather than in close compact, as other birds.

They have a great enemy in the moor-buzzard or marsh-harrier, but when attacked or threatened by that carnivorous enemy they exhibit admirable discipline, and—just as if taught and trained to military tactics—in an instant, on a given signal from the sentinel on duty, they close up the ranks, and huddle together, forming a solid mass which would seem to defy the daring of the most ferocious hawk. When so ranged in a dense body, the buzzard seldom ventures to attack; if he does, or continues hovering about them, they swim rapidly round and round in a circle, fluttering their pinions, clashing and flapping the water with their wings, and throwing up clouds of spray, by which means they dazzle the sight of their enemy, and altogether present so threatening an aspect, that the buzzard decamps and watches his more favourable opportunity of pouncing upon one of a small party of stragglers, off which, if his attack be successful, he makes a hearty meal, the raw flesh of the coot being one of his most delicious morsels.

Pliny speaks of these scufflings between the hawk and waterfowl as a very amusing sport to behold. 'Spectanda dimicatio, ave ad perfugia litorum tendente, maxume si condensa harundo sit.[1]

Coots prefer fresh water, and never forsake a chosen haunt until fairly frozen out, when they take to their salt-water retreats.

Their habits, in some respects, are the very reverse of other wild-fowl; for instance, coots feed by day and roost at night, their accustomed places of repose being among reeds, rushes, or sedges by the water-side, or on some secluded island about their haunts.

No water-fowl have suffered more, nor been so completely driven from their places of refuge by the draining system, as coots; these birds used to breed by thousands in the fens and broads on the eastern coast, and though there are still a great many bred annually in this country, yet in no proportion to the number of years gone by. Their nests, too, are now plundered, and their eggs, as well as those of scores of other water-fowl, are sent to the market, and *all* are called 'plovers' eggs!' Such is the innocent deception practised with impunity upon those who may not be familiar with the size and colour of the genuine plover's egg.

Coots are sometimes so reluctant to leave a favourite haunt (such as a decoy, where they are always a nuisance), that they may be driven to and fro like sheep, and will put up with a good deal of noise and threat rather than leave the pond.

The call-note of this bird represents the sound of the word

'krew!' or 'kreow!'

––––––––––––––

[1] Drayton's 'Poly-olbion,' song xxv.

[2] The author of 'British Field Sports' says he 'has actually beheld upon the Manningtree river, in Essex, a shoal of coots reaching *two miles in length*, as thick as they could well swim, and half-a-mile over.'

[1] 'Nam in pelago gravissima tempestatem futuram esse certissimim est, quando merguli fugiunt ad litus cum clamore.'—*Glantvilla de Rerum Proprietatibus.*

[2] Aristotle, 'Hist. Anim.' book ix. cap. 35.

[1] Pliny, lib. x. cap. 3.

CHAPTER XLIX

THE MOOR-HEN

(*Gallinula chhropus.*)

'Come up by Glenduich, and down by Glendee,
  And round by Kinclaven, and hither to me;
  For Ronald and Donald are out on the fen,
To break the wing o' my bonny moor-hen.'—ARMIGER.

THE Moor-hen, or Water-hen, though very much resembling the coot in colour and form, is in many respects of different habits; yet the two species associate together during the breeding season, and their young are reared in company the one with the other. The moor-hen never seeks the salt water, but confines itself entirely to fresh; and is never seen *confertus*. It is by no means shy, but when undisturbed is as tame as a domestic fowl. The croak of the moor-hen can never be mistaken when once the sportsman has become acquainted with the sound, and it is familiarly known to every rustic. Its flesh is not generally much esteemed; but when dressed as a coot it is really a very inviting dish.

Moor-hens offer good practice to the young sportsman; they may sometimes be easily driven from their hiding-places at the waterside by a clog; and they generally present so fair a mark that it would seem impossible to miss them; but they will occasionally lie so close when anyone is near, that they require much pressing before taking wing. The moor-hen makes but a sorry attempt at flying, its wings being so far forward that its body and legs hang down in a most awkward manner; but this deficiency is made up in its pedestrian powers: it runs with great rapidity, flicking up its tail, and exposing the white feathers beneath it with apparently insulting contempt. This bird also swims fast and with graceful attitude, nodding its head at every stroke of the leg.

The moor-hen is abundantly common on almost every lake, pond, and swamp throughout the country; and is equally so in Ireland, Holland, and various parts of the Continent.

No water-fowl suffers so much from severe frost; a hard winter is generally fatal to many of them. They creep into holes by the banks of ponds and rivers during such trying occasions, or hide in the thickest willow-beds in the neighbourhood.

When closely pursued they are very reluctant to fly, and the sportsman is constantly disappointed of his shot by seeing his dog emerge from the thicket with a live moor-hen in its mouth.

The moor-hen of Ionia is highly commended, and was

formerly in high estimation: 'Attagen maxumelonius celeber et vocalis alias.'[1]

It is also said, by ancient writers, that so soon as this bird is taken captive it loses its voice and becomes mute, but at other times is noisy enough. Of old it was reputed a rare and singular bird: 'Captus vero obmutescens quondam existumatus inter raras avis.'[2]

---

[1] Pliny, lib. x. cap. 48.

[2] Ælian, 'Hist. Anim.' lib. xv. cap. 27. Pliny, lib. x. cap. 48.

CHAPTER L

SHOVELLER SHOOTING

'The shouler, which so shakes the air with saily wings,
 That ever as he flies you still would think he sings.'

SHOVELLERS (genus *Spathulea*) are sometimes very troublesome birds to pursue with punt and gun; they swim at an extraordinary rate, leading the punter a smart chase and causing his arms to ache ere they can be overtaken. Directly they find the enemy in close pursuit they make use of the power with which nature has so liberally gifted them, and 'shut the door' upon their pursuer; and probably, when next rising to the surface, they are either very wide of him, or so far ahead as to be out of his sight altogether.

The punter who would be successful at this sport must carefully observe the direction taken by these birds at the moment of diving, and then keep his punt moving quickly ahead in the same track, or as nearly as he can guess, bearing in mind that the shoveller is a bird which can swim nearly as fast under water as upon the surface.

When these birds find they are thus closely pursued they

generally cease diving, and swim away on the surface as fast as their legs can propel them; they seldom take to their wings, except as a *dernier ressort*.

If the punter is active and skilful in the management of his punt, he may be pretty sure of a shot when he chances to meet with birds of this species, and whether by daylight or moonlight, but if the latter, it must be on a very bright night, or he will assuredly lose sight of his birds, which keep constantly diving when first pursued, but cease after being chased some little distance.

Wounded shovellers are among the most difficult of waterfowl to capture, and lead a long, determined, and cunning chase ere they can be taken. Their powers of diving are so great, and their vigilant cunning equally so, that unless their legs are broken or their bodies severely wounded, they entirely elude their pursuers.

They are sometimes sought by the more undignified sportsman with shoulder-gun, in a rowing-boat propelled by one or two rowers, whilst the sportsman sits abaft; but in this case they generally fly, or, diving, take a backward route when a fast boat pursues them.[1] By looking out sharply, and firing the moment they come to the surface, the young sportsman may sometimes have very fair sport. Calm weather and a smooth surface are best for shoveller shooting.

None of the species of shoveller can be recommended

for the table. In a work by an eminent physician, which lias been already alluded to as one of great rarity and antiquity, they are classed with herons and bitterns, and are considered indigestible as an article of food.[2]

THE BURROW-DUCK.

(*Tadorna vulpanser.*)

The punter is often tempted to make a shot at the sheldrake or burrow-duck (by the latter name it is better known), though for edible purposes it is of little value, the flesh being coarse, and requiring great care and culinary skill in dressing before it can be made a palatable dish.

They are called burrow-ducks from their habits of breeding in rabbit-burrows and holes by the waterside, in sandy cliffs and banks. They are larger than most others of the species, swim very fast, and dive with great dexterity; but a shot may generally be obtained at them, with punt and gun, by following them up closely and expeditiously. When pursued they seldom take wing until closely pressed, by which time they are within the range of a punt-gun. In consequence of their having so many white feathers about them, they cannot be seen on the water at night; it is therefore only by daylight that there is any chance of shooting them.

They come to our coasts in small numbers every winter, and may often be found near the shore or in shallows, but seldom in deep water, unless wounded; in which case, if pursued, they make for the deepest places at hand.

THE VELVET DUCK.

(*Anas fusca.*)

Most wild-fowl shooters have occasionally met with these birds. They are of little use when killed, but very trying to the sportsman's skill: if he pursues them they dive with remarkable facility, and, rather than fly, will trust to their under-surface powers, never taking wing till very hard pressed.

They are almost exclusively a sea-bird, and are seldom seen inland, except during the heaviest gales, when they come no farther from the coast than compelled, but accept the nearest refuge, and that only as a temporary retreat.

The flesh of the velvet duck is of no estimation; but their black soft plumage is very beautiful.

THE SCAUP-DUCK.

(*Fuligula marila.*)

This is a species which is always to be found, in hard winters, up almost every river and arm of the sea on the coast. They are most frequently in little doppings of six or eight, and are by no means difficult of access, though very active divers. They give preference to oozy rivers rather than sandy bottoms, but never travel far from the sea. The sportsman will frequently be tempted to make shots with his punt-gun at these birds.

Their food consists of Crustacea and mollusca, obtained by diving, in which art they are very expert.

They arrive late in the season, and appear to prefer the eastern coast, where in some seasons they are very numerous.

THE SCOTER OR BLACK-DUCK.

(*Anas nigra.*)

These are well known to every wild-fowl shooter on the coast, from the smack's cabin-boy down to the practised gunner. They are the hardest birds to kill and capture of any of the species. The oldest sportsmen are often astonished at the hard hitting they require before falling to the shot; and when fallen, wounded, it is often impossible to recover them. I have fired the stanchion-gun at large flights of these birds, scattering a pound-and-a-half of shot amongst them at a charge; and, though within fair range, have seldom seen more than ten or a dozen fall to the charge, and have never been able to recover more than four or five of those which actually fell directly beneath the shot. Colonel Hawker may well remark, that he never saw such creatures 'to swim, dive, and carry off shot.' And the Colonel adds, 'They take as hard a blow as a swan; and will even swim for a short time after being shot in the head.'

They are met with in large numbers on the coast in winter, and are often mistaken at a distance for a more desirable class of wild-fowl.

The flesh of the scoter is not palatable. They have a thick coating of feathers and down, which seems to render them almost invulnerable to the effects of gun-shot.

------

[1] 'The great difficulty is always to keep in view the exact spot where the birds come up; once lose sight of it, your progress is

stopped, and in recovering your advantage the birds are almost certain to see you, and fly.'—*Colquhoun's Moor and Loch.*

[2] 'These fowles be fishers, and be very rawe and flegmatike, like unto the meate wherof thei are fedde; the young are beste, and ought to be eaten with peper, sinomon, and ginger, and to drinke wine after them, for good digestion; and this doe for all water fowles.'—*The Book of Simples*, fol. lxxij. By Dr. William Bulleyn. London: 1562.

CHAPTER LI

DIVER SHOOTING

'Now up, now down again, that hard it is to prove
  Whether under water most it liveth or above.'—
DRAYTON.

THE species of birds which fall under this denomination are many, and sometimes afford the wild-fowl shooter excellent sport; but they are altogether useless as an article of food, the flavour of the flesh being disagreeable to the palate, on account of their subsisting entirely upon fish. And, totally different to other wild-fowl such as are fit for the table, they have bills peculiarly formed by Nature for the purpose of assisting them in obtaining their food. The bill of the diver species is, for the most part, serrated, sharp-pointed, thick in substance, and strong; possessing, in exquisite arrangement, five rows of sharp, tiny teeth, thereby vesting in them the power of holding the most slippery of the finny tribe with the greatest ease. The teeth are arranged in a position slightly inclining inwards, so that it would seem impossible for any small fish to escape when once within the grasp of so powerful a mandible.

In pursuing divers as objects of sport, the only way to succeed in killing them is, to follow them up closely, in the same manner as that already stated in the previous chapter, under the head 'Shoveller Shooting.' The sportsman should fire the instant they come to the surface; unless killed, they generally contrive to escape, so cunning and expert are they in the art of diving, and they never resign the chase whilst they have sufficient power left to hold themselves under water. They seldom fly, always preferring to trust to their wonderful diving powers to evade their pursuers.

They are, for the most part, savage birds when taken alive (as they often are, accidentally, in fishing-nets[1]), striking their bills, with fierce onslaught, at man or dog, and are capable of inflicting a severe wound in the flesh.

They are seldom seen in doppings of above five or six, but more frequently entirely by themselves.

The numbers which visit our southern shores always depend on the temperature of the season; they are only driven there by stress of weather.

THE RED-BREASTED MERGANSER.

(*Mergus serrator.*)

'Mergansers came many, with fish in their throat,

By gluttony prompted their bodies to bloat.'

JENNINGS, Ornitholegia.

Although this is a species wholly disregarded by the modern apician, it is a bird of so beautiful a plumage, and so often crosses the track of the wild-fowler, sometimes challenging him to a trial of his best skill as a punter, that it would be wrong to pass it over without some comment.

The species is rather abundant on the coasts of Scotland and the north of England, but scarce in the south, seldom visiting the southern counties except in hard winters.

They are among the most distrustful water-fowl I ever met with, and it is seldom that a shot within range can be had at them. They are, besides, expert divers, and, when wounded, make determined efforts to elude the shooter's grasp.

A few seasons ago, five of these birds puzzled me a long time ere I could obtain a shot at them. They were seen from day to day on the waters; and I made several attempts to approach them in my rowing-punt, but without success. One fine day, however, during a steady breeze, I launched my *sailing*-punt, hoisted a small lateen-sail, and proceeded to look for these same five unapp roach able mergansers, which I discovered after a short search, and bore down towards them. Having first cocked my punt-gun, which was charged with one of Ely's patent cartridges, I placed myself flat upon my chest on the floor of the punt, using the greatest precaution not to move

limb or feature above the gunnel; and so well did my plan
succeed, that in a few minutes I found myself within range;
the birds sitting well for a shot, I instantly sent the charge after
them, and stopped all five, three of which were killed outright,
and the other two so severely wounded that they made only
feeble efforts to dive, and were easily secured. They were two
cocks and three hens; the cock-birds in beautiful plumage,
with their graceful topples in perfect order. I have two pairs of
these birds—the result of the shot above recorded—stuffed,
and preserved in glass cases.[1]

In the summer season, the male bird loses his beautiful
plumage, and approaches in colour to that of the female.

The call-note of this bird is harsh, and sounds like 'Kerr!
kerr!'

THE HOODED MERGANSER.

(Mergus cucullatus.)

This is also a bird of beautiful plumage, not unfrequently
met with on the eastern coast. It is of similar habits to the last
species, and gifted with similar powers of catching and holding
its slippery prey. It is a most expert diver, and would seem
almost to defy capture when only winged, if there be weeds at
the bottom of the water, or any such temporary resort.

The hooded merganser prefers inland waters to the open

coast; indeed, it is very seldom seen on the sea-coast, but frequently in both salt and fresh water rivers, ponds, and pools.

Its power of flight is very great; it can rise up from the water in a perpendicular line when suddenly alarmed, thus puzzling young sportsmen to knock it down. When flying straight off, it proceeds with astonishing rapidity.

The note of this bird may be expressed by the monosyllables 'Kroo! kroow!'

THE GOOSANDER.

(*Mergus merganser.*)

'The gosander with them, my goodly fens do show,
  His head as ebon black, the rest as white as snow.'—
DRAYTON.

This is also an exceedingly beautiful bird, and is the largest of the British mergansers. It very rarely visits the southern counties of England, although in hard winters there are generally a few killed by the punters.

The flesh of the goosander is not palatable; but the skins of these birds are often sold at high prices, for the purpose of stuffing and putting in glass cases.

Goosanders are generally pretty numerous in the Orkney

Isles, where they abide throughout the whole year, unless driven farther southward by the severity of frost. In the outer Hebrides they are also frequently to be met with, in doppings of fifty and upwards.

They are difficult birds to approach, and their powers of diving are so great, that they puzzle the oldest sportsman with their tricks and dexterity; when merely winged or slightly wounded, it is almost impossible to capture them.

In every hard winter some of these birds are shot on the Eastern coast, and on the sea-going rivers and bays of Essex and Suffolk.

THE GREAT NORTHERN DIVER.

(*Columbus glacialis.*)

'The divers were many, and various in hue;
  Of the Northern, the Imber, Black-throated a few.
  By tribes hyerborean their pelts often sought,
  Into robes warm and flexile are frequently wrought.'—
JENNINGS.

This is the largest of the genus *Columbus*, and by far the most beautiful in plumage of the diver species. They are sought after by the wild-fowl shooter more as trophies of successful sport, wherewith to grace his hall, than for any other purpose. The flesh is dark in colour and unpalatable.

They are so accomplished in the art of diving, that when pursued they do not appear to make the least exertion on disappearing from the surface, but sink gradually under water without throwing themselves forward, the head being the last part that disappears.

They are bold and tenacious of life, but extremely shy and difficult of approach; and, from the facility with which they dive and the rate at which they swim, it is very puzzling to follow them up in such a manner as to secure them, for, unless shot dead, the chances of recovering them are very small. When wounded, they manage to remain below the surface several minutes, and can with ease go a distance under water of one hundred yards at a time, then, when rising again to the surface, they are so cunning, and possess such extraordinary powers, that they sometimes only show their heads above water, when, if their pursuers are near by, they again instantly disappear.

The best chance of killing them is to follow them with a sailing-vessel when they dive, and despatch them with a charge from a large shoulder-gun the instant they rise to the surface.

They live out at sea among the fish. It is seldom that they come far southward of the Orkney and Shetland islands. They are said to breed on the Faroe islands, as well as in many other northern countries, and also in Canada.[1] They prefer cold and icy regions, and in summer they visit Spitzbergen, Greenland,

Iceland, and other coasts in those latitudes.

They are taken under water in those countries by meaos of baited hooks, and are sometimes caught alive by fishermen in herring-nets. They require cautious handling when taken alive, as they are very savage, and make dangerous attacks upon man or beast, sometimes inflicting serious wounds with their pointed beaks, which they are capable of using with much power and injurious effect.

The skins of these birds are used freely, in hyperborean latitudes, for articles of clothing.[2]

THE BLACK-THROATED DIVER.

(*Colymbus articus.*)

This is also a large and handsome bird, though smaller than the great northern diver. It is still more rare than the great northern diver, and is seldom seen on our southern coast, except during very severe winters; its habits are similar, and it is as shy and difficult of approach as the other. It dives with immense facility, and always seems reluctant to take wing when pursued, preferring to trust to its powers of evasion under water. Like others of its species, its flesh is not fit for domestic purposes.

THE RED-THROATED DIVER.

(*Colymbus septentrionalis.*)

This bird, better known by the name of the 'sprat-loon,' or 'speckled diver,' is very common about the English coast, particularly off Kent and Essex, and other parts, during the sprat season, when it is sometimes seen, in company with others of its species, following and diving among shoals of sprats, on which it seems to subsist.

The red-throated diver may often be shot from the deck of a sailing-vessel, by watching for its appearance above water after diving. When closely pursued it takes wing, and flies some little distance, but very low in the air, sometimes only a few inches above the surface of the water.

It is only in summer that it has a red hue about its neck; in winter, the red is replaced by a dark brown.

These birds are also frequently taken alive in nets by fishermen. They are so abundant, and of so little use when killed, that the wild-fowl shooter is seldom tempted to waste powder and shot about them.

The note of this bird is peculiar, a loud and wailing cry, sounding like 'Kakeerah.! kakeerah!'

———————

[1] In reference to water-fowl being sometimes surprised by the fishing-net, Mr. Daniel records the following remarkable story: 'An extraordinary occurrence took place March, 1810, near Drumburgh. A fisherman placed a flounder-net in the river Eden, which is subject to the flux and reflux of the tide; and, on his returning to take up his net, instead of finding fish, he found it loaded with wild-ducks. During his absence, a fleet of these birds had alighted below the net, and, on the flowing of the tide, were carried, from the contraction of the channel, with great, impetuosity, into the net, and were drowned. He caught *one hundred and seventy* golden-eyed wild-ducks, supposed to be from the Orkneys, as very rarely any of that species frequent that part of the country.'—*Supplement to Daniel's Rural Sports*, p. 430.

[1] Lubbock mentions the circumstance of a red-breasted merganser being once killed very near the city of Norwich, and adds: 'This was near Surlingham; and I was present when it was shot by one of the sons of Parkjr, who kept the ferry-house. Upon shaking the bird, five roach dropped from its throat, large enough to be used as baits for pike. They seemed

all to have been taken in the space of a few minutes; all their brightness remained on the scales.'—*Lubbock's Fauna of Norfolk.*

[1] 'The great northern diver is a resident of Canada. It nests on an island, or in a meadow or marsh, near the borders of the interior lakes; laying two or three eggs of a reddish brown colour, with an olive tint.'—*The Birds of Canada* (2nd edition). By Dr. M. A. Ross. 1872.

[2] *Vide* Latham's 'Nat. Hist.;' Pennant's 'Arctic Zoology;' Gass's 'Journal,' and other books of northern travel.

CHAPTER LII

WILD-FOWL SHOOTING ON THE COAST BY DAYLIGHT

.... 'The fowling-piece
Was shoulder'd, and the blood-stain'd game-pouch slung
On this side, and the gleaming flask on that;
In sooth, we were a most accordant pair;
And thus accoutred, to the lone sea-shore
In fond and fierce precipitance we new.'—*The Fowler*. By
DELTA.

WILD-FOWL shooting as practised ashore is a general and
varied diversion, with some of the branches of which most
men are more or less familiar; but it is a distinct and totally
different pursuit to that of wild-fowl shooting at midnight or
in boats. The 'shore-gunner' has a variety of minor chances and
advantages over the others of obtaining by less laborious means
shots from the coast at wild-fowl under various circumstances,
but the amount of success is generally very far inferior to that
of the punter. The shore-gunner will frequently find, in his
excursions along the coast, that success depends mainly on

his skill in stalking and obtaining a good ambuscade; for this purpose he must be prepared to incur much disagreeable exposure, to act promptly, boldly, and in defiance of trifling obstacles and obstructions.

There is not a branch of the sport of wild-fowl shooting but is fraught with occasional trying exposure to the severity of the weather, and the man who exposes himself most, and energetically pursues the diversion, is not only the least liable to suffer constitutionally, but is invariably the most successful.

The shore-gunner will sometimes find it necessary to crawl upon his knees through snow or mud, but, regardless of both, he must face all such difficulties manfulty, without a murmur, and success will the more frequently crown his efforts.[1]

> 'Crouch down, as low, as still as death.
> Heed not that the swamp is deep,
> Through the marshes you must creep;
> If the victory you would win.'[2]

Many a wild-swan, goose, and other fowl are killed in this manner.

The sportsman should always bear in mind that, having stalked the birds, it is useless to fire at them in their sitting posture if their breasts are turned towards him; the shot in such a case strikes the feathers, and glides off with harmless effect; the only chance of killing under such circumstances is, that a stray shot may hit the bird in the head; such, however, must be very remote if they are small birds. It is generally better to wait a few moments to see if they turn tail, or to put them up at once and fire under their wings, which is the most vulnerable part of all the feathered tribe.

Wild-ducks and widgeon generally keep to lee-shores when feeding; the wild-fowl shooter need not be disconcerted at finding the birds to leeward; he will be able to stalk them, with skill and precaution, if he has no strong scents about him, and allows not the slightest noise to reach their ears. Wild-fowl detect the enemy quickest in calm weather, but during a strong wind there is less occasion for such extreme caution.

The best time for pursuing this sport is during windy weather, or whilst snow and sleet are falling; when—

'Earlier than wont along the sky,
Mixed with the rack the snow mists fly.'

It is also a favourable opportunity during the prevalence of an easterly wind with snow (especially on the eastern coast), or in foggy or hazy weather. At such times wild-fowl do not fly nearly so high in the air as when the atmosphere is clear. The first day or two, on the breaking-up of a long-continued frost, when the ground has been some time covered with snow, are exceedingly favourable opportunities for shore-gunning.

The wild-fowl shooter must at all times pay regard to the colour as well as the warmth of his sporting costume, and in no branch of the pursuit is it more essential than in this. When the ground is thickly covered with snow, the wild-fowl shooter's dress cannot be too white; at other times a light drab, or that nearest resembling the colour of the coast where his diversions are pursued, will be best. Jacket, waistcoat, cap, and trowsers should all be of the same colour, that no contrast may attract notice or create suspicion among the flights of wild-fowl which may be hovering in the air far or near. It is always the business of the 'shore-gunner' to stand still and motionless as a statue, or lie down on the ground, when he sees wild-fowl on the wing, which, perchance, may approach within range, as such would purposely avoid him if he were moving; they are so very keen-sighted and vigilant when high in the air, that the least movement of a human object on land is quickly detected and avoided.

When the surface of the country has long been buried in snow, it is an excellent though very ancient artifice on the part of the sportsman while ranging the coast to envelop himself in a white sheet, or clothe himself from head to foot in garments of spotless white; and immediately on observing wild-fowl on the wing, whether near or distant, to stand perfectly still and motionless as a snow cliff, by which means he may escape detection, and the birds will probably come unsuspectingly within range of his gun. The whiteness of the sportsman's attire being in accordance with the tint of the country, they do not detect him until they feel the effects of the shot.

This method of wild-fowl shooting seems also to be practised on the banks of the Rhine,[1] and even in Scandinavia.[2]

In stormy weather, accompanied by severe frost and snow, there is no lack of sport for the wild-fowl shooter on the lee coast, if he judiciously selects a spot frequented by those birds. When any are seen hovering in the air near by, the best plan is—whether clad in white raiment or otherwise—to lie flat on the beach in a motionless position until the birds are within range, and then suddenly to rise up and fire:

> 'Silent upon the chilly beach we lay
> Prone, while the drifting snow-flakes o'er us fell,
> Like Nature's frozen tears for our misdeeds.'[1]

The services of a dog are indispensable for this sport, as most of the shore-gunner's victims fall into the water. If into shallow places, the dog retrieves every bird, whether dead, winged, or otherwise wounded; but deep water is very trying even to the best of dogs, because wounded wild-fowl, when closely pursued, frequently dive, and so lead a severe and difficult chase.

A pocket telescope will be found of great service for this sport, particularly in the locality of lochs and inland waters, where it becomes necessary to stalk the birds. Having discovered a number of wild-fowl on the water through the aid of the telescope, the sportsman should keep his eye upon them a few moments if doubtful as to the species; by so doing he will soon discover what they are, through one or more of the party treading the water and flapping its wings, an irresistible habit of wild-fowl, especially widgeon, when not suspecting danger.[2]

When the frost is so severe as to interfere with the navigation of broad tidal rivers which become blockaded with ice, the shore-gunner will find no difficulty in obtaining good sport. It is then an easy matter for a sportsman with tolerable endurance to kill his two and three pair of duck or widgeon daily, by looking out sharply along the coast or boundaries of the blockaded waters. He has only to conceal himself behind some large piece of ice which the tide may have turned up edgewise a few feet above the surface of the ground, and the probability is that he will not remain long concealed ere his efforts are rewarded with a shot; for the colder it is, the more restless aie the birds, and the more indifferent they are to danger.

At such times they are flying about in every direction, cold and hungry, eagerly searching for food and water; resting here a minute and there a minute on bits of floating ice, and flying to and fro, calling to their companions with wailing and clamorous notes.

Another mode of pursuing this sport on the coast, and one

that is often highly successful, is that of making an ambuscade by digging pits or holes about five or six feet deep in the beach; or by sinking empty hogsheads, tubs, or boxes by the margin of tidal waters or in low-lying marshes frequented by wild-fowl, where, otherwise, no shelter could be had. The top and edges of these hiding-places are carefully concealed with shingle or tufts of grass; and from such sunken positions the wild-fowl shooter is enabled to take deliberate aim, as he watches unobservedly the approach of the birds. He can also frequently obtain a shot at birds on the wing; his position in the pit being so advantageous that he may, on the most open coast, screen himself from observation, and watch all the movements of the unsuspecting fowl.

These artifices of pits and sunken tubs are frequently resorted to for the purposes of flight-shooting: they are also used on the banks of the Ehine with good success, where the sportsman, having descended into the pit, draws a hurdle of brushwood over his head[1] to complete his concealment, then, by merely raising the hurdle a few inches at one end and resting it upon a stone, he is enabled to observe the approach and position of such fowl as venture within range of his gun, and to shoot with deliberation.

[1] The ancient fowler was thoroughly awake to the necessity of caution and hard toil in stalking wild-fowl. It is observed by Markham, 'If you have not sufficient shelter by reason of the nakednesse of the bankes and want of trees, then you shall creepe upon your hands and knees under the bankes, and lying even flat, upon your belly, put the nose of your piece over the banke, and so take your levell; for a fowle is wonderfully fearefull of a man.'—*Hunger's Prevention, or the Art of Fowling.* By Gervase Markham. A.D. 1655.

[2] Bishop Tegnér, 'Translations from Swedish Poetry.' By J. E. D. Bethune.

[1] *Vide* 'Rambles in Germany, France, Italy, and Russia in Search of Sport.' By the Hon. F. St. John. A.D. 1853.

[2] 'Scandinavian Adventures.' By Lloyd, A.D. 1854.

[1] 'The Fowler.' By Delta.

[2] Colquhoun says of the shore-gunner: 'His first object should be to see his game without being seen himself, even if they are at too great a distance to show signs of alarm. To effect this he must creep cautiously forward to the first point that will command a view of the shore for some distance; then, taking out his glass, he must reconnoitre it by inches, noticing every tuft of grass or stone, to which wild-fowl asleep often bear so close a resemblance, that, except to a very quick

eye, assisted by a glass, the difference is not perceptible. If the loch be well frequented, he will most likely first discover a flock of divers; but he must not be in a hurry to pocket his glass until he has thoroughly inspected the shore, in case some more desirable fowl may be feeding or asleep upon it.'—Vide *The Moor and Loch.*

[1] 'Rambles in Germany, France, Italy, and Russia in Search of Sport.' By the Hon. E. St. John. A.D. 1853.

CHAPTER LIII

FLIGHT-SHOOTING

'Vainly the fowler's eye

Might mark thy distant flight to do thee wrong;

As darkly painted on the crimson sky

Thy figure floats along.'—W. C. BRYANT.

THE term 'flight-shooting' signifies shooting wild-fowl by twilight in the evening, as they fly overland from the sea, or from rivers, lakes, or decoys which they use by day, to marshes, fields, and fens where they feed by night; and by twilight in the morning as the birds return from their feeding haunts to their places of daily resort.[1]

The flight-shooter awaits his sport in ambush behind an embankment, a hedge, sea-wall, or any temporary screen thrown up in the track of flight usually taken by the wild-fowl as they fly to and fro morning and evening; or he may conceal himself in a boat, up a creek or rill in some large river, and indeed anywhere in their track.

From some such place of concealment the flight-shooter keeps a sharp look-out during the space of about an hour and a-half, or so long as twilight lasts. He must be very expert at handling his gun, and ever watchful, or his attempts will be fruitless. Wild-fowl move very rapidly through the air at flight-time, but generally low enough to be brought down by a dexterous sportsman, even with a small, short gun. The tyro will be sorely puzzled at first as trip after trip passes over his head in rapid succession: no shooting is more difficult than this, and none requires a keener eye or greater dexterity. The sportsman should load again after a discharge with as little delay as possible, as another shot may offer within a minute or less.

Wild-fowl generally follow the main current or channel of large rivers as far as it goes, flying very low all the while until approaching land, when they immediately rise higher in the air. Whenever wild-ducks are plentiful at sea there is assuredly plenty of sport for flight-shooting, as they are sure to come inland to feed, and return again to sea in the morning.

The secret of success at this sport is dexterity in handling the gun, and the amount of success depends on whether or no the sportsman has been fortunate enough to place himself beneath the aerial track of the fowl. Novices at the sport are very apt to miss fair shots by not making sufficient allowance for the rapid flight of the birds. The young sportsman should remember to allow the birds to pass over his head before firing, and then to send his shot after them under their feathers, and he must fire well forward, aiming well ahead, at least a foot in front of them, so as to make allowance for the rapidity of their flight, or he might as well keep his charge in the barrel. On a calm night he will hear his birds come down with a thud on the marshes when he kills, though out of sight before they fall. In fact, many which fly away wounded drop several hundred yards off. The sportsman should be accompanied by a good retriever when he goes flight-shooting.

There is now a good deal of uncertainty attending this sport in any but severe winters; but before the destruction of the breeding haunts of wild-fowl by the drainage of moors and fens it was a very popular diversion. I have known sportsmen drive ten miles with their guns to a favoured locality, for the purpose of flight-shooting, taking their chance as to obtaining a shot or two at the wild-fowl on their evening flight; and in those days, in the locality of which I am speaking, every sportsman who stood his watch one hour at flight was disappointed unless he had at least one pair of fowl to carry home with him, and he often had as many as four or five pairs of duck and mallard.

When the flight-shooter is fortunate enough to get a shot at a good number of birds, he may bring down his four or five at a charge with a double gun, if he be expert at the sport and fire at the critical moment, which is the instant after they have passed over his head.

The most propitious night that can be chosen for this sport is at the first and last quarters of the moon, or at the half-moon, and during a strong wind, as the birds then fly very low. A cloudy sky, or rather a sky which presents a mixture of dark and white clouds with only a little moonlight, is also highly favourable; neither bright moonlight nor clear starlight evenings are so suitably adapted for successful flight-shooting.

When the course of the birds is westward, and a lurid sky illumes the scene, the fowler has an excellent chance of seeing his birds clearly at the critical moment of shooting—just as they have passed over his head.

The majority of birds killed in flight-shooting are duck and mallard. They generally fly in small trips to their feeding haunts at night, but return in the morning in larger flights. They fly very low as they proceed over water and mud, but rise higher in the air on reaching the land.

In windy weather they keep more together and go in larger flights; but very swiftly, if their course be down wind. The sportsman must be doubly quick in taking his shots, or the birds will have passed by him before he can bring the gun to his shoulder. If, on the other hand, the course of the birds be against wind, their flight will be steadier, and he will have time to take deliberate aim.

When the moon rises before twilight, the flight-shooter's sport is often considerably prolonged, as many of the fowl reserve their flight an hour or two later on such occasions.

Wild-fowl generally fly much lower in the morning flight than in the evening, sometimes only just topping the hedges, and they appear less wary of danger; probably this may be accounted for by their crops being full and their appetites appeased.

As a general rule, the more the wild-fowl fly about during the day, the less they do so at night. Open weather is far more favourable to flight-shooting than sharp frosts; indeed, the less frost there is the better for this sport.

In some places flight-shooting is practised from boxes or tubs sunk into the ground on open plains and plashes; often in the very heart of the best feeding-grounds. From these positions the flight-shooter fires at the birds both on the wing and as soon as they alight, whichever appears to present the better chance. So indefatigably do some men pursue this particular branch of sport, that they remain throughout the whole night in these sunken boxes.[1]

[1] In some parts of America this sport is termed 'Slaking.'—*Vide* Krider's 'Sporting Anecdotes.' By H. M. Klapp. 1853.

[1] Captain Lacy, in speaking of sunk boxes being used on the coast of Durham as places of concealment, says:—'The Greatham flight-shooters are, for the most part, what the greyhound men call *rare good stickers;* for they will sit in these boxes till the icicles hang down from the hairs of their head, so long as there remains but the *hope* even of a good shot to be made!'—*The Modern Shooter.* By Captain Lacy. 1842.

CHAPTER LIV

WILD-FOWL SHOOTING ASHORE BY NIGHT

> 'Now wand'ring by the river's winding side,
>   Its mazy course we trace, explore each creek,
>   Islet, and shelter'd cove, the wild-fowl's haunt.'

Fowling, a Poem, book v. p. 141.

IT will sometimes happen during long and severe winters that there are many days and nights when it would be imprudent to venture on a punting excursion, and when but little sport can be indulged in by the wild-fowl shooter, except by ranging at nigbt, with dog and shoulder-gun, the shore and the margins of lakes and rivers, inland and near the sea. This may arise from various causes: either the frost may be so severe as to blockade the waters with ice, so that it is impossible to stir with the punt, the wind may be too high, or the night unpro-pitious for any other adventure than a stroll ashore with dog and gun. There are some men who prefer this sport to any other, and who, by long experience in it, become highly successful.

In the neighbourhood of inland rivers, lakes, or broads, where the tide ebbs and flows, the time chosen by the midnight sportsman for this diversion should be an hour or two previous to high water, when wild-fowl which may not have gone to the fens at flight-time are busily feeding on the ooze and saltings, and, if not disturbed by the punters, they will gradually approach towards the shore as the tide flows and brings them on. In some seasons, when wild-fowl are abundant, an experienced shore-gunner is enabled to kill more than a bad punter. Notwithstanding that it is the nature of wild-ducks to seek fens and moors at evening-twilight, there are many which remain in salt-water rivers all night, for they find abundant feeding in such places.

The sportsman should be ever ready for a chance shot when ranging the coast of a tidal bay or river at night, though it may be many hours after high-water; because, if any wild-ducks have approached the shore with the flood-tide, and have come upon good feeding among the grasses at the brink of the shore, or, what is still more enticing to them, a fresh water tributary, they will not recede with the ebb-tide, but, on the contrary, will most assuredly remain there until daylight next morning, if undisturbed. But in the absence of white water to assist the fowler he will find a difficulty in discovering the precise position of the birds; and, in all probability, will have to shoot entirely by guess, with nothing to direct him but their noises:

'All's hush'd, except the sea-fowl's notes,
Hoarse-murm'ring from yon craggy brow.'

It is advisable that the sportsman be warmly clad for this pursuit, as he will often find it necessary to lie in ambush an hour or more at a time, and to retrieve his birds he will require the services of a well-trained dog, one that is obedient to the most silent commands, obeying its master's signs and signals, and mute in all its actions. A perfectly-trained wild-fowl shooter's dog is seldom to be met with at the present day, but is a most valuable animal to the shore-gunner.

The sportsman will only be able to see the birds *when on the water* at night, their figures then showing as dark objects upon a white and glittering surface; but when the birds are feeding on grass-lands or elsewhere ashore, they cannot be discerned with sufficient accuracy to enable him to shoot with any certainty unless there be bright moonlight, though he may sometimes succeed in making a good random shot, being directed to the position of the fowl by their clamorous notes. Having crept closely to the spot, by watching carefully a few minutes he will be enabled to discern their movements.

On moonlight nights he will have to observe the same rules, as to placing himself in the loom, as have been previously prescribed with regard to punting[1] in order that he may not be discovered by the birds.

It will be almost a useless adventure to go in quest of sport on the marshes by night, or, indeed, anywhere inland, unless there be a pond, pool, or stream of water to assist the fowler in discovering the exact spot where the birds are.

In some places, where there may be a particular haunt or favourite spot frequented by wild-fowl night after night, though on open grass-lands, if there be the smallest ambush, such as reeds, bushes, sedges, or long grass, within range, the midnight wild-fowl shooter may be pretty certain of a shot, unless the night is very dark. He should creep up to the ambuscade with all possible caution, and from that position take aim.

He must carefully observe the direction of the wind, and always approach from the lewarclmost available position, unless the wind be high, in which case he may pay less regard to the position from which he approaches, as sound does not travel so accurately in strong winds as in steady breezes. On calm nights he must be very guarded in his movements when within hearing of the birds.

When wild-fowl are busily feeding, the fowler is enabled, on still nights, distinctly to hear the clatter of their bills as they dabble in the water, which noise, with that of the notes of the fowl, will be sufficient to guide him.

The midnight fowler should take careful observation during daylight of all the rills, rivulets, and dykes which run into the main lake or river, and note those in which feathers and other traces of the resort of wild-ducks are found. Wherever wild-ducks discover food and quietude they return again at their customary feeding hours. The sportsman should stalk cautiously up to such spots, and in open marshes, in the absence of a screen, he should erect a temporary one during the day-time. Shore-gunners are generally enabled to kill more wild-fowl at midnight and early morning in rills, rivulets, and dykes than on other parts of the coast.

It is the nature of wild-ducks, on arriving at their destination after their evening flight from the sea-coast by night, to seek the rills and dykes of the freshes, which to them are rich feeding grounds, as are also shallow waters and the margins of lakes and rivers. Although, on first alighting, they take up a position in the centre of inland pools and flooded meadows, as soon as they gain confidence and feel assured of the safety of their retreat, they swim to the brink of the water and commence their dabblings in the shallowest places, where they can obtain easy access to the bottom. Ducks in particular, in frosty weather, feed close along the water's edge, as the mud there does not freeze so readily.

On these excursions the shore-gunner must never forget, whilst stalking wild-fowl, that their ears are ever open to suspicious sounds, and that they invariably take wing on the slightest intimation of an enemy's approach. The least rustle, noise, or crackle under-foot, whether of crispy snow, briar, or shingle, will assuredly alarm them if it reaches their ears; and then perhaps the gunner's best or only chance during the night is gone.

When frozen out of the river, and unable to use a punt because of the complete blockade of ice, or when driven from my customary pursuit of punting, my inclination has often led me to night excursions on the shore with dog and gun; and if I may be excused for so frequently thrusting narratives of my own adventures upon my readers, I would venture to place before them a somewhat stirring incident, as the best means of giving a faithful description of the pleasures and hardships of this particular branch of the sport.

It was past twelve o'clock on a cold snowy night, when, after walking several miles along the shore by a river-side, I halted at the foot of a large oak tree, whose hundred arms, when loaded with green foliage, had sheltered me on many a summer's day from the scorching rays of the sun. Whilst partaking of a sandwich and draught of sack, I stood musing on the tales the old tree could tell—of merry-makings, pic-nic parties, and rural frolics which had taken place in that retired locality, under the auspices of warm summer weather; when, suddenly, my faithful dog 'Sambo' arrested my attention by a low whining noise. I instantly forgot the summer scenes, and listened to the signal. Would that all my friends were as faithful as that dog! But human nature is too prone to err; too apt to raise, by false professions, hope where hope is vain. I never knew that dog deceive me. Nay! I would not keep a dog that told a lie. I listened! but hearing nothing, attacked another sandwich and took another cup of sack. Sambo softly whined again! I offered him part of the sandwich, but his attention was too riveted upon something—I knew not what—to heed the proffered food, and, though hungry, he refused it. A few seconds more, and he whined again! peering all the while in the direction of the river. At this moment I distinctly heard the note of a wild-duck or mallard not very far distant; and so, patting the dog, took my gun and proceeded with cautious steps to follow through the falling snow my unerring guide.

> 'Silently, silently, on we trode and trode As if a spell had frozen up our words:
>   White lay the wolds around us, ankle deep
>   In new-fallen snows, which champed beneath our feet.'

We proceeded several yards along the shore, every step seeming to bring us nearer to the birds, and I soon discovered that there was more than one noisy mallard of the party. The marshes were quite open and unsheltered: there was but one screen—a small bed of reeds on the brink of the river—a position behind which it was highly desirable to obtain; but the difficulty of getting there unseen was great, it being more than a hundred yards across open marshes, which were covered with snow, and wet, cold, and muddy: but what of that—whilst my water-boots extended far above the knees? So down I knelt and proceeded to crawl along the marsh, through the snow, as noiselessly as possible, Sambo following close in the rear; when, having nearly gained the reeds, I was puzzled to know what the clog meant by every now and then walking a few yards in front, and then returning, growling and rubbing his nose against my arm. Having never known him to act so strangely, I could not divine his meaning. A few moments solved the mystery; for, on approaching the reeds, to my great surprise, they were already occupied by a snow-covered sportsman, who had not observed my stealthy approach, and was so startled, when I gently pinched his leg, that I feared the birds would take alarm, but was glad to find they did not. The already ensconced sportsman was a young farmer living near by, who had reached the spot as stealthily as myself an hour or more in advance of me; consequently the falling snow had removed all trace of his footsteps. He told me in a whisper he had long been watching the movements of the ducks, which had hitherto been out of range, but were now just approaching within shot. As he was first there, by the rules of sporting, it was his shot; but as there seemed to be from twenty to thirty birds together, it was at once arranged that we should both shoot; and, having so agreed, we waited a few minutes until they afforded us both a fair chance, when, at a given signal, we fired simultaneously—the farmer at one side the paddling, and I at the other—and in less than five minutes Sambo fetched us from the muddy ooze thirteen cluck and mallard, the result of our joint shot. How the farmer had thought of recovering his birds without a dog I cannot tell; but I imagine he must have been very glad of Sambo's assistance, the ooze being too soft and rotten to bear human weight without mud-pattens.

Punters have, generally, a great antipathy to shore-gunners, who often spoil their best sport; when, just as they are about approaching large numbers of fowl, and almost within shot, the report of a small gun ashore disturbs the whole lake, and every bird rises in the air. Shore-gunners have a similar antipathy to punters, and their best sport is sometimes spoilt by the roar of the punter's artillery.

On one occasion I remember an event which gave rise to much gossip at the time it occurred—now many years ago. A fowler, named 'Ted Steele,' who pursued his calling more by night than by day, was in the habit of skirting a certain bay in a river on the eastern coast famous for wild-fowl shooting. In the bay alluded to he had bagged many a pair of wild-fowl, and on the occasion to which our anecdote relates was in eager pursuit of his calling. But before proceeding farther with Ted Steele on his midnight excursion with punt and gun, the reader must follow me ashore to a sea-wall or mound thrown up close by the river side, behind which two men lay concealed, with shoulder guns of long barrel pointed in the direction of a paddling of wild-ducks which were unsuspectingly swimming in-shore towards the tumulus before mentioned, the flowing tide assisting and encouraging them onwards. Both the men had their guns primed and cocked, and their fingers on the triggers: a dog was lying at their feet, ready to obey instant orders when required. In a few seconds they would have fired: the signal had already passed between them to 'stand by!' when, 'bang!' roared an unexpected and startling gun from the punt, which then instantly emerged from the shade, and which the ensconced sportsmen had only that instant detected, though within fifty yards of the mound.

' 'Tis that fellow Ted Steele again,' said one of the men from behind the mound; 'this is now the third time he has spoilt our sport this moon! Let us see if we can't make him steer another course, instead of poking and groping about here directly in our way every night. I say, Ted! why don't you go lower down the river with your punt, and leave this little bay to us shore-gunners? 'Tis the only place within two miles that we have a chance of a shot. We were *just* going to shoot at those ducks as you came up.'

To these remarks Ted Steele replied:—

'How could I tell you were lying behind the bank? I could not see you. I have a living to get at the sport, and follow it up wherever I think there's the best chance. I don t know why you should claim the exclusive right to the shooting in this bay, and I don't intend to give it up to you,' said Ted, as he picked up four pairs and a half of wild-ducks, the result of his charge.

After some further jangling, and as soon as Ted Steele had re-loaded his gun and bade the shore-gunners a good night, the men behind the tumulus agreed among themselves to be prepared for Ted on the following night, intending to endeavour to put him off his course, and have some fun into the bargain.

Accordingly, the night following they placed themselves behind the mound as usual, and patiently awaited the appearance of their victim. It was a fine moonlight night, and, as the tide gradually flowed towards the bank, they distinctly heard the sound of wild-fowl approaching; very shortly afterwards they caught sight of a punter, apparently watching the wild-fowl and awaiting the flow of tide.

'Here comes Ted, or I'm a sinner!' said one of the two shore-gunners, with much glee. They directly drew the shot from their gun barrels, and placed each a charge of *hard peas* a-top of the powder, and silently awaited the flowing tide, keeping watch on the movements of the unsuspecting punter. As the tide rose, the birds came onwards towards a tiny stream of fresh water which ran from beneath the bank at the foot of the secreted shore-gunners. The punter now laid himself down in the customary attitude, and proceeded to paddle cautiously towards the birds. He had arrived nearly within range, as he lay prostrate in the punt about fifty or sixty yards from the mound, when 'bang!' 'bang!' roared a couple of guns from the shore, plump at Ted Steele, who, in most indescribable fright and smarting with pain, roared out lustily—'Oh Grod! you have killed me! You have done for me outright, you villains! I'm killed from head to foot!'

'Good heavens, Ted, what's that you? We thought it was the wild-fowl we shot at!' said one of the men behind the mound. Having somewhat recovered from his fright, Ted began to look about him and found he was not seriously hurt, though severely stung. On observing the peas scattered about the punt he immediately suspected the hoax, and thirsting for vengeance pulled ashore, and set off in pursuit of one of the offenders, who, as preconcerted, ran off as hard as he could on being pursued by the punter. The other man concealed himself; and, taking advantage of the opportunity thus afforded him of inspecting Ted Steele's punt, jumped into it and rowed away from the shore. On Ted's return from, the pursuit, the saucy shore-gunner coolly wished him 'a good night and pleasant walk home,' adding that he intended having a night's punting at Ted's expense, by way of change from shore-gunning.

It would not be prudent to follow the highly-exasperated Ted Steele through the catalogue of curses he heaped upon the heads of the shore-gunners, or to accompany him in his disconsolate walk home—a distance of no less than six miles, the scene of action having taken place, unfortunately, on the opposite bank of the river to that of Ted's cottage; so retired, too, was the locality, that no boat could be had along the coast in which to cross the river. The nearest bridge was a long way distant, and the walk tedious and rugged, particularly for one clad as Ted Steele was, with heavy water-boots and double thick woollen clothing, which the inclemency of the season rendered necessary. Poor Ted waited at the mound some little time, thinking the man would return with the punt; but, finding there was no probability of his so doing, he set off to walk home; and after many slips and slides in the snow, and other obstacles, weary and tired, he reached his cottage home, when he threw himself on his bed, and slept as soundly as his rage, disappointment, and annoyance would admit. Next morning he shoved off in a small boat to search for his punt and gun, which he ultimately found carefully made fast to a stake on the shore, a long distance down the river. The punt-gun had evidently been fired two or three times, judging from appearances and the diminished state of the powder and shot; apparently, also, with some effect, as there were blood-stains and feathers of wild-fowl in the punt. Without making further ado, Ted took the punt in tow and brought her home, endeavouring to forget and forgive the offenders, though he ever afterwards, on passing the tumulus at night, cast suspicious glances at its significant appearance, and always gave the shore-gunners a wide berth on his future expeditions.[1]

----

[1] *Supra* 'Night-punting.'

[1] This anecdote was originally published by the author in the 'Sporting Review,' vol. xxxv. p. 16.

CHAPTER LV

WILD-FOWL SHOOTING IN THE FENS.

'Sportsman! lead on, where through the reedy bank
The insinuating waters, filter'd, stray
In many a winding maze. The wild-duck there
Gluts on the fattening ooze, or steals the spawn
Of teeming shoals—her more delicious feast.'

SOMERVILLE.

PUEVIOUS to the drainage and cultivation of the fens, Lincolnshire was termed the 'Aviary of England' for wild-fowl,[1] and that county, conjointly with Cambridgeshire, was the best of all for fen-bird shooting. Those were the falconer's and wild-fowler's halcyon days. The best of sport was always to be had in the wild and uncultivated regions of those counties. Thousands of wild-fowl and fen-birds used annually to be bred upon the quiet and undisturbed islets which abounded in those parts, and formed the very strongholds and nurseries of the aquatic species; and whilst fens, meres, islets, and broads remained as nature left them, the numerous and beautiful varieties of water-fowl revelled in the luxuriant feedings of those sequestered spots, which seemed specially planned by nature as the habitations and breeding haunts of birds, whose home is upon the waters, and whose food and sustenance are in the fens and meres.

In those days their greatest enemy was a species of rapacious bird, called the moor-buzzard, which is alluded to by Pliny as haunting lakes, fens, and standing waters for the purpose of preying upon water-fowl.[2] But now there are but few large fenny districts in England that have not been drained and cultivated to some extent, so as to have seriously injured, if not completely uprooted and destroyed, many of the best retreats of the aquatic species.[3]

Thus the sportsman learns with regret that whilst the enterprising land-owner and agriculturist have attained their ends, and converted many thousand acres of swamps and fens into arable and meadow land, such conversion has only been acquired at a partial sacrifice of some of our most healthful and interesting diversions, and the driving from our shores of a variety of the largest, rarest, most beautiful, and useful of the wild feathered tribe. But notwithstanding the heavy blows which have thus been struck at our good old English recreations, there are yet remaining in some of the neighbouring counties, as elsewhere, some of the best and fairest retreats for wild-fowl that can be imagined; and though a good number are annually bred in those places, yet in no proportion to the thousands which were reared in the fens in days gone by.[1]

The aerial wanderers are now wary of the haunts of their ancestors, and hover suspiciously in the air over miles of acres of cultivated land that used to be fens and meres, and where in former days a glance sufficed to satisfy them that they had found the food and rest they sought.

Those days can only be looked back upon by wild-fowlers with regret, for never now, can those extensive wilds of fenland be restored to what they were.

The Great Bedford Level contains a tract of sixty computed miles in length and forty in breadth. It was originally a wooded country: the sea is supposed to have burst in upon it and overwhelmed the whole tract, leaving a thick deposit of silt, beneath which modern excavators have discovered whole forests of firs and oaks; some of the latter, fifteen feet in girth and sixteen yards in length; many of them burnt at the roots, thus indicating the ancient method of falling timber to be the same as that adopted by uncivilized nations. Others appeared to have been uprooted by the force of the current rushing upon them.

Many years after these encroachments of the sea, and when a thick alluvial deposit had. been extensively spread over the level, the Romans, with indefatigable perseverance, which has never been equalled by the people of any other nation (unless it be by those of the Netherlands), raised an embankment, and thereby regained many thousand acres of land which the inundations of the sea had converted from forest into fen.

Pennant remarks that it was the complaint of Galgacus that the Romans exhausted the strength of the Britons 'in sylvis et paludibus emuniendis.'[2]

There are abundant evidences of these facts; and among them Eoman tumuli, coins, and other relics, which were found in the immediate neighbourhood of the level.

It appears that the laborious exertions of the Eomans were not immediately inherited by the Britons; for when that industrious people deserted our island, the drains and embankments which they had made were neglected, and in process of time the sea again burst over them, when the level became a region of fens, lakes, and swamps, and so continued through many centuries, offering by far the most extensive and favoured haunts for wild-fowl of any in the kingdom; so that thousands of water-fowl thronged the district of the level at all seasons of the year.

After the inundations of the sea, and embankment by the Romans, the Great Bedford Level contained upwards of 300,000 acres of fenland.[1] In addition to which it was bounded by other extensive districts of fens and broads, extending into the respective counties of Lincoln, Norfolk, Suffolk, Cambridge, Huntingdon, Northampton, and the Isle of Ely.[2]

There were eight principal rivers formed by Nature[3] for conveying to sea the waters of this extensive waste; these were the main arteries of the fens, and most of them originally united by connecting or tributary veins or streams, forming themselves at different situations into large estuaries, and thus making natural and excellent resorts for water-fowl.

Art has long since changed the current of these tributary streams and estuaries, so that scarcely a trace can now be found of the original works of nature.

Those extensive tracts of land, in their wild and uncultivated state, abounded with game, were studded with lakes, and afforded admirable scope for the sports of the field.[4] Such a country, as might be expected, was far better adapted to those pursuits than the regular operations of husbandry. The opportunities it afforded for enjoying the pleasures of hunting, fowling, and fishing were unrivalled.[5]

'Th' abundance then is seen, that my full fens do yield,
That almost through the isle, do pester every field.'[6]

According to the same authority, the wild-fowl that were taken in the Lincolnshire fens (part of the Great Bedford Level) were considered of superior flavour to those of the 'foggy fens' of Holland.

'These fowls, with other soils although they frequent be,
Yet are they found most sweet and delicate in me.'

Whittlesea Mere and Ramsey Mere were two of the largest pools in the fens; the former was especially celebrated for its great variety of water-fowl and abundance of fish.

It was strongly urged at the time of the proposal for draining the Lincolnshire fens that the scheme, when carried out, would drive away the feathered and finny occupants of the meres, and spoil both the fowlers' and fishers' sport. A bold standing in behalf of these two classes was made in opposition to the promoters of the undertaking, when the defence was, that there were many meres and lakes which would be left in their original state, that the fish and fowl preferred rivers and channels to wide-spreading waters, and that the additional number of such receptacles would tend to the greater preservation and increase of fish and fowl rather than the extermination of them.[1]

The drainage of the Great Bedford Level was undoubtedly the greatest blow ever dealt to the sport of wild-fowling in England. It is therefore with some consolation that we turn at the present day to neighbouring counties, and find many thousand acres of fen-land preserved in their natural, uncultivated, and good old primitive garb.

The far-famed Norfolk Broads remain much the same as they were a century ago. The plough and draining pipes of the agriculturist have effected but little change in those wild districts, which for the most part are preserved by the proprietors for the special diversions of hunting, shooting, fishing, and fowling.

And notwithstanding that the iron-way of the engineer has been driven to the very verge of the Norfolk Broads, and the timid fowl are occasionally disturbed in their midnight revels by the screaming whistle and fiery snorts of the steam engine, there yet remains many a tranquil spot within the area of those extensive broads where no such sights and sounds can reach them.[1] Many of the broads are very shallow, and navigable only by means of flat-bottomed boats. Some of them, as at Eanworth, Barton, Wroxham, and Horsey, present a wide expanse of water surrounded by reed-beds and rushy borders, with occasional islets of a similar growth, or shrubs and plantations of birch and alder, sloping gradually to the water's edge; others with a variety of little channels traversing the reed-beds in all directions, or with small reed-locked pools opening into each other by narrow 'gat-ways.'[2]

The formation of the Norfolk Broads is in other respects peculiarly adapted to the habits and requirements of the waterfowl which frequent them, being for the most part fleet and shallow, with rich, loamy bottoms, on which sweet weeds and grasses grow within easy reach of their bills. And, as Mr. Stevenson observes, 'everywhere the rich aquatic herbage teems with bird-life.'[3]

A sportsman living in the country of broads and fens near

543

the seacoast may even at the present day have sport without end, and wild-fowl shooting, in severe winters, to his heart's content, provided he takes that delight in the sport which will incur the necessity of early rising, with energy and indefatigable exertion:

> 'Ye fowlers! manly strength your toils require;
> Defiance of the summer's burning sun
> And winter's keenest blast, of hail or storm,
> Of ice or driving snow; nor must the marsh
> That quivers to your step deter you.'[1]

The movements of wild-fowl are always regulated by the severity or mildness of the season; accordingly, the severer the winter, the further the birds travel southward, the larger their flights, and the more numerous the variety. It is in the severest winters that we meet with the rarest specimens from high northern latitudes. It is, besides, during the most nipping frosts that the birds are tamest, but more especially so on the first breath of a thaw, after long-continued and severe frost, when they are so hungry and eager to feed, that they may be approached with less difficulty than at other times; but in general they are not near so fat and full-flavoured whilst the weather continues severe as during a long continuance of mild or open weather.

It is by no means to be inferred that it is only during severe winters that good wild-fowl shooting may be had.

Every winter, whether severe or not, brings large numbers of the aquatic tribe to our shores, but they are extremely wary, and not to be approached on the open waters by any but experienced hands, for which purpose the gunning-punts recommended in former chapters in these pages are the best means to be employed for getting at them, and afford by far the finest sport to the ardent sportsman. But to those who object to punting, or prefer the sport on *terra firma*, and who reside near the locality of fens, broads, or marshes skirting the sea or any large river, there is generally, during winter, some good and certain sport to be had by walking beside the largest of the dykes and delfs which always abound in such localities; the sportsman, however, must be an early riser, and on his ground before daylight, as the birds generally begin to move off to the open waters at morning twilight, returning again to their feeding-haunts at eventide. Where there is good feed and a quiet retreat, wild fowl will sometimes remain during the greater part of the day, or until disturbed, and, having once discovered such a spot, they are almost certain to return to it again.

Many and many are the pairs of duck, mallard, and teal that I have brought down with the shoulder-gun before day-light, when there was only just sufficient light to see an object clearly enough to shoot it, and without knowing, until my dog brought it to my feet, what species of fowl it was.

A dog is almost indispensable for this sport, not so much to *find* the birds, as to *fetch* them when shot; because they as frequently fall on the opposite side of a wide ditch as on that from which the sportsman fires. If he has no dog he loses half his time in going a roundabout way to pick up his birds, which, after all, he may entirely lose if only winged or wounded. A young dog with a good mouth is apt to be outwitted by the cunning of an old duck that is not very badly wounded, as shown in the engraving opposite of 'Sambo's First Lesson in the Fens;' but after Sambo had once griped the feathers of a wild-duck, and found they were not firm fixtures, I never afterwards knew him allow a captive to escape.

One of the secrets of success in this branch of our pastime is to rise early, and be at the most likely dykes just at dawn of day. The sportsman should move on briskly from one dyke to another, and if there be any wild-fowl among the sedges or reeds, and the dyke not very extensive, they will rise without the assistance of a clog or any extra alarm from the sportsman, whose object should be to pass on quickly, that he may get as near to his birds as possible and be the more certain of killing.

An old mallard requires a hard hit from the shot of a small shoulder-gun; and to carry a very large gun on such excursions would seriously interfere with the pleasure attending the sport, and bring no greater success than that of a well-made double-barrelled gun of No. 8 or No. 10 gauge.

This kind of wild-fowling when the birds are moderately abundant is an enviable sport, and they may be considered tolerably plentiful when a sportsman is able to kill, on an average of two hours' walk every morning, four or five pair a week. The sport is, to my mind, unequalled by any with dog and gun, but success depends mainly on the time chosen for the walk. The sportsman should be on the moor, of a morning, as soon as he can see an object in the air with sufficient distinctness to knock it down.

The charm of this kind of sport is, that whilst walking the fens, birds of such various species are to be met with; and when the sportsman has tried likely places for wild-fowl, if without success, he need not return home with empty pockets; he has only to draw the large shot from his gun, put in smaller, and go in search of snipes and plovers.

Sawbo's first lesson in the fens

Even at the present day (1875) the London markets are well supplied with fen-birds of every kind (excepting ruffs and reeves),[1] and the demand for them is considerable. They may also be had alive in the Leadenhall Market.[2] The dealers there receive them from 'their correspondents' in various parts of the country.

---

[1] Fuller's 'Worthies of England.' By Nuttall.

² 'Illa quam tertiam fecimus aquaticas avis circa stagna adpetit mergentis se subinde donee sopitas lassatasque rapiat.'—*Lib*. x. cap. iii. s. 9.

³ As to which it is remarked in Fuller's 'Worthies of England' that, 'if the plenty of birds have since been drained with the fens in this county, what Lincolnshire lacks in her former fowl is supplied in flesh (more mutton and beef), and a large first makes amends for a less second course.'

¹ The author of 'Sport and its Pleasures, Physical and Gastronomical,' A.D. 1859, asserts, without fear of contradiction, that even at the present day thousands of wild-fowl are hatched annually in this country; an assertion in which I unhesitatingly concur.

² Pennant's 'Arctic Zoology.'

¹ Well's 'History of the Drainage of the Fens,' 1830.

² See Map of the Fens, by Hondins, A.D. 1680; also Elstobb's 'History of the Fens.'

³ Wells, p. 6.

⁴ Well's 'History of the Drainage of the Fens,' p. 55.

⁵ *Ibid*, p. 423.

[6] Drayton.

[1] 'As for the decoy of fish and fowl, which hath been no small objectn. agst. this public work, there is not much likelihood thereof; for, notwithstanding this general draining, there are so many great meers and lakes still continuing, which be indeed the principal harbours for them, that there will be no want of either; for in the vast spreading waters they seldom abide, the rivers, channels, and meers being their principal receptacles; which being now increased, will rather augment than diminish their store.'—*Dugdale on Embanking.* A.D. 1772.

[1] Mr. Henry Stevenson, speaking of the Norfolk Broads, in allusion more particularly to the far-famed Breydon, says:— 'It is impossible to imagine a spot more attractive than this both to the grallatorial and natatorial tribes, the "flats" at low water affording throughout the year an inexhaustible supply of food in the shape of crustacea, mollusca, and various aquatic insects. The harder the winter the greater are the flocks of dunlins and other tringæ, gulls, and wild-fowl collected here as to one common banquet, when frozen out from more inland waters; and incredible almost are the numbers killed in some seasons by the gunners, whose flat-bottomed boats float in the little creeks, or are pushed easily over the "muds" when a "lumping" shot presents itself.'—Introduction to *The Birds of Norfolk*, 1866.

² 'At Lynn, as may be seen by a glance at the map, a perfect maze of sands and shoals, extending from the mouth of the harbour to the open "deeps," are traversed in all directions by the main channels, or the outlets of minor streams. Such feeding-grounds are at all times attractive to the oceanic ducks and other marine fowl, but in severe weather, or when heavy gales outside have driven them in for shelter, enormous flocks of fowl and waders are collected together, and large numbers are killed by the gunners.'—Stevenson's *Birds of Norfolk*, Intro.

³ A most interesting description of the Norfolk Broads, in an ornithological point of view, is to be found in the Introduction to Mr. Stevenson's 'Birds of Norfolk.'

¹ 'Fowling, a Poem,' book i. p. 7.

¹ *Infra*, page 293.

² The author has (December 1874) just seen there a coop of live lapwings which were about to be sent off to New Zealand.

CHAPTER LVI

PLOVER SHOOTING AND NETTING

'The Plover safe her airy scream
Circling repeats, then to a distance flies,
And, querulous, still returns, importunate,
Yet still escapes, unworthy of an aim.'

The Birds of Scotland. By JAMES GRAHAME. 1806.

PLOVER SHOOTING affords much variety of amusement to the sportsman during mild winters, or when there are but few wildfowl. England of all other nations has always been a favourite resort of plovers: and, be the season mild or severe, these beautiful and delicate fen-birds may be found in their favourite localities. Previous to the inroads made by agricultural drainage, they were specially abundant in the fens of Lincolnshire, Cambridgeshire, and Norfolk:

'For near this batning isle, in me is to be seen,
More than on any earth, the plover, gray and green.'[3]

And they still adhere with determined pertinacity to the soil of those and other counties wherever a vestige of fen-land remains.

Plover shooting affords the sportsman good practice in the fens with his snipe-gun; and on the coast, shores, and margins of lakes, broads, and rivers, by loading his punt-gun with small shot, he may have opportunities of trying it at the large 'congregations' of plovers in early season, before the wild-fowl arrive.

It appears by Latham that they were formerly objects of the falconer's diversion,[1] and came under the denomination 'green-fowl.' And, according to Drayton, all wild-fowl frequenting inland waters, except the duck and mallard, were so termed; for he sings—

'The duck and mallard first, the falconer's only sport
(Of river-flights the chief, so that all other sort
They only *green fowl* term), in every mere abound,
That you would think they sate upon the very ground.'

The golden plover (*Charadrius pluvialis*) is esteemed a bird of choice delicacy for the table, and is therefore well deserving the sportsman's pains to bring it to bag. The grey plover (*Squatarola cinerea*) is scarcely less inferior in flavour, and affords equal sport in certain seasons of the year. The pewit, or lapwing (*Tringa vanellus*), is also a species of plover, though inferior, as a table delicacy, to the others.

Plovers are generally found in small 'congregations' by the river-side, about marshes and salt-water plains, and sometimes in meadows, inland fields, and uplands. They are very distrustful of the human form, and their flight is rapid and graceful. When plovers are observed on the wing the sportsman should remain perfectly still. They may then very probably pass within shot, but they are at all times shy and difficult of access. The best means of getting at them by land is by lying in ambush behind a bank or mound in the direction they are known to take in their flights, and then, by sending a boy round to put them up, a shot or two may be had as they pass over—

————. 'Beneath this hedge

Screen we ourselves and dogs—close o'er our head
The birds will skim; they come, compact and close;
When instant 'mid their ranks the whistling shot
Spreads dire destruction.'[2]

The instant plovers take alarm at any object on the land, when flying over or when fired at, they dart down suddenly in their flight towards the ground, and then, rising in the air, scatter themselves in every possible direction, dodging and flitting about in such a manner as to try the skill of the most practised sportsman.

They are fond of associating in small parties; a solitary plover always shrieks and whistles as if the most unhappy bird on the moor. At such a time, the sportsman who can mimic their call-note may assuredly decoy the bird within gun-shot, if himself in a place of concealment; but it can seldom be done otherwise except in foggy weather. Rather than remain by itself, a plover will seek the society of other birds, as oxbirds, godwits, and sandpipers.

The punter who pursues his sport on inland waters sometimes meets with very inviting shots at these birds, more particularly if in the locality of a tidal river and oozes.

I have killed large numbers of them at a shot with my punt-gun, and I once saw two punters approach a mixed 'congregation' comprising several hundreds of grey and golden plovers and lapwings. The two punters killed in their joint-shot upwards of a hundred. They fired simultaneously at the birds when huddled together on their last legs, on a small space of uncovered ooze, which the flowing tide was every moment creeping upon, and rendering smaller and smaller, so that the birds stood closer and closer, presenting one of the most favourable chances at plovers I ever saw. I afterwards understood that these two men had *two guineas* to share between them, the result of their shot at the plovers.

Plovers are much in the habit of picking and feeding in the wash of a flood-tide as it gradually flows towards the shore. On watching them narrowly they appear to revel in the surf, as it washes their slender and delicate little legs, causing them to skip and jump with interesting delight. They may then, with caution, be approached in a recumbent position in the punt; but it is useless to attempt getting at them by land unless some bank or screen be at hand. They sometimes run along the ground with great velocity; and, however mournful the tone of their call-note, they appear the happiest little creatures of the feathered tribe when running to and fro on the beach, flirting and whistling with pleasing and happy-looking movements. All which I have frequently observed by cautiously peeping over the gunwale of the punt when within twenty yards or less of scores of them.

Another of their most interesting actions when running about the shore in unsuspecting security is that of opening their elegant little wings, as if intending to fly off, but not actually doing so. It is merely a playful movement, by which they expose the white feathers beneath their wings, and thus put themselves for a few moments in very graceful attitudes. I have observed godwits and oxbirds performing the same antics.

There is no better time and opportunity for making successful shots at grey and golden plovers than early in the morning, just at daybreak, and an hour or so later, when they are less wild, and may be risen on the marshes within range of gunshot. Whenever plovers are observed on the wing near by, they are very likely to pass close to the sportsman if he stands quite still. As they are generally in a closely-packed flight at that time, a good number may sometimes be killed at a single discharge.

Golden plovers are frequently found in fields and uplands during the day; indeed, a great portion of their time is spent in ploughed fields and inland meadows.

The punter should keep a sharp look-out for plovers when rowing near the shore; they are often passed by unobserved when feeding and running about in the surf, or by the brink of the water, on a beach of small shingle.

It is said to be a sign of bad weather when these birds are very restless: they fly to and fro, shrieking as if in dismay at some incontrovertible danger.

Plovers are to a certain extent migratory, usually arriving about our coasts towards the end of October. They are much more abundant at some seasons than at others, though not apparently in actual accordance with the severity of winter; for they are sometimes as numerous in mild winters as in hard ones. Grey plovers are not generally so abundant as others, though often found in great numbers. These are more exclusively coast-birds, and seldom visit fields and uplands.

The lapwing, or pewit, is the bird so famous for its eggs, which in some places are of more value as a marketable commodity than the birds themselves. The plundering of their nests with so much avidity has tended materially to diminish the numbers of these beautiful birds, which used to breed in thousands about the English fens, fields, and marshes. They have curious artifices for endeavouring to mislead intruders as to the whereabouts of their nests, flying round and round with much clamour, and pretending to hover over a particular spot; which is never found to be the place where their nest is actually situated, but always many yards apart from it. The poet Thomson says:—

> 'Hence around the head
> Of wand'ring swain, the white-wing'd plover wheels
> Her sounding flight, and then directly on,
> In long excursion, skims the level lawn,
> To tempt him from her nest.'

The call-note of the lapwing is very simple, expressing most distinctly the word 'pee-wit!'

In some parts of Scotland the lapwing is spoken of as a treacherous bird, and is looked upon with detestation by the inhabitants, because of having been the means of betraying the fugitive Presbyterians during the reigns of Charles II. and James II.[1] Chaucer also speaks of this bird as

'The false lapwing, alle full of trechirie.'

The flesh of the lapwing is not held in high estimation as a cibarious commodity, though it may be rendered very palatable by an experienced cook. The ideas of some ancient writers as to this bird being a dirty feeder[2] are erroneous, as are also other strange delusions of the author of 'Grlantvilla,' who states that philosophers assert of this bird that when it becomes old, and unable to see or fly, its companions pull away the feeble feathers and anoint its eyes with juice of herbs. They then brood the aged patient under their wings till its feathers are grown, again and its sight restored.[3]

But notwithstanding these crude ideas, it appears that the lapwing[4] was, during the fifteenth century, in higher (or at least quite as high) estimation for its dietary excellence as other plovers.[5]

When these birds were more abundant than now, and at an age when fattening fen-birds for the table was a regular trade, lapwings were taken from the nest just before being able to fly; they were then shut up in coops and fed on curds a short time, upon which diet their flesh much improved in flavour;[1] thus they brought a liberal remuneration to the fen-fowler, who sold them at an advanced price to such as could afford to invest in such delicacies.

Lapwings are still tolerably abundant in the fens and

marshes of the eastern coast, and they used to be especially so in the parish of Little Oakley, near Harwich, where there is an island consisting of about two hundred acres, called 'Pewit Island,' from the numbers of birds of that species which frequent it.[2]

CAPTURING PLOVERS WITH NETS AND SNARES.

Plovers are also taken by fen-fowlers in day nets, a practice as old as any method of fowling extant, and one which is used in Germany, France, and the Netherlands, as well as in England, Scotland, and Ireland.

The proceedings connected with the day or clap net have been already described under the head 'Ancient Fowling.' The net is spread just before twilight, and in the dusk of the evening the plovers are enticed by call-birds to alight within its meshes, when the fowler immediately secures them. Helme states that he has seen a dozen, and sometimes two dozen, taken at a pull, they come in such closely-packed flights.[3]

They are easily captured in these nets during open weather, but not so during the frost. A great many are caught with nets in fields of green corn, in which they delight to turn up the ground for worms and seeds. But the greater numbers are captured on grass lands in the fens.

Plover-catching is by no means a difficult art: these birds always roost on the ground: the fowler, therefore, with ordinary precaution, is also enabled to take them with a snipe or lark net, which is simply a drag net with small meshes made of fine twine, but of large size, sometimes fifty or sixty yards in length by ten or twelve feet in breadth. This net is quietly dragged by two men over meadows and marshes, the nightly haunts of plovers. It is a very profitable employment for the poor fowler in a district where these birds are abundant, provided there is a market for them when captured; and, it may be added, provided the fowler abstains from poaching or dragging his net for partridges, a temptation to fen-fowlers not at all times irresistible.

Plovers are also freely taken with lime-strings pricked out in the marshes, fens, and fields—their customary haunts. They are fond of resorting to ploughed fields, particularly when sown with corn. The time of day for capturing them with lime-strings is the night or just after twilight; they are too wary to be taken by moonlight.[1]

PLOVER NETTING IN THE NORFOLK FENS.

Since the agricultural drainage of some of the fens and meres of Norfolk, the fen-fowlers of that neighbourhood have employed a very ingenious means for capturing plovers, which, upon the reliable authority of Mr. Stevenson (the author of a recent work of great merit on 'The Birds of Norfolk'), is used at the present day by the Norfolk fen-men.

Mr. Stevenson states that the Gruyhurn and Whittlesea Washes were at one time periodically flooded, and many varieties of wild-fowl visited them. Since the improved drainage of those parts of the fens it is seldom that the marshes are naturally flooded, and the fowler's occupation would be gone were not artificial means adopted. This latter mode of flooding is by means of a 'slacker' or small sluice through which water is admitted, and an area of eight to twelve acres is thus covered with water from six to eight inches in depth. In one portion of this lake the fowler constructs a small island about thirty-six feet in length and from four to five feet in breadth. Upon this his net is spread, which is stained the colour of the ground, and its meshes proportioned to the size of the birds he is likely to take: some nets having meshes one and a half inch and others three inches in size. The fowler keeps some live decoy birds (lapwings or ruffs) and a dozen stuffed skins or 'stales,' and these are placed on the island close outside the range of the net. The living birds being tethered are made to flutter their wings, whilst the fowler with a whistle imitates the call of the birds on the Wash; they are thus tempted to alight on the island, and are ultimately captured. The net covering the surface is so arranged that the fowler, who sits at a distance of upwards of 200 yards, by means of a string attached to pulleys, throws over the net, and the birds are jerked into the water and covered by it. The fowler rapidly approaches, and either takes the birds alive or at once breaks their necks and draws them through the meshes. The following is the method of arranging the net:—When stretched on the ground, the net is fastened down with small pegs on the side nearest to the fowler. It is held out in its narrow width by two poles, four feet in length, having a groove at the end, through which a rope passes from pulleys fixed parallel to the poles and some few feet from them, and from which is also carried, at right angles, the long line held by the fowler. The two poles work in joints, and at the fitting moment the fowler pulls the line; then the net is suddenly cast over and falls towards the pulleys, throwing the birds into the water and covering them as before stated.[1]

The same author observes that on one occasion within the last twelve years he purchased, alive, a small flock of nine dusky sandpipers or spotted red-shanks which had been taken in a plover net in the Norfolk fens. And the author also says he personally knows a Norfolk fowler who has taken as many as four dozen and nine lapwings at one time, and twenty-four dozen in the course of a single day.

It appears that the Zoological Society's Gardens in Regent's Park have frequently been enriched with live fen-birds caught by nets in the locality of the Norfolk Broads.

––––––––––––––

³ *Drayton.*

¹ 'Also the haggard doth prey upon green fowl where she espieth her advantage—the green plover, the bastard plover, and of divers other fowls that might be named.'—*Latham's Faulconry*, A.D. 1658.

² 'Fowling, a Poem,' book v.

¹ In the 'Glossary to the Complaynt of Scotland,' v. Thuesnek, we are told that 'in the south and west of Scotland this bird is much detested, though not reckoned ominous. As it frequents solitary places, its haunts were frequently intruded upon by the fugitive Presbyterians, during the persecution which they suffered in the disgraceful and tyrannical reigns of Charles the Second and James the Second, when they were often discovered by the clamours of the lapwing.'

² 'Avis enim est spurcissima et immunda.'—*Glantvilla de rerum proprietatibus.* See also *Aristotle, Hist. Anim.* book ix. cap. 15.

[3] 'De hac ave dicunt Physici, quod cum senuerit, eo quod nec videre nec volare queat, pulli eius evellunt ei pennas invalidas, et liniunt ei oculos herbarum succis et fovent sub alis, donee recrescant plumse eius, et sic renovata perfecte volet et videat clare sicut et ipsi.'—*Ibid.* Vide also *De proprietatibus Rerum.* By Bartholomews. A.D. 1582.

[4] Lapwings were then termed wypes. 'Wipa' is still the Swedish name for these birds.

[5] See the 'Northumberland Household Book' of that period:—

'Item: It is thought goode that *wypes* be hade for my Lordes own mees onely and to be at jd. a pece.'

'Item: It is thought good that *no pluvers* he bought at noo season bot onely in Chrystynmas and princypall Feestes and my Lorde to be servyde therewith and his Boordend and non other and to boght for jd. a pece or jd. ob. at moste.'

And in the Account-book of the Bursar of the Priory of Durham, A.D. 1530 to 1534, are entered:—

'3 plovers et 1 wype 5d.' '1 plover et 1 snype 2 1/2d.'

[1] 'Being young, they consist only of bones, feathers, and lean flesh, which hath a raw gust of the sea. But poulterers

take them then, and feed them with gravel and curds (that is physic and food); the one to scour, the other to fat them in a fortnight; and their flesh, thus recruited, is most delicious.'— Puller's *Worthies of England; by Nuttall*, vol. i.

² Fuller's 'Worthies of England; by Nuttall,' vol. i. p. 491.

³ 'Jewell for Gentrie.' A.D. 1614.

¹ 'A novel mode of netting most kinds of shore birds, suggested by the shallow waters and flat shores of the Wash, has been occasionally adopted of late years at Lynn in Norfolk with much success. Long nets, stretched on poles about six feet high, are placed in double lines upon the sands towards dusk, one line below high-water mark, and the other beyond the reach of the tide. A dark still night is most favourable for this sport, as the nets are not only invisible but are in no danger of being blown down. In this manner some eighty or ninety birds have been taken at one time, having struck the nets in their nocturnal flight and become hopelessly entangled. When gathered in the morning a large proportion of the birds are secured alive, including godwits, knots, plovers, woodcocks, oyster-catchers, sheldrakes, and other fowl.'—*The Birds of Norfolk*, by Stevenson, Introduction, vol. i. (1866).

¹ 'The Birds of Norfolk,' by Henry Stevenson, F.L.S., vol. ii. (1870), p. 111.

CHAPTER LVII

THE CURLEW

(*Numenius arquata.*)

'The corlew ly veth by kynde of the eyr
Most clennest flesh of birddes.'

PIERS' *Ploughman's Vision.*

THESE birds sometimes afford the wild-fowl shooter good sport, but they are extremely shy: he who would get within range of a 'herd' of curlews by daylight must be a cunning sportsman. They are, besides, very watchful: other water-fowl seek their society because they are such excellent sentinels. The smallest suspicion will excite alarm in the curlew, and cause it to rise in the air with a loud shrill whistle, encouraging all its companions to follow.

Curlews differ so much in size and length of beak, that it is supposed age has a great deal to do with this discrepancy, and that the older the bird the larger it is; but not being prepared to assert this as a positive fact, I leave it to ornithologists to determine: certain it is, that as a distinct species the common curlew is found in a greater variety of sizes than any other fen-bird. In further support of my humble opinion as to increasing in size according to age, it may be added that the larger the birds the more wary they are, and the more clamorous on the approach of the sportsman.

About harvest time, or very soon after, the curlew season commences: they come in small herds of from ten to twenty; and these are generally of the largest size, and are known in some places by the name of the 'great harvest curlew.'[1]

It is not very difficult for a good mimic to imitate the note of the curlew with such good effect as to attract a straggler within gunshot; but the art is seldom successfully practised upon more than one or two birds. I have seen the mimicry so exactly performed as to induce a curlew to run many hundred yards on the mud and marshes in search of its supposed call-mate, until a shot from behind a bank or bush has cruelly settled the deluded victim. They sometimes take wing and fly around in the direction of the false call, until, hovering at last within range of the deceiver, they are greeted with a charge of shot.

The note of the curlew is harsh, and resembles a loud whistle sounding like 'kor-r-ew!' or 'whor-r-r-euh!' Jennings says the common notes uttered by the curlew are 'hoë hoë hoë;' but I have never been able to recognise such a sound in the actual note of the bird.

The punter will frequently be tempted to try his skill at curlews when wild-fowl are scarce. He must not forget that they have long legs, and stand high on the mud; and unless his gun be elevated as for long shots, he must take a turn or two at the barrel-rest-screw, slightly raising the muzzle, or the shot will probably fly among their legs without touching any vulnerable part, and he will not recover a bird.

Another mode of sport which often succeeds better than any other with these birds is by means of the wild-fowl canoe already described. Two persons proceed in the canoe up creeks at low-water, or grope about among islands and oozes frequented by these birds; and having found a 'herd,' await their time until the tide rises high enough to lift the canoe so that the prow is upon a level with the land on which the curlews are feeding; the fowler then takes deliberate aim with a large fowling-piece, too heavy to hold out to the shoulder, except by resting the barrel upon the prow of the boat or upon a crotch; meanwhile the other occupant steadies the canoe with one of the oars, which is thrust through a sculling hole in the stern piece. Numbers of curlews may sometimes be killed in this manner.

The fowler is frequently able to stalk them just after dusk, in his boat, on the muddy flats of a river, or by creeping within range from some screen on land.

There are various tricks and means resorted to for getting

within range of the wary curlew, such as digging holes in open marshes, burying casks on the beach, and lying in ambush in those unenviable positions, thus taking the birds by surprise. Such proceedings may answer once or twice, but curlews soon forsake a place of resort when so assailed.

The plan recommended by Colonel Hawker, as to making an island on the ooze by means of a few boat-loads of rubbish, is far better. Curlews always remain on the highest ground, nor do they leave it until the tide reaches their legs; so that by proceeding in a punt, and using great caution, a good shot may sometimes be made. These birds are among the very last of the water-fowl to leave the coast in spring; therefore the sport of curlew-shooting lasts longer than that of any other fen-fowl.

Curlews which feed chiefly on the oozes and marshes of saltwater rivers are very good eating; but those which feed far inland in ploughed fields and fresh-water meadows are not so palatable.

The curlew was anciently esteemed by the *gourmet* as one of the finest-flavoured water-fowl in the land; and, as it was supposed to feed after the manner of woodcocks, which were erroneously imagined to obtain their sustenance entirely by suction, it was pronounced by Piers in his 'Ploughman's Vision' as the cleanest flesh of birds.

There are abundant records of the high estimation in

which the curlew was held during the fourteenth century, when the heron, from its superior size, majestic proportions, and notoriety as the falconer's most distinguished quarry, was first in order at all principal feasts: still it would seem that the curlew was the greater luxury, as the prices paid for it were equal to those of the heron,[1] and higher than those of any other wild-fowl.

In the account-book of Eobert Benett, Bursar of the Priory of Durham, from Whitsuntide, 1530, to Whitsuntide, 1534,[2] are entered (*inter alia*) as purchased:—'1 curlew, 3*d.*;' '3 curlews et 1 whympernal, 13*d.*' The prices of other fowl were less; but a Barnacle goose was 3*d.*

A strange and erroneous notion once prevailed that the curlew fed on poisonous seeds,[3] and that its flesh was, in consequence, not good for food. But in opposition to the authority of Batman, the very contrary appears from the extract already quoted from the Northumberland Household Book, which must have been compiled about the same age as that in which Batman wrote.

The whimbrel, or little curlew, is less difficult to shoot than the other, because not so wary.

The stone curlew, or great plover, is altogether an upland bird, feeding in turnip and fallow fields, therefore not a subject for these pages.

―――――――――

[1] Lubbock speaks of them as 'probably old *females* collected together after the breeding season.' I should, however, be more disposed to believe they are *male* birds, which have preceded the females and their young in their flight from the low countries.

[1] 'Item: *Kyrlewes* to be hadde for my Lordes own mees at pryneipall feestes and to be at xij a pece.'—*Northumberland Household Book. Temp*. Hen. VIII.

[2] Printed for the Surtees Society, 1841.

[3] 'Coturnix is thought to feede on venemous seedes, and therefore not to be very wholesome.'—*Batman vppon Bartholome.*

CHAPTER LVIII

METHOD OF CAPTURING DOTTERELS

'The dotterel, which we think a very dainty dish,
Whose taking makes such sport as man no more can wish;
For as you creep, or cowr, or lie, or stoop, or go,
So marking you (with care) the apish bird cloth go;
And acting everything, doth never mark the net
Till he he in the snare which men for him have set.'

DRAYTON, *Polyolbion*, Song XXV.

IN former days the Dotterel (*Gharadrius morinellus*) is said to have afforded the fowler abundant diversion; and, according to numerous authorities, was not difficult to capture. Through centuries past it has been highly esteemed as one of the rarest delicacies of the table, consequently eagerly sought by the fowler. And it appears by the 'Northumberland Household Book' (*temp*. Hen. VIII.) that whilst stints were purchased at *twopence per dozen*, dotterels were bought at *one penny each*—a high price for so small a bird in those days. And when we consider that teal and widgeon were bought at the same price (one penny each), the dotterel must have been held in *very* high estimation as a table delicacy.

The dotterel is termed by Aristophanes a mirth-making bird; and according to that authority, was easily caught by the ancient fowler: or, as has been quaintly remarked, it catcheth itself by its over-active imitation.

'The dotterell that folyshe pek.'[1]

The method of taking dotterels by lamp or candle light on dark nights is as follows: The fowler proceeds with a lanthorn to their most frequented haunts in the fens, when, by disturbing them, they run along the ground rather than attempt flying, and are thus easily taken with nets, which are spread for them. They always run towards the light; so that the fowler fairly entices them to his net. History and tradition both speak of this bird as imitating the gestures and movements of the fowler; whereby it is asserted that when the fowler stretches out an arm or leg, the dotterel performs a corresponding movement with leg or wing. If the fowler runs, the dotterel runs; if he crawls slowly along, the dotterel does likewise:

> 'Most worthy man, with thee it is even thus—
> As men take dottrels, so hast thou ta'en us;
> Which as a man his arm or leg doth set,
> So this fond bird will likewise counterfeit.'[1]

Dr. Key, in his letter to Gesner, describes the movements of the dotterel when pursued at night, after the manner already explained; and expresses his belief in the actions of the bird as in imitation or mockery of the fowler. Another author also inclines to the same opinion.[2]

In reference to the practice mentioned in the note below, of capturing apes by inciting them to mimicry, there is in a curious work (already referred to in these pages) 'Venationes ferarum avium,' &c, the following inscription at the foot of an engraving representing the capture of apes by the art of mimicry:

'Quo Venatores oculos lavêre catino,
Pro lymphis indunt viscum: mox Simia visco
Os oculosque lavat: capitur lento uncta liquore,
Incidit et caligata in idem quandoque periclum.'

It would seem that Ray doubted the veracity of Dr. Key as to the mimicry of the fowler by the dotterel; he subjoins a statement communicated to him by his 'very good friend Mr. Peter Dent, a person well skilled in the history of plants and animals,' whereby it is stated, that it was thought the imitation was not regarded by the birds, nor did such conduce to the taking of them.[3]

Dotterels are naturally sluggish birds, more especially at night: the time when the ancient fowler used to put his plans in operation for taking them. And it is a habit of sluggish birds on being aroused, when unsuspicious of danger, to stretch their legs and wings, regardless of the fowler's movements and without intending in the least to imitate his actions. I have seen stints and red-shanks, as well as dotterels, perform these supposed acts of mimicry by broad daylight, when I have been rowing leisurely along the banks of the water in a gunning punt; having approached gradually upon them, and without sudden appearance or noise, I have frequently found them in an apparently lethargic state, when they stretched out their legs and wings, singly, before running off along the shore with their companions. But beyond this I have never found them more mimical or easy of capture than stints, redshanks, and others of the species. It is easy to believe that the dotterel imitates the fowler to the extent only of running after the lamp or lighted candle at night; but sparrows, and many other birds, will do this. Wild beasts, on the contrary, always shun a light, and purposely avoid it; so that the natives of countries infested with such animals burn a fire all night outside their huts for the express purpose of keeping wild animals away.

As a further proof of the tame and lethargic habits of the dotterel, it was customary for six or seven persons to proceed together in attempting to catch them with the candle and nets employed by the ancient fowler; each of these persons was provided with two large stones, and by holding one in each hand, and clapping them together, after the net was cast, as much clatter was made as possible, so as to rouse the dotterels, and drive them into the net.[1]

The dotterel has evidently obtained notoriety as being one of the most foolish and ridiculous of birds, so that it has become proverbial to speak of a foolish or dull person as a 'silly dotterel,' an expression heard even at the present day.

---

[1] In Skelton's 'Lament for Phyllyp Sparowe' the dotterel is thus introduced as one of the mourners.

[1] Drayton.

[2] 'There is a sort of apes in India caught by the natives thereof after this manner: They dress a little boy, in his sight; undress him again, leave all the child's apparel behind them in the place, and then depart a competent distance. The ape presently attireth himself in the same garments till the child's clothes become his chains, putting off his feet by putting on his shoes, not able to run to any purpose; and so is soon taken. The same humour, otherwise pursued, betray eth the dotterels. But, it is observed, the foolisher the fowl or fish (woodcocks, dotterels, cods-heads, &c.) the fairer the flesh thereof.'—Fuller's *Worthies of England: by Nuttall*, vol. ii. p.

263.

[3] Willnghby's 'Ornithology,' by Ray.

[1] Willnghby's 'Ornithology,' by Ray.

CHAPTER LIX

THE RUFF AND REEVE

(*Machetes pugnax.*)

An epicure, of dainty whim,

Who lived in ages long since past,

    Was asked one day,

    In friendly way,

What best he liked for his repast?

And 'mong the list of choicest game

His greatest favourite to name.

The gourmet smiled, and stroked his chin;

Then quaff'd his cup, and prompt replied:

    'Of tid-bits rare,

    Of princely fare,

Of flesh of birds—roast, grilled, or fried;

Of hare or rabbit, woodcock, snipe;

Of partridge, pheasant, plover, wipe;[1]

Of larks for breakfast, or for supper

All these I relish well enough:

    But, tho' such dishes

    Are delicious,

There's nothing nicer than a fattened ruff;'

And little any taster leaves,

Except the gizzards of the reeves.   THE AUTHOR.

THESE birds were formerly abundant in this country, but are now so scarce as to be known only by name: they are exclusively fen-birds, and seldom found elsewhere. The male bird is the ruff, the female the reeve. When in full plumage, during the breeding-season, the ruff is eagerly sought by taxidermists, as an object of great attraction for the glass-case; and by the fowler as one of the rarest luxuries of the table.

They are summer visitants to this country, arriving in the fens early in the month of April, and departing late in September; consequently they breed and rear their young whilst residents here. They are generally very shy; and from their present scarcity, it is seldom the sportsman meets with them in the shooting season. Their favourite haunts are fens and marshes: they feed in wet and swampy grounds, but seldom, if ever, on salt oozes. During the breeding season they frequent drier grounds, and assemble on small hillocks, in numbers of about ten, twenty, and sometimes more. Seventy or eighty have been seen together in the Norfolk fens, but not of late years.[2]

When so assembled they are termed 'hilled,' and, just as if in pitched battle, the ruffs engage in apparently desperate combat one with another, the object of their interesting fights being, it is said, the possession of the reeves, about which they are extremely tenacious, and contend with much fierceness and prolonged quarrel:

> 'The ruff is pugilistic, bold, and *debonair*;
> And in bloody battle wins his fair.'

The fens of Lincolnshire were long celebrated as the favourite resort of these birds. Wells, in his History of the Fens, mentions that 'those rare and delicate birds, called the "ruff and ree," are found here, and are trained with considerable expense and difficulty.'

There are two methods resorted to by the fowler for taking these birds, one during spring, when the ruffs hill, the other in autumn. The fowler having discovered the spot where the ruffs have held their love-battles, repairs thither in the morning before daybreak; an experienced fenman soon finds out their blood-stained hills, by the trodden turf, which in some places, where much fighting has been engaged in, is often quite bare, from the incessant trampling of their little feet, as they run to and fro, dashing at their antagonists with a courage and determination quite astonishing. Arrived at the spot, the fowler spreads a clap-net about seventeen feet in length by six in breadth,[1] the net being furnished with a pole at each end, precisely similar to an ordinary clap-net for catching other land-birds at twilight. This net is fixed to the ground by means of small stakes,[2] and being furnished with sheaves (or pulleys) and lines, it is so placed that it may be suddenly jerked and folded over, on drawing a cord at a distance from the hill of about one hundred to four hundred yards, according to the time of season; the later it is the more wary are the birds, and the fowler stations himself in concealment accordingly.

Pennant says it is usual to spread the net over-night, in order that the marsh may not be disturbed in the morning.

It is the habit of these birds to repair at dawn of day to their battle-fields, and the fowler who wisely chooses his ground and judiciously places his net, is generally rewarded with success, frequently taking the whole hill at a single fold of the net. It is usual after making the first pull, and taking those within scope of the net, to place stuffed birds or stales to entice those which are continually traversing the fen;[1] but it is seldom that more than two or three are taken at a time by aid of the stales.

582

The other method of taking ruffs when not hilled is, by means of decoy-birds and nooses. It is better that the decoy-birds be live ones, though stuffed skins and other artificial resemblances are sometimes successfully employed. The stuffed skins are connected with the fowler's hand by a long string, which by jerking causes the dummy to jump or leap from the ground, a space of a yard or more, in representation of the habits of live ruffs; by such enticements the wanderers are induced to alight among the fowler's snares, and thus become captives.[2]

The method of setting these snares is thus explained by Lubbock,[3] and, it would seem, is employed by the Norfolk fowler when the ruffs are hilled, but never with that success which attends the clap-net employed by the Lincolnshire fenman.

'The Norfolk fowler prepares about a dozen pegs sharpened at one end, and split at the other; into the split he introduces the middle of a loosely-twisted link of long horse-hair, so as to form two nooses, one with each half of the link. The peg is then driven into the ground, so as to be perfectly level with the surface, and one noose is placed horizontally, just raised by the herbage, perhaps half-an-inch from the soil, whilst the other is disposed perpendicularly, the lower part resting on the ground. These snares are disposed on the outskirts of the hill, rather than the middle, as the ruffs in their flutterings generally spring *from* the circumference of this chosen spot.'

The live decoy-birds are tied by the leg to small stakes placed near the snares, and have a latitude allowed them of about two feet of string, that they may be enabled to play and jump about, so as to attract notice of the wild birds.

The scarcity of ruffs and reeves at the present day is not entirely attributable to fen drainage, but to the pernicious system long pursued by fenmen, of taking them during the very time of nesting, when they are unusually tame, and may be caught with nooses by any country bumpkin, so that every ruff and reeve in some fens has been known to have been captured.[1]

It is not, therefore, at all a matter of surprise, though it be of regret, to find from an author of reliable authority on the subject, writing in the year 1866, that ruffs, reeves, andgodwits had vanished as inhabitants of the fen districts in Norfolk.[2]

If ever those interesting and highly-prized birds again become abundant in this country, it will be owing to the good judgment of the fowler in carefully abstaining from taking them at any other than the autumnal season, a stipulation which ought to be regarded by all fowlers and fenmen. And indeed they cannot now be taken in the breeding season, as they are specially included in the Schedule to the Wild-birds Protection Act, which prohibits the taking or offering for sale of any of the birds therein enumerated between the 15th of

March and the 1st of August in any year.[3]

The flight of the ruff, when in perfect plumage, is slow and laboured, resembling that of a newly-arrived woodcock;[4] but having thrown off the much-admired frill of staring feathers which encircles its neck, the ruff then flies with the same buoyancy and velocity as his partner, the reeve.

The high estimation in which the flesh of these birds is held cannot be better authenticated than by simply referring to the enormous prices they fetch in the market. At the present day the price paid for fattened ruffs (when obtainable, which is seldom) is as much as *four guineas* per dozen—almost as expensive as ortolans, and they are considered by some gastronomes as equally delicious.

But the demand for these birds has nearly ceased, by reason of the difficulty of obtaining them at the proper season. There are game and wild-fowl dealers in Leadenhall Market at the present day (1875) who remember the time when, forty or fifty years ago, they used to receive these birds alive from 'their correspondents,' the fen-fowlers, and when they fattened them in the market, under coops, with bread-and-milk. The reeves used to fatten quicker than the ruffs, and the prices then, as they became scarce, was *ten and fifteen shillings per bird*, when fat and fit for the table! If not fattened they sold them at about five shillings per bird.

Yarrell mentions the regular price of fattened ruffs to be

two guineas per dozen, and states that they are never less than thirty shillings when fit for the table.

Pennant speaks of the regular price of fattened ruffs (at the time he wrote) being 2*s.* or 2*s.* 6*d.* a-piece.

Lubbock states that the price of a ruff, fresh caught in the fens, was formerly tenpence or a shilling.

Ruffs and reeves, as well as many other fen-birds and wildfowl, are now imported from Norway and other countries, and sold by the poulterers in London.[1]

Fatting ruffs for the table was once a regular trade carried on in the fens. The birds being taken alive, they were placed in aviaries and fed with great care and attention, bringing considerable remuneration to the feeders. Montague states:— 'Mr. Towns, the noted feeder at Spalding, assured us his family had been a hundred years in the trade, and boasted that they had served Greorge the Second and many noble families in the kingdom.'

They are fattened for the table with bread-and-milk, hempseed, and sometimes boiled wheat, but if expedition is required, sugar is added. This latter method of feeding makes them perfectly fat in a fortnight.[2]

Their condition should be watched during the process of fatting, and they must be killed at the juncture of extreme fatness, or they soon fall away.

When killed with good judgment at the critical time, and dressed after the manner of a woodcock, they are considered by epicures as extremely delicious.[3]

Pennant speaks of forty-four birds having been taken by a fowler at a single haul, and that the same man took in all six dozen in one morning! At four guineas per dozen this would be a pretty prize for a poor fowler. He also says that a fowler is sometimes able to take forty or fifty dozen in a season.

And Mr. Stevenson,[4] in allusion to the fowlers of the Norfolk Fen District, says there are, or at least until very recently were, people who recollected that a comfortable living might be made by netting ruffs and reeves in summer, and in winter by snaring snipes, when the true fen-man who was seriously believed in other counties to be born with a 'speckled belly' and a web between his toes, did not think his Sunday's dinner complete unless he had a roast bittern on his board.

---

[1] The ancient name of the lapwing.

[2] Lubbock, in his 'Fauna of Norfolk.'

[1] Montague. Pennant speaks of the clap-net used for

this purpose as being fourteen yards in length and four in breadth.

[2] In Oliver Goldsmith's 'History of the Earth and Animated Nature,' it is stated that the nets in which these birds are taken are supported by sticks at an angle of near forty-five degrees, and placed either on dry ground or in very shallow water, not remote from reeds, among which the fowler conceals himself till the birds, enticed by a stale or stuffed bird, come under the nets; he then, by pulling a string, lets them fall, and they are taken; as are godwits, knots, and grey plover also, in the same manner.—Vol. iii. p. 384 (edition 1824).

[1] Pennant. Vol. ii.

[2] Rennie.

[3] See Lubbock's 'Fauna of Norfolk.'

[1] Montague.

[2] Stevenson on the 'Birds of Norfolk,' vol. i.

[3] See *infra*, p. 320.

[4] Lubbock.

[1] Since the two previous editions of this work, the Author saw on one occasion, three or four years ago, scores of ruffs

and reeves hanging up for sale in Leaden-hall Market at a shilling each; but at a time of the year when not in season, viz. the month of May, the very height of the breeding-season; consequently not worth eating, and, therefore, dear at any price. Who can be surprised at the scarcity of these beautiful birds when such facts are known?

[2] See Goldsmith's 'Animated Nature;' also Nuttall's 'Ornithology of the United States and Canada,' 1834.

[3] Pennant.

[4] 'The Birds of Norfolk,' by Henry Stevenson, 1866, Intro.

CHAPTER LX

GODWIT SHOOTING

'The puet, godwit, stint, the palate that allure
The miser, and doe make a wasteful epicure.'—DRAYTON.

THERE are several different species of godwit (*Scolopax limosa*) which annually visit our shores. They arrive during the prevalence of easterly winds, and are more numerous in mild winters than severe ones. They are then abundantly scattered about our shores, and afford young sportsmen excellent amusement; not being a very shy bird, nor by any means difficult to kill, as they do not require hard hitting, and small-shot will bring them down. They frequent marshes and fens, as well as the seacoast: their habits are to run about with brisk and interesting movements; and they will sometimes allow the sportsman to walk directly up to them on the open marshes within easy gunshot. Grodwits are in much estimation with the sporting gastronome; and are preferred, by some people, to snipe.

Sir Thomas Browne quaintly remarks of them, 'Grodwyts, taken chiefly in marsh land, though other parts are not without them, are accounted the daintiest dish in England; and I think for the bigness of the biggest price.'

The female godwit is larger than the male, which is also the case with sandpipers.

Ben Jonson, in his 'Praises of a Countrie Life,' says, with a rapture and indelicacy scarcely suited to the present age:

> 'Th' Ionian godwit nor the ginny hen,
> Could not goe downe my belly then
> More sweet than olives that new gathered be
> Erom the fattest branches of the tree.'

OXBIRD AND DUNLIN SHOOTING.

> 'Then every fowler who so cozens,
> Sells you in markets strung by dozens.'
>
> *Translation from Aristophanes.*

THE Dunlin, Oxbird, or Stint (*Tringa variabilis*), is well known as an annual visitant to our coast, appearing in immense 'flings,' and moving through the air with wonderful velocity; performing the most graceful evolutions, when on the wing, of any gregarious birds. They seem to go through regular gradations and figures, closing up their ranks and keeping in a body so compact, and yet flying so swiftly, that their volitations are as interesting as they are extraordinary: on sunny days, when they turn and twist in the air, the whiteness of the feathers beneath their wings glitters in the sky like bright white metal; and the whole 'fling,' however large or numerous, every now and then presents the identical appearance of a beautiful cloud of frosted silver. The sight is one never to be forgotten, as a marvellous illustration of instinct, in the perfect order and compactness of their evolutions.

When the weather is mild and open they are more scattered, and are seen only in small flings. It is in cold and frosty weather that they perform their grandest and most picturesque volitations. They are the tamest birds on the coast when in small numbers, but are more wary when numerous. Like other waders, they will not take wing until the tide fairly washes them off their legs. They huddle together in cold weather on the last bit of mud that is not covered with water, and struggle to retain possession of it until the tide touches their feathers. When in such positions they are frequently killed in large numbers by punters, who use small punt-guns. By loading with half-a-pound of No. 7 shot, more than a hundred are sometimes killed at a shot.

Directly the ebb-tide leaves them a resting-place on the ooze, there they alight and feed, frequently in company with grey plovers, a stray bird or two of which is sometimes seen among them when on the wing, looking like the parent of the fling from its superior size; but which drops out of the ranks whilst they perform the evolutions before mentioned, and joins them again afterwards.

It is puerile sport to kill them, though affording excellent fun to young sportsmen. They are very good eating, and are frequently palmed upon the inexperienced purchaser as snipes, especially in London, where some persons call them 'sea-snipes,' because of their bills being long, and of similar shape to a snipe. The prices charged for these birds are far advanced of late years, though they have always been esteemed as great delicacies.[1] At the present day they sell for 2*s*. 6*d*. to 5*s*. per dozen.

The dunlin belongs to the tribe of sandpipers, the various species of which afford good diversion to young sportsmen.

---

[1] 'Item, it is thought good that *styntes* be hadde for my lordes own mees, and non other so they be after vj. a jd.'— *Northumberland Household Book: temp*. Henry VIII.

In the account-book of Robert Bennett, bursar of the

Priory of Durham, they are charged, in 1531–2: '1 doz. dunlynggs 4d., et 3 doz. styntes 6d., 6 doz. stynts 12d., 1 1/2 doz. dunlyngs 6d.' And there is another entry in 1533–4: '6 dunlyngs 2d.'—*Printed for the Surtecs Society*, 1814.

CHAPTER LXI

SNIPE SHOOTING

'A lively sport,

Affording to the fowler's varying hand,

As wheeling, oft returns, though often sprung,

The noisy bird.'

Fowling, a Poem, Book v.

THE subject of snipe shooting is one upon which so many authors have written, that the reader will probably find less novelty in this than in any other part of our treatise. There are, however, several interesting discussions connected with the fowler's art of shooting and capturing snipes, which have hitherto escaped notice by the numerous writers upon the subject, and which it will be our purpose to enter upon.

The drainage of fen-lands, though seriously detrimental to the well-being of these birds, the increase of their numbers, and the encouragement of their immigrations, operates with less effect upon snipes than upon wild-fowl. In every ditch with a moist bottom the snipe finds food and sustenance; and, though in a measure driven from its favourite fens, there is generally no lack of food and shelter for it elsewhere within our island.

Ireland, too, abounds with snipes; the moisture and richness of the soil, and the extent of bog and marsh land, rendering that country a favourite resort of the species. The sportsman who has trod an Irish hog in pursuit of snipes, has partaken of the sport in its true nature; and, though distasteful to some people, the best and finest snipe shooting within many thousand miles of this country may be had in the Emerald Isle. It often happens, whilst wading up to the knees in an Irish bog after snipes, that the sportsman meets with wild-duck and teal; so that, whatever may be the disadvantages, there are varieties attending it which repay the sportsman for his most indefatigable exertions.

Snipes abound in every quarter of the globe. In North and South America they are generally abundant,[1] though much more so in some of the States than in others.[2]

During the rainy season they are found in tropical climates; and in winter, the rice-fields of Egypt swarm with them.[3] In Madagascar they are abundant. In the arctic regions of Siberia, in Sweden, and many other countries, travellers allude to the excellent snipe shooting they found. Mr. Lloyd[4] speaks of having had excellent snipe shooting near G-othenburgh, also in the marshes and bogs in the vicinity of Trollhattan. Though the marshes at the latter place are not extensive, yet a good shot might bag without difficulty fifteen or twenty couple in the course of a few hours, and thirty couple in seven or eight hours; and these the common or double snipe. Sportsmen in that locality being careless of expending their ammunition on jack-snipes. Major Forbes, in his 'Eleven Years in Ceylon,' says he found snipes more abundant in Ceylon than any other game. Indeed, every travelling sportsman should be prepared for snipes, in whatever quarter of the globe his steps may take him. A game certificate is required before shooting them in this country, and a *port d'arme must* be obtained before shooting them in France.

A difference of opinion prevails among those who have written upon the subject of snipe shooting, as to the proper manner of talking a 'snipe-walk.' Some writers affirm that it is best to walk clown-wind; others, that the sportsman should walk up-wind. Of the two opinions, I agree with the former, as the easier and more successful method of killing snipes, because these birds invariably fly up-wind; consequently, they pass to the right or left of the sportsman, within easy range; whereas, if he walks up-wind, the snipe flies off straight ahead with such rapidity that it is out of range before the gun can be brought to the shoulder.

There is another point with regard to snipe shooting, in which there is also great difference of opinion, which is, as to the services of a pointer or setter; some advocating that the snipe shooter is best without either, others that the services of one or the other are highly desirable. In the latter opinion I entirely concur. But the dog must be fast and stanch: a setter is as good as a pointer for this sport, but a slow dog is worse than none at all.[1]

The effluvium of snipes is very powerful on the olfactory organs of the dog, which, if he be stanch to his point, the faster he ranges, the better. It is very easy to train a dog for snipe shooting; but he should be taught to hunt at right-angles to the wind.

The great snipe (*Scolopax major*) is very irregular in its visits to this country. It is the easiest to kill of any of the species, not simply on account of its large size, but because it lies closer, is more sluggish in its habits than the common snipe, flies steadier, and seldom goes far on being flushed. It may be instantly distinguished from the common snipe, on rising from the ground, by its red-looking tail, which it spreads out like a fan: the under part of its body showing very white.

These birds are so indolent in their nature that they often lie as close as a jack-snipe, or until nearly trodden upon; indeed, they very much resemble jack-snipes in their habits.

The great snipe often arrives early in August, and is generally found in drier marshes than other snipes.

The common snipe (*Scolopax gallinago*), which is the most

abundant species in this country, arrives about the latter part of September; and by the first or second week in October they are pretty freely dispersed.

These birds, though apparently wild and distrustful, are by nature very inactive. If undisturbed, they spend the whole day in eating and sleeping, merely making a few volitations morning and evening.

They are very uncertain in their movements: the sportsman should, therefore, make the most of his sport when he finds them; for, on going over the same ground every day during the week following, he may find them all absent.

They are generally abundant during the first few days of a gentle frost; but if the weather becomes severe they migrate to the uplands, and pitch in rivulets and ditches that are the most free from frost.

During windy and cloudy weather snipes lie closer and fly straighter than on bright or frosty days.

The reason why young sportsmen so frequently miss these birds is that in taking aim they do not make sufficient allowance for the sudden rise and rapidity of their flight. It should not be forgotten that, whilst darting off, they are gradually rising higher in the air, and that to kill, aim should be taken above as well as in advance of them, taking care to fire at an elevation proportionate to the distance. The author of the 'Dead Shot' is ve-y impressive as to this, and states that some sportsmen, good shots in other respects, do not shoot at snipes because of the difficulty they experience in hitting them; and he attributes the fact of missing them to their having never carefully considered the flight of the snipe in its varied and beautiful gyrations, or they might kill them as certainly as they do any other birds.[1] The sportsman should never use larger shot for snipes than NOS. 7 or 8, otherwise he will often be disappointed with the result of fair chances.

When walking *up-wind* the most experienced sportsmen find snipes difficult to kill; but on going down-wind they fly in a semicircular course, and afford plenty of time for a deliberate shot.

From the inaccessible positions of some snipe-walks it is difficult to adhere at all times to the rules as to up and downwind, so that it sometimes becomes necessary to make snapshots, in which case it is generally found that he who is quickest in handling his gun and fires oftenest kills the most birds, though it is impossible but the best sportsmen frequently miss random shots.

Whenever a snipe rises within a few yards of the gun, the sportsman need not be in a hurry; the fault with young hands is that they fire too soon.[1]

'Her rapid rise, and vacillating flight,
In vain defend her from the fowler's aim.'

A good snipe-shot is generally a man of active spirit, full of

energy, and indifferent to toil and hardship. 'Craven'[2] says:—
'Taken in all its bearings, this sport is a very true general test
of a marksman's quality.'

The spot where a snipe falls should be carefully noted,
and the eye kept upon it until the bird is bagged. On a snipe
falling into the water it should be wiped before being put into
the pocket, or it will not keep so long as others.

Not a word should be spoken when going down a snipe-
walk: silence must prevail, or the birds will rise out of
range—darting off like arrows, crying as they go, 'Shaich!' or
'Schaÿich!'

On passing beside dykes and along the banks of rivulets
and snipe-walks the sportsman should keep a look-out for
snipe-trails, the unerring index of their whereabouts.

The jack-snipe (*Scolopax gallinula*) generally arrives in
small numbers about the third week in September. They are
the most sluggish little birds to be met with, seldom stirring
until within a few inches of the sportsman's feet, when they
rise in silence, and dart off in a zigzag flight, which puzzles
young sportsmen exceedingly, as they discharge barrel after
barrel without effect.

Late in the season they sometimes emit a feeble sort of
squeak on rising.

The greater numbers of snipes that are vended in the

London and provincial markets are not killed with dog and gun, but are caught in nets similar to those used for taking plovers and larks by drawing them over fens and marshes at night, after the manner of poaching for partridges. Hampers-full of these delicate table luxuries are captured in this manner. Netted snipes always fetch a better price than those killed with powder and shot; and so the poacher (if such he may be called) has the advantage of the sportsman.

---

[1] 'They are found in the middle and Northern States only in the spring and fall, when they are frequently shot in great numbers. In the winter they frequent the rice-grounds of the South.'—*Skinner's Dog and Sportsman:* America, 1845.

[2] 'The great multitude breed far to the northward, not only of the United States, but of the British provinces, in the vast marshy tracts which extend inland nearly to the Arctic Ocean. Many, however, make their nests and rear their young in the secluded morasses of Maine, Nova Scotia, and New Brunswick, and a few pairs here and there throughout the Eastern and middle States; becoming less frequent as they advance toward the South, so far, probably, as the north of

Pennsylvania.'—*Herbert's Field Sports in the United States;* A.D. 1848.

[3] Krider's 'Sporting Anecdotes:' A.D. 1853.

[4] *Vide* 'Field Sports of North Europe,' by L. Lloyd, Esq.: A.D. 1830.

[1] 'They know practically little of what they are writing about who assert, in these days, that a slow dog is to be preferred in this species of sport.' *Krider's Sporting Anecdotes,* by II. M. Klapp: A.D. 1859.

[1] 'The Dead Shot, or Sportsman's Complete Guide: with rudimentary and finishing lessons in the art of shooting.' By *Marksman,* p. 187 (4th edition), 1866.

[1] 'If you are naturally a sportsman, you will soon learn how to approach and to kill them, albeit, on the first few trials, the eccentricities which they practise on the wing, and the elfish ease with which they seem to evade the contents of both barrels, will leave an impression on your mind which, however annoying then, becomes a very pleasant and exciting reminiscence, after you have learned how to knock them down right and left *secundum artem.'*—*Krider's Sporting Anecdotes.*

[2] *Vide* Craven's 'Recreations in Shooting.'

CHAPTER LXII

WOODCOCK SHOOTING

. . . . 'Hark! that quest proclaims

The woodcock's haunt. Again, now joining all,

They shake the echoing wood with tuneful notes.

I heard the sounding wing; but down the wood

He took his flight. I meet him there anon.

As fast I press to gain the wish'd for spot,

On either side my busy spaniels try:

At once they wheel—at once they open loud,

And the next instant flush th' expected bird.

Right up he darts amongst the mingling boughs;

But bare of leaves, they hide not from my view

His fated form; and ere he can attain

Th' attempted height, with rapid flight to cleave

The yielding air, arrested by the shot,

With shatter'd wing revers'd and plumage fair,

Wide scatt'ring in the wind, headlong he falls.'

Fowling: a Poem. Book iv.

THOUGH scarcely within the category wild-fowl, the woodcock (*Scolopax rusticola*) is generally classed with migratory water-birds, and forms so attractive an object to the English sportsman, and so frequently crosses the path of the aquatic fowler, that to exclude all notice of it from a treatise of this kind would, it is considered, be a grave omission. There is this important resemblance to wild-fowl in the habits of the woodcock—it is to be found in every land,[1] and affords infinite variety of amusement to the fowler and the sportsman.

The autumnal flight and arrival of woodcocks to this country generally take place about the beginning of October; the time of their vernal flight is March or April. On first arrival they keep to the open ground, taking temporary refuge in the grass, rushes, brushwood, heather, clumps of trees, or whatever offers in the locality where they chance to alight. They do not long remain in these exposed places, but as soon as they have partially recovered from the effects of their tedious passage across the sea they hie to the woods, as their favourite and natural places of resort.

Woodcocks generally arrive in falls of from ten to fifty,

always choosing night for their migrations or a mist. When they have arrived and rested sufficiently they disperse, and though a few come in October, the greater numbers arrive in November and December, generally between the hours of sunset and sunrise. It is erroneous to suppose that moonlight either hastens or determines the arrival of woodcocks; their movements are regulated by the wind rather than the moon.

It sometimes happens, after encountering adverse gales in their passage across the sea, that they reach their destinations in a very exhausted state. In allusion to this, I remember a very remarkable circumstance which occurred in my own immediate neighbourhood, on an estate abutting upon the sea-coast, part of which comprised several hundred acres of woodland. It happened, during a hard winter, that early in the morning one of the gardeners employed on the estate flushed a number of woodcocks in the pleasure-grounds around the house; they appeared to be in a sort of semi-lethargic state, and to have scarcely power to suspend themselves in the air. The gardener caught three or four couple alive, in the space of a few minutes. With, hands full, he ran to the house to deposit them, and tell of the singular adventure; when others having joined in the pursuit of capturing them, upwards of a dozen couple were secured alive without injury; but on examining their bodies they were found to be almost skeletons, and totally unfit for the table. The poor captives were, therefore, immediately set at liberty in the woods.

Wild-fowl are sometimes found in the same condition, and have been taken in a similar manner, during very severe weather; but like the skeleton woodcocks they afford no sport to the wild-fowl shooter, are useless for the table, and are, therefore, best set at liberty.

A good marker is indispensable for woodcock shooting, because the birds often pitch in such improbable places as many sportsman would not think of beating, and after being once flushed, they lie so very close that the most careful beating is necessary if the sportsman expects to find them. It is desirable that the dogs should not be hurried over the ground too quickly, or the probability is that many a close-lying cock may be passed. And it should be borne in mind that woodcocks, at the instant of alighting, sometimes run along the ground many yards from the spot at which they pitch.[1]

Whilst beating a wood, one or more markers should be placed on the highest ground in the locality, or on a tree commanding the best view of the surrounding country: if he attends to his business he will be able to mark the flight of every cock which leaves the wood.

On being flushed, they make for the clearest openings, and soar as high as the tops of the trees, over which they fly in a straight line, and often pitch on the opposite side of the covert; they not unfrequently make a circuit of the whole covert, and then drop close to or in the same spot from whence they were sprung. The sportsman will generally find the cocks at which he has been unable to obtain a shot in the same places on the day following as those from which they were sprung the day previously. The practical sportsman will, therefore, judiciously station himself in or near an opening where he may obtain the best chance. When fairly sprung, they take the same route of flight, passing the same openings and topping the same trees as before. Any person who may take the trouble to watch their evolutions will soon become familiar with the sameness and regularity of their course. If the sportsman goes on the following day in the opposite direction to that taken the day before, he will probably find that the woodcock has likewise an opposite course of retreat. Familiarity with such habits, which are peculiar to the woodcock, invariably ensures success to the sportsman: after once or twice observing their line of flight in any particular locality, a very fair idea may be formed as to the best position to take on a future day. Sportsmen so instructed have a considerable advantage over their fellows when beating large coverts, the route of the birds flushed seldom deviating from a once chosen passage through the wood.

This propensity on the part of woodcocks for taking a regular line of flight has been the subject of remark by Mr. Colquhoun.[1]

The woodcock is generally considered an easy shot to an

experienced sportsman, but to a tyro very puzzling. Its flight is deceptive, and varies considerably, according to time of day, season, and wind; it is sometimes slow and laboured, at others rapid and direct, as if bent on a determined destination.[2]

Notwithstanding these peculiarities, some of which would seem to favour the sportsman's aim, there is no bird of equal proportions so frequently missed, though flushed at the very feet of its pursuer; sometimes rising very awkwardly, and crossing through openings within a few yards of his position, creating a temptation to fire often too irresistible for an anxious man.

It often happens that when a woodcock is first flushed it offers the fairest shot that could be desired; when the sportsman, wishing to kill the bird cleanly, by taking time loses the chance, as the cock suddenly turns and darts through a narrow opening among trees, where it is impossible to obtain a view sufficiently clear to make effective use of the gun.

More random shots are fired at these than at any other birds, because of the uncertainty of their movements, and the eagerness to get possession of so choice a prize. The remotest chance is instantly embraced, and thus they are popped at through impenetrable brushwood, trees, and branches. The sportsman should closely watch their flight in the openings, and shoot the instant a fair chance offers, or he may lose it.

When cock-shooting in woods where the trees are lofty,

it is generally advisable to shoot before the bird rises so high as the branches. The sooner aim can be taken the better; but when the covert is low more time may be given, and the bird allowed to rise above the branches of the trees.

The sportsman will do well before leaving the covert to take a turn round the outside, more particularly if the dogs and beaters have done their work properly. Many a woodcock on being flushed in thick covert drops again just on the skirts of the grove.

Holly-bushes and evergreens should always be well beaten; they are among the most likely places in the wood to shelter a cock:

> 'Content he wanders, or beneath the shade
> Of scatter'd hollies turns with curious bill
> The fall'n leaves, to find his hidden food.'

In very severe and long-continued frosts woodcocks forsake their inland resorts, and depart to woods near the sea-coast, where they remain during the day, and fly to the saltings at twilight, instinct teaching them that the frost has less effect on the sea-ground than on fresh-water localities; but woodcocks never seek such places except as a last resource during a trying season. The western coast of Scotland is a favourite resort of woodcocks during severe weather; the frost drives them from northern and eastern parts to a coast on which the snow never remains very long, the aspect being warmer and more favourable. Mr. Colquhoun makes special allusion to the western coast of Scotland as an extremely favoured locality of woodcocks, particularly such parts of it as afford an aspect of the morning and mid-day sun.[1]

There is no doubt but they are fond of warmth, and endeavour to choose a resort which faces the sun.[2]

The best kind of clogs for finding woodcocks are Clumber spaniels; but they should be carefully trained to the pursuit, and under the perfect control of their masters; should be persevering in their nature, of good courage, and inured to hard work; for it sometimes happens that woodcocks lie very close, and are most reluctant to rise from their favourite haunts; and after being driven up, settle again, like jack-snipes, within a few yards of the spot from which they were flushed.

The sportsman sometimes meets with extraordinary good sport with these birds in the month of March, when they seek the coast, in order to be ready for departure on the first favourable opportunity: if the wind be fair they go at once, but if otherwise they remain in the neighbouring woods, awaiting a more suitable chance. They may then be easily flushed, and on these occasions afford much sudden and unexpected diversion to the sportsman: but they are not so good eating then as in the winter.

During the early season of their arrival woodcocks may frequently be found on the moors and meadows near the sea, where they quickly recruit their condition. But be those spots ever so rich in food, and the productions of the moors ever so dainty, the first frost warns them that an open country is not suited to their habits or their nature, and they then seek shelter in the nearest woods, always preferring the thickest and most impenetrable covers by day; and at twilight, in the evening, and early in the morning, visiting swamps and fens such as are least affected by frost. It is the nature of the woodcock to feed and fly by night, and, when undisturbed, to roost and shelter by day.

The time of their evening flight is rather earlier than that of wild-fowl. It is just at the commencement of twilight that the woodcock moves from its daily retreat to its nocturnal feeding-grounds. Colquhoun says, when the shrill chirp of the blackbird is heard in the grove, it is a good warning bell that the woodcock is about leaving its haunts.[1]

A careful observer of the route taken by woodcocks on leaving or returning to the wood in their daily flights may generally make pretty certain of a shot by occupying a secluded position, so as to intercept them either on leaving or returning to the wood. It is the habit of woodcocks, when uninterrupted, to leave their retreats at eve, and return in the morning with great regularity through the very same glades, and frequently to the same spot as that in which they rested on the day previously.

Everyone accustomed to the sport of woodcock shooting is familiarly acquainted with the signal 'Mark, cock!' and the pleasurable excitement and anxious expectation which follow the sound of those words as they echo through the wood.

The note of the woodcock is a guttural cry, sounding like '*Pa-a-ck!*' or '*Pa-a-ik!*'

Excellent woodcock shooting may be had in Ireland; and though there may sometimes be a difficulty in finding dogs, there are plenty of Irish peasants with their shillelaghs ready and willing, for a small remuneration, to proceed in line through the woods and flush the cocks for the sportsman.

Mark Cock!

As to the abundance of woodcocks in that country, it is recorded of the late Duke of Richmond that many years ago, when Lord Lieutenant of Ireland, he received as a present an immense pie, which when opened was found to contain *twenty score of woodcocks!*[1]

---

[1] 'Woodcocks are to bo had all over the world, in the ancient as in the new; in Siberia as in Senegal—from the Land's-End to John o' Groat's house—from the city of the Sultan to the city of the Czar. . . . . At Constantinople, in Greece, in the Islands of the Archipelago, in all the Ionian Islands, in Sicily, Sardinia, and Corsica, they abound.'—*Sport and its Pleasures*, A.D. 1859.

[1] The Duke of Argyll, in his interesting work 'The Reign of Law,' says:—'The colour of the plumage of this bird bears so striking a resemblance to decayed fallen leaves, that it has been said to be a provision of Nature for its protection, in rendering it invisible, and standing in clear relation to the habits of the bird, resting all day upon the ground under trees.'

[1] 'The extreme regularity of the woodcock's flight has been proved to me even after putting him up a second time. We flushed one in the Kilmun coverts out of reach. He flew straight for a bit of marshy ground: some woodcutters were at work there, and prevented his settling. In a short time we

noticed him come back, and light close to the same spot where he was first put up.'—*Rocks and Rivers*, p. 145.

² See 'The Dead Shot,' by Marksman, p. 160 (4th Edition).

¹ 'The snow never lying long on this coast, nor on the adjacent grounds, nor those sides of the covers facing south-east, and the coverts being filled with numerous springs which are never frozen, may be the united causes of attracting cocks in severe weather, their instinct apparently directing them to the most suitable localities.'—*Bocks and Rivers*.

The same author remarks:—' During severe frost I have seen nine out of ten cocks in those parts of the cover facing the south-east.' He also adds that the 'north-west covers, though suitable in every respect, are not much frequented by woodcocks in severe weather.'—*Ibid.*

² 'The woodcock cloth usually lye on banks by hedges and ditches, against the sun.'—*Blome's Gent's Rec.*

¹ *Vide* 'Rocks and Rivers,' by John Colquhoun, Esq. A.D. 1849.

¹ *Vide* Craven's 'Recreations in Shooting.'

CHAPTER LXIII

METHODS OF CAPTURING WOODCOCKS WITH GLADE NETS, SNARES, AND OTHER ARTIFICES.

'At morn and eve he seeks the limpid streams,
And springing thence, his stated flight he takes,
By the dim light, through op'ning glades: there oft
The treach'rous net his rapid course cuts short,
And his fast flutt'ring pinions beat in vain.
But if with steep ascent he top the snare,
Or sidelong 'scape it, through the wither'd ferns
He picks his silent way.'

Fowling: a Poem. Book iv.

THE art of capturing woodcocks by means of glade nets is a very ancient one. I found an engraving of it in the British Museum, in a curious old work entitled—' Venationes Piseationis et Avcvpii. Typis *Antonia Tempesta.* Claes *Janss Visscher* excudit'. The engraving alluded to represents fowlers in the act of capturing woodcocks and partridges with nets, snares, and nooses. The glade nets are hung between trees, and are represented as being raised or lowered by the aid of ropes rove through sheaves (or pulleys) affixed to the trees. Some of the fowlers shown are in active performance capturing the birds in nets, others are taking either snipes or woodcocks out of nooses and snares: these appear to have been caught by their legs at the water-side.

It is evident that the glade net was sometimes used for capturing partridges as well as woodcocks: the former are mentioned in the Latin inscription at the foot of the engraving:—'Rustica sic Perdix laqueis vel retibus amplis, Falsitur umbrosis nemora intra frondea ramis.'

It appears from this inscription that the glade nets were hung in shady groves among boughs full of leaves: the object of which seems to have been, that the birds might not see the net until they found themselves entangled in it.

The proceedings connected with the use of glade nets appear to be very simple. The nets have to be of lengths and breadths proportioned to the glades in which they are to be suspended. They are simply square pieces of fine thread netting, edged with cords adapted to the extent of the lint or netting. The glade net so formed is suspended between two trees directly in the track of the woodcocks' flight, or rather in the 'cock roads,' as they are termed by Blome.[1] Both the upper and lower corners have each a rope attached to them, which, as regards the upper part of the net, is rove through sheaves, iron rings or thimbles, fastened to the trees on either side, at the top of the glade, at a moderate height, varying from ten to twelve or fifteen feet.

The falls of the two upper ropes are joined, or so adjusted that they form a bridle, to the central part of which a single rope is attached of several yards in length, which the fowler holds in his hand, in a place of concealment; and thus commands full power over the net, being able to drop it down suddenly and intercept the flight of any birds, which may attempt to escape through the glade; or he can draw it up as suddenly from the ground to a perpendicular position.

A stone of about 5 lbs. weight is attached to each of the lower cords of the net, so that when the fowler lets go his controlling rope, the weight of the stones forces the lower part of the net down in an instant with a strong fall, and at the same time they draw up the upper part of the net.

The fowler having stationed himself in such a position as to command a full view of the glade in which his net is placed, beaters are employed to flush the cocks from their retreats; immediately on one or more. flying in the direction of the fowler a signal is given, and just as the bird approaches the net is suddenly let down or drawn up, when the woodcock, flying forcibly against it, is immediately ensnared.

The instant the birds have struck the net the fowler lets go another cord, which is generally looped to a stake within reach of his arm, and the whole net, with the birds entangled, then drops to the ground. In forcing themselves forward, in their endeavours to escape, they form the net into a sort of bag, which makes their capture more certain.

Coveys of partridges, and occasionally hares, are taken in these nets. Many game-keepers (as well as poachers) use them, and make a good deal of money by the pursuit; the extravagant prices offered, and the ready sale for woodcocks, being frequently too great a temptation for some men to withstand.

The method of capturing woodcocks by means of glade nets is almost universal; but is now more frequently resorted to on the Continent than in this country. Some of the French fowlers are particularly skilful in this art of taking woodcocks (*bécasses*) with the glade net, which they term *la pantière*.[1]

Daniel, in his 'Rural Sports,' speaks of great havoc being made among woodcocks by the fowlers of Cornwall and Devon, through the medium of glade nets; and he states that the Exeter stage coach used to bring as many as thirty dozen in a week to the London markets, where they sometimes fetched the exorbitant prices of from ten to sixteen shillings per couple! But since the time when Daniel wrote the prices have advanced. In seasons when they are very scarce woodcocks are sold in London at one guinea per couple!

In further assurance of the high market value which has always been put upon these much-coveted birds, a fact is recorded by Daniel of one person having been known to send woodcocks and snipes from the neighbourhood of Torrington in Devonshire to the London markets to the amount of 1,900*l.* in the course of one season; and this upwards of thirty years ago!

Besides the system of taking woodcocks in glade nets, numbers are captured with traps and snares: those taken by such means, and in glade nets, form the chief supplies of the London and provincial markets.

The method of taking woodcocks by means of lime twigs was freely resorted to by the ancient fowler, as was also the art of capturing them with horse-hair nooses. These nooses were generally made of black horse-hair, with a running knot and spring-stick.[2] For capturing woodcocks they should be laid flat upon the ground, so as to snare them by their legs. In this manner poachers take scores of partridges by placing the hair nooses in furrows, particularly if a few grains of corn be scattered among them. Thus it appears the woodcock is exposed to constant perils and incessant persecutions by the fowler;

> 'Yet not the perils of the aerial voyage,
>   Nor varied death, that hovers on the shore
>   From guns, and nets, and hairy springes, serve
>   The fruitful race t' extirpate.'

Woodcocks are also taken by snares and nooses in various

ways in continental countries.[1] Mr. Bell, in his 'Travels in Asia,' speaks of a singular method of taking the *coc-limoge*, the heath cock, and others, by the Osteacks. They erect a sort of paling of stakes about four or five feet in height, so as to form a pathway from some wood, and if possible along a sandy bank leading to the brink of a river. These stakes are placed sufficiently close that no cock can pass between them. But at certain intervals there are openings or passages for the purpose of inviting the birds to pass through; and it is found that, rather than take wing, the cock will seek a passage from one end of the enclosed space to the other. In each of these openings are set springs or snares connected with flexible rods, which fly up and catch the bird either by the neck or legs the moment it ventures to touch or approach the fowler's apparatus. The Osteacks catch numbers of cocks in this manner.[2]

In the woods of Finland and Lapland, where woodcocks are very abundant, numbers of them are captured in snares. The natives are also very fond of their eggs, which they take in great quantities, disposing of them as an article of food. They are also very skilful in their modes of capturing the woodcock; and by judiciously placing stones on each side, the birds, in endeavouring to avoid the obstructions, pass directly into the snares.

Woodcocks are found throughout the United States and in Canada; they pass towards the south as winter approaches.

They are also generally very abundant in New Jersey[3](America), and in many other parts of the western hemisphere.

It appears by some authorities that there are are no woodcocks in India; but Mr. Williamson asserts the contrary, though he states they are very rarely met with in that country.[1]

In 'Le Moyen Age et la Renaissance,' tome 1, tit. 'Chassée,' p. xxiv., is an amusing description of a most incredible method of capturing woodcocks, said to have been used in France during the fourteenth century.

At that period the French hunted woodcocks after the fashion *à la folatrerie*. The fowler had a dress of the colour of dead leaves (feuille-morte); his face covered with a mask of the same colour, having two holes in the place of eyes. As soon as he saw the woodcock he went upon his knees, resting his arm on two sticks to keep himself perfectly motionless. Whilst the woodcock did not perceive him, he walked gently upon his knees to get near to the bird. He had in his hand two small *baguettes*, the ends of which were dressed with red cloth. When the woodcock was stationary he gently knocked the *baguettes* one against the other: this noise amused or distracted the attention of the bird: the fowler approached nearer, and ended by casting over its neck a noose which he had at the end of the stick. 'And know this,' says the French writer, 'that woodcocks are the most silly birds in the world.'[3]

If they can be caught in this manner, that opinion cannot be disputed.

––––––––––

[1] *Vide* Blome's 'Gentleman's Recreations.'

[1] *Vide* 'Aviceptologie Française,' p. 43, par C. Kresz Aîné. A.D. 1854.

[2] *Vide* 'Jewell for Gentrie,' and Blome's 'Gentleman's Recreations.'

[1] *Vide* 'Aviceptologie Française,' before referred to.

[2] Bell's 'Travels in Asia.'

[3] 'The extensive wild and wet meadows of that State are favourite places of resort for them during the drought so usual in America in July and August. They congregate in such places at those seasons in numbers truly astonishing, and incredible to those who have not witnessed it.'—Skinner's *Dog and Sportsman* (America), A.D. 1845.

[1] 'Woodcocks are so extremely scarce that most of the best and oldest sportsmen doubt whether one is to be found in

India. However, two or three have to my knowledge been shot; indeed, I am greatly mistaken if I did not one day see several brace, as I was following the course of a small spring through an extensive jungle of underwood near Hazary Baug. They flitted before me for at least a mile, suddenly dropping as they got out of my reach, and taking great care to dog in such a manner through the bushes as to destroy every possibility of taking an effectual aim. It was in the month of January, when we had as sharp a frost as ever I can remember to have experienced in India.'—Williamson's *Oriental Field Sports, with drawings by Howett*. Elephant quarto. Anno 1807.

[2] Not wishing to give so long a text in a foreign language, I have simply given a *translation* of this extraordinary proceeding from the French work referred to above.

CHAPTER LXIV

LAWS AFFECTING WILD-FOWL, SEA-FOWL, WOODCOCKS, SNIPES, AND FEN-BIRDS.

IN legal language wild-fowl were anciently termed *fluminecv volucres*. There were formerly several statutes, which threw around the wild-fowler a similar protection to that which was given to the game-shooter, but most of which are now repealed.

Wild-fowl were formerly considered game, and are distinctly enumerated as such in the preamble to the statute 2nd Jac. I., cap. 27; but, according to the present laws, they are not within the prescribed definition of the term '*game:*' they are, nevertheless, recognised by law as creatures of value. There are no lack of precedents, in the earliest volumes of the Statute-book, of laws specially framed for the preservation of wild-fowl and the prevention of their destruction. This recognition of the law in favour of the sport of wild-fowling is confirmed by several subsequent Acts of Parliament, extending over three centuries. The strictest of those laws were enacted in years long since past, when falconry was the prevailing recreation in the country, and hawking by the brook-side the favourite diversion of every nobleman in the land.

The first trace which appears in the nature of a law affecting wild-fowl relates as far back as the year 1209, when a proclamation was issued by King John forbidding the taking of wild-fowl, by any means, in England. Holinshed assigns as a reason for this proclamation that the King, going in progress about the tenth year of his reign, and finding little or no game wherewith to solace himself or exercise his falcons, and being at 'Bristow' in the Christmas ensuing, he restrained all manner of hawking or taking wild-fowl throughout England for a season, 'whereby the land within few years was thoroughly replenished again.'[1]

By the 13th Richd. II., stat. 1, cap. 13, laymen who were not possessed of 40s. a year freehold, and clergy of 10*l.* a year, were prohibited from keeping dogs, or using ferrets, hays, nets, cords, or other engines, for taking deer, hares, conies, or *other gentlemen's game*, on pain of one years imprisonment. It is conceived that wild-fowl were at that period within the ancient definition of 'other gentlemen's game.'

The first statute ever passed in England[2] specially affecting the sport of wild-fowling was that of 25th Hen. VIII., cap. II[1]—'An Act against the Destruction of Wild-fowl.' In the preamble' of that statute it is stated that, whereas before that time there had been plenty of wild-fowl, as ducks, mallards, widgeons, teals, wild-geese, and divers other kinds of wild-fowl, whereby not only the King's most honourable household, but also the houses of noblemen and prelates of the realm, had been supplied with them at convenient prices, and also the markets were sufficiently furnished with wild-fowl: nevertheless divers persons next inhabiting in the countries and places within the realm where the same wild-fowl had been accustomed to breed, in the summer season, at such time as the old fowl were moulted and unable to fly, nor the young fowl fully feathered, had, by certain nets and other engines and policies, yearly taken great numbers of the same fowl, in such wise that the breed of wild-fowl was thereby almost wasted and consumed, and was likely daily to become more wasted and consumed if remedy was not therefor provided. By section 2 it was enacted that it should not be lawful for any person, at any time between the last day of May and the last day of August, to take wildfowl with nets or other engines, upon pain of one year's imprisonment, and a forfeit for every fowl so taken of the sum of four-pence. Section 3 gave power to justices to hear and determine offences. Section 4 provided that it should be lawful for any gentleman, or any other person who had a 40s. freehold, to hunt and take wild-fowl with a spaniel, but without using any net or other engine for the same, except a long-bow. Section 5 prohibited the taking of the eggs of wild-fowl, by day or night, between the 1st of March and the last day of June, under pain of one year's imprisonment, and the penalties of twenty-pence for every egg of any crane or bustard, eight-pence for every egg of bittern, heron, or shoveller, and one penny for every egg of any mallard, teal, or other wild-fowl.

It appears, however, that this statute was found to be oppressive, and a part of it was repealed by the 3rd and 4th Ed. VI., cap. 7, in. the preamble of which it is stated (after briefly reciting the former statute) that, forasmuch as the occasion for passing the previous statute appeared to have arisen out of a private case, and that no manner of common commodity was perceived to have grown of the same, it being proved by daily experience that there had since been less fowl brought into the markets than there was before the making of the said act; which was taken to come of the punishment of God, whose benefit was thereby taken away from the poor people, that were wont to live by their skill in taking the said fowl, whereby they were wont at that time to sustain themselves and their poor households, to the great saving of other kind of victual; of which aid they were then destitute, to their great and extreme impoverishing, especially of such as had their habitations near the fens; therefore the whole of the former statute was repealed, except the section which prohibited any person from destroying or taking away the eggs of wild-fowl.

By 2nd Jas. I., cap. 27,[1] in the preamble, herons, mallards, and such-like, are distinctly recognised as game; and after stating that the game therein enumerated having been 'more excessively and outrageously spoiled and destroyed than hath been in former ages, especially by the vulgar sort, and men of small worth making a trade and living of the spoiling and destroying of the said game,' who are not of sufficient substance to pay the penalties imposed by the statutes, or to answer the costs and charges of a prosecution against them, by reason whereof few suits had been attempted upon the said laws, and thereby there was great scarcity of game throughout the realm; it was therefore enacted, that no person should shoot at, kill, take, or destroy any of the game therein enumerated, under certain pains and penalties. A proviso follows, authorising qualified persons to take pheasants and partridges at certain seasons of the year with nets only; but there is no proviso regarding wild-fowl or any other of the species enumerated as game.

By a very oppressive statute, 4th and 5th William and Mary, cap. 23,[1] any person having game, &c. (wild-fowl included), in his possession, and not being able to give a satisfactory account of the manner in which he obtained it, was liable, on conviction, to a fine not exceeding 20*s*., and not less than 5*s*., for every bird; and, in default of payment or a sufficient distress, to be committed to prison for a term not exceeding one month, and not less than ten days, and there to be whipped and kept to hard labour.

By the same statute, unqualified persons having, keeping,

or using dogs, ferrets, bows, nets, or snares for taking game, fowl, &c, were liable to the like pains and penalties.

In a subsequent reign (9th Anne, cap. 25)[1] it was considered necessary to revive some of the provisions of the original statute, by reason of the immense destruction of wild-fowl, by driving them into hays, tunnels, and other nets, during the moulting season, and at a time of year when the flesh of the fowl 'is unsavoury and unwholesome, to the prejudice of those that buy them, and to the great damage and decay of the breed of wildfowl.' It was, therefore, enacted that, if any person should, between the 1st of July and the 1st of September, 'by hays, tunnels, or other nets, drive and take any wild-duck, teal, widgeon, or any other fowl commonly reputed water-fowl, in any of the fens, lakes, broad waters, or other places of resort for wildfowl in the moulting season,' such person, on conviction, should forfeit 5s. for each bird so taken; and the hays, tunnels, and nets used in taking such wild-fowl were to be seized and destroyed in the presence of the justice before whom the party was convicted.

The 10th Geo. II., cap. 32,[1] recites that the said Act of Queen Anne had been found ineffectual, by reason of the wildfowl begining to moult before the 1st of July, and that they had not done moulting by the 1st of September; the time was therefore extended to between the 1st clay of June and the 1st of October.

LAWS NOW IN FORCE.

Wild-fowl.—As the law at present stands, no game certificate is required to authorise a person to kill wild-fowl,[2] whether in a decoy or elsewhere, but no person is allowed to shoot wild-fowl so near to an old-established decoy as to disturb it, or prevent wild-fowl from resorting there (*vide ante,*' The Law of Decoys'); nor may any person kill wild-fowl on private property without leave of the owner or the person legally authorised to give permission.

By the Sea-birds Preservation Act, 1869,[1] passed for the protection of 'sea-birds' during the breeding season, it is enacted by section 2 that any person who shall kill, wound, or attempt to kill, or wound, or take, any sea-bird, or use any boat, gun, net, or other engine or instrument for that purpose, or shall have in his possession any sea-bird recently killed, wounded, or taken, between the 1st of April and the 1st of August in any year, shall, on conviction of any such offence before any justice of the peace in England or Ireland, or before the sheriff or any justice of the peace in Scotland, forfeit and pay for every such sea-bird so killed, wounded, or taken, such sum of money, not exceeding one pound, as to such justice or sheriff shall seem meet, together with the costs of the conviction; provided always that this section shall not apply where the said sea-bird is a young bird unable to fly.

By section 3 the Home Office as to Great Britain, and the Lord Lieutenant as to Ireland, may, under certain restrictions and upon application to justices at quarter sessions, extend or vary the time during which the killing and taking of sea-birds is prohibited by this Act.

The words 'sea-birds' shall for the purposes of this Act include the different species of Auk, Bonxie, Cornish Chough, Coulterneb, Diver, Eider-duck, Fulmar, Gannet, Grebe, Guillemot, Gull, Kittiwake, Loon, Marrot, Merganser, Murre, Oyster-catcher, Petrel, Puffin, Razor-bill, Scout, Sea-mew, Sea-parrot, Sea-swallow, Shearwater, Shelldrake, Skua, Smew, Solan goose, Tarrack, Tern, Tystey, and Willock.

The operation of the Act is not to extend to the Island of St. Kilda.

By the Wild-birds Protection Act, 1872,[2] any person who shall knowingly or with intent, kill, wound, or take any wild-bird, or shall expose and offer for sale any wild-bird, recently killed, wounded, or taken, between the 15th of March and the 1st of August in any year, shall, on conviction, for a first offence be reprimanded and discharged on payment of costs, and for any subsequent offence fined a sum not exceeding with costs 5s. for every bird so killed, wounded, or taken, or exposed or offered for sale.

The schedule to this Act includes (among others) most

kinds of wild-fowl and fen-birds, as Curlew, Dotterel, Dun-bird, Dunlin, Grodwit, Kingfisher, Lapwing, Mallard, Moor (or water) hen, Oxbird, Pewit, Phalerope, Plover, Ploverspage, Pochard, Ruff and Reeve, Sandpiper, Shoveller, Snipe, Spoonbill, Stint, Summer Snipe, Swan, Teal, Widgeon, Woodcock, Wild-duck, &c, &c.

Snipes and Woodcocks.—By the 52nd Geo. III., cap. 93, any person using a dog and gun for the purpose of shooting or killing snipes or woodcocks is liable to, and must obtain, a game-certificate. This enactment is still in force. But snipes and woodcocks may be taken with nets or springes by persons who have not obtained a game-certificate, such methods of fowling being specially exempted from game-duties by the same statute.

Wild-fowl, Snipes, and Woodcocks are not Game.—Neither wild-fowl, snipes, nor woodcocks are game. The statute 9th Geo. IV., cap. 69, sec. 13, defines the species of all birds that are, by law, considered game. The Game Act of 1st and 2nd Wm. IV. cap. 32, specifies the same creatures to be game as the former statute of 9th Geo. IV.

Killing Wild-fowl, &c, on a Sunday.—Sec. 3 of this statute (1st and 2nd Wm. IV., cap. 32) prohibits, under certain penalties, the killing of game of all kinds, and bustards, on a Sunday or Christmas-day, but it does not mention wild-fowl, woodcocks, or snipes; consequently, persons shooting such birds on those days are not liable to the penalties imposed by this section of the Act.

Tenants' Rights.—Where the landlord reserves to himself simply the right to kill the game, the tenant may kill snipes and woodcocks, as well as quails, landrails, rabbits, &c. But if the tenant, not having the right to kill game on the occupation, gives leave to a stranger to kill snipes, woodcocks, &c, the stranger will do so at his peril; if he acts on the tenant's leave, he will be liable to a penalty, and, in default of payment, to imprisonment.[1] The tenant, however, may *bonâ fide* employ his servants to kill them.[2]

Trespassers.—Persons (not having game-certificates) trespassing by clay, in search of snipes or woodcocks, are liable to a fine not exceeding 2*l.*, and if such persons trespass together, to the number of five or more, they are liable to a penalty not exceeding 5*l.* each person. Wild-fowl are not within the pale of this law, but trespassers in pursuit of wild-fowl, by breaking and entering another's land without lawful authority, would be liable for an ordinary trespass, and, if no other damage could be assigned, the treading down and bruising the herbage would be sufficient.[1]

Penalties and Exemptions.—A person liable under sec. 30 to the 5*l.* penalty for killing game without a certificate is not liable for killing woodcocks or snipes; but is liable to the 20*l.* penalty under 52nd Geo. III., cap. 93, and also to the further duty charged on a game-certificate. The latter penalty and duty are expressly referred to in sec. 23 of the statute 1st and 2nd Wm. IV., cap. 32, which enacts that the present statute is not to affect the existing laws as to game-certificates.

Eggs of Wild-fowl, Penalty for taking or destroying.—By 1st and 2nd Wm. IV., cap, 32, sec. 24, it is enacted, 'That if any person not having the right of killing the game upon any land, nor having permission from the person having such right, shall wilfully take out of the nest, or destroy in the nest, upon such land, the eggs of any swan, wild-duck, teal, or widgeon; or shall knowingly have in his house, shop, possession, or control, any such eggs so taken, every person shall, on conviction thereof before two justices of the peace, forfeit and pay for every egg so taken or destroyed, or so found in his house, shop, possession, or control, such a sum of money, not exceeding 5*s.*, as to the said justices shall seem meet, together with the costs of the conviction.'

See also 'The Law of Decoys,' *ante*, page 77; 'Herons,' page 191; 'Swan Laws,' page 203.

———

[1] Holinshed, vol. i. p. 374, quarto edition. 1807.

[2] In Scotland several statutes have been passed concerning wild-fowl—*inter alia:*

JAMES I., anno 1427. 'Anent wylde foulis.'
JAMES II., ,, 1457. 'Anent the keping of wylde foulis that ganis to eit for the sustentacione of man.'
JAMES IV., ,, 1493. 'Anent the distroying of heron sewis.'

MARY, anno 1551. 'Anent thame that schutis with guns at deer and wylde foulis.'
  ,,   ,,   ,,   'Anent the executione of the act maid vppon the prices of all wylde foulis.'
  ,,   ,,   1555. 'Anent the slaying of poutis, pleuver, mure foule, duke, draik, teil or goldeine.'
  ,,   ,,   ,,   'Anent the execution of the actis maid for stanching of the slaying of wylde foulis and wylde beistes with additioun.'

[1] This statute was partially repealed by 3rd and 4th Ed. VI., cap. 7; was revived by 21st Jac. I., cap. 28; and further continue I by 3rd Car. I., cap. 4, and 16th Car. L, cap. 4.

[1] Repealed by 1st and 2nd Wm. IV., cap. 32.

[1] Repealed by 1st and 2nd Wm. IV., cap. 32.

[2] A gun licence is, however, now necessary. See the recent

statute, 33 and 34 Vic. cap. 57.

[1] 32 & 33 Vic. cap. 17.

[2] 35 & 36 Vic. cap. 78.

[1] *Vide* 1st and 2nd Wm. IV., cap. 32, sec. 30.

[2] Spicer and others *v.* Barnard, vol. vii. W. R., p. 467.

[1] Blackstone's Com. vol. iii. p. 209; 2 Selwyn's Nisi Prius, p. 1295, 12th ed.

CHAPTER LXV

WILD-FOWLING IN FOREIGN COUNTRIES

'Birds! birds! ye are beautiful things,

With your earth-treading feet and your cloud-cleaving wings!

Where shall Man wander, and where shall he dwell,

Beautiful birds, that ye come not as well?'—ELIZA COOK.

WILD-FOWL are undoubtedly much more abundant in foreign countries than in England at certain seasons of the year, and it is natural that migratory birds should be more inclined to settle in wild and thinly-populated lands than in such as are thickly-inhabited and avariciously cultivated.

One of the oldest and most sportsman-like methods of fowling employed in Eastern nations is that of falconry, and in this branch of the pursuit the people of some countries exceed the best skill and tactics of the English falconer. Down to the present time the practice of 'hawking by the brook' is pursued in Eastern countries as ardently as ever,[1] and upon the most modern and scientific principles, so that it is evident if we wish to see falconry to perfection we must go to Eastern lands, where too there is an extent of wild country and other advantages favourable to the sport which are not to be found in England.

Everyone who is familiar with the works of voyagers and travellers in foreign countries must have marked the astonishment expressed by some of them at the numbers of wild-fowl they encountered in their travels. This occurs in books of travel through every quarter of the globe.

The voyagers engaged in the various expeditions in search of the late Sir John Franklin also speak of the vast flights of wild-fowl they met with in the Arctic regions.

An instance is recorded by a French writer in which the whole crew of a vessel would inevitably have perished with hunger had it not been for the extraordinary abundance of wild-ducks.[2]

It also appears that wild-fowl are very numerous in parts of Russia, and, according to the experiences of a sportsman, they are killed there in great numbers.[3]

Another author informs us that he found the rivers and lakes in Lapland literally covered with wild-fowl.[4]

In Hudson's Bay thousands are annually shot by the inhabitants of the surrounding country; their flesh is highly esteemed by the people of those parts as a valuable article of food.[5]

'The lakes and rivers of Scandinavia,' says Lloyd,[6] 'swarm with aquatic birds.'

On the coast of New Guinea they abound in every variety, so that at certain seasons of the year the whole country seems covered with wild-fowl.[1]

Adamson, in his voyage to Senegal, speaking of the morasses between the villages of Nguiago and Tokrod, says they abound with aquatic birds such as curlews, teal, and wild-ducks. The latter species are sometimes so abundant in those parts that they cover a very large tract of ground or water. They appear in flights comprising several thousands, and they are killed in great numbers, so that it is no uncommon circumstance to see thirty drop at one shot, and often twice that number. Those lucky shots, however, seem to be reserved to the negroes, some of whom are very good marksmen. They use none but large fowling-pieces, called '*buccaneers,*' which are rather formidable pieces of artillery: they take aim with these only upon level ground, and in large plains. The natives are enabled to draw near to the birds unobservedly on the savannas by reason of their bodies being of a colour which is confounded with the verdure of the plain.[2] The white faces of the Europeans are said to frighten the birds away, and it is only the natives who can approach them successfully in this manner.

Even among the burning plains of India, where, of all other lands in the world, one would least expect to find wild-fowl, they may be met with in abundance during the monsoons, when the rivers are swollen and the whole country drenched with tropical rains; but as soon as the sun and heat have dried up the waters, wild-fowl are no longer to be seen in that country.

Captain Williamson speaks of large flights of water-fowl arriving in Bengal soon after the monsoons.[3]

Even the impenetrable swamps of Central Africa swarm with wild-fowl. Sir Samuel Baker tells us that he and his party shot them right and left; and that wild-ducks and geese were bagged freely, though they had many exciting adventures in stalking them.[4]

On the banks of the Yang-tse-Kiang, and along the shores of the Po-yang-hou, during the progress of Lord Amherst's embassy, wild-geese and ducks occurred in large flights on both the lake and river, and were so tame that they might be approached within a few yards.[1]

The bays, lakes, fjords, and rivers of Iceland are very numerous, and some of them of considerable extent; many of the larger bays and fjords are studded with innumerable islets, the home of myriads of eider and wild-duck. Almost every species of wild-fowl that visits England is common in Iceland.

The eider-duck is protected by law in Iceland, on account of the great value of its down. A penalty is inflicted on those who kill an eider-duck during the breeding season. These birds therefore become so tame in the breeding season as to build their nests and lay their eggs on the roofs and in the windows of the farm-houses. The birds strip their breasts to line their rudely constructed nests, and the down thus pulled off is removed by the native peasants. The duck then pulls off a fresh supply, and this also is removed from the nest. If the third lining of down be carried off, the bird will desert its nest. The eider throughout Northern Europe is the chief friend of man amongst birds. It is almost a domesticated fowl; wherever it breeds it is preserved, as it pays valuable toll in down and eggs.[2] Eider down is in fact one of the principal exports of the island. Eider-duck farms are common in Iceland, and so stringent are the laws for the preservation of those birds, that it is forbidden to fire a gun in the neighbourhood of an eider-duck farm, for fear of disturbing the birds.

Sir G. S. Mackenzie, in his travels through Iceland, speaks of the multitudes of eider-ducks he saw nestling on the ground through which he passed at Vidoe; they were 'so numerous,' the author states, 'that it required caution to avoid treading on their nests.'

Another author also speaks of similar experiences in his travels.[3] Sir Leopold McClintock[4] mentions that at Waigat Strait, Greenland, on a smooth day, he found its surface only-rippled by the myriads of eider-ducks, which extended over it for several miles; most of them were immature in plumage, and were probably the birds of last year moulting. He also mentions that off Godhavn eider-ducks were very abundant but extremely shy.

The eider-duck is also common in the Baltic, and on all the western coasts of Scandinavia, from Scania to the North Cape, but more especially on certain islands called *Fugel-vass*, or bird preserves, on the north-west coast of Norway.[1] In parts of Norway the down of the eider forms a valuable article of commerce. But the flesh of these birds is considered coarse and not very palatable.

The eider-duck breeds in abundance in Labrador, and in Northern Canada. During the fall and early winter it is occasionally shot near Toronto. But the king duck or king eider is a more northern species than the other, and is seldom seen in Ontario, though specimens are occasionally obtained in the Gulf of St. Lawrence.[2]

Instances might be multiplied by reference to works of travel, both ancient and modern, of the abundance and variety of wildfowl in every quarter of the globe, though at certain seasons of the year in greater numbers in northern countries than elsewhere.

---

[1] *Vide* 'Falconry in the Valley of the Indus.' By R. F. Burton, A.D. 1852. 'Oriental and Western Siberia.' By T. W. Atkinson, A.D. 1858.

[2] 'Promenade autour du Monde.' By Jacques Arago.

[3] 'Pray, Sir, let us go and shoot at Lgoff,' said Ermolai to me; 'there we shall shoot ducks by hundreds and thousands.'—*Russian Life in the Interior; or The Experiences of a Sportsman.* By Ivan Tourghenieff. A.D. 1855.

[4] Regnard in his 'Voyage en Laponie.'

[5] *Vide* Pennant's 'Arctic Zoology,' vol. ii.

[6] 'The Game-birds and Wild-fowl of Sweden and Norway by L.Lloyd. 1867.

[1] *Vide* Bosnian's 'Description of the Coast of Guinea.'

[2] Adamson's 'Voyage to Senegal, the Isle of Goree, and River Gambia.' A.D. 1759.—*Translated from the French.*

[3] 'The flights of water-fowl that arrive in Bengal immediately as the rains subside are astonishing. The *cyruses*, and all the larger kinds, may be seen during the early time of the rains

in immense flights, each string forming an angle, led by one bird, which at times is relieved by some other. They invariably fly to the same quarter.'—*Oriental Field Sports*. By Captain T. Williamson.

[4] 'Ismalia,' by Sir Samuel Baker; 'A Narrative of the Expedition to Central Africa for the Suppression of the Slave Trade.' 1874.

[1] Murray's 'China,' vol. iii. p. 427; and see also Abeel's 'China.'

[2] 'Iceland, its Scenes and Sagas.' By Sabine Baring-Gould, M.A., 1863.

[3] 'Travels through Sweden, Norway, and Finmark.' By A. De Capell Brooke, M.A., A.D. 1823.

[4] 'Narrative of the Fate of Sir John Franklin.'

[1] Lloyd's 'Game-birds and Wild-fowl of Sweden and Norway,' p. 347.

[2] 'The Birds of Canada.' By Dr. A. M. Ross, 2nd Edition, 1872.

CHAPTER LXVI

WILD-FOWLING IN SWEDEN, NORWAY, AND LAPLAND

'From the frozen North, where Winter's hand,
With sway despotic and untamed, locks up
The shrinking world; o'er the wide ocean, borne
On vigorous wing, pour forth the feather'd tribes
Diverse and strange.'—*Fowling: a Poem.*

THE lakes and rivers of Scandinavia are among the most attractive waters on the face of the globe to the various species of wild-fowl. And although many thousands are taken in the course of every year, by various arts, from the primitive horsehair noose to that of the *Fogel-Nät*, the cry is still—' they swarm!' and when one considers the numbers that are bred in the inland waters of Sweden, Norway, and Lapland, the few that are killed seem comparatively small, which is probably in part owing to decoys being altogether unknown in the Peninsula; or at all events, if known, they are not employed, though it would appear that the fairest facilities are afforded for the construction and employment of such to considerable profit and advantage.[1]

The stalking-horse, under the name of the Skjut-jo, or artificial cow, seems to be freely used for wild-fowl shooting in most parts of Scandinavia.[2]

That destructive weapon the punt-gun, which might be so successfully employed on the lakes and rivers of those countries, appears at present to be but little used, though the echoes of the less formidable artillery of many an enterprising English sportsman have resounded throughout the length and breadth of many of the lakes and bays of those parts, and with merited success.

The usual plan of shooting water-fowl in the Gothenburg and neighbouring *Skärgardar* is out of a small sailing-boat: tolerable sport is always obtainable, particularly among the eider-ducks, which are abundant in those parts.[3]

Another plan of shooting water-fowl in the Gothenburg and others of the Scandinavian Skargardar is by aid of the so-called 'Wettar,' or artificial decoy birds. These consist either of such as are stuffed, or of blocks of wood so fashioned and painted as to resemble live water-fowl. The fowler anchors his 'Wettar' by means of pieces of string and small stones, within easy gunshot of some headland the fowl are in the habit of passing in their morning and evening flights.

The fowler, having concealed himself on shore behind a boulder or other screen, should be provided with at least two guns. A boat is also indispensable, as well to moor the 'Wettar' as to collect the killed and wounded; but it should be hidden in some neighbouring creek.

Another mode of taking water-fowl in Scandinavia is by means of the Fogel-Nät (or fowl-net); and this appears to be one of very ancient origin. In the ancient *Jagt-Stadgar* (or laws relating to the chase) the use of the Fogel-Nät is mentioned as one of the privileges of the inhabitants of the Skargardar.

The Fogel-Nät is from eighty to one hundred fathoms in length by four to six fathoms in depth. It is made of stout twine, with meshes from three to four inches square. The upper part of the net is furnished with rings at intervals of about three feet, by means of which it is made to traverse a rope stretched between two posts each about thirty feet in height, placed one on each side of a narrow strait or sound through which wild-fowl are known to pass *på drag* (or at flight-time). By the aid of a tackle or pulley the net can be spread across the water or drawn together with facility, and in like manner to a curtain on its rods.

The Fogel-Nät being spread, the fowler stations himself behind one of the posts, holding in his hand the end or fall of the rope to which the net is appended, and so awaits the coming of the birds. If they are few in number, and are flying in compact order, he, just as they are in the act of striking the net, lets go the rope 'by the run,' when both birds and net fall together into the water; but should the flight be a numerous one and scattered, the fowler eases the rope gradually, so that not even the rearmost ranks can escape capture. By the mere act of striking against the net the fowl become entangled in the meshes; but in their endeavours, by diving or otherwise, to recover their liberty, they become more so, and are made captives by the fowler or his assistant in a boat, or by folding the net and drawing it ashore.

When the fowl first strike the net in their flight they do so with considerable force; and unless the fowler takes the precaution, at the moment, to slacken the rope, and so yield to the pressure, they would break through the net, the meshes of which fly with a twang like that of a bowstring.[1]

The Fogel-Nät seems more especially designed for the capture of birds of the pochard species, as well as the long-tailed hareld, the velvet duck and the eider, the flight of these being rapid and direct, and seldom more than six or eight feet above water. Others which fly higher in the air and are less heedless in their flight discover the net in time to pass over it.

The best time of day for the Fogel-Nat is at flight-time— just after dawn in the morning or towards dusk in the evening. In broad daylight fowl cannot be captured with it.

In the winter-time, again, such of the fowl as pass that inclement season on the more southern coasts of Scandinavia, are subject to much persecution; for when compelled by hunger to resort to *wakar*, or openings in the ice, caused by currents or otherwise, they are slaughtered in great numbers, by various expedients: nets, for instance, are set in these openings for such birds as obtain their food by diving; at other times snares are substituted for nets in the *wakar*, or it may be in square holes that are cut in the ice for that purpose; at others large numbers are taken without either nets or snares by men armed with poles, who creep up to the brink of the *wakar* unseen, when they suddenly start up and knock the fowl on the head as they rise, or attempt to rise, from the water. Mr. Lloycl says that the quantity of aquatic birds, such as widgeon, golden eye, and long-tailed harelcl, that at times congregate in *wakar*, and other openings in the ice, is enormous. When, in the winter of 1853, which was a severe one, Mr. Alexander Keiller in an ice-boat was crossing the Great Belt, then entirely frozen over, with the exception of a very narrow channel in the middle, he saw such multitudes of fowl as filled him with astonishment. 'Billions,' said he, 'would give no idea of their numbers; and when they took wing it was not simultaneously, but in succession, like unto clouds of dust that arise on a highway when swept by a whirlwind. Owing to their being so closely packed together it would have been impossible for the whole of them to have flown up at once; and when they were ail fairly on the wing they literally darkened the air. The open channel spoken of was fringed with the dead and dying.

Many had perished from starvation, whilst not a few, owing to their helpless condition, had been killed with sticks; others, again, had been destroyed by birds of prey, more especially eagles, several of which were seen perched on hummocks of ice, gorged with the blood of their victims.[1]

Mr. Lloyd also speaks of an ingenious expedient adopted by the Northern *chasseurs* to beguile wild-fowl late in the autumn, the same being also practised by the workmen at the ironworks of Gysinge and Söderfors. Quoting M. Bedoire, lie says:

'During the autumn ducks collect in large flocks on the neighbouring lakes and rivers, the strands of which are in general flat. The fowler, on observing the birds, walks as near to them as he can with safety, when, falling on his hands and knees, he makes his further approaches slowly and cautiously. In the meanwhile he causes his well-trained dog, who should be of a reddish colour, to gambol before him, which he effects by every now and then throwing the animal a crumb of bread that it catches in its mouth. The ducks, attracted by the antics of the dog, gradually approach the strand, and thus the man is often enabled to get sufficiently near them to fire with effect.' 'According to the account of the men in question,' M. Bedoire goes on to say, 'it was from seeing the way in which the fox at times secures his prey that they were induced to adopt the plan spoken of, for that cunning animal in the autumn resorts to a similar ruse to capture young clucks. He then promenades near to the water's edge, sometimes vaulting high in the air and at others crawling on his belly, his brush in the meanwhile trailing along the ground. These manœuvres of his so excite the curiosity and tickle the fancy of the ducklings that they gradually swim towards him, occasionally so near, it is said, as actually to seize hold of his tail with their bills; but they usually pay dear for their temerity, for the wily fellow seizes his opportunity and pounces on one or other of them. To this device of the fox,' M. Bedoire continues, 'I myself have been an eyewitness, and it was only last autumn that my bailiff shot one of these animals in the very act of beguiling young ducks in the manner described.'[1]

Another device used in Scandinavia for the capture of water-fowl is called the *Fogel-ref*, which consists of a very long line, to which are attached wooden pegs, at distances of about three feet apart, to fasten it to the ground. On both sides of each peg is a black horsehair snare, or noose, about twenty inches in length, and at its base a piece of a quill to keep it in its proper position. The Fogel-ref is placed along the shore or marshy edges of the waters frequented by ducks and other water-fowl, so that on coming ashore in search of food they get caught by the neck or feet in the snares.[2]

METHODS OF CAPTURING WILD-FOWL IN LAPLAND.

In parts of Lapland a kind of snaring raft, called the *Lintu-Lauta*, said to be of Finnish invention, is commonly used for the capture of wild-ducks and other fowl. It consists of a small raft about four feet square, constructed of wooden planks, to each of the four corners of which a short stick is secured, standing about twelve inches high; and a line being rove through the top of each stick, a kind of rail is formed on each of the four sides of the raft; another line is rove through the four corner sticks, and passes along the base of the raft, resting upon the planks on each of the four sides or edges, and by means of short cords knotted to the upper and lower line, about twelve inches apart, small squares or apertures are formed, in each of which a noose of horsehair or other suitable material is placed, hanging from the upper or rail-line. The Lintu-Lauta so constructed is then moored in an opening in the ice at the breaking up of the frost; and being baited with roots and leaves of aquatic plants, the hungry fowl in their attempts to get at them are snared by the neck, and so very many are captured.[1]

Wild-geese are also taken in Lapland by the ingenious means of snares placed along the shores of the lakes. The locality preferred by the Lapland fowler for the purpose is generally a low sandy *landtunga*, or tongue of land, about fifty paces in length by twenty or thirty in breadth, stretching into a lake. Around the more central parts of the *landtunga* he constructs an artificial barrier, or low zigzag railing. This consists of a number of sticks about the thickness of one's finger placed about ten or twelve feet apart in zigzag line, at the several angles of which two of the sticks should be placed so as to form an opening about ten inches wide. The sticks should all stand at a uniform height of ten or twelve inches from the ground, and must all be linked together by a string or wire, so as to form a dwarf or diminutive fence, with an opening at the angle of each zigzag. The snares or nooses, from twenty to thirty in number, are then set one at each of the angles or openings before-mentioned, being kept in their places by notches cut in the bark of the stick at the sides. Broken straw, barley, and the like are strewn both outside and inside of the barrier, but the greater portion within it. When the geese, which always in the first instance alight in the water, see the scattered grain they swim ashore and waddle towards it; and when they come to the dwarf fence, instead of attempting to pass over or under it, they follow along the zigzag obstruction to the nearest opening, when, in attempting to pass through it, they are caught by the neck in the snare that is there spread for them.[1]

Numbers of water-fowl of various kinds which obtain their

food by diving for it are taken in Lapland with common iron traps, similar to English rat-traps. These traps are set at the bottom of the lakes, in shallow water, at the mouths or openings of rivulets and other small tributaries or places where the ice is first ready to melt, and to which the aquatic fowl are sure to resort. Those intended for the capture of pochards and others which feed on the herbage which grows at the bottom of the lakes are baited with the roots and choice sprigs of aquatic plants, as the *Ranunculus aquatilis*; but those intended for the loon and merganser species, which have serrated bills, and subsist on small fish, are baited accordingly, generally with a small fish of the genus *Coregonus*. The fowl on diving for their food and seizing the baits spring the traps, and are thus caught by the neck in those submerged engines.

It appears, however, that the greatest destruction made amongst wild-geese and other wild-fowl in Lapland, as also in Sweden and Norway, is during the moulting season, when, being unable to fly, they are hunted and caught by dogs or knocked down with sticks.

———————

[1] 'Decoys are, I believe, unknown in Scandinavia, though the country is in many parts very favourable for the purpose.'—

Scandinavian Adventures. By L. Lloyd, 1854, vol. ii. p. 457.

[2] Lloyd, in his 'Game-birds and Wild-fowl of Sweden and Norway,' p. 280, quoting M. von Grieff: where see ludicrous illustrations of the Skjut-jo.

[3] See Lloyd's 'Game-birds and Wild-fowl of Sweden and Norway,' p. 354.

[1] See Lloyd's 'Game-birds and Wild-fowl of Sweden and Norway,' from which the above description has been taken.

[1] 'The Game-birds and Wild-fowl of Sweden and Norway,' by L. Lloyd, 1867, p. 370.

[1] Sen Lloyd's 'Game-birds and Wild-fowl of Sweden and Norway,' p, 283.

[2] See the 'Oländska Resa,' by Linnæus, 1741, p. 203.

[1] See Lloyd's 'Game-birds and Wild-fowl of Sweden and Norway,' 1867, p. 285.

[1] See a description and illustration of this mode of fowling in Lloyd's 'Game-birds and Wild-fowl of Sweden and Norway,' 1867, p. 286.

CHAPTER LXVII

ROCK-FOWLING IN NORWAY.[2]

'The baron hath the landward park;

The fisher hath the sea;

But the rocky haunts of the sea-fowl

Belong alone to me.

'The baron hunts the running deer;

The fisher nets the brine;

But every bird that builds its nest

On the ocean-cliffs is mine!'

Song of the Sea-fowler. By MARY HOWITT.

THE system of rock-fowling as practised from the precipitous cliffs of Norway is extremely perilous, though frequently attended with considerable success and remuneration to those who have the hardihood and daring to pursue it. The Norwegian rock-fowlers, at imminent hazard of their lives, climb rocks of startling altitude, leap over yawning chasms, and, with a rope attached to their waists, throw themselves with grace and agility over the most fearful precipices, some of which present a perpendicular frontage of from four to five hundred yards in height, and are washed at the base by a turbulent sea.

The men who perform these feats of daring are termed 'bird-men,' many of whom are trained to the pursuit from boyhood.

A long staff, called a 'bird-pole 'or 'fowling-staff,' about five or six ells in length, is used by the fowler in climbing the rocks; and a rope, called a 'rock line,' several fathoms in length, is also used for the purpose of descending from the upper part of the cliffs, or for pulling up a comrade from below.

The bird-pole is furnished at one end with an iron hook, which is fastened to the waistband of the fowler when climbing from a boat at the base of the cliff; it enables his comrades to hold him steadily, and assist him up the rocks to the extent of the length of the bird-pole; or, if the cliff is very perpendicular, the flat head of the pole (which is about six inches in diameter) is applied to the seat of honour for the same purpose. In this manner the fowler is enabled to climb to some *helde* or projection where he can obtain a footing; then those below help another up to the same place; and when both have climbed to the *helde* bird-poles are handed to them. The two adventurers are then linked to each other by means of the rock-line, one end of which is secured to the waist of one, and the other end to that of his companion. One of them then climbs as high as he can; and where the climbing is difficult the other, by applying his bird-pole in the manner before mentioned, pushes his fellow-mate up to a standing-place. The uppermost of the two then draws up his comrade with the rock-line, and so they get to apparently inaccessible holes and clefts in the rocks, where the birds roost or build.

Whilst one of the fowlers is climbing the other seeks a firm standing, and has to be prepared for the most sudden emergency, so as to be able to hold his comrade fast in case he should slip or fall.

Accidents often happen, for if the one whose duty it is to be watchful be not standing firmly, or is not strong enough to support the other should he slip, they are both precipitated to the bottom, from whatever height, one dragging the other after him to certain death; both are inevitably killed in the fall, by being dashed to pieces against the rocks, or drowned in the water beneath them; and in this frightful manner several bird-men perish every year.

‘ "Stay, ye fools," he cried; "ye madmen, stay! Nor further prosecute your vent'rous way." ’

On arriving at the bird-roosts in the rocks about twilight, or later, the fowl are sometimes found very tame, and are easily taken with the hand; but when wild the fowler takes a small light net from his pocket (with one or two of which he is always provided) and throws it over the holes and clefts in the rocks, and sometimes over the birds that may be hovering within reach of his arms. The bird-poles are sometimes used with the nets appended to them, so as to entangle any bird that ventures within reach, or that the fowler may chance by his skill to ensnare in that manner. If he contrives to throw the net so as to touch either the head, feet, or tips of the wings of any bird it generally becomes his captive.

During these operations a boat awaits the fowlers at the foot of the rock; into this the fowl are taken, after being let down in bundles by a cord, or thrown down singly into the water by the bird-men, if not at so high an elevation as to injure them by the concussion.

In fine weather, and during favourable seasons, when the fowlers have climbed to difficult places and found an abundant number of birds, they sometimes remain on the rocks six or eight days at a time. There are generally holes and clefts sufficiently large to admit the body of a man; into these the fowlers creep, where, resting in safety by day, they pursue their calling at night.

On such occasions provisions are supplied them from the top of the precipice, by being let down with a small rope.

During the fowlers' sojourn in the rocks their companions in the boats are regular in attendance once or twice at certain specified hours—generally at dawn of day—to take away the birds or eggs which are let down in the manner before mentioned, and to respond to the signals and supply the requirements of their more adventurous companions.

The fowling is performed chiefly by night; but the egging, which is done at a different season of the year, is generally pursued by day. There are stated periods of the year for this perilous work; the first takes place in May, when they go after the eggs of gulls, kittiwakes, and such like, which are of excellent flavour; those of the razor-bill, puffin, and guillemot are rank and unpalatable.

The other method of fowling resorted to by the Norwegian bird-men is attended with equal if not greater hazard, though sometimes with astounding success. Some of the rocks are inaccessible to the climber; the fowler is therefore let down to the bird-colonies by means of a bird-rope; this proceeding is termed 'to sie.' The bird-rope is made of hemp, and is generally from one hundred and sixty to two hundred yards in length, and about the substance of three fingers in thickness. One end is made fast to the back part of the bird-man's belt; or, as is more frequently the case, there is a belt fitted to the end of the rope, so as to fasten securely at the back. It is then drawn betwixt the bird-man's legs in such a manner that he sits upon it, and so is let down with the bird-pole in his hand. Another plan is by fastening the end of the bird-pole to a small beam or pole, upon which the fowler sits; but this is not considered a safe method unless a lashing be passed round the waist of the bird-man, so as to fasten him to the rope.

Some fowlers are so expert in this art that they pursue the perilous calling without the aid of assistants. Having fastened the rope to a post, they let themselves down over the cliffs; and in the same manner work themselves up again by simply climbing the rope. In the absence of any stake or other holdfast within reach of the cliff, six men, at the top, stand by the rope and hold it, letting the fowler down by degrees. A semicircular socket is sometimes stuck into the ground at the brink of the precipice for the rope to slide over, and in order to prevent its chafing on the sharp edges of the stony rock; in the place of the socket a piece of smooth timber is sometimes used.

A small signal-line is also fastened to the fowler's waist, by means of which he telegraphs to his assistants who have the command of the bird-rope; and by certain preconcerted arrangements the fowler is enabled to make them understand his wishes—as to being drawn up higher, let down lower, held in the same place, or howsoever otherwise he may desire.

In addition to the perils already alluded to the bird-man has many minor casualties to encounter, even under the most careful precautions: pieces of stone loosen by the friction of the rope and fall on his head. To guard against serious wounds from such occurrences he wears a thick-furred cap, well stuffed with pliable substance.

The fowler, with the aid of the bird-pole, casts himself several fathoms from the rock, and thus shoots himself to whatever part he wishes to explore. He is able to sit on the rope in the air, and, with both hands at liberty, to use with ease the fowling-staff and net for taking such birds as fly within his reach. He has also a particular method of plying his feet against the rock. In moving and swinging to and fro the bird-pole is of great service in skilful hands; it is also sometimes used for preventing birds from leaving the holes in the rocks until the fowler is enabled to capture them with his hand. It will thus be seen that the bird-pole is a very necessary appendage to the proper equipment of a Norwegian rock-fowler.

Some of the rocks, by reason of excavation at the base, the unceasing fluctuations of the tide, or other natural causes, project over the sea beyond a perpendicular to a *leaning* position; and it is generally found that these, of all others, from the apparently inaccessible security they offer, are the favourite roosts and resting-places of rock-fowl. The places under these projections are termed 'sielings;' to obtain access to these constitutes the very summit of the rock-fowler's art: none but the most skilful can perform it. The bird-man has to swing himself as far as he can from the cliff, and then to dart under the projecting rock, and all whilst suspended in the air by the bird-rope. When he has succeeded in swinging himself under the projection it requires a good deal of experience and skill to know how to hold on by the feet to a leaning rock, and at the same time make use of the hands for the purpose of taking the birds.

The most skilful bird-men delight in this perilous practice, and swing themselves from rock to rock with great dexterity, an accomplishment peculiar to the art, which requires much practice.

When the bird-man comes to a good standing and plenty of birds he sometimes unfastens the rope and secures it to a large stone, whilst he pursues his art unfettered, climbing and catching the birds with his hands or by aid of the bird-pole. When he has taken a reasonable number he ties them to the signal-line, and on telegraphing to his companions above the birds are drawn up, and the line is let down again.

On ordinary occasions, when suspended by the bird-rope from the brow of a precipice, the fowler, having taken merely a belt full, is drawn up with the birds attached to his belt, on signalling such his desire to his companions.

Some of the rocks scaled by these intrepid fowlers are fearful to look upon, and so perilous that to a stranger it appears almost incredible how the fowlers dare venture to scale them. In the most precipitous cliffs, however, there are but few if any clefts that are not explored by these dauntless fellows. They sometimes venture into places where they can but just pitch their toes or lay their fingers on some narrow ledge; and this where a gulf of two hundred fathoms' descent lies yawning beneath them.[1]

The occupation is often very lucrative; a great profit is sometimes derived from the feathers of the birds, and the flesh is dried and salted in large quantities as a staple article of food during the winter.

By the ancient laws of Norway, when a fowler on climbing the rocks in that country happened to be killed by a fall, the nearest male relative of the deceased was compelled to climb by the same route as that from which the deceased fell. If he declined, or lacked the skill and courage necessary to incur the risk, the deceased was adjudged to have been guilty of suicide, and was not allowed a Christian burial, but treated as a criminal, who had, by means of too hazardous fowling, been his own executioner.

But Peter Clauson, in his 'Description of Norway,' says there is nothing done under that law at the present day.

------

[2] *Vide* 'Natural History of Norway,' by Bishop Pontoppidan. 'Færoa Reserata,' by Lucas Debts; 'Description cf Norway,' by Ilcrr Pader Clauson, &c., &c.

[1] Pontoppidan says: 'There are some, indeed, who say there is no great danger in it, excepting that when they have not learnt the practice, or are not accustomed to it, the rope runs about with them till their heads are turned, and they can do nothing to save themselves. But those who have learnt it make play of it.'

CHAPTER LXVIII

ROCK-FOWLING IN THE ORKNEY ISLANDS

'The wild sea roars and heaveth

    On the granite crags below;

And round about the misty isles

    The fierce wild tempests blow.

'And let them blow! roar wind and wave!

    They shall not me dismay:

I've faced the eagle in her nest,

    And snatched her young away.'—*Song of the Sea-fowler.*

A SIMILAR system of fowling to that practised in Norway is pursued in the Orkneys. Many of the poor inhabitants subsist chiefly, during the spring season, on the eggs of birds which nestle in the lofty cliffs and rocks of those islands, the height of some of which is above fifty fathoms, and many of them are nearly perpendicular, with here and there shelves or ledges sufficient only for the birds to roost and lay their eggs upon, yet the venturous fowlers of those islands ascend, pass intrepidly from one to the other, collect the eggs and birds, and descend with the same indifference.

These excursions are generally attempted from the table-land or top of the precipice. The fowler is let down by a rope, in the same manner and under precautions precisely similar to those already described in the preceding chapter.

The Orkney bird-men sometimes trust themselves to a post and a single assistant, who lets his companion down, over stupendous precipices, with apparently careless incaution; and the rope is often shifted from place to place along the cliff whilst the fowler, with his game, is all the while suspended.

Pennant, in his 'Arctic Zoology,' asserts, apparently without authority, that the bird-men of the Orkney Isles are sometimes let clown over the rocks by means of a rope made of straw, and not infrequently of *Hogs' bristles!* adding, that the fowlers prefer the latter even to ropes of hemp, because they are not liable to be cut. But this is evidently one of those careless assertions of Mr. Pennant on which no reliance can be placed, and which shake the authority of that otherwise able and amusing writer. So illogical a statement should never have been put forth. It is utterly inconsistent with common sense to suppose that a rope of some thirty or forty fathoms in length, capable of enduring considerable strain, could be made of straw, and much less out of hogs' bristles, which, everyone knows, do not grow to above three inches in length, and the very nature of which, stiff and brittle as they are, renders them totally unfit for the purpose of making a rope; besides, too, all the hogs in the Orkneys could not produce sufficient bristles for such a purpose, and, if they could, the ingenuity of man would be most sorely taxed to make a forty-fathom rope of such material; moreover, hogs' bristles are of far too great a value for other purposes than to be used in making a bird-rope.

Mr. Pennant must have mistaken *horse-hair* for hogs' bristles. Horse-hair bird-ropes are said to be used by the fowlers of the Island of St. Kilda (*infra*, chapter lxx.), as also bird-ropes made of strips of cow-hide.

Few men who practise these hazardous systems of fowling come to a natural death. There is a common saying among rock-fowlers, that 'such-a-one's gutcher went over the sneak.'[1]

Similar systems of fowling to those already described as practised in Norway and the Orkneys are employed in the Faroe Islands, where some of the cliffs are two hundred fathoms in height,[2] and are explored by the fowlers of those islands, both by ascent and descent. The sea surrounding many parts of the Faroe Islands, where the rock-fowler ventures, is extremely turbulent, and the currents varied, rapid, and whirling; but notwithstanding such threatening horrors, the fowler climbs about rocks projecting over the sea at considerable altitude, with as little concern as if he were but a few feet from the bottom, and had a feather-bed in readiness below to receive him in case he fell.

The birds which form the chief objects of attraction to the fowlers of the Faroe Islands are termed *Lundes*, which are simply described as large birds, 'black on the back, and white under the belly.'[3]

The Faroe fowlers have a method of capturing these birds flying. They provide themselves with a net similar to a cripple-net or a landing-net, but with a longer staff and larger meshes. This net they term a 'stang of staffe.' Equipped with one of these, the fowler places himself, at twilight, on a cliff near the bird-colonies, or in the '*ures*' between the rocks (which he terms 'flight-places ') most frequented by the birds. On the 'lunde' flying either to or from the cliffs he suddenly raises the net, so as to intercept its flight, and if he be expert in the art he captures the birch A skilful performer is sometimes enabled to take two hundred lundes in a few hours.

The proceedings connected with this method of fowling are more difficult and dangerous to behold than can be described. The fowlers sometimes climb up from below, where the cliffs are steep as a wall, or they are let down from above by a stout hemp rope.

A portion of the birds taken by the fowlers are eaten whilst fresh, others are hung up, dried, and preserved as provisions for the winter.

The perilous pursuit of rock-fowling by means of hair or leathern ropes suspended over cliffs and precipices appears to be also practised in Iceland, on the island of Drangey, which in spring is said to be visited by a great number of men, who descend the cliffs, slung by hair or leathern ropes, and rifle the nests of the numerous sea-birds which build upon the ledges. They also catch the birds themselves at the foot of the rocks by means of floating snares formed of boards, and provided with nooses. The unsuspecting creatures fly down and perch on the planks, when they are caught by the threads and held till the fowler visits his *fleke* in the evening.[1]

---

[1] Pennant.

[2] 'It cannot be expressed with what pain and danger they take these birds in those high and steep cliffs, whereof many are above two hundred fathoms high.'—*Færoa Beserata.* Also Jacobson's *History of the Faroe Islands.*

[3] *Vide* 'Færoa Reserata,' translated from the Danish by Jno. Sterpin.

[1] 'Iceland,' by S. Baring-Gould, M.A., p. 243.

CHAPTER LXIX

ROCK-FOWLING IN THE SHETLAND ISLES

'The billows burst in ceaseless flow
 Deep on the precipice below;
 And steepy rock and frantic tide
 Approach of human step defied.'—SIR WALTER,
SCOTT.

A SIMILAR and equally dangerous method of fowling to those described in the two preceding chapters is practised in one of the Shetland islands, at the Holme of Noss, a precipitous rock which stands severed from the Isle of Noss, only sixty-five feet distant, as if by some long-forgotten convulsion, or other unaccountable phenomenon. The Holme, which is little more than five hundred feet in length by one hundred and seventy in breadth, rises abruptly from the sea in the form of a perpendicular cliff, one hundred and sixty feet in height. The chasm which intervenes between it and the no less precipitous banks of JSToss cannot be looked upon or contemplated without horror.

The woodcut is a small sketch of the Holme of Noss, with

cradle and rock-fowlers engaged in the pursuit of fowling. The height of the rocks renders it impossible to show the figures very clearly; the cut will therefore give the reader only a very indistinct notion of the scene. From the cradle to the water the height is one hundred and sixty-two feet,[1] and the depth of the water is twenty-seven feet eight inches, as measured by Dr. Scott, of Lerwick.

Dr. Hibbert[1] states that the original temptation to reach this Holme was caused by the inumerable birds which visited it during the season of incubation, when the grass became literally whitened with their eggs. The writer also gives an interesting narrative of the manner in which the perilous feat was accomplished; but whether a traditional statement or otherwise it does not appear, though it is evidently well-authenticated. It appears that upwards of two centuries ago an adventurous fowler was induced, for the tempting reward of a cow, to ascend the Holme from its base, a hardy and almost incredible undertaking, which lie accomplished; and having reached the top, two stakes were thrown across to him from the island, with tools for fixing them in the rock at the projection nearest the opposite precipice. Having firmly fixed the stakes, the object of the perilous adventure was accomplished, and the fowler was entreated to avail himself of the communication of ropes for the purpose of returning across the gulf. This he refused to do, preferring to descend by the way that he had climbed, and in the rash attempt he fell, and perished. Strange to say, it does not appear that the unfortunate man waited to complete the undertaking by twisting a rope round the stakes, nor is it stated that such was thrown across to him for that purpose.

The manner in which the islanders availed themselves of this ill-fated hero's success, and completed the hempen tramway across the chasm, was by first conducting a small double cord across it, attaching a stone at one end and throwing it over; then, by means of a long pole or fishing-rod, the cord was slightly elevated, so as to be drawn round the stakes, a thicker rope was then attached to the cord, and upon the latter being drawn in, the other was, in its turn, brought round the post. This operation was repeated until a strong and firm cordage formed the medium of transport from the island to the rock. The tramway so far constructed, an oblong box or cradle was contrived, at the extremities of which two holes were made, through which the ropes of the tramway were drawn, and thus the cradle was safely slung. The first passenger across the chasm then seated himself in the cradle, when, there being a slight descent towards the Holme, he glided easily across, regulating the celerity of his conveyance by means of lateral cords. The return trip was not so easily accomplished, it being on an ascent, assistance was required from those on the island, who drew him up by means of a rope attached to the cradle.[1]

At the time when Dr. Hibbert wrote (1822) the Holme was used as a pasture for twelve sheep, which were conveyed across the chasm one at a time, the cradle being just large enough to accommodate a man and one sheep at each transit.

For the purposes of fowling the cradle is slung twice in the year; once in the egging season, and again in the fowling season. The proceedings of crossing the chasm are still conducted in the same manner as that which has always been practised since the line of communication was first made.

In the island of Foula the bird-man makes fast his rope to a small stake or a dagger driven into the ground. He sometimes incurs the rash folly of trusting his life to a fishing-cord, which is twisted round the stake or dagger, and, with no other assistance, he descends from the top of the precipice and collects his spoils. He then ascends by aid only of the fishing-cord.

It appears that the perilous system of rock-fowling is now very little practised in Shetland, except by some of the old hands: but considerable quantities of eggs are taken annually, either for home consumption or for the local dealers. The cause of this decline has not been any failure in the supply, but the steady manner in which the proprietors have endeavoured to persuade the men to turn their time to a better account.[2]

---

[1] This height, however, is nothing in comparison with that of the rocks scaled by the Norwegian rock-fowlers, some of which present a perpendicular frontage of from four to five hundred yards in height.—*Supra*, chap, lxvii.

[1] *Vide* Hibbert's 'Description of the Shetland Isles,' p. 285:

A.D. 1822.

[1] *Vide* Hibbert's 'Description of the Shetland Isles.' Also Gorton's 'Topographical Dictionary,' vol. iii.

[2] Saxby's 'Birds of Shetland:' A.D. 1874.

CHAPTER LXX

ROCK-FOWLING IN ST. KILDA

'Come on, then, Jock and Alick,

 On to the sea-rocks bold;—

I was trained to take the sea-fowl

 Ere I was five years old!

'Come on, then, Jock and Alick,

 To the splintered sea-cliff's brow!

Where are the lads?—I wot ye,

 On the topmost crags ere now!'

Song of the Sea-fowler.

THE island of St. Kilda has always been a favourite place of resort for sea fowl; the numbers frequenting the cliffs and rocks of that locality, at certain seasons, being truly astonishing. During summer the natives subsist chiefly on the birds captured by the rock-fowlers, and on the eggs of the various species which build in the rocks. It has been affirmed that during the fowling and egging seasons, out of the abundance of fowl and eggs that are taken in the island, there is a sufficient surplus, after amply supplying all the natives, to support *two thousand persons* besides!

The fowlers of St. Kilda are said to be the most intrepid and expert in the world: but it would appear that the Norwegian rock-fowlers perform even greater feats of daring and alertness, inasmuch as the rocks and precipices scaled by those adventurous fowlers are much higher and more stupendous than any in St. Kilda.[2]

When the fowling season commences in St. Kilda the native fowlers have a merry-making, and feast together, as of one fraternity, over the first productions of their adventures. At this meeting they arrange themselves into distinct parties (generally each of four persons) for the purpose of fowling. Each party has at least one fowling-rope, which should be about thirty fathoms in length.

A fowling-rope is an indispensable requisite for the operation; and was formerly considered the most valuable implement a man of substance could be possessed of in the island. It was looked upon almost in the character of an heirloom, and descendible through the family from generation to generation. It formed the first subject of bequest in the will of a St. Kildian, and, on intestacy, fell to the share of the eldest son. In default of male issue, on falling to a daughter's portion, it was reckoned equal in value to two of the best cows in the island.

This fowling-rope, upon which so high a value is set, is not made without considerable labour and expense, the material employed being raw cow-hide, salted and dressed for the purpose, and, when so prepared, the hide is cut into thongs of equal length, three of which on being closely woven or twisted together form a threefold rope of great strength, capable of sustaining considerable weight, and sufficiently durable to last through two generations. In this manner, with a succession of trios of the cow-hide thongs, the fowling-rope is made of the length required. The whole is then coated with sheep-skins (dressed in the same manner as the cow-hides), in order to preserve it from injury, to which it is constantly exposed on coming in contact with the sharp edges of the rocks. Trusting to the strength of a rope of this kind, and the care and skill of those who have the command of it, the practised fowlers of St. Kilda stalk about from rock to rock, and over precipices terrifying to behold, performing their feats of daring with grace as well as intrepidity. They go clown into the most impenetrable clefts and shelves of the rocks with apparent ease and delight; and they signal to their companions above by means of a string tied to the rope within reach of the fowler's hand.

The operations of rock-fowling are chiefly performed in the night-time; but the egging is done by daylight. The method by which the fowler captures his birds by night is very ingenious; it is as follows:—He clothes himself in garments as nearly resembling the colour of the rocks as possible, but upon his breast he wears a broad piece of white linen; when, having descended, by aid of the bird-rope, to some shelf on the rock where he has obtained a footing, he places himself in a position with his back to the rock near the roosts of the birds, where he remains perfectly still; the birds, mistaking the white on the fowler's breast for a resting-place in the rock, fly directly towards it, and endeavour to cling to it; when the fowler immediately takes them with his hand, and after wringing their necks suspends them to his girdle, or throws them in a heap at his feet. The fowler generally continues these operations throughout the whole night, and sometimes with astounding success—as many as four hundred fowl being sometimes taken by an expert fowler in one night.

When there is no room on the rock to lay the birds as they are taken the fowler, as soon as his belt or game-bag is full, ties the signal-line to it, and telegraphs to his companions to haul it up, which they do; and having secured the birds, instantly haul back the line to the fowler. But when there is space sufficient on the rock to deposit the birds as they are captured the fowler never signals, except in case of emergency, until the morning.

The St. Kildians have used this art of fowling in connection with the piece of white linen on the breast through many ages. It was purely the invention of the ancient natives of that island.

Besides the more costly and valuable fowling-rope already described the fowlers of St. Kilda use another made of horsehair, termed a rock-line. But this is of far less value, and is only about nine or ten fathoms in length. It is used in places less stupendous and less difficult of access than those explored by means of the principal rope.

St. Kilda is also a well-known resort of solan geese, and the St. Kildian fowlers are particularly expert in capturing them; but to such persecution are those birds subjected, that it is almost astonishing there are any left in the island.[1] They are objects of the fowlers' attacks at all seasons of the year. In the month of March, just before they begin to lay, the rock-fowlers seek them in the night-time, and creep upon them so stealthily that they snatch them from their roosts without disturbing others which may be roosting beside them. The fowler employs, besides, the very cunning stratagem of depositing the first captive goose, as soon as killed, among its living companions; the latter immediately begin to mourn over their departed friend with much grief and groaning, when the fowler, taking advantage of the mournful ceremony, secures many captives from among the mourners.[2] In these expeditions the fowlers climb over steep and dangerous rocks linked together in couples after the same manner as that pursued by the fowlers in Norway;[1] so that one, having climbed to a shelf, draws up his comrade by the rope which unites them; and in case of one of the two slipping or losing his hold, the other, by standing firm or holding on, checks the fall and saves the life of his companion, as in Alpine climbing.

In the month of May the fowlers climb and scale the rocks in the same way in pursuit of the eggs of solan geese; and about August and September they take the young ones (called 'goug'), which are then just ready to fly, and in prime condition for the table, being so redundantly fat, from the constant feeding of the parent birds, that they are, just at that particular age and season of the year, larger and heavier than the old birds. Macauley asserts that the fat on their breasts at that time is three inches in thickness. They are also well covered with valuable down, which is stripped from them after being killed, and they are then sent to market.

The young solan goose is quite a favourite dish of the St. Kildians, and at festive entertainments is the crowning delicacy of their humble board.

The rock-fowlers of St. Kilda also use gins, made of horsehair, for the purpose of taking birds on the rocks; and they use nooses of the same material, which they attach to the ends of light poles or fishing-rods, and reach over, at night, to opposite cliffs (otherwise inaccessible) and snatch birds off the ledges whilst at roost there, by quietly slipping the noose over their heads, and drawing it round their necks one at a time: in this manner they sometimes capture dozens of fowl in a few hours.[2]

The rocks of this island are allotted once in every three years, in exact proportions, among the inhabitants, according to the extent of land each person possesses: and this whether for the purposes of fishing or fowling. At the expiration of every three years, which terminates the tenancy, the allotments change hands; and any disputes which arise are finally decided by drawing lots. Encroachments upon a neighbour's rock are treated as serious offences, and punished with as much severity as a felony.

Some of the rocks which lie beyond the principal island are most difficult to land upon; the adventurous fowlers who approach them in boats incur very great risks, but nothing seems to daunt them, though they are in danger of staving their boat, and being swept off the rocks the instant a footing is obtained. They manage with extraordinary dexterity to effect a landing, which, though never a dry one, they boldly attempt, clinging to the rock with hands and feet, and often with their teeth besides, after leaping from the boat when at the top of a wave.

A singular method of fowling is used in Hirta, which is performed chiefly by females,[1] with the assistance of dogs specially trained to the pursuit. The only birds they capture in the manner about to be described are puffins, which burrow under ground with their beaks, and there deposit and hatch their eggs.

The maids of Hirta make early morning excursions on the beach, attended by a dog, which hunts the holes at the foot of the rocks and about the shore. Some of these dogs are so well trained that they never pass a hole containing a puffin's nest but they smell it out, and capture the old bird without killing it or breaking the eggs. In the cold weather, when these birds sit closely huddled together in large numbers in the deep holes and clefts of the rocks, on one of the little dogs being sent in it seizes the first bird by its wing, and proceeds to drag it out; the bird, to save itself from persecution, lays hold with its powerful beak of the wing of another, which, to save itself, seizes the next; this in like manner clings to its nearest neighbour, and so on, the dog continuing to drag them out steadily. In this way a whole string of puffins falls into the hands of the fowler, as every bird from first to last grasps the one nearest to it, and so all are dragged out one after another as if linked together. Thus, the wife or daughter of a family in the short time of an hour, or less, secures sufficient provision to supply for one day or more all the inmates of her household. Every family throughout the island has one at least of these little fowling-dogs. The breed of the animal is simply a mixture of the terrier and water-spaniel, and is sometimes so regularly trained to its duties, that it is sent unattended in search of puffins, when it goes about its business with the same sagacity as if its young mistress accompanied it. On a dog being sent on an errand of the kind it generally returns in a few minutes with a live puffin in its mouth; then, if required, it is sent on a second and third excursion, and so on, until sufficient are caught for the day's subsistence.[1]

And so during a considerable portion of the year the chief subsistence of many a family in the island consists of the flesh of puffins; and, during the egging season, of their eggs; whilst the feathers and down of these birds are of great use and value, both for domestic comforts and as an article of commerce.

---

[1] *Vide* 'History of St. Kilda.' By the Rev. Kenneth Macauley: A.D. 1764. Also Jacob son's 'History of the Faroe Islands.'

[2] *Supra*, chap, lxvii., 'Rock-fowling in Norway.'

[1] 'In some localities, as on the island-rock of St. Kilda and others of the Hebrides, the gannets congregate in vast numbers. Twenty-two thousand birds, besides immense numbers of eggs, are annually consumed in St. Kilda alone,

without seriously injuring the colony. The birds are still so numerous there that it is supposed they destroy annually a hundred millions of herrings.'—*The Sea-side Book*. By W. H. Harvey, M.D., 4th edition, p. 294: A.D. 1857.

[2] Yarrell, in his 'British Birds,' alludes to the remarkable tameness of solan geese whilst sitting upon their eggs; so tame, he says, as to allow themselves to be stroked with the hand. Such, however, is rather a dangerous experiment, as they are not all so tame; on the contrary, they are sometimes very fierce; and moreover are capable of inflicting a severe wound with their sharp and powerful beaks.

[1] *Supra*, chap, lxvii.

[2] This method of taking rock-birds is also practised in Siberia by the Kamtschadales.—*Infra*, chap. lxxiv.

[1] The maids of ancient Sparta were much employed in fowling.

[1] This method of fowling is also practised in several other rock-fowling localities, and is alluded to in the 'Fseroa Reserata.' *Vide* also 'Travels through Sweden, Norway, and Finmark,' by A. De Capell Brooke, M.A.

CHAPTER LXXI

WILD-FOWLING IN FEANCE

'Or in a darksome night,

Fires on the margin of the river light:

Struck with the dazzling flame, ne'er seen before,

Surprised, they slow approach the shining shore.'

THE fens of France, like those of England, have been drained and cultivated with considerable skill and industry. Their appearance, when viewed at a distance, is wooded and picturesque, most of them being planted with tastefully-arranged avenues of willow-trees; and whole districts being intersected with dykes and canals, varying in width from six to thirty yards, thus forming hundreds of little islands of rich and fertile soil, many of which are cultivated as market-gardens, and the products conveyed to neighbouring towns in *marais*-boats.

But some of the interior parts of the fens of France which have not been reached by the arm of husbandry are still in a swampy and uncultivated state, covered with sedges and rushes, thus presenting a wild appearance, and affording excellent haunts for water-fowl.[2]

In some of the wildest districts of the French fens numbers of wild-fowl are killed in winter by the marais-fowlers, who of late years have resorted almost exclusively to their guns, rather than the more captivating system of decoy, which in Picardy was formerly much in vogue.

At the present day there are only a few decoys in France employed upon the English system, though there are huttier's decoys innumerable, which will be treated of in the latter part of the present chapter.

Previously to the invention of guns, and improvements in the art of gunnery, the means employed by the ancient French fowler were similar in many respects to those of the English. He used nets, snares, springes, nooses, bird-lime, and such-like devices;[1] and we learn from a high authority upon French fowling[2] that decoys, as practised in England and Holland, were employed in various parts of France.

The most attractive method of wild-fowl shooting in France is that in which a little dog is used for the purpose of enticing the birds within range of the sportsman's gun; for this art the dog performs a similar part to that of an English decoy-piper,[3] being taught to obey its master's signs in silence, and to skip round reed-screens erected for the purpose on the banks of lakes or other resorts of wild-fowl.

The French sportsman, however, does not entice the birds up a decoy-pipe and capture them alive; but, having allured them within range of his gun, he thrusts the latter through a loophole in the screen, and fires into the midst of the paddling just as they turn tail to swim away. Sometimes two or three gunners are stationed behind the same screens, and when the birds are numerous they all fire at once.

This practice is attended with far inferior success to that of the quieter operations of the English decoyer. After the discharge of a gun every bird leaves the lake; and those which have once been enticed by the dog to approach the shore and then shot at are afterwards wary and distrustful, which makes their companions equally so. The practice is only moderately successful in the best fowling districts throughout the country.

Mr. O'Connor recommends those who may wish to see a French decoy, admirably arranged for wild-fowl shooting, with a reed-fence surrounding it, to pay a visit to a pond in the marais of Soubruie, occupied by M. Pierre Dewert, who lives upon an island, and supports himself by his exertions as a wildfowl shooter.[1]

In many parts of France little skiffs, somewhat resembling English gunning-punts, are used for wild-fowl shooting, the occupants lying flat down in the boat, and pushing it ahead with a pole furnished at the upper end with a ring or grommet, and at the other end with a forked iron. Some of these boats are fitted with guns as large as English punt-guns: with these the French fowlers often make highly successful shots.

A singular artifice for shooting wild-fowl in the night-time in France is that of enticing the birds within gun-range by means of a reflector (*réverbère*).

This deception is made to represent as well as it can the rising sun, at the appearance of which the birds assemble together and swim towards the shore, from which the rays of light are emitted. The reflector is neither more nor less than a copper dish, well polished, which, when the sport is pursued on the banks of a river, is suspended from the neck of one person, who also carries in his hand a caldron or pan containing oil and four or five lighted wicks. The caldron being held immediately below the reflector, bright rays of light are cast upon the water, which, if seen from afar by the wild-fowl, are so announced by their cries and quackings.

Immediately on hearing from the feathered tribe these indications of attraction the sportsman, together with the bearer of the reflector and caldron, accept them as a signal to observe strict silence and precaution. They walk very slowly and lightly in the direction of the birds, which at the same time are probably advancing towards the attraction. The sportsman stands in obscurity behind the bearer of the reflector; and as soon as he finds the birds are within range, and are sitting close together, he takes deliberate aim and fires his gun at them. The killed and wounded are then captured by the fowlers, who get into a boat and pursue them.

When this attraction is used on the banks of a pond or small space of water it may be performed by one person alone, in which case the reflector is suspended from a post or staff; and the caldron is placed upon the ground in front, at the necessary distance to throw the reflection at the required range on the water. Everything should be in readiness before lighting the wicks in the caldron; and the fowler should be cautious not to show himself between the light and the water, but immediately on lighting the wicks he should retire behind the reflector.

After shooting once it is useless to attempt it again on that night, in the same place; the fowler must, therefore, change his position to another spot, beyond the sound of his former discharge, where he may probably be again successful.

This method of wild-fowl shooting is much practised at Burgoyne and many other places on the continent of France.[1]

Another very general method of shooting wild-fowl in France is by firing from small huts, temporarily erected for the purpose in the fens, and on the margins of lakes, rivers, ponds, and such-like places, the resort of water-fowl. The sport is called '*la chasse à la hutte.*' These huts are built in the form of a beehive,[2] and generally among trees or brushwood, or in a bed of reeds. The little building is rudely constructed of turf, and covered with a light roof of dried reeds; or it is sometimes formed with branches of trees, and not infrequently entirely with reeds, or, indeed, of the roughest though readiest materials at hand. Two or three small apertures are left in front of the hut, immediately facing the water, and commanding a full view of the lake. Through these apertures the French fowler thrusts his gun and slaughters his victims. The entrance to the hut is in the rear.

The huts are sometimes constructed in such a manner that the level of the gun bears in a line only one foot higher than the surface of the water. This is done by simply digging a hole for the foundation of the hut, and from these very effective shots are sometimes made. The guns generally used for the purpose are as large as can be fired from the shoulder without injury; that is to say, guns carrying from two to five ounces of shot at a charge.

In front of the hut, and parallel with the sides, or a little wide of them, small posts are driven into the ground, to which strings are attached, drawn tight, and secured to similar posts, also placed in parallel position, about a hundred yards distant. To each of these strings live tame ducks are secured. These are the 'call-birds,' intended, by their incessant quacking, to entice the wild ones to alight among them, when, if they do, the huttier, from his place of concealment, scatters a charge of shot straight up the water, between the two strings of call-birds; the effect of which is to kill numbers of the wild ones, without injury to the call-birds on either side beyond seriously alarming them, and causing them to chafe their legs and bodies with the strings in their endeavours to free themselves from their fetters.

The time of day for this murderous sport is twilight, moonlight, and day-dawn, it being seldom that the huttier is able to make a shot by daylight.

When the water chosen by the huttier is shallow, instead of securing the call-ducks to a string drawn from post to post, each call-bird is tethered to a separate post or stake. These are carefully placed so as to leave a clear centre, about twice the width of a cart-way, for reception of the wild-fowl, and in order that such may be shot without injury to the tame ones. Duckweed is cultivated and permitted to grow in profusion about the water, in the central track where the wild-fowl are enticed to resort.

The number of call-birds generally employed to each hut are five—two mallards and three ducks. A few skins of ducks, stuffed with straw, are often interspersed with the live fowl, when the huttier's decoy-ducks are few in number.

As soon as daylight appears the huttier leaves the decoy, takes up the call-birds from the strings, and, having placed them in a basket, which he slings across his shoulder, he walks off to his cottage, returning to the shooting-hut again in the afternoon, in time to fix his call-birds to their stations before the hour of evening-flight. The poor captives are frequently in their fetters all night long.

In shallow water, instead of performing his operations in a boat, the huttier provides himself with a pair of water-boots, and wacles about the decoy, the spot chosen for which is generally shallow, so that he may wade at pleasure knee-deep in the water, to pick up his birds after shooting.

The French markets depend chiefly upon the supplies furnished them by the huttiers; in some seasons the supply is very abundant.

A number of fowling-huts are scattered over the *marais* districts, and when the birds are plentiful the huttiers keep them constantly flying from one decoy to another during the night, the quacking of the decoy-ducks enticing the wild ones to alight. A huttier sometimes makes three, four, or five shots in one night. A more simple method of shooting wildfowl cannot be imagined. No skill is required; the veriest *nigaud* might kill his dozen birds with the first trigger of his life; and the old huttier could kill a score with his eyes blindfolded.

The fens and waters of favourite or extensive resorts of water-fowl are let to the huttiers in convenient portions. Many of these men obtain their chief means of subsistence from the pursuit.

Wild-duck and teal are the only birds they kill in great numbers; widgeon do not often drop to the enticements of the call-birds.

When the huttier has made a good shot during the night, and has reason to believe that some winged or wounded birds have escaped him, he proceeds with a dog on the next morning to hunt the reeds and rushes about his aquatic domain, and thus secures them without difficulty.

On some of the French lakes wild-fowl are particularly numerous, more especially in Picardy and the lakes of Gratte-mare and Peronne; the latter is peculiarly well adapted for the sport, being very shallow, and intersected by numerous small islands and beds of reeds and rushes, where hundreds of wild-fowl annually breed in summer; the huttiers taking care to preserve the broods of ducklings[1] with as much care and concern as are used by the English decoyman.

Other artifices of French sportsmen to get within range of wild-fowl, though of ancient origin, are still employed in some parts of France; these are the Stalking Horses, the artificial Cow (*la Vache artificielle*), and the Walking Hut, or *la Hutte ambulante*, the latter an arrangement of boughs and sprigs of shrubs on a light circular frame, like a lady's crinoline, only longer, but certainly not any *larger* in circumference than those commonly worn by English ladies. Concealed from observation in a bower of the kind, the French fowler stalks about the *marais* and other open places the resort of wild-fowl, halting occasionally when birds are near or suspicious of his movements, and for the purpose of taking deliberate aim with his fowling-piece.

In many parts of France large coverts of coots frequent the open waters, and, from the habit which these birds have of taking up a central position in large ponds or lakes, they are (at least to the French sportsman) quite unapproachable; but few are killed, and those only on such occasions as *grandes battues*, when, according to preconcerted arrangements, at a precise time of day parties embark in boats from different banks of the lake, each advancing gradually towards the centre of the water occupied by the coots; and so these unfortunate victims ultimately find themselves surrounded on all sides by the enemy, when, escape being impossible, they rise in the air, the boats having closed upon them, and they are then immediately assailed in every direction with murderous artillery. The attack generally ends in a dispute, it being almost impossible to divide the spoils of such a *chasse* satisfactorily.

Professor Yarrell[1] gives an account of scoters and other ducks being attacked *en grande battue*, in a similar manner, according to arrangements directed by the Mayor of the *Commune*.

697

FRENCH GAME LAWS AFFECTING THE SPORT OF WILD-FOWLING.

Before hunting or shooting Game, Birds of passage, or waterfowl, in France, it is necessary to procure a *Permis de chasse*, or *porte d'arme*, which is analogous to an English game certificate, or Gun-licence. It may be obtained on application at the office of the Mayor in any town, whose duty, though he cannot grant it himself, is to transmit the application to the *Prefet* of the *Département;* and that official, if all is satisfactory, will immediately issue the *Permis* to the *Bureau des contributions directes* in the town where the application was first made; it will then be delivered to the applicant on payment of *twenty-five francs*.

Private individuals have no right to demand from a sportsman, the production of his *Permis de chasse*; the only persons invested with that authority are the Mayor, his assistant or deputy, the *Garde-champêtre* or *Forestier*, and the *Gendarmes*.

In the event of a sportsman being found by either of these officials shooting without a *Permis de chasse* he will be taken before the Mayor of the *Commune* in which the offence was committed. This *Dignitaire* is generally a village farmer, who exercises a sort of summary jurisdiction.

The *Permis de chasse* confers the personal privilege of hunting and shooting throughout the entire kingdom of France for *one year*, computed from the day of its date.

The *Prefets* of the several departments are required to determine by formal decrees, duly promulgated at least ten days previously, the precise day on which the *chasse* shall be opened, and also that on which it shall be closed. Shooting and hunting are strictly prohibited at any other time than whilst the *chasse* is open.

The *Prefets* also determine: '1. The proper time for shooting birds of passage (except quails) and water-fowl. 2. The time during which water-fowl may be shot in the *marais* districts, and upon ponds and rivers.'

It is also provided that the *Prefets* shall make proper regulations 'to prevent hunting and shooting while the ground is covered with snow.'

The punishment inflicted upon persons infringing these laws is fine and imprisonment, and the confiscation of the gun, nets, engines, or implements employed.

---

[2] *Vide* 'Introduction to the Field Sports of France.' By R. O'Connor, Esq.: A.D. 1846.

[1] Olina on Fowling. See also 'Traitté de toute Sorte de Chasse et de Pêche,' before referred to.

[3] Selincourt. And *vide ante*, p. 30.

[3] *Vide ante*, p. 59.

[1] O'Connor's 'Introduction to the Field Sports of France.'

[1] *Vide* 'Aviecptologie Franҫhise,' p. 43, par C. Kresz Ainé; Paris, 1854.

[2] O'Connor.

[1] In France half-grown wild ducks are called *halbrans*—a word derived from the German tongue, and used to designate the young of the wild-duck.

[1] *Vide* 'History of British Birds,' vol. iii.

CHAPTER LXXII

WILD-FOWLING IN AMERICA

'A weary waste!—

We passed through pools, where mussel, clam, and whelk

Clove to their gravelly beds; o'er slimy rocks,

Ridgy and dark, with dank fresh fuci green,

Where the prawn wriggled, and the tiny crab

Slid sideway from our path, until we gain'd

The land's extremest point, a sandy jut,—

Narrow, and by the weltering waves begirt

Around; and there we laid us down and watch'd,

While from the west the pale moon disappear'd,

Pronely, the sea-fowl and the coming dawn.'

The Fowler. By DELTA.

WILD-FOWL are, probably, as numerous in America as in
any quarter of the globe. Some of the States of that country

are most favourably adapted for their reception.

The drowned lands of Orange County, the meadows of Chatham and Pine Brook, the Passaic and its tributaries, before the modern system of draining and embanking, offered the fairest possible retreats for wild-fowl. In those parts thousands of acres of luxuriant soil were annually covered with shallow water; and those inundated flats were sometimes literally blackened with all the varieties of wild-fowl known throughout the land.[1]

But it is not in those parts of America only that wild-fowl are so numerous. They abound in all the States of the country, wherever there are lakes or moist feeding-grounds to which they can resort for food and shelter.[2]

In Canada wild-fowl are in great variety and abundance. Immense skeins of wild-geese are sometimes seen almost daily in some parts of Canada during the latter part of October and through the month of November.[3]

In the province of Ontario (late Canada West) the most extensive grounds for wild-fowl shooting are those of Long Point and St. Clair. The St. Clair river runs from Lake Huron at Sarnia down to Lake St. Clair, and forms one of the links of the great chain of lakes and rivers which extend from the seaboard into the far North-West, beyond the Red River settlement, a distance probably of two thousand miles. Hurson's Island, about thirty miles down the St. Clair from Sarnia, and five from Lake St. Clair, is a favourite resort of wild-fowl shooters, and the country around is admirably adapted to the sport. The marshes are clothed with grass, reeds, and sedges, and divided into innumerable islands, studded with pools, creeks, and rills, affording most inviting resorts to the web-footed species; and some parts of the St. Clair flats during the proper season abound in snipe.

The neighbourhood of the Champlain Lake is at some seasons frequented by extraordinary numbers of water-fowl of every species. The fowlers there make huts, on and near the water, with branches of trees, placing stuffed decoy birds about the spot they wish the wild ones to resort to. When the latter alight the fowlers shoot them; and sometimes they shoot at them as they fly, if they approach within range: after which the natives get into their canoes and gather them up.

Excellent sport may sometimes be had by proceeding on moonlight nights in a small canoe; when, by gliding noiselessly amongst the islets of the lake, the birds may be suddenly surprised within easy range of a shoulder-piece. The fowlers have also a method of catching them in nets, which they spread upon the surface of the water at the entrance to some of the rivers. Wild-fowl have been found so abundant in the vicinity of the Champlain Lake that one traveller states, 'in a word, we ate nothing but water-fowl for fifteen days.'[1]

Long Point, on Lake Erie, is detached from the mainland

about eight miles. From Long Point a succession of sand-bars, forming islands, run twenty miles into the lake, with marshes on the one side, chiefly beds of wild rice and high reeds, which are the resort of countless water-fowl. The flight-shooting when the wind sets in from the lake for half an hour is magnificent. Stationed in a punt among the reeds, near a rice-bed, one may fire as fast as possible, and bag from fifty to sixty wild-ducks in the course of an evening. Sir Richard Levinge[2] says it is the best place in Canada for wild-fowl shooting, the next being Ballidoon, near Lake St. Clair.

The marshes on either side of the Chippeway Creek are full of snipes in the months of September and October; and from the Falls in a direct line along the left of the road to Queens-town, and in the Cedars, in the vicinity of this village, woodcocks are to be found in the same months in considerable quantities.

At the mouth of the Miramichi, and on the whole northeastern coast of New Brunswick, there is abundance of every kind of wild-fowl. Sir Richard Levinge also informs us that the immense flights of geese, ducks, and other migratory birds which annually pass over to the northernmost parts of America, to breed during the summer season, remain on this coast for some time, returning to the south in the autumn. Those who have read Audubon's work may form some idea of the countless thousands of birds which constitute 'a flock' on these shores. But those only who have seen these wonderful collections of waterfowl, and heard their surprising clamour, can form any idea of their extent, and, one might almost say, grandeur, for they are indeed wonderful.[1]

Wild-Fowl Shooting on Lake Champlain by Moonlight

Wild-fowl also breed in large numbers on the small uninhabited islands of the Gruff of Mexico; though their nests are often plundered by persons who go in quest of their eggs in boats; and who frequently return with two or three bushels, the result of a few hours' work.

Wild-ducks, canvas-backs, and others arrive in the Susquehanna about the first week in October, and they generally remain in the neighbourhood of the Chesapeake until the middle of the following March.

That incomparable bird, the *Wood* or *Summer Duck*, is well known in Canada. Dr. Boss[2] says it is without exception the most beautiful of all the Canadian ducks, its whole plumage being beautifully variegated with purple, green, chestnut, white, and ash-colour. It builds its nest in a hollow tree, or on a branch overhanging the water, in which it lays twelve or thirteen eggs of a yellowish white colour. The wood-duck is easily domesticated, and becomes quite tame, breeding and soon acquiring all the habits of the common duck.

The Canvas-back Duck is a bird of delicious flavour, particularly when it has fed and fattened on the wild-celery grass of the Susquehanna, the roots of which the canvas-back and other wild-ducks are very fond of. This grass grows in abundance under water on the mud and shoals of the Susquehanna and other rivers that empty into the Chesapeake. The root of the grass is about three inches long, and terminates in a small white bulb, in colour and flavour like celery. Canvas-back ducks, pochards, and other wild-fowl tear it up and feed greedily on the roots. The canvas-back breeds in Northern Canada, but, according to Dr. Boss, is becoming quite rare in Ontario, where a few years since it was abundant.[3]

TOLING WILD-FOWL.

The art of toling wild-fowl as practised in America is curious and interesting, and bears a close resemblance to one of the principal stratagems employed at the English decoys. What the origin of the term may be we do not know, unless it implies simply a *death-knell*, for such it assuredly assumes to those birds which approach within range of the secreted sportsman. The singular proceeding is said to have been first introduced upwards of fifty years ago, near Havre de Grace, in Maryland; and, according to traditional testimony, the art was accidentally discovered by a sportsman whilst patiently lying in ambush, watching a paddling of wild ducks that were a little beyond the range of his gun. Whilst in a state of doubt and anxiety as to whether they would approach near enough to be shot he suddenly observed them raise their heads and swim towards the shore, apart from his ambuscade; and whilst wondering at the cause of so strange a proceeding his attention was directed to a fox skipping about on the shore, and evidently enticing the clucks to approach. The accidental discovery of so weak a point in the nature of the feathered tribe led the sportsman to turn it to his own advantage, and thence arose the curious art of toling. To practise it successfully the sportsman requires simply the services of a dog, which he uses in a similar manner to that of a piper, as employed at an English decoy.

For the purposes of toling, the American sportsman erects blinds or screens on the margin of some lake the resort of wild-fowl. When wild-fowl are in sight upon the water he with his dog takes up a position behind the screens, and by throwing chips of wood or small pebbles up and down the shore he keeps the dog in active motion, so as to attract the attention of the birds and induce them to swim towards the shore within a few yards of the screens, which if they do the sportsman immediately discharges his fowling-piece at them, and sometimes kills large numbers at a shot. The principal things to be observed are a strict silence, and to keep the dog constantly in motion and all the time in sight of the ducks. The little animal should be encouraged to skip and bound over the rocks or stones in front of the screens, and to flourish his tail about with playful vivacity. He must never bark, for that would alarm the fowl and cause them to fly away immediately.

Red or chestnut-coloured dogs, with long bushy tails, are best for the purpose of toling; the nearer they approach in colour and appearance to a fox the better.

Generally, as soon as the birds see the dog skipping about on the shore they stretch out their necks as if struck by an irresistible impulse, which, either through fear, curiosity, or revenge, attracts them towards him; and so they approach nearer and nearer, until within range of the fowler's gun.

The least interruption, as the movement of a boat or human form, within sight or sound of the eyes and ears of the birds, spoils the toler's sport, by inducing the birds to swim or fly away. Their whole curiosity must be riveted to the one attractive object—the dog. If their attention be diverted the charm becomes broken, and the dog ceases to have any influence over them: when, as if a curtain suddenly fell from their eyes, they become awake to surrounding dangers and no longer yield to canine enticement. One dog only at a time can be used successfully: if two are started at once, the birds take alarm and fly.

A dog perfectly trained to this sport is seldom to be met with, though such an animal is a most valuable creature, and to a fowler is truly worth its weight in gold. When the dog is thoroughly awake to its master's signs and wishes the proceeding of toling wild-ducks is a highly interesting one. As the clucks approach, the well-trained dog gradually lessens the height of his jumps and bounds; and when they advance within range he almost crawls upon the ground.

Herbert, in his 'Field Sports of America,' states that he has seen thousands of wild-fowl under the influence of the toler swimming in a solid mass direct for the object; 'and by removing the dog farther into the grass, they have been brought within fifteen feet of the bank.'

An imperfectly trained dog causes the fowler much anxiety. When first started in pursuit of the chips the dog pays no attention to the ducks, because they are then perhaps four or five hundred yards off; but as they approach nearer the toler cares less and less about the chips, and casts whining and longing looks at the clucks, as if eager to bound into the water and attempt to seize them. It sometimes happens, after the ducks have been enticed within sixty or seventy yards of the blinds, that the dog refuses to run after the chips, preferring rather to stop and gaze at the birds; exhibiting all the while a whining anxiety, as he expects every moment that his master will fire.[1] This impatience on the part of the dog frequently spoils the sport, and induces the fowler to fire before the birds are near enough, when he probably kills only two or three; whereas, had the dog toled them a few yards nearer, he might have slaughtered a dozen or more.

It would seem that a dog could never be trained to perform his part at toling so steadily and accurately as an English decoy-piper, because of the discharge of the gun which is used in toling, and which so excites a dog that the animal is always expecting it when birds are near. But, as no gun is fired at the English decoy, the fowler there has his dog under perfect control, free from that anxious excitement, though the ducks approach within a few yards.

A dog trained to the practice of toling should never be suffered to retrieve the birds from the water, or it will always be anxious to rush in after live ones, and spoil the toler's sport. A Newfoundland dog, or a retriever, should be kept within hail or trained to lie perfectly still behind the blinds during the operations of toling; and as soon as the fowler has discharged his gun the toling dog should be kept back whilst the other retrieves the birds.

The spot usually selected for toling is one where the birds have not been much disturbed; where the fowler can command a sufficiently extended space to preserve it from the interruption of all intruders, and where there is water enough for the birds to swim freely and approach close to the shore. They cannot be toled into shallow water.

The best time to shoot is, when the birds have satisfied their curiosity, have turned tail, and are in the act of swimming away. The sportsman should never shoot as they approach with their breasts towards, him, though they be ever so close. He will be enabled to kill twice the number by waiting until they swim or fly from him with their tails towards the gun.

There are generally two or more fowlers behind the same blind during the process of toling: the one who manœuvres the dog gives the signal for firing. If the fowl are numerous the sportsmen distribute themselves widely apart, so that neither of them should shoot at the same birds. When the fowler is alone behind the screens, and has succeeded in toling the birds within range, he is sometimes enabled to start the dog in such a manner as to huddle them together: he then fires into the most crowded part of the flight or paddling, and makes a very effective shot.

Young ducks are very easily toled. It is of great advantage to the fowler when there are such among others in the paddling: the old ones generally follow them. Sometimes a few only, as a dozen or more, part of a much larger number, may be toled; but more frequently the whole paddling, be it ever so extensive, swims in at once; and they have been seen to exhibit uncontrollable curiosity by rushing ahead in such an eager manner that those in the rear fly over the heads of the leading birds, as if anxiously endeavouring to get ashore first. Although this is not a usual scene, it is a well-authenticated fact.

In the absence of a dog they may sometimes be *toled* by simply waving a small red flag or handkerchief, but they seldom approach so near the shore by this stratagem as by that of the dog.[1]

It is stated by those who are familiar with this sport that the canvas-back ducks and pochards are among the easiest captives to the toler; but the two species appear to have distinct peculiarities: the canvas-back responds to the enticements of the dog with head erect, a wild look, and body sitting buoyantly on the surface. The pochard, on the contrary, appears unconscious of danger, keeps its head low and body much sunk in the water.[2]

Great numbers of wild-fowl are killed in America by the singular stratagem of toling. The time of day best adapted to the sport is, from sunrise till nine o'clock in the morning, though they may generally be toled at any hour of the day, and they are sometimes toled on bright moonlight nights; but then a white dog must be used instead of a red one; or, in absence of a white one, a clog of another colour may be employed, by covering it with a white coating. Wild-fowl may also be toled with a white flag by moonlight.

In America every experienced wild-fowl shooter is supposed to be familiar with the art of toling wild-fowl.

THE AMERICAN SCOW AND BATTERY.

The *Scow*, or American shooting-yacht, is a vessel about ten tons burthen, and of peculiar form and construction. Although answering in some respects the purposes of an English shooting-yacht, it is not used for chasing wild-fowl with a stanchion-gun; indeed, it appears to be totally unfit for such a purpose. The most approved dimensions of a Scow are—forty feet in length, by nine feet beam. In form the Scow is flat-bottomed, with straight, upright, but low wall-like sides; and rigged in a similar manner to some of the Thames river-barges, with sprit-sail and fore-sail. The Scow is also fitted with lee-boards, which, in deep water, enable it to be sailed very close to the wind; but in shallow water it makes much leeway. Setting-poles and large sweeps also form part of the equipment of a Scow, in order that the occupants on board may not be left on the mud or become becalmed in light winds.

The Scow carries no ballast beyond her necessary equipment, which is somewhat extensive; the whole of the space abaft the mast is occupied with the battery, or sunk-box, used for wildfowl shooting apart from the Scow, as will be explained presently. Piled in heaps abaft the battery, and on each side of the decks, are numbers of decoys, or wooden ducks, each fitted with a cord and weight at the end, which serves as anchor and cable to the wooden imitation. The cords are carefully wound about the decoys, and fastened with a slip-knot, so as not to become entangled with others, but to be ready for instant service. In addition to this cumbrous armament, the Scow tows at her stern two large flat-bottomed boats, termed 'yawls:' these are used for towing, anchoring, and arranging the battery, when launched from the Scow.

Bulkheads divide the fore part of the vessel from the aft; the interior of the space before the mast being furnished as a cabin, with stove, sleeping-berths, ammunition lockers, and other fittings necessary to the comfort of the hardy sportsmen, who are frequently absent on wild-fowling excursions in the Scow several days, and sometimes weeks.[1]

The fowlers having arrived at their destination, and anchored the Scow in some quiet bay or remote space of water where the wild-fowl resort, the battery is lowered down over the sides of the vessel with very great caution, or it gets filled with water in the performance. On being safely launched, the floating wings which are attached to the sides of the machine are unfolded, and the guards or wash-streaks turned up. Several pigs of iron-ballast are then placed in the bottom, in order to sink the frame of the battery upon a level with the surface of the water, the floating wings preventing its being swamped in ordinary weather; a platform is then placed over the ballast in the bottom of the battery, and a blanket, rug, or a little straw being spread over the platform, the machine is ready for the reception of its solitary occupant, who, after taking his guns on board, with ammunition and other requisites, casts off the rope by which it is held to the Scow, and the battery is then taken in tow by the flat-bottomed yawls to the spot chosen for the sport, where it is anchored fore and aft. The stools and dummy decoy-ducks are then placed in a judicious manner around the battery by those in the yawls. Some fowlers are very fastidious as to the disposal and adjustment of the decoys; they should ride freely, so as not to come in contact with each other. These dummies, to the number of one hundred and fifty or two hundred, cover a large space of water; they are placed principally at the stern of the battery, and a few of the lightest on each of the wings. Several wooden heads of decoys are permanently fixed on pins on the deck of the battery; these are painted in imitation of red-heads, black-heads, and a few bald-pates. The outermost dummy, or that anchored in the rear of the others farthest from the group, is generally in imitation of an old canvas-back duck, and is facetiously termed 'the toler.' Some of the dummies are made to imitate the living fowl so admirably that they appear, when kept in motion by the ripples of the water, like veritable live ducks. When the decoys are all anchored and the battery fixed, the men in the yawls pull back to the Scow, which remains at anchor some distance apart from the battery, and the fowler is left alone to his operations. The box or interior of the battery is not more than eighteen or twenty inches in depth, but is sufficiently commodious to receive the fowler, and enable him to lie down at full length on the platform. In such a position he is almost invisible to every object on the surface of the water; he shoots at the fowl with a large shoulder-piece when they approach and offer a fair chance.

Sometimes he allows the fowl to alight and swim in among the decoys before shooting; at others he fires at them on the wing as they fly overhead. The fowler is enabled to load his guns in safety on board the battery, but immediately after shooting, the men who watch his actions from the deck of the Scow proceed in the yawls to gather up the slain and chase the cripples.[1] The battery is generally fixed of an evening, and the fowler's sport is sometimes continued throughout the night, but his best chance is at dawn of day. It is only when the water is smooth that the guards or wash-streaks are turned down level with the surface of the water. On a sudden breeze springing up, or rough water flowing around, the battery is in peril of being sunk, in which case, in the event of the yawls not being at hand, it becomes necessary for the fowler to throw the iron-ballast overboard to lighten his perilous machine and enable it to ride more buoyantly until assistance arrives.

Taking up the stools and towing the battery, with its ponderous frame and accompaniments, is a work requiring some time and labour in performance. Each of the two hundred decoys, with its leaden weight, has to be taken up separately, the cord carefully wound about it, and the whole stowed away in the yawl. There are two occupants to each yawl, one to manage the boat during the process of collecting the decoys, and the other to take them up. The fowler in the battery collects the few dummies which may be near the wings of the machine; he also turns up the guards, and assists as far as he can in the tedious operations.

Many persons who pursue the diversion of wild-fowl shooting in a Scow do so for profit, and supply the Canadian and American markets with the results of their sport. The principal channels for shooting with the Scow are the Shematagan, the Chenal Ecarte, and the Baswood.

Such are the proceedings connected with the American method of fowling with the Scow and Sunken Battery.[2]

OTHER METHODS OF WILD-FOWLING IN AMERICA.

The manner of punting as practised on the Delaware and some other parts of America is very remarkable, if we may judge from Wilson's description of the artifices employed on the Delaware, and other rivers in that country, for the purpose of getting within range of the birds. He speaks of painted wooden ducks being used as decoys, and, it appears, in a very extraordinary manner.[1] Sometimes the American punt is loaded with stones, in order to bring the gunwales down nearly upon a level with the surface of the water, and, with a projecting framework, on which several painted wooden ducks are fixed, the laden craft is sculled ahead by the punter with a small oar. When employed by daylight this system of punting is not objected to, but when pursued by night it is considered so destructive, that very reprehensible and illegal attempts have been made by unprincipled fowlers to put it down. On the Chesapeake, some years ago, the use of the swivel-gun by a successful fowler became so unpopular, that he was compelled for his own personal safety to abandon its use;[2] but notwithstanding, there are at the present clay many American waters on which the punter enjoys uninterruptedly his sport, and almost invariably with very great success.

Excellent flight-shooting ('slaking') maybe had in many parts of America, more especially in Susquehanna and in the rivers and creeks which flow into the Chesapeake. Spesutia Island is also a noted spot for wild-fowl shooting, as indeed are many other parts of both Americas.

Pochards, and such other fowl as obtain their food at night by diving, are captured, in some parts of America, by means of gilling-nets; these are placed under water, in the evening, in the feeding-haunts of the birds; so that, when they dive for their food, their heads, feet, or wings become entangled in the net and they are drowned. The fowler, having judiciously placed his nets over-night, on taking them up next morning frequently finds several pairs of pochards entangled in his snare.

It is mentioned by Wilkes, in his 'Narrative of the United States Exploring Expedition,' that in the course of his travels on the Nisqually and Columbia River he was informed that in the neighbourhood of Protection Island the Indians suspend nets at night on long poles along the shore, for taking the wildfowl that frequent those parts in great numbers. The nets are set up on the poles at night, at which time the geese search those grounds for food; fires are then lighted, which alarm the birds, and cause them to fly against the nets, by which they are thrown upon the ground, where, before they have time to recover themselves, they are caught and killed.[1]

---

[1] *Vide* Herbert's 'Field Sports in the United States:' A.D. 1848.

[2] 'In every region of the United States, from the rock-girdled, pine-embosomed lakelets of Maine and the Eastern States, to the limestone pools of the Pennsylva-nian Alleghanies, to the limpid basins set in the oak-openings of Michigan and Illinois, to the gleaming waters that lie unsheltered from the sun's brightest beams in the centre of boundless prairies, all of which, in their proper seasons, are absolutely alive with wild-fowl of every description.'—*Herberts Field Sports.*

[3] 'The Birds of Canada,' by Alexander Milton Ross, M.D., &c., 1872.

[1] *Vide* 'Travels in Canada,' by the Baron Lahontan.

² 'Echoes from the Backwoods.'

¹ 'Echoes from the Backwoods,' by Sir Richard G. A. Levinge, Bart., 1859.

² 'The Birds of Canada,' by Alexander Milton Ross, M.D., 2nd edition, 1872.

³ 'The Birds of Canada,' by Dr. A. M. Ross, 2nd edition, 1872.

¹ 'There are few dogs gain celebrity in this practice; they generally become too fond of the ducks, and either stop to look at them as they approach the shore or lie down; in either case your sport is spoiled.'—*The Dog and the Sportsman.* By J. S. Skinner, Philadelphia: A.D. 1845.

¹ Mr. Skinner says of the art of toling: 'Ducks act very strangely sometimes. I have seen a dog play without effect at one spot, when, by moving a short distance to another blind, the same ducks would run in to him as fast as they could swim. At other times I have seen them take no notice of a dog, when they would run immediately in to a red silk handkerchief tied to the end of a ramrod, and kept in constant motion on the outside and in front of your blind.'—*The Bog and Sportsman.* By J. S. Skinner.

² It will be remembered that, although the pochard defies

the English fowler to capture it in the decoy-pipe, it may be easily enticed along with other fowl to the mouth of the pipe, but it always beats a retreat under water. (*Supra*, p. 82.) The American toler gives it no chance of returning, but greets it with a charge of shot.

[1] Mr. Klapp, speaking of the cabin of an American Scow, says: 'It was well pitched, so as to be water-tight, and was entered by a small scuttle with a slide; here the fowler cooked, ate, slept, kept tally of his game, manufactured the heads and necks of decoys, cut his gun-wads, spun his yarns, drank his grog or coffee, and kept care outside—from October until April—during the severest season of the year.'—*Krider's Sporting Anecdotes*, by Klapp.

[1] 'In the year 1838 a law was passed in the State prohibiting the use of batteries. Eor a short time it was respected; but the gunners who depend on waterfowl shooting for a great part of their living considered it such an invasion of their rights, that they defied it: at first shooting with masks, at the same time threatening to shoot the informer, should one be found. They finally laid aside their masks, and the law became a dead letter, and has since been repealed.—*Field Sports in the United States*, by Frank Forester. 1848.

[2] The amateur fowler who wishes to pursue the subject farther may consult with, advantage 'Krider's Sporting

Anecdotes,' by II. M. Klapp, 1853; and 'Field Sports of the United States,' by Frank Forester, 2 vols. 1848.

¹ 'Sometimes eight or ten painted wooden ducks are fixed on a frame in various swimming postures, and secured to the bow of the gunner's skiff, projecting before it in such a manner that the weight of the frame sinks the figures to their proper depth; the skiff is then dressed with sedge or coarse grass in an artful manner as low as the water's edge, and under cover of this, which appears like a party of ducks swimming by a small island, the gunner floats down sometimes to the very skirts of a whole congregated multitude, and pours in a destructive and repeated fire of shot among them. In winter, when detached pieces of ice are occasionally floating in the river, some of the gunners on the Delaware paint their whole skiff or canoe white, and laying themselves flat at the bottom, with their hand over the side, silently managing a small paddle, direct it imperceptibly into or near a flock, before the ducks have distinguished it from a floating mass of ice, and generally do great execution among them.'—Wilson's *American Ornithology*, vol. iii. p. 142.

² 'Paddling upon them, by night or day, drives the birds from their places of resort, and, although practised to some extent on Bush River, is highly disapproved of by persons shooting from points. For the last three years a man has been occupied on this stream with a gun of great size, fixed on a

swivel in a boat; and the destruction of game on their feeding flats has been immense; but so unpopular is the plan, that many schemes have been privately proposed of destroying his boat and gun; and he has been fired at with balls so often, that his expeditions are at present confined to the night.'—*Field Sports in the United States*, by Frank Forester. 1848.

[1] Vol. iv. p. 298.

CHAPTER LXXIII

PERSIAN METHODS OF CAPTURING WILD-FOWL

'Ah, wretched me!
These men are bird-catchers.'

Translation from Aristophanes.

WILD-FOWL are particularly abundant in some parts of Persia, especially in the extensive tracts of wild and uncultivated swamps which skirt the shores of the Caspian Sea. Thousands of coots and other water-fowl are annually bred there; in addition to which, innumerable flights of migratory fowl visit those parts in the winter season.

The fowlers of Persia have some very primitive notions of the art of capturing wild-fowl alive; others which are peculiar, and different to those generally employed in European nations.

In the neighbourhood of the lakes and swamps they use long nets made of very fine thread, which they suspend in the air at an elevation of several feet above the surface of the water, by the aid of long poles thrust into the mud, and standing in perpendicular positions about the lake. The nets are not placed in line, but in various directions, so as to form a sort of labyrinth, and intercept the flight of the birds in every direction. A number of live decoy-ducks are stationed upon the water, below the nets, and secured by their legs to stakes or a sunken weight. Wild-fowl flying over these at night are attracted by the callings and quackings of the decoy-ducks, and induced to alight on the water and join their supposed companions; when, on swooping in flight, they are caught by the neck in the meshes of the net,[1] or, on striking suddenly against it, they fall fluttering into the purse or lower folds of the net, from which they cannot escape.

The proceedings of the Persian fowler succeed best on dark and stormy nights: they are impracticable by daylight, moonlight, or at any other time than when the darkness is sufficient to obscure the nets from observation. The Persian fowler, by this means, is sometimes enabled to take ten or fifteen wild-ducks during the night, unaided by any other assistants than his decoy-birds. Numbers of wild-fowl are thus captured during the season, in the lakes and swamps which abound along the coasts both of Gheelaun and Mauzunderoon.[2]

Another of the fowler's arts employed in the Persian fens is that of spreading a large net at the brink of a pool or on a *marais*; and, by means of a cord and flexible staff, raising it to a perpendicular position, but so that on a slight pull it falls, and covers a large space of ground. The fowler, having suspended his net, conceals himself in reeds, rushes, or other ambuscade, taking care to keep the leading cord in connection with the net taut, and looped to a stake by his side. A few decoy-fowl are stationed outside the immediate scope of the net, and the fowler, on discovering that a number of wild ones are within reach of the meshes of his snare, by casting off the cord by which it is held in its upright position, it suddenly falls, or is drawn over such birds as are within range, which, on attempting to escape, thrust their heads through the meshes, and are thus completely ensnared.[3] This method is practised by twilight or moonlight, rather than by daylight or in darkness.

Another device of the Persian fowler, and which may be considered the most ingenious of the three, though it can only be performed on dark nights, is that in which three persons embark in a small canoe, one of whom sits at the stern, whose duty it is to devote his whole attention to the management and steering of the boat; another, generally a boy, occupies a position in the waist of the canoe, holding in one hand a circular plate of bell-metal, upon which he has to keep up a rapid succession of strokes with a small staff; the third occupant stands at the prow of the canoe, close beside a curiously constructed apparatus formed of felt and wool; but having a firm and fire-proof hearth, on which a small fire is kept burning during fowling operations, the fuel consisting of cotton stuff or tow, steeped in naphtha.

The apparatus thus fitted is placed in the bows of the canoe, and a reflector is fixed to a socket at the back of the machine, in such a position that the light from the burning naphtha is cast directly in front of the boat, the sides and back regions being kept in obscurity by the same means.

The boat being manned and equipped in this manner, the fowlers proceed on their midnight excursion to waters frequented by wild-fowl. The foremost occupant of the boat, who stands at the prow, has by far the most exciting and interesting part to perform. He is provided with a hand-net of special construction, attached or suspended to two canes of solid substance, and about twelve or fourteen feet in length.

The glare of light from the reflector, combined with the noise of the gong, appear to have such remarkable influence upon the birds sitting upon the water, that they remain motionless on the surface, as if bedazzled or otherwise rendered powerless. The man at the stern, meanwhile, propels the boat stealthily along, whilst the fowler at the prow stands behind the reflector with net in hand, which he dexterously pops over them as they sit upon the water; then by suddenly twisting it and holding up the canes the instant he finds the bird struggling, it falls into the bag of the net, from which it cannot escape: the fowler then takes the captive into the boat.

Two or three are sometimes taken in the net at once. The splashing noise occasioned by their struggles generally disturbs other wild-fowl which may be near, causing them to take wing; they then fly round about the reflector as if bewildered, making first towards the light, and sometimes, as if unable to see, dashing themselves both against the men and the boat; such as approach so near are frequently knocked down with a staff, or taken with the hand.[1] Those which are taken in the net the fowler removes; these he does not kill at once, hut simply twists their wings one in the other; and after turning their legs over their backs, throws them into a basket or upon the floor of the canoe, the whole proceeding occupying but a few seconds. Killing the fowl so captured is quite another operation, and has to be performed by cutting their throats in a very orthodox manner, with their heads towards Mecca, or they would not be proper food for a strict Mussulman.[2]

Coots, as well as widgeon and other species of wild-fowl, are caught in this manner; and, under favourable circumstances, as many as fifty head of fowl are sometimes taken by one boat's crew on a single night's excursion. Holmes mentions one locality where there are twelve or thirteen boats constantly employed during the season in this particular branch of wild-fowling. The neighbourhood not offering very promising advantages to the cultivation of the land, and the inhabitants not possessing much energy in regard to agricultural pursuits, the wild-fowl captured by the Persian fowlers at certain seasons of the year furnish an important article of food for the inhabitants.

The general average price of wild-ducks in those parts is 3 1/2*d.* per pair, and of coots 2 3/4*d.* per pair.[3]

———————

[1] Holmes's 'Sketches on the Shores of he Caspian.' See also 'Travels in Persia.'

[2] 'Travels in Persia.

[3] Holmes.

[1] A somewhat similar method of capturing wild-fowl appears to have been employed by the ancient Egyptians; but the precise method of operation is not clearly defined.—*Vide* Champollion-le-Jeune, *Monuments de VEgypte*, vol. iv. planche ccccx.

[2] Holmes.

[3] Holmes's 'Sketches on the Shores of the Caspian.'

CHAPTER LXXIV

FOWLING IN RUSSIA, SIBERIA, GREENLAND, AND OTHER NORTHERN COUNTRIES.

'Who can recount what transmigrations there
Are annual made? what nations come and go?
And how the living clouds on clouds arise?
Infinite wings! till all the plume-dark air
And rude resounding shore are one wild cry.'—
THOMSON.

THERE is a species of wild-goose, which Pennant recognises as the "White Brant, or Snow Goose, which annually visits the north of Asia, in gaggles of several thousands.

The method of taking these birds, as described by Pennant in his 'Arctic Zoology,' seems extraordinary, and yet so simple as almost to excite a feeling of incredulity as to the authenticity of that author's statement. It is, however, confirmed by other writers.[1] The art is said to be practised with considerable success in Jakut and other parts of Siberia.

A large net is placed on the bank of a river, near the nightly haunts of the wild-geese, in such a position that, on the fowler

731

suddenly jerking a line communicating at a distance of several yards from the net, it falls, and ensnares any birds which may be within its compass. On the net being spread the singular proceedings connected with it are put in force. One of the fowlers (generally a man of diminutive stature) covers himself with the skin of a white reindeer, or wraps a white sheet about him, and in that disguise, at twilight or later, crawls along the ground towards the geese, not near enough to allow of detection, nor so as to alarm them. The distance he advances must be regulated according to the humour of the birds. If they are unsuspecting and indifferent to his movements he approaches within a few yards of their whereabouts; but if they show symptoms of distrust he is wary in his advances. His actions have, therefore, always to be regulated by the caprices of the birds; and the more discretion he displays in this part of the proceeding, the greater are his chances of success.

Having approached, in the disguise aforesaid, as near the geese as he considers prudent, he suddenly turns round and proceeds in a contrary direction, crawling away from the birds. His companions, who station themselves at a distance, on the opposite side of the geese to that taken by the fowler, narrowly watch his movements; and the instant he turns round to retreat they show themselves, and by making a noise drive the geese forward; the fowler, meanwhile, waddling along on hands and knees, as if frightened at the noise of the men, and anxious to avoid them, but, in reality, all the while acting the part of a decoyer.

The geese, apparently mistaking the fowler for one of their own species, and afraid to approach the water, because of the presence of the men on the opposite side, are deluded, in their attempts to escape, by obeying the dictates of their own nature, which is to follow a leader; and, fancying they see such in the disguised figure before them, they pursue it, when, of course, they are led directly to the net; and as soon as they have arrived within scope of its meshes they find themselves irretrievably ensnared.

In the absence of a net the fowlers of those parts construct a hovel of the skins of animals, sewed together, which they place in a convenient position, near the brink of the water, or where the geese most commonly sit at night. The hovel has an inlet and outlet; and the fowler, in the disguise of a reindeer's skin or white sheet, leads the way, in a manner precisely similar to that in which the net is used; and having waddled along under the hovel, and enticed the geese to follow in his wake, he does not remain inside, but emerges at the outlet; and, closing the door after him, awaits the arrival of his followers. As soon as he finds them all, or a good number, within the hovel he runs round, or pulls a string communicating with a trap-door, which, on falling, instantly closes the entrance, and thus his deluded followers are imprisoned within the hovel.[1]

The numbers of geese taken by the fowlers of Northern

Asia by means of these singular stratagems appear almost incredible. A family of five or six persons sometimes captures several hundred in a season, which thereby afford them a substantial means of subsistence. Of the feathers they make a good price; and the flesh of the geese is preserved by being simply thrown in heaps into holes dug for the purpose. These, when filled, are covered with earth, which, quickly freezes, and forms a crust over the heap. The larder so formed and filled is only opened in the severest weather, when food is scarce; and the flesh is then found sweet and good as if preserved in hermetically-sealed cases. Whole families are sometimes kept from starving by means of supplies afforded from the stores of a larder of this simple contrivance.[1]

Another of the most successful arts employed in Siberia for taking wild-fowl is as follows:—A spot is chosen for the purpose where a wood happens to stand between two lakes, or between a lake and a river. A straight opening is then made through the wood from one lake to the other, by felling and clearing away the trees. Wild-fowl soon acquire a habit of passing through a vacuum of this description. The fowler then provides himself with two, three, or four glade-nets of sufficient breadth and extent to reach across the vacuum, and at night he suspends them on poles as high in the air as the fowl are in the habit of flying as they pass from one lake to the other. As soon as all is ready the fowler's assistants disturb the ducks on one of the lakes, and cause them to take wing, when, in passing through the vacuum, they fly against the nets and fall captives to the fowler. Connected with each net is a small rope, of sufficient length to reach the arm of the fowler in a place of concealment, where he awaits the arrival of the birds; and, as soon as he finds they have struck the net in their flight, he pulls a rope which brails it up, and completely secures the birds within it. Sometimes, however, they are in such a body, and fly with such velocity, that on striking the net it breaks away; the wild-fowl then dash through it as if it were a mere cobweb, though, on such occasions, a few of the leading birds are generally killed on the spot by the severity of the concussion.

Wild-fowl are also taken in the lesser rivers of Siberia by means of small nets stretched across the streams, when, during night, the birds are disturbed, and in swooping over the waters fall into the nets and are captured.

The Kamtschadales are awake to many devices for taking water-fowl—

'In those cold regions where no summers cheer,
Where brooding darkness covers half the year,'

and so during inclement seasons when food is scarce they resort to various means for capturing some of the wild-fowl which swarm around them.

During the moulting season, when there are thousands of

wild-fowl of every variety in those parts, they pursue them with boats or hunt them with dogs, in the same manner as swans are hunted and killed in Iceland.[1]

The Kamtschadales also catch numbers of wild-geese during the moulting season by a very primitive artifice. They dig pits near the brink of such lakes and rivers as those birds are in the habit of resorting to. The pits resemble those employed in some countries for taking wild beasts, and are lightly covered with grass in the same manner, when the geese, on stepping ashore and walking about the land in search of food, fall into them and become easy prey to the fowler. It would seem that a similar method of taking wild-ducks was known to the ancients. Pliny says, '*Itaque in foveas quibus feras venamur delapsæ soke evadunt.*'[2]

They also take large numbers of wild-fowl in the moulting season by surrounding them with a fleet of small boats, and driving them into a shallow river or bay with the flood-tide; then by watching them and waiting many hours in their boats at the mouth of the river, the birds are prevented from returning, and are so compelled to remain there until the ebbtide has run out and left them upon the land, when the boatmen and inhabitants fall upon them and generally kill or capture every bird. These droves of fowl are sometimes so large that twenty or thirty birds fall to the share of each person who partakes in the scramble.

At the entrance to the river Ochotska this practice of wild-fowling is very frequent, and often abundantly successful.[3]

The Kamtschadales also freely use fishhooks for the purpose of fowling; they bait them with small fish, and take many of the crane and heron species in that manner. This is one of their few modes of fowling at other than the moulting season.

They are also particularly expert in taking rock-birds with nooses attached to long poles. They climb the highest and most precipitous rocks in search of birds; and, at the hazard of their lives, sometimes crawl to the brink of fearful-looking precipices, where they cautiously slip the noose over the heads of their victims and snatch them from their roost one at a time as they sit on the ledges of the rock. When skilfully performed a whole roost of fowl may sometimes be taken one after another, with so little noise as not to awake or disturb their next companions on the same ledge.

The Green landers, in their little sporting kajaks, or canoes, which they manage with such incomparable skill and dexterity,[1] pursue wild-fowl and kill them with darts. They watch the course taken by the bird on diving, and, following in the track of the air-bubbles, strike the moment it rises to the surface.[2]

In Eussia large numbers of wild-geese are caught with day-nets. These birds are so abundant in some parts of that country that a much higher value is put upon their down and feathers than upon their flesh, though numbers of them when captured and stripped of their valuable coatings are smoked and hung for winter food.[3]

The manner in which the Russian fowler conducts his operations is as follows:—He spreads his net on an open plain encompassed with wood and water; and having leading-strings attached to the net, after the same manner as the English day-net, he conceals himself in a small hut formed of branches of trees, placed at some distance apart from the net. He is also provided with a number of dummies or stuffed skins of geese, which he judiciously arranges in various attitudes on the grass round about the nets; and, having so far completed his arrangements, he watches, from his place of concealment, the approach of his prey. By an ingenious whistle, made of birchen bark, which he applies to his lips, he so accurately mimics the gaggle of wild-geese that they seldom approach within sound of the false call without being induced to alight among the dummies. On hearing the call they whirl round in the air, as if to gain assurance before alighting of the quiet and safety of their supposed companions, and, after making a few such evolutions, they come down among the nets in gaggles of hundreds at a time, when numbers of them are immediately captured in the flaps of the nets. The Russians by another device capture wild-fowl in large nets fixed to lofty poles, probably resembling the ingenious contrivances of the Siberian fowlers referred to in another part of this chapter.

---

[1] *Vide* 'History of Kamtschatka,' translated from the Russian of Krasheninicoff, by James Grieve, M.D. 1761.

[1] *Vide* Pennant's 'Arctic Zoology,' vol. ii. p. 549, *et seq. Vide* also 'History of Kamtschatka,' by Grieve.

[1] Pennant, p. 551.

[1] *Supra*, p. 201.

[2] Pliny, lib. x. cap. xxxviii. sec. 112.

[3] Krasheninicoff's History of Kamtschatka.

[1] See 'The Sailing Boat,' 4th edition, p. 356.

[2] Sir Leopold McClintock speaks of Disco Fiord, in Greenland, as a most enticing spot for a week's fishing, shooting, and yachting. Hares and ptarmigan, he says, may be found along the bases of the hills; ducks are most abundant upon the fiord; and delicious salmon-trout very plentiful in the rivers.—*Narrative of the Fate of Sir John Franklin*, 1859.

[3] *Vide* Bell's 'Travels in Asia. Description of a Journey from Surgute to Moscow.'

CHAPTER LXXV

FOWLING IN INDIA, CHINA, ARABIA, AND OTHER COUNTRIES.

'There is a Power whose care
   Teaches thy way along the pathless coast,

The desert and illimitable air,
   Lone wandering, but not lost.'—W. C. BRYANT.

ON the Ganges, and in some other parts of India, wild geese and ducks are taken by a simple though very remarkable artifice. The fowler covers his head with a calabash[1] hollowed out in such a manner as to admit the whole of his cranium, and pierced with small eyelet and respiration holes. Wild-fowl are very fond of the fruit of the calabash, which they peck at and feed upon when found floating about the rivers and inland waters. The fowler therefore cuts away part of the rind of the gourd, whereby the fruity part is exposed in such a way as to make it a very enticing bait to hungry birds. In this disguise the fowlers of India wade up to their necks in water, among the wild-fowl as they sit upon the surface; and, as no part of the head, limbs, or body of the fowler is seen above water, if he acts cautiously he may snatch the birds down one after another without awakening suspicion, or alarming others which may be sitting among them.

A fowler, so disguised, is careful to keep himself deeply immersed, in order that the gourd only may be visible upon the surface; and, as gourds are constantly floating about the Ganges, and afford excellent food for wild-ducks and geese, those birds become thoroughly familiarised with the sight of them, and in that peculiar disguise suffer the amphibious fowler to intrude among them, not in the least aware of his presence or suspecting his design; on the contrary, the geese approach and peck at the gourds with their bills. The fowler then quietly seizes the birds one at a time by their legs, draws them under water, and dislocates their necks; he then tucks their heads beneath his girdle, from which they remain securely suspended, until he has captured two or three, or as many as are within reach, when he walks or swims towards the shore, and emerges from the water with the captives in his belt. The cut at the head of this page will give the reader a notion of this singular mode of fowling.

In a work of extreme curiosity,[1] which I discovered in my researches in the Library of the British Museum, and have already referred to more than once in these pages, this remarkable method of capturing wild-geese is very clearly depicted in a beautifully executed engraving; beneath which is the following inscription:—

'Anserum agreste genus stagnante in aqua capit Indus.
Ipse cucurbita habet tectum caput illecebris
Allicit: esuriens anser visse in vol at escæ.
Indus pascentem facile capit arte volucrem.'

None of the aquatic fowlers, emerging from the water, are represented by the original engraving as having captured more than three birds, the result of one wading; though several figures are in different attitudes, with the manner of approaching the fowl and drawing them under water.[1]

Strachan[2] mentions that in Ceylon wild-ducks and geese are caught in a similar manner in shallow loughs and waters; but, instead of using a gourd as a decoy, the fowler is said to cover his head with an earthen pot pierced with eyelet-holes; so that when he wades nothing is seen above the surface but the earthen pot which covers his head. In this disguise he enters among the wild-fowl; and they, mistaking the deception for a block of wood, or the like, regard it with indifference, and unsuspectingly admit the fowler to move amongst them, when he almost imperceptibly draws them under water by their legs, and secures them in the manner before described.

If Mr. Strachan's statement stood unconfirmed we should be disposed to doubt its veracity as to earthen pots being used for this purpose in the place of gourds; but he is confirmed on the subject by other writers, who also speak distinctly of earthen pots being employed in this peculiar method of wild-fowling. At the same time the disguise of the gourd must be by far the more enticing; and, indeed, the very fact of the gourd, as offering food to the wild-fowl, would seem to form one of the principal attractions by which the ancient fowler was enabled to practise his artifices successfully, for the Latin inscription expressly states, 'Esuriens anser visæ involat escæ.'

It is not improbable, however, that Mr. Strachan and others who have written upon the subject may have overlooked the fact that the earthen pot, when used instead of the gourd, is made similarly enticing, by having a few grains or ears of corn, or some other food, sprinkled upon or stuck about it. This assertion is further confirmed by engravings of the art in works by different authors of travel, where the fowl are represented as actually pecking at and in some instances perched upon the head of the amphibious fowler.[3]

The modern Egyptians also rise this mode of fowling,[1] and employ similar means to those of the Indian fowler for capturing some of the thousands of wild-fowl which resort to the banks of the Nile during the annual inundations of the lowlands.

The same artifices are also employed in China; and (though it may be difficult to trace at this remote period) it is highly probable that the artifice originated with the people of that nation. The whole proceedings are very clearly explained and illustrated by Du Halde.[2]

It appears to be a mode of fowling that can only be employed where the water is shallow, or, at all events, not beyond a certain depth; for no man could swim in such a manner as to keep his whole body under water with three or four wild-geese suspended from his girdle. It is also a pursuit peculiarly adapted to Eastern countries. No one could remain under water up to his neck for any length of time in a cold country, though the natives of warm climates are able to do so with impunity.

Niebuhr, in his 'Travels in Arabia,' mentions that Pococke and some other travellers were not credited when they spoke of this mode of taking wild-fowl as practised in China; 'but,' he adds, 'no fact can be more certain.'[3]

A precisely similar method of capturing wild-geese is practised on the lake Cienega de Tescas, near Carthagena. The water of this lake is salt, and is frequently visited by large gaggles of wild-geese, to capture some of which the fowlers in that locality throw into the water, at such times as the wild-geese are in the lake, fifteen or twenty large calabashes, which they call *totumos*. These are merely decoys, with which the fowl soon become familiar; and, having repeated the proceeding of setting the totumos adrift three or four days successively, the fowler goes to the lake in early morn with his head disguised in one of the totumos; and, observing all possible stillness and precaution, he contrives to swim or creep among the birds, when he pulls them down under water, and secures them to his girdle,[1] after the same manner as that pursued by the Indians and Chinese.

Bewick speaks of this peculiar art of capturing wild-fowl as attended with much watching, toil, and fatigue, and comparatively trifling in point of success.

The Arabs are also awake to a similar mode of disguising
the head and wading neck-deep in pursuit of wild-fowl; but
instead of a gourd or calabash the Arabian fowler simply piles
a few handfuls of sea-weed upon his head, and in that excellent
disguise approaches wild-fowl by wading up to his neck in the
water, when he snatches them down one after another; whilst
their companions are quite unconscious of the presence of
the submerged fowler, much less of the destruction he deals
among them.[2]

The Arabs, who delight in fowling, also use the artificial
stalking-horse: they carry in front of them a piece of canvas,
on which is painted a leopard, the whole stretched on two
reeds or sticks; with this they walk through brakes, &c. A little
below the top of the canvas is one or more peep-holes for the
fowler to look through and see what is passing. At sight of the
canvas the birds do not fly, but stand still in astonishment, or
rush into covey. The fowler then presents and fires through the
holes. The Arabs are up to many of the arts of wild-fowling.[3]

---

[1] '*Calabash*, a gourd or pompion, the fruit of the
Adansonia, or baobab tree, the shells of which are employed
by the Caribbee Islanders for drinking-cups, kettles, measures,

musical instruments, and various other purposes.'—*Encyclo. Met.*

'*Calabash Tree.*—It bath a flower consisting of one leaf, divided at the brim into several parts, from whose cup rises the pointal in the hinder part of the flower, which afterwards becomes a fleshy fruit, having a hard shell.'—*Miller.*

[1] Venationes Ferarum, Avium, &c., depietæ a Joanne Stradano: editæ a Philippo Gallæo: Carmine illustrate a C. Kiliano Dufflæo. *No date.*

[1] There is a work hearing the same title as that from which the Latin text is taken published, at Amsterdam, anno 1627: said to be 'Delineates ab Antonio Tempesta;' but many of the engravings appear to be ill-executed *piracies* from the valuable works of art of Stradano.

[2] *Vide* 'Philosophical Transactions, Abridged,' vol. v. A.D 1701.

[3] Captain Thomas Williamson, in his 'Oriental Field Sports,' states, with reference to this mode of fowling: 'In *jeels* the natives often catch wild-fowl by means of large pots; at first left to float aboutamong the birds, which soon become reconciled, and approach them without fear. When this effect is produced a *shecarry* wades, among the birds with his head in a similar pot, and pulls them under water, fastening them

to a girdle prepared for the purpose. The *braming*, or red-and-white goose, is, however, very wary, and is seldom taken by any device. A pair of them, with a flock of grey geese, will commonly keep tip such an alarm as to defy the powers of small shot.'

¹ *Vide* 'Manners and Customs of the Ancient Egyptians,' by Sir J. Gr. Wilkinson, vol. iii. chap. 8.

² 'La manière dont ils les prennent, mérite d'être rapportée; ils se mettent la tête dans des grosses citroüilles seches, où il y a quelques trous pour voir et pour respirer, puis ils marchent nuds dans l'eau, ou bien ils nagent sans rien faire paroître au dehors, que la tête couverte de la citroüille. Les canards accoûtumez à voir de ces citrouilles flottantes, autour desquelles ils se jouent, s'en approchent sans crainte, et le chasseur les tirant par les pieds dans l'eau pour les empêcher cle crier, leur tord le col, et les attache à sa ceinture. Il ne quitte point cet exercice, qu'il n'eu ait prix un grand nombre.'—*Description Géographique, Historique, Chranalogique, &c.*, par Du Halde, vol. ii. p. 138. Folio edition.

³ See also Nieuhof's 'China,' Murray's 'China,' and Navarette's ditto; also Pococke's 'Travels.'

¹ Ulloa's 'Voyage to South America.'

² 'Travels in Arabia,' by Carsten Niobuhr.

³ See 'Travels in Barbary.' Pinkerton's 'Voyages and Travels.'

Printed in Great Britain
by Amazon